MARTA MINUJÍN

MARTA MINUJÍN
Menesunda Reloaded

Edited by Helga Christoffersen and Massimiliano Gioni

NEW MUSEUM

Contents

Foreword

—

Lisa Phillips

Over the past sixty years, the epoch-defining Argentinian artist Marta Minujín (b. 1943, Buenos Aires, Argentina) has developed happenings, performances, installations, and video works that have greatly influenced generations of contemporary artists in Latin America and beyond. A pioneer of Latin American Conceptual art, Minujín combines elements of experimental theater, film, television, advertising, and sculpture to create total environments that place viewers at the center of complex social situations. At once monumental and fragile, Minujín's works challenge artistic conventions while testifying to her unyielding engagement with both radical art forms and the artifices of popular culture.

In 1965, at the Center for Visual Arts of the Instituto Torcuato Di Tella in Buenos Aires, Minujín and Rubén Santantonín devised the now-legendary environment *La Menesunda*. The work led visitors on a circuitous journey through eleven distinct spaces. This intricate, interactive labyrinth sought to provoke visitors and spur them into action, offering new modes of encounter with consumer culture, mass media, and urban life. While *La Menesunda* was created as a direct response to street life in Buenos Aires—the title is slang for a confusing situation—the work, alongside that of Niki de Saint Phalle, Christo, Claes Oldenburg, and others, counts among the earliest large-scale environments made by artists, demonstrating how Minujín anticipated the contemporary obsession with participatory spaces, the lure of new pop-up museums, and the quest for an intensity of experience that defines social media today.

I would like to thank, Massimiliano Gioni, *Edlis Neeson Artistic Director*, and Helga Christoffersen, Associate Curator, who worked tirelessly to bring this extraordinary work to the United States for the first time. They worked very closely, across continents, with Minujín and her team to realize the exhibition. Francesca Altamura, Curatorial Assistant, provided invaluable assistance at various stages of the project's development, with help from curatorial interns Natalia Almada and Gregory Ng. This complex exhibition is the result of immense efforts of the entire New Museum staff. In particular, I would like to thank Karen Wong, Deputy Director;

Dennis Szakacs, Chief Operating Officer; Diane Vivona, Director of Development; and their respective teams for all of their support in making this exhibition possible. I am grateful to David Hollely, Director of Exhibitions Management, and his team—Patrick Foran, Chief Preparator; Stephen Nunes, Production Preparator; Christine Navin, Preparator; Kevin Kelly, Audio Visual Preparator; Abby Lepold, Senior Registrar; Maria Lostumbo, Registrar; and Carlos Yepes, Registrar—who were essential to the planning and installation of the show.

The New Museum gratefully acknowledges our Board of Trustees and sponsors for their support of "Marta Minujín: Menesunda Reloaded." Lead support for the exhibition is provided by the Artemis Council of the New Museum. Major support is provided by the Federal System of Public Media and Contents of Argentina through the Centro Cultural Kirchner. The exhibition is generously supported by Fundación Proa, Maria Belen Avellaneda of Compass, Estrellita B. Brodsky, and Kathleen O'Grady and the O'Grady Foundation. Additional support is provided by Amalia A. Amoedo. I would like to extend special thanks to Minujín's galleries: Herlitzka + Faria, Buenos Aires, and Henrique Faria Fine Art, New York. Thanks to the Bowery Hotel. Support for this publication has been provided by the J. McSweeney and G. Mills Publications Fund at the New Museum.

In 2015, the Museo de Arte Moderno de Buenos Aires presented a reconstruction of *La Menesunda*. This second iteration of the work at the New Museum is coproduced with the Museo de Arte Moderno de Buenos Aires, and is its first-ever presentation in the US. We are extremely grateful for the tremendous support of the entire team of the Museo de Arte Moderno de Buenos Aires, and especially to Victoria Noorthoorn, Director, for her dedication to the work and legacy of Marta Minujín and for her support throughout this process. We would also like to thank her staff, especially Micaela Bendersky, Head of Exhibitions; Agustina Vizcarra, Producer; and Iván Rosler, Head of Design and Exhibition Production, for their expertise and insight, which has been an invaluable resource throughout all phases of the exhibition planning, alongside Vizcarra's tireless help during the installation phase. In addition, we would like to thank Henrique Faria and Mauro Herlitzka, whose insight has supported the development of the whole project.

This catalogue includes a conversation between Minujín and curators Massimiliano Gioni and Helga Christoffersen, and an interview with the legendary artist Christo, who witnessed Minujín's very early activities in Paris in the 1960s. It is also a great pleasure to publish new scholarship on Minujín's work, with newly commissioned texts on *La Menesunda,* its relationship to the emergence of media art in Buenos Aires and beyond, and Minujín's activities in New York and Washington, DC, in the 1960s and 1970s by Zanna Gilbert of the Getty Research Center and Argentinian art historian Aimé Iglesias Lukin. We are grateful to all of the authors, and to Lily Bartle, Editor, for her attentiveness in editing this publication with the assistance of Dana Kopel, Senior Editor and Publications Coordinator. The catalogues in this series have been beautifully designed by Brendan Dugan, David Schoerner, and Grant Schofield of An Art Service.

Most importantly, I would like to thank Marta Minujín for her groundbreaking vision and work, which continue to transform the cultural landscape across the globe. It has been an incredible joy to experience her generous enthusiasm at every stage of this exhibition's development.

Lisa Phillips
Toby Devan Lewis Director, New Museum

Mediating Menesundas: Marta Minujín from Informalismo to Media Art

—

Zanna Gilbert

Menesunda means to begin to live through art. ~~An act of life—to commit an act of life with art.~~
—Marta Minujín

By 1965, Marta Minujín was already a well-known artist in Argentina. Despite only being in her early twenties, she had already won the Di Tella National Art Prize, staged so-called happenings on television, generated a great deal of press coverage, visited Paris for extended stays, and was acquainted with not only the major artists of her own milieu in Buenos Aires but also with those of *Nouveau réalisme* in Paris.[1] She was also championed by Jorge Romero Brest, the influential director of the Centro de Artes Visuales at the ambitious Instituto Torcuato Di Tella in Buenos Aires. It was in this position of increasing success and celebrity that Minujín, along with her collaborator Rubén Santantonín and a team of artist accomplices—Floreal Amor, David Lamelas, Leopoldo Maler, Rodolfo Prayón, and Pablo Suárez—embarked upon the singularly ambitious project of *La Menesunda*, an eleven-room environmental installation that opened to the public in May 1965.[2] Its title, meaning “chaos” or “confusion” in *Lunfardo Porteño* (Buenos Aires slang), proclaimed a new, indeterminate art of experience and, in Romero Brest’s words, “was the first insult to Art with a capital A in Argentina.”[3]

At the heart of *La Menesunda*, however, was another first: no Argentinian artist had included the newly ubiquitous technology of closed-circuit television in a work of art before.[4] Nevertheless, the emergence of the *arte de los medios de comunicación* [media art] movement in Argentina, spearheaded by Roberto Jacoby, Eduardo Costa, and Raúl Escari in 1966, has often been historicized independently of Minujín’s explorations of the media.[5] This essay seeks to position *La Menesunda* within the context of the Argentinian *arte de los medios* movement, considering the media elements contained within it, the technological landscape of 1960s Argentina, and Minujín’s employment of what I call *live-mediated* events.[6] Through close examination of Minujín’s artistic production between 1964 and 1966—the period in which she abandoned her earlier cardboard and mattress constructions in favor of participatory experiences, we

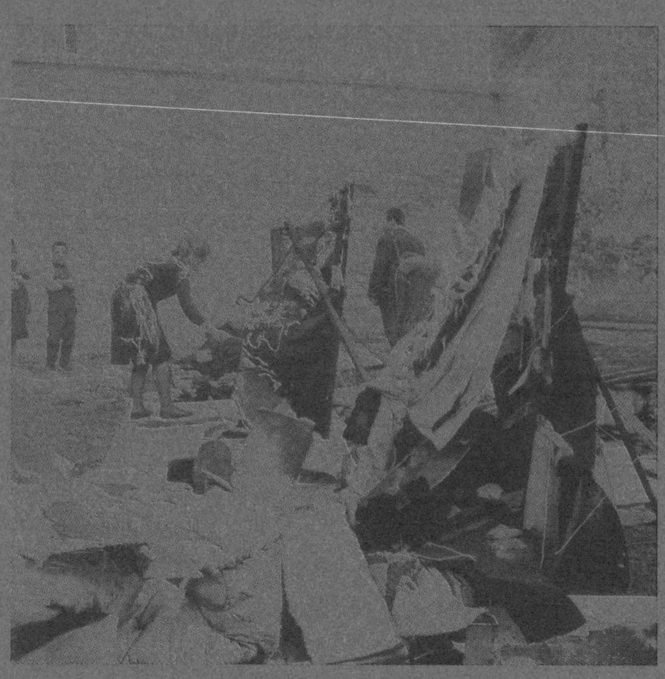

Marta Minujín, *La destrucción* [The Destruction], 1963. Installation view: Impasse Ronsin, Paris, 1963

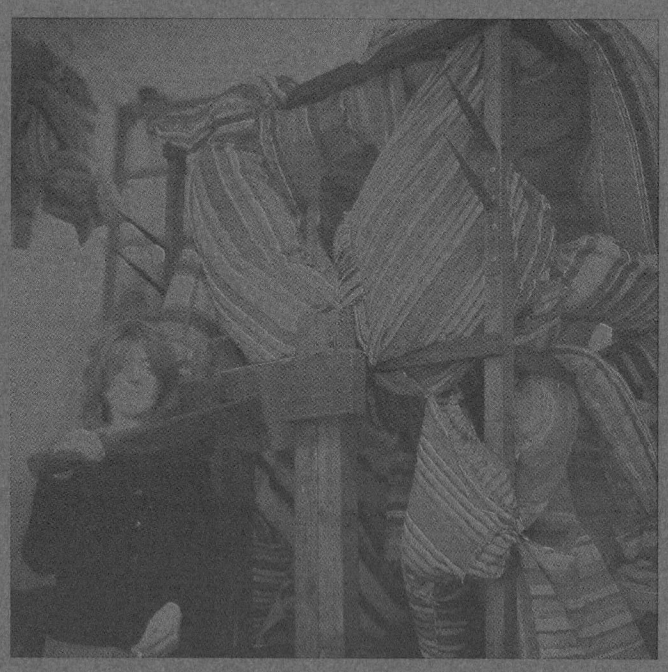

Marta Minujín and Mark Brusse, *Chambre d'amour* [Room of Love], 1963

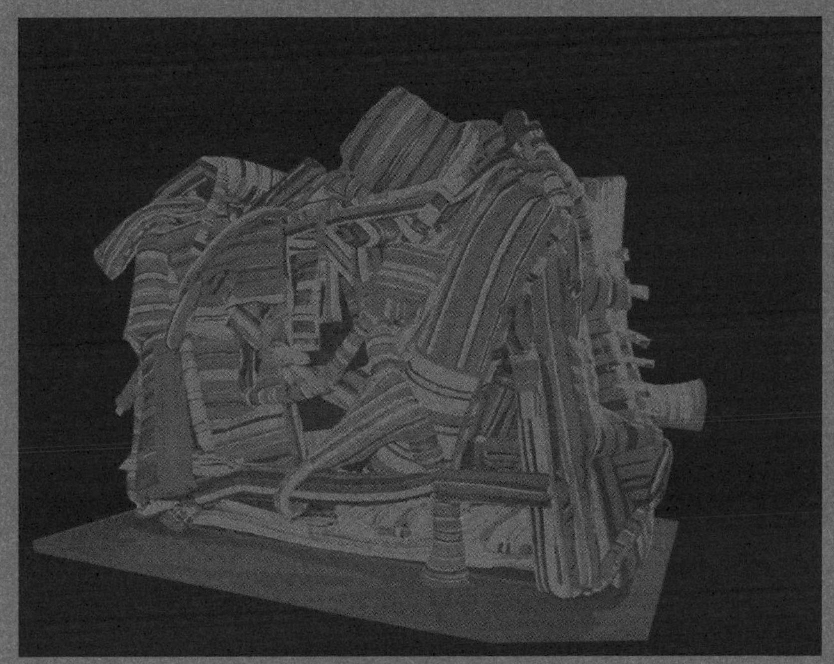

Marta Minujín, *¡Revuélquese y viva!* [Wallow Around and Live!], 1964

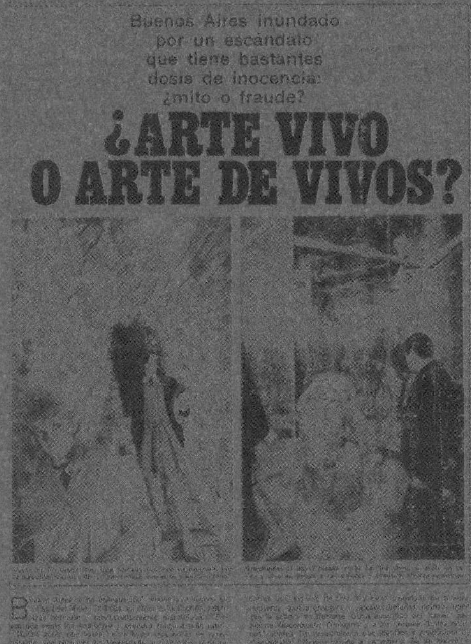

Buenos Aires inundado por un escándalo que tiene bastantes dosis de inocencia: ¿mito o fraude?

¿ARTE VIVO O ARTE DE VIVOS?

Review of *La Menesunda* published in *Atlántida*, Buenos Aires, August 1965

may better understand her unique contribution to discourses around mass media in the Buenos Aires art scene. I argue that the artist's prescient ability to command and critique the media allowed her to forge a distinctive mass-media art that both engaged and parodied spectacle and reckoned with media as live, sensorial, and immediate. Not withstanding this particular aim, the story of the conception, execution, and reception of *La Menesunda* is a rich and multifaceted one, which I will attempt to trace as I highlight some of the underexplored aspects of its history: the collectivity at the center of its origin and the importance of Argentinian Informalism to some of its key characteristics. In the concluding section, I will consider the unstable territory of resurrecting *La Menesunda* based on memory and historical documents as another instantiation of mediation.

EXPERIENCING *LA MENESUNDA*

It is now folklore that the lines for *La Menesunda* extended around the block of Calle Florida. This was partly because the labyrinthine installation could only be experienced by eight people at a time, who were let in one by one. The mega-installation comprised eleven distinct spaces that were designed to provoke and unsettle those who entered, and, ultimately, to "liberate" them from their passive acceptance of a Christian society and bourgeois consumerism by exposing them to a series of "multisensory, aesthetic and ethical stimuli."[7] The exhibition's somewhat cryptic pamphlet read: "'LA MENESUNDA'/is a caprice/a nonsense/way of creating difficult/strange/embarrassing 'situations'/ for those who are willing to accept them/INTENSIFYING EXISTENCE/ beyond gods and ideas/feelings/mandates and desires."[8] According to Minujín's archival notes, *La Menesunda* was designed to "shake human consciousness" to achieve a "superior reflection on the spirit of life."[9] Indeed, the filmmaker Leopoldo Maler's contemporaneous documentary depicting visitors as they exited *La Menesunda* did record expressions of displeasure, affirming, to a certain degree, the artists' success in creating "embarrassing situations."[10] By 1965, Minujín had categorically decided that *arte nuevo*, or "the new art," would not be static but would instead invoke a sensory experience akin to the sensorial bombardment of the public by popular culture and mass media. In the now-iconic environment of *La Menesunda*, Minujín's belief in this new art was productively combined with Santantonín's interest in phenomenology. Indeed, art historian Andrea Giunta has suggested that since 1961, Romero Brest had become increasingly convinced that the new art was one of *experience*, that is, an art that was no longer centered on the object but was instead an approximation of life. The term *experience* was to become central to Romero Brest's defense of the Di Tella generation, and in 1967 he changed the name of the Di Tella Prize exhibition to "Experiencias."[11]

To experience *La Menesunda*, the visitor would pass through a translucent, hot-pink entranceway in the shape of a human silhouette that led to a tunnel filled with flickering neon signs and the scent of frying oil—intended to replicate the experience of walking down Calle Lavalle, a busy city street in Buenos Aires. The visitor would then arrive at a set of stairs leading to the sparse black *TV Tunnel* containing seven televisions, two of which were connected to closed-circuit cameras recording the visitor themselves and five of which were tuned to local television stations, with programs ranging from music to news, all with the sound blaring. After another brief ascent by stairway, the visitor would enter a bedroom in which a couple, played by actors, lay in bed listening to the Beatles. Then, by way of a steep descending staircase, the visitor would enter the interior of an enormous painted sculpture of a woman's head.[12] The domed walls and ceiling were adorned with cosmetic products while two attendants—a beautician and a masseuse—offered treatments to visitors.

Next, the visitor was required to jump onto a spinning carousel called *The Rotating Basket*, with walls woven from multicolored strips of vinyl. They could choose one of two doors to exit this space. From there, one might enter a spiral-shaped room containing roughly 821 feet (250 meters) of polyethylene tubing, which was stuffed with sawdust and painted bright pink to resemble intestines.[13] As the visitor moved through the spiral, the ceiling gradually became lower and the floor gradually inclined. At the end of this corridor was a hole, through which clips of Ingmar Bergman films could be seen. To proceed,

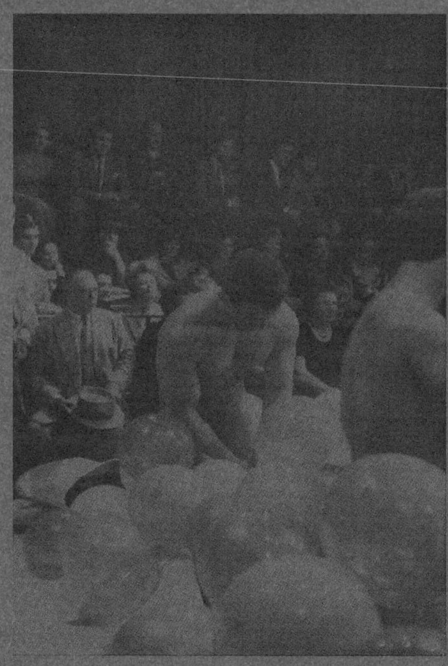

Marta Minujín, *La Cabalgata* [The Procession], 1964. Performance aired live on the television show *La campana del cristal* [The Glass Bell] on channel 7. Executed with the collaboration of Pablo Suárez, Marilú Marini, Alfredo Rodríguez Arias, and Graciela Martínez

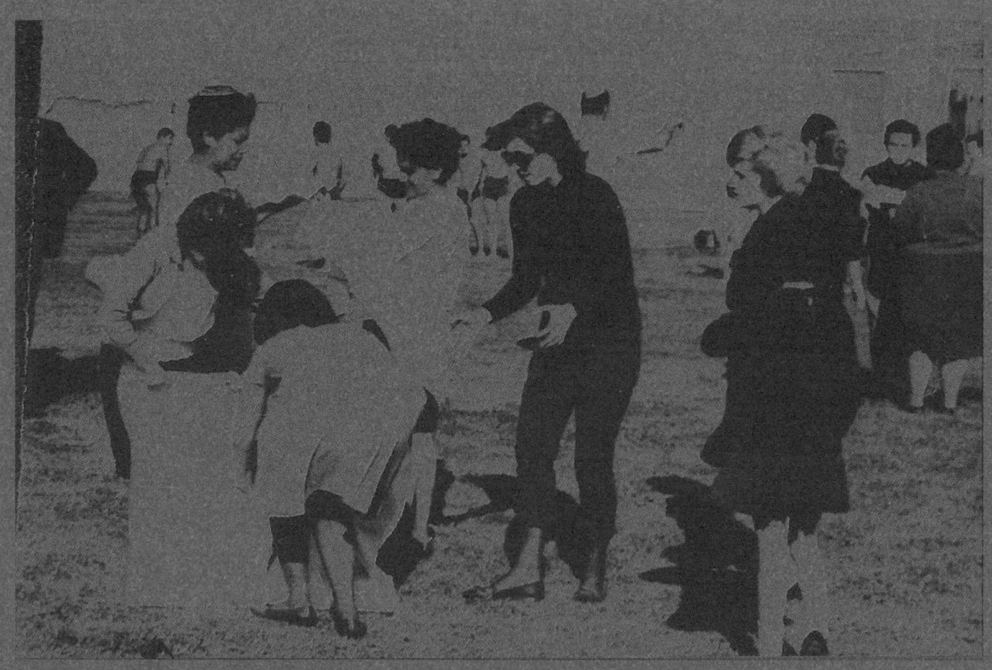

Marta Minujín, *Suceso plástico* [Visual Event], July 25, 1965. Happening at the Club Atlético Cerro, Montevideo, Uruguay

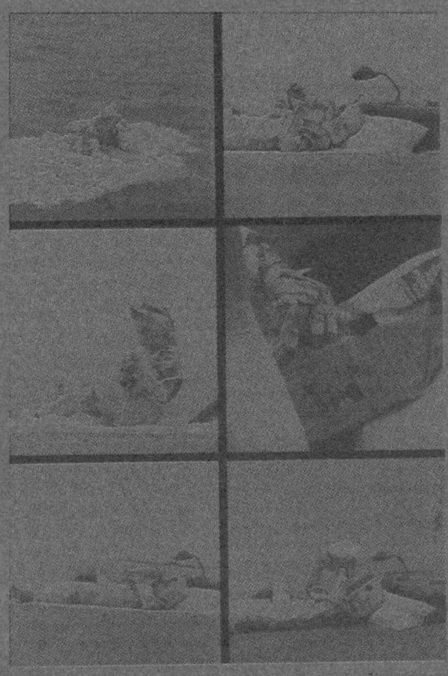

Marta Minujín, *Leyendo las noticias en el Río de la Plata* [Reading the News in the Río de la Plata], 1965

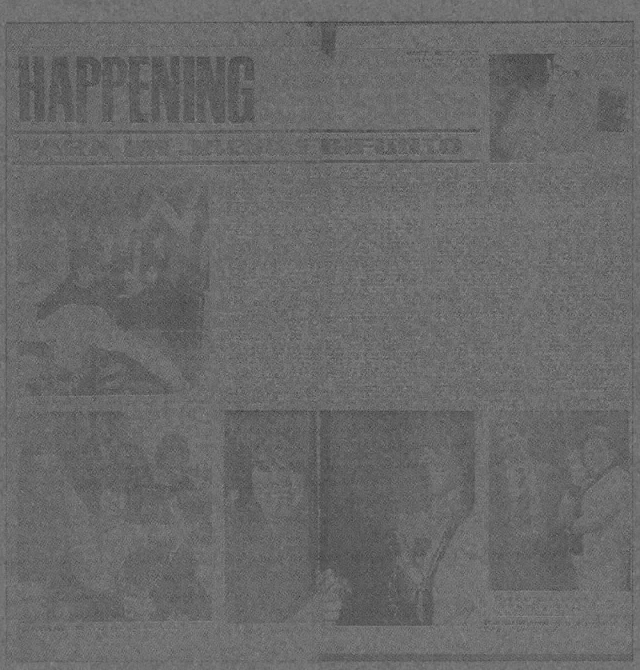

HAPPENING

Review of Eduardo Costa, Roberto Jacoby, and Raúl Escari's "non-event" *Happening para un jabalí difunto* [Happening for a Dead Boar], 1966, which mentions Minujín's participation, published in *El Mundo*, Buenos Aires, August 21, 1966

the visitor would have to jump back on the carousel and choose the other door, which led to *The Swamp*, a difficult-to-traverse corridor covered from floor to ceiling in foam. Along the side of the wall, peepholes offered glimpses of the exterior of *The Woman's Head*. Next, visitors would arrive in a dark room—which smelled strongly of a dentist's office—with a huge telephone dial, a locked door, and a sign reading: "Select the correct button to leave." After trying all the buttons, the participant would eventually be released from this claustrophobic setting. They would then proceed through a refrigerated room that led to *The Forest of Shapes and Textures*, in which forms stuffed with foam and encased in a variety of materials—ranging from "sandpaper, lambskin, coat lining fabric, hessian, sisal twine, floor-cloth, artificial grass, leather, satin, [and] metal"—hung from the ceiling.[14] The final space was more celebratory: an octagonal mirrored room, the center of which featured a transparent booth. When the visitor stepped on a platform, their presence would activate ultraviolet lights and fans that blew confetti around. This room of mirrors effectively shattered the unified self-image previously seen on CCTV, obliterating the ego and allowing the participant to exit transformed.

THE "MANZANA LOCA": ARTISTIC COLLABORATIONS FROM INFORMALISM TO ARTE DE LOS MEDIOS

La Menesunda could not have taken place without Jorge Romero Brest's organizational, financial, and intellectual support. The critic had previously been the director of the National Museum of Fine Arts and had remained a staunch supporter of abstraction throughout the 1950s. However, by 1960, Romero Brest began to embrace the work of an emerging generation of young artists who shunned the notion of the work of art as it was traditionally circumscribed.[15] Founded in 1958, the Instituto Torcuato Di Tella became a hub for new art, comprising three programs: two centers dedicated to musical and theatrical experimentation, respectively, and the Center for Visual Arts, which opened in 1963 under Romero Brest's leadership. The undertaking was sponsored by the Di Tella family, wealthy industrialists who sought to establish a modern, international institution.[16] The institute was part of a wave of new infrastructure for modern art established after Argentinian president Juan Perón was overthrown in 1955, during the country's brief and tentative return to democracy in the 1960s, a period brought to a close by the military coup of the *Revolución Argentina* in June 1966. This period of relative stability marks the advent of an official economic program known as *desarrollismo*, or "developmentalism," which emphasized internationalism as a core tenet of economic development and led to the establishmentof new museums and prizes for modern art.[17] At Di Tella, Romero Brest advanced this internationalism by inviting critics such as Lawrence Alloway, Pierre Restany, and Clement Greenberg to be jurors for the Di Tella prizes. In a notorious disagreement between Romero Brest, Restany, and Greenberg over the 1964 prize winner, Romero Brest ultimately sided with Restany, who wanted to award the prize to Minujín. This episode is now considered symbolic of the shift in Argentinian art away from Greenbergian modernist principles and toward a new aesthetic.[18]

The Di Tella was located on what became known as the *manzana loca*, or "the crazy block," on Calle Florida. For the better part of the 1960s, an atmosphere of transgressive experimentation was to be found at Di Tella, as well as in the galleries in the surrounding area, such as Lirolay and Bonino. Minujín and her peers were even known as *los locos del Di Tella*.[19] Romero Brest's support for new art provided institutional backing for these young artists. As Sofía Dourron has explored in her essay "La Menesunda," the newly established Di Tella Prize "did not just legitimize and embrace the practices of these young artists, it institutionalized a series of issues linked to intimacy, sexuality, and the forced inclusion of the spectator's body in the work, pushing the boundaries of morality and decency of the time."[20] Furthermore, the Di Tella family's conglomerate SIAM Di Tella provided expensive hardware for artists' increasingly technological and ambitious environmental installations.[21] The good times were, however, short lived. After the coup of 1966, the political climate grew increasingly contentious, as did the relationship between Romero Brest and the artists, the latter having become highly critical of the military dictator, General Juan Carlos Onganía. In 1969, the CAV was forced to close.[22]

At the time of its original installation, *La Menesunda* marked the heady intersection of Informalism, *Nouveau réalisme*, Pop art, happenings, and mass media, all of which were hotly debated in artistic circles and the popular press in Buenos Aires. Despite these manifold lineages and influences, Minujín has often been categorized as a Pop artist, especially by institutions in the US and Europe.[23] This classification—which was contested even at the time—stems from her early Informalist interest in everyday, popular materials, the multicolored environments she constructed with mattresses, her engagement with and frequent appearance in the mass media, and her high-profile friendship with Andy Warhol; indeed, she has styled herself as a media icon throughout her career.[24] However, a thorough analysis of her work from the 1960s reveals a more complex picture in which Minujín's practice incorporates the genres of Informalism, *Nouveau réalisme*, Pop, and happenings to arrive at a distinctly hybrid form of media and environment art, and—in collaboration with Santantonín—an art of totalized experience that would envelop both the body and the senses.[25] According to scholar Marcelo E. Pacheco, *arte nuevo* began to crystallize around 1956 after the fall of Perón's decade-long government one year earlier.[26] Pacheco contends that the art forms that subsequently emerged were "bounded at one end by the spread of Informalism, and on the other, by Pop and conceptual art; and included the appearance of object art, video art, environments, Happenings, installations and media art."[27] Scholars have previously pointed out that Pop art was received, digested, and reformulated in Buenos Aires through international legitimization on the part of institutions and individual artists alike.[28] However, as theorist Oscar Masotta and Romero Brest pointed out, Argentinian Pop amounted to a complex refraction of US Pop that would eventually birth both media art and participatory environments.[29]

While living in Paris from 1962 to '63, Minujín worked primarily with cardboard boxes, found mattresses, and industrial paint. In June 1963, she enacted her first happening, *La destrucción* [The Destruction], in which she meticulously staged the destruction of her works. First, the artist organized an exhibition of her work in her studio—alongside works by Lourdes Castro and Miguel Otero—in which none of her works were actually for sale, since, as Minujín puts it, they were "destined for the butcher."[30] Then, one month later, on June 6, artists were invited to come and "symbolically destruct" the works by intervening in them—an act of overwriting that would modify or erase her authorship.[31] Notably, the prolonged execution of this event in various stages over the course of a month (during which the artist successively produced an invitation, an exhibition, a catalogue, and the final event) anticipates what would become a hallmark of media art: the increasingly deliberate augmentaion of the discontinuity between information and event.

Minujín was part of a generation of artists who, as Brest put it, "[questioned] the basis of creation with an unprecedented freedom," and *La destrucción* was one of the inception points of Minujín's radical opposition to artistic conventions.[32] Describing her thinking at the time, Minujín writes: "I felt and believed that art was something more important for human beings than the eternity that only a few cultured ones could attain in museums and galleries; for me art was a way of intensifying life, of having an impact on the viewer by shaking him up, rousing him from his inertia. Why, then, was I going to keep my work? . . . So that it could die in cultural cemeteries, the eternity in which I had no interest? I wanted to live and make others live."[33] It was this attitude that led Minujín to a live, participatory art that would envelop the viewer and shun traditional conceptions of the artwork and the museum.

In Paris in 1963, she had collaborated with the Dutch artist Mark Brusse on *La chambre d'amour* [The Room of Love], a participatory installation comprising a room constructed from sewn mattresses. And in 1964, while back in Buenos Aires, Minujín won the prestigious National Di Tella Prize with a similar environment, titled *¡Revuélquese y viva!* [Wallow Around and Live!] (1964), in which visitors were invited to discard their inhibitions and crawl inside the works. These works created the foundation upon which Minujín would develop her approach to participatory art and her stance on art's relation to everyday life. Winning the prize also catalyzed her transformation into a controversial public figure and a staple of press coverage of the *manzana loca*.

In 1965, Romero Brest gave the go-ahead to Santantonín and Minujín to begin coordinating *La Menesunda*. How exactly did Santantonín, an introspective Informalist artist from an older generation, and Minujín come to work on this project together? Minujín remembers that they were "absolute partners" from the beginning.[34] Both were interested in popular—meaning vernacular—culture, and as Minujín recalls, "We looked at the window displays on Lavalle and Florida [Streets]. . . . Everything kitsch interested us."[35] In 1963, Santantonín had addressed a letter to the Instituto Torcuato Di Tella proposing a project he called *Arte-cosa-rodante* [Mobile-Thing-Art], an "immense mobile mechanism" that the public could enter to encounter a "magical and different world, much of which they themselves would create."[36] This environment would include "lights, textures, dancing objects animated by people, popular or symphonic music, humor, lotteries, and literature."[37] In 1961, Santantonín defined this notion of *arte cosa*, or "art thing," as seeking "to provoke a challenge to the imagination," and as something that "works hard at trying to prevent man from persisting in contemplating things from a distance."[38] At the time, the use of the term *thing* to describe an artwork represented a radical departure from medium-specificity because of its implicit rejection of the term *object* and the traditional notion of objecthood, which was considered coterminous with bourgeois standards of acceptability in art. Santantonín's desire to stimulate the senses led him to produce phenomenological *cosas* that bore vital traces of their human transformation from matter into art. He began to conceive of the spectator's participation as central to his work: "We are concerned with the spectator," writes Santantonín. "We would like to turn him around, like one turns a glove inside out. For him to have different sensations from all the aesthetic experiences he has had in his life before."[39] To this focus on participation and new sensorial experiences, Minujín added what she considered the unavoidable theme of mass media's invasion of human subjectivity, which resulted in the live elements within *La Menesunda*—the *TV Tunnel* and the human actors.

Describing a meeting with Minujín in late 1964, Leopoldo Maler recalls that "Marta effused with her traditional enthusiasm for just a few minutes [while] outlining the idea for *La Menesunda*. Romero

Brest had asked her to conceive a work different from everything she had done up until then. The first ideas came out of her first meeting with Rubén Santantonín. Quickly we gathered more participants."[40] One of these participants was artist David Lamelas, then just nineteen years old, who remembers being included in the group only after completing a "test" from Minujín in which she asked him to do a series of quasi-automatic word association exercises in her studio. They would meet at Minujín's family home to brainstorm potential ideas, which were recorded on a typewriter. A document in Minujín's archive—possibly a record of one of these brainstorming sessions—lists ideas for the installation (presumably of 1965, but undated). The list included, among other entries: "Swamp floor," "Collective journey," "Chinese torture moveable walls that crush the spectator," " Successive enclosures," "A room full of objects that the spectator has to throw away in order to pass through," "Frying room with an essence of flowers," "Room full of placards," "Change of temperature (fridge doors that open but are hot inside, cold turkish baths)," "In order to continue you pay to enter and shit in a black hole," and "Gymnastics room with obligatory gymnastics."[41] These proposals reveal the outlandish collective imagination that produced *La Menesunda*, as well as that imagination's distinctly sadistic tenor.

THE LIVE-MEDIATED EXPERIENCE

After several months of rigorous work, *La Menesunda* opened to the public and immediately garnered a great deal of attention from the national press, with headlines such as, "Menesunda? Bah!", "La Mene . . . Que?" [The Mene . . . What?], "Sinvergüenzas?" [Shameless?], "Sobre un Lamentable Espectáculo" [About a Lamentable Show], and "'Algo' para locos o tarados" ["Something" for the crazy or stupid].[42] Much of the press's criticism focused on the half-naked couple in bed, and this aspect of the environment—which was, according to Lamelas, "pure Marta"—does, in fact, seem to have shocked the Buenos Aires establishment. [43] Reflecting on his experience of *La Menesunda* and his conversation with the artist afterward, art collector Ignacio Pirovano recalls that he challenged

Minujín about the couple, an addition he considered "useless, superfluous and puerile," and she replied by explaining that the scenario was "indispensable to introduce to the spectator the improvisation in everyday reality."[44]

This was not the first time that Minujín had incorporated living beings, besides herself, into her work.[45] Her first televised happening, *La Cabalgata* [The Procession], aired live on the Argentinian television show *La campana de cristal* [The Glass Bell] in October 1964. According to researchers Ana Longoni and Mariano Mestman, "The artist brought on stage chickens, balloons, voluptuous athletes in their underwear, and a pony loaded with paint buckets."[46] The ponies "painted" the mattresses with paintbrushes that were strapped to their tails. Minujín herself performed a so-called "Sioux dance" before being ejected from the program's stage. The sheer number of live elements and their conflicting instincts created chaos—a kind of proto-*Menesunda*—amounting to a suspension of the normative order that keeps everyday habits in place. Art historian Daniel R. Quiles writes, "The increasing abundance of materials and scale suggest that each project was laboring to outdo the last one in terms of spectacle and subsequent publicity," positing that the referent of Minujín's events is "spectacle itself, the perceptual conditions engendered by the mass media."[47] She had absorbed theorist Marshall McLuhan's writings about how media fundamentally affects human faculties by, as he puts it, creating "an entirely new set of perceptions."[48] With this event, Minujín thus draws together two seemingly opposed aspects of her work between 1964 and 1966: that of "intensifying existence" through liveness and chaos, and the mediation of that same experience to critically examine the power of mass media to achieve that intensification.

As critic Jacqueline Barnitz argues, "Living things are essential to the purpose of [Minujín's] work. They are a plastic extension of inanimate soft objects, and they increase the intensity of the experience"; echoing the principles espoused by Allan Kaprow, Minujín claims that her work is "complete only from the moment the spectator walks inside and participates."[49] However, the chaos and immediacy facilitated by live action was always enhanced, perhaps paradoxically, by its mediation. As Victoria Noorthoorn observes, "Minujín already perceived the need to focus less on the happening understood as the art of the *immediate* which Kaprow had championed for years and rather on the new universe of intellectual exploration that, on the basis of the writings of Marshall McLuhan, focused on mediations."[50] Almost immediately after *La Menesunda* closed, Minujín was invited by the *El Pais* newspaper's Center for Arts and Literature in Montevideo to stage a happening. On July 2, 1965, She produced a live televised event, *Suceso plástico* [Plastic Event], in a stadium in the Uruguayan capital. It was composed of "two hundred audience members, fifteen police motorcycles, fifteen fat ladies chasing fifteen athletes, and young girls who went around kissing the audience while others wrapped themselves in paper. Five hundred live chickens, along with lettuce and talcum powder, were dropped from a helicopter."[51] Notably, the artist had been invited to do this by a newspaper—a mass-media entity—and thus the event both originated from and was performed for media structures (newspapers and television, respectively).[52]

Before Minujín's mediated stunts and *La Menesunda,* another Argentinian artist, Alberto Greco, had employed publicity as a strategy in his work. Greco was a major figure in Minujín's life up until his suicide in October 1965, and his practice provided key elements that she would further develop: the use of live animals (including people), mass-produced media (posters), and a confrontational attitude toward institutionalized art. Greco notoriously orchestrated publicity stunts that ironically celebrated his own artistic prowess.[53] In 1961, for example, he pasted posters around Buenos Aires with slogans like "Alberto Greco: El pintor informalista más importante de América" [Alberto Greco: America's Most Important Informalist Painter] and "Alberto Greco: ¡¡Qué grande sos!!" [Alberto Greco: How Great You Are!!]. Addressing the link between the two, Andrea Giunta writes, "For Minujín, like Greco, it was important to have been noticed."[54] Additionally, as Daniel R. Quiles observes, Greco's posters also explore the disjunction between the media's messages and lived reality—an important precedent for media art.[55] It wasn't only Minujín who would take up Greco's notion of self-promotion; other artists in Di Tella's orbit cultivated similar publicity-as-art strategies. In August 1965, Edgardo Giménez, Dalila Puzzovio, and Carlos Squirru—three artists closely associated with Pop in Argentina—appeared on a billboard on Calle Florida. Their so-called "advertisement," created by the agency Meca, was intended to resemble a movie poster and depicted each of the artists holding items related to their work above the bold-lettered question, "¿Por qué son tan geniales?" [Why are they so brilliant?]. While these artists foregrounded mass-media messages in the public sphere, challenging artistic conventions along the way, the inclusion of media elements in *La Menesunda* referenced the invasion of these cultural products into the population's everyday sensorium.

Within the context of Minujín's live-mediated happenings, a consideration of *La Menesunda*'s *TV Tunnel* raises two questions: Was it important that the seven television sets were some of the first things encountered by visitors? And what was the significance of the televisions and CCTV? As described above, upon entering *La Menesunda*, spectators would climb a staircase and find themselves confronted with their own image on a television screen, along with several other televisions broadcasting Argentinian television. The disparity between the images of oneself and those from the local stations highlights the distinction between the participant as media protagonist and the corporate- or state-sponsored media that was delivered to and passively absorbed by viewers. In the catalogue for the 2015 presentation of *La Menesunda*, Sofía Dourron points out that the *TV Tunnel* was "a microcosm of the rest of the itinerary," explaining:

> The presence of the television sets, which were only beginning to become widespread in family homes in Argentina, and the novelty, for most people, of seeing themselves on television for the first time, addressed a series of issues that would later recur: the unstoppable progress and domestic spread of technology and the media, the invasion of the spectator's body and privacy, [and] their absolute immersion in a structure as precarious as it was spectacular. . . . Would television be a new and improved form of entertainment or a power-serving and alienating mass medium?[56]

Indeed, it is important to remember the novelty of television for Argentinians in the '60s. While the television was one of the commodities becoming increasingly available for mass consumption by the middle class in Argentina due to economic development—which also facilitated access to appliances like refrigerators and telephones—this was still a new phenomenon. In his study of the effect of television on Argentinian private life, Gonzalo Aguilar notes that the increasing proliferation of televisions in private homes effected an enormous shift in behavior and customs.[57] Minujín, however, went so far as to characterize the incredible spike in television ownership in Argentina—rising from 450,000 sets in 1960 to 1,600,000 in 1965—as an "invasion" into people's homes.[58] Revealing a technologically deterministic logic, Aguilar argues that television changed from a public service accessible in communal spaces such as bars and cafés to a commercial vehicle that ushered sedentary consumption in to the private sphere. This development was widely considered the result of Argentina's adoption of an "American way of life."[59]

In interviews with the press, Minujín often stressed that she abandoned static easel painting as a response to media's increasing invasion into people's daily lives. Interestingly, this cultural shift established the conditions in which Minujín herself would flourish as the iconic public face of *La Menesunda*. Indeed, resistance to the totalizing image of an artwork was a key proposition of the new art.[60] Forgoing traditional pictorial art for one of experience hindered the production of an easily codifiable representation of the work itself, creating a void that was filled by an increasingly media-conscious and stylized Minujín. One report depicted her in an explicity Warholian fashion: the artist, the very image of rebellious youth, looks frankly at the camera while holding a cigarette in her right hand. In the weeks after *La Menesunda* opened, she was both celebrated and attacked as "La cara de *La Menesunda*" [The face of *La Menesunda*]. By 1968, however, Minujín would become "La Diosa de *La Menesunda*" [The Goddess of *La Menesunda*].[61] The press certainly zeroed in on her, while Santantonín, who could not provide such bona fide Pop imagery as the fashionable and female Minujín, rarely appeared beyond his name in print. Notably, Maler's documentary about

La Menesunda—commissioned by Romero Brest—includes the media's reports in its record of the installation, demonstrating the degree to which reportage became one with the work itself.

Perhaps in response to her increasing presence in the newspapers, soon after making *La Menesunda*, Minujín performed the action *Leyendo las noticias en el Río de la Plata* [Reading the News in the Río de la Plata] (1965), in which she wrapped herself from head to toe in an outfit—featuring a hood with a peephole—constructed entirely from newspapers. She lay down close to the tidal river and read the papers, equipped with a pillow, nightstand, and reading lamp, as she waited for the tide to rise. Then, as she waded in, the river gradually dissolved the newspapers that clad her body. In a contemporaneous interview, Minujín expresses her desire to show that "the mediums of communication have invaded us, one lives as a prisoner of them: cinema, television, radio have interfered in our life in such a brutal way that we still don't want to accept it."[62] Minujín recast the media as bodily invasion, precluding her own representation by covering her head and face. The media, conceived as a form of imprisonment, is ultimately destroyed as the artist triumphantly dissolves her costume in the river. Invoking the dichotomy between nature and culture addressed in her other works, she reduces the newspaper to pulp—mere matter, like the water around it.[63]

MINUJÍN AND *ARTE DE LOS MEDIOS*

In July 1966, the famed *Happening para un jabalí difunto* [Happening for a Dead Boar] was widely covered by Argentina's press. However, its authors—artists Raúl Escari, Eduardo Costa, and Roberto Jacoby, who deemed their work *arte de los medios*—defined it as an *anti-happening*, in that it only occurred within the circuits of mass media. The artists were responding to what Masotta described as the "phenomenon of overreporting in the mass media [which] was inversely matched by very few effectively realized Happenings."[64] The artists sent a press release and photographs taken by Santantonín to all the main newspapers, resulting in the wide coverage of the supposed event. Featured in the photographs were all the requisite components of a happening: well-known artists, dancers, and intellectuals engaged in group actions. The press release detailed ideas for actions the artists had collected from their friends as if they had really been undertaken, including one by Minujín.

Initially, the event was given the ironic title *Total Participation Happening*. Described by Daniel R. Quiles as a "fictional happening," the event had no direct participants, but as a widely-circulated media story, there were many more viewers than the group of art world insiders that would have been present had it occurred in physical space. The piece played upon questions that had begun toarise regarding the media's coverage of happenings. In effect, the ephemeral happening appeared more "real" once it was reported on because media coverage created the structure and tangibility that it otherwise lacked. By entering these activites into the printed record, the newspaper reports in particular gave materiality to what was otherwise completely ephemeral. Key to this disjunction betweenthe event and its representation was the notion of a happening's liveness and ephemerality.

Since early that year, Jacoby, Costa, and Escari had been under the tutelage of Masotta in a reading group, which Marta Minujín also attended, focusing on media theory and French structuralism.[65] Having read texts by Marshall McLuhan, Umberto Eco, Roland Barthes, Susan Sontag, Claude Lévi-Strauss, Gregory Bateson, and Roman Jakobson, this "grupo masottiano," as Jacoby dubbed it,[66] explored the capacity of the media to *create* and *construct* events, rather than simply report on them.[67] As the group declared in their manifesto, "It is of no interest to information consumers if an exhibition took place or not; all that matters is the image of the artistic event *constructed* by the media."[68]

One of the newspapers reported, "Marta Minujín was one of the most brilliant of the [event's] 'intervenors': she recorded the dialogues of the guests, who she photographed and a while later gave them a copy of the photo, to 'give each one back their image,' she then explained."[69] Both Masotta and Minujín, along with several other artists, had participated in the planning of this anti-happening.[70] Minujín's conceptual contribution to the project offers us some art historical clues as to the reasoning behind her inclusion of CCTV in *La Menesunda*, thus prompting a reevaluation of Minujín's role in *arte de los medios*. In both *La Menesunda* and *Happening for a Dead Boar*, the participant's image is, at a certain point, captured and then fed back to them, facilitating in the viewer a heightened, critical awareness of the whole circuit of media production, an aim comparable with that of Jacoby, Costa, and Escari.

By the fall of 1966, this strategy of recording the participant and then transmitting that information back to them was fully developed in *Simultaneidad en Simultaneidad* [Simultaneity in Simultaneity], planned as part of *Three Country Happening* with Wolf Vostell and Allan Kaprow. Minujín met the two artists in New York in early 1966, and together they conceived a transcontinental happening comprising three simultaneous events in Germany, the US, and Argentina, to be connected by satellite—although this particular element ultimately proved too complex and expensive. The structure of the event was elaborate; critic Michael Kirby claims that *Simultaneity in Simultaneity* was "probably the first performance piece in history to make use of several coordinated [types of] mass media."[71] The first of the two elements, *Instantaneous Invasion*, took place on the evening of October 24, 1966. One hundred twenty preselected participants, who all lived alone and had previously agreed to be filmed, photographed, and recorded in their private domestic settings during the weeks prior, were "invaded" at home.[72] Participants were instructed to turn on their televisions, which broadcast instructions from Minujín to turn on their radios and receive an audio component that complemented the television image and message. According to a document in Minujín's archive, the participants "received their images reflected on the screens of their sets, hear[d] themselves over the telephone and on the radio and received telegrams where they could read their names, in this way, through the media, each spectator could objectivize his gestures, movements, the intonation of their voices. He *was* the 'Event.'"[73] The experience lasted ten minutes, during which time the participant was dubbed by Minujín as a "prisoner of the media."[74]

The second part, *Enveloping Simultaneity*, occurred on the same day, but in the public setting of the Di Tella Institute. Sixty preselected people were invited to attend, all of whom were related to the news media in some way. According to Minujín's notes, the selection criteria was based on a role reversal for reporters and media personalities: "Instead of taking notes and pictures of the show, they were photographed, filmed and recorded. They *were* the show. . . . As they went to their corresponding seats, each of them with a TV set in front of them and a radio set in their hands, could see their images, their gestures, and movements through different mass information means."[75]

Art historian Rodrigo Alonso notes that Minujín's happening was "so complex that neither Kaprow nor Vostell were able to reproduce it, as it was planned, because of the impossibility of obtaining in their respective countries all the required technology."[76] Indeed, Maler describes himself as having been the "magician manager" of the project, recalling, "Marta needed 200 TV sets with their tables. In those days, television sets were only black and white and each one required a separate antenna. Can you imagine . . . 200 antennas on the roof of the Di Tella building? So . . . my friend Arnoldo Werthein came to our aid [by] lending the equipment and [providing] its installation, which I supervised."[77] The preparation for the event began in June 1966, but was interrupted by the military coup. According to Maler, at the time of the coup, he and Minujín were recording the "freedom of mind" message that would be broadcast to participants during *Instantaneous Invasion*. The military occupied the television stations, taking control of Argentina's broadcast media. "We tried to explain [to] the officers there that it was only the innocent play of some artists," Maler recalls. "I got the camera and recorded Marta's message which, totally by [the] mistake of the usurpers, was broadcast the next day."[78] Importantly, the planning for *Simultaneity in Simultaneity* began in April 1966—the first announcement for *Three Country Happening* is dated April 27, 1966—before *Happening for a Dead Boar* and the publication of Jacoby, Costa, and Escari's manifesto, "An Art of Communications Media," in July 1966. However, despite its prescience, Minujín's contribution to the earliest inceptions of media art has not been fully appreciated in accounts of the movement; she is usually considered to have begun working more intentionally with media *after* the publication of Jacoby, Costa, and Escari's manifesto. Once *Simultaneity in Simultaneity* was complete, Minujín returned to New York on a Guggenheim fellowship, where she would stay for one and a half years, continuing to develop her enveloping media-related projects, including *Circuit Super-Heterodyne* (1967), *Minuphone* (1967), and *Minucode* (1968).

Simultaneity in Simultaneity manifested the clear contrasts between individual and communal use of the media. It also imitated therapy practices popular in the 1960s, in which patients were encouraged to observe themselves through closed-circuit televisions.[79] While an in-depth analysis of these aspects exceeds the scope of this essay, I would like to consider Minujín's contribution to media art and her work's anticipation of the movement's critical project—that is, to reveal the codes and structures of the media itself. Masotta understood the anti-happening as facilitating the public's consciousness of the "environmental power of the media," and in the prologue to his 1967 book *Happenings*, he ruminates on the relationship between happenings, the press, and the political events of 1966—all of which, he argues, led to the development of *arte de los medios*.[80] Masotta believed that happenings and media art were deeply interconnected but fundamentally differentiated by their respective relationships to mediation, arguing that a happening is a live, unmediated event, whereas media art is by nature reported on and thus mediated.[81] Minujín carved out a path connecting Masotta's seemingly opposed notions, arriving at an innovative and nuanced understanding of the happening merged with media art. She conceived of an art that, through the media's bodily and physical invasion of the senses, was itself both immediate and mediated, or *live-mediated*.

As Masotta writes, "There was something within the happening that allowed us to glimpse the possibility of its own negation, and for that reason the avant-garde is built today upon a new type—a new genre—of works."[82] That negation was constituted by a missed encounter between the event and audience, either temporally or through dissemination in the media. In contradistinction, *La Menesunda* and *Simultaneity* both stage mediation as an *encounter* through the use of closed-circuit television and the concept of recording, developing, and returning participants' images. Minujín eludes the negation at the (empty) center of *Happening for a Dead Boar*, offering in its stead a sensorial—and potentially restorative—form of participation. The cerebral tricksterism of *arte de los medios* reduced the art event to information, rendering it entirely conceptual in order to expose the codes intrinsic to media systems. Minujín, however, would not relinquish experience and object altogether—she remained committed to environments that immersed participants in overwhelming situations—focusing on the media's invasion of the body, in the vein of McLuhan, while, at the same time, attempting to reveal its implicit code or structure.

MENESUNDA AS ITERATIVE CONCEPT

In 1965, Minujín was already planning an adapted version of *La Menesunda* for television called *La Telesunda*, but it never came to fruition.[83] This was not the only planned reiteration of the piece. The realization of *La Menesunda* did not preclude the possibility of realizing further experiences within a similar framework, and the term *menesunda* became more of a working concept for Minujín, rather than simply the name of a work she had created in 1965. In fact, this concept gave way to the ambitious desire to enact a *Menesunda* in New York. Planning to use her 1966 Guggenheim grant to fund the project, she envisioned "a space that would fit 60 people with 10 uneven levels" with "discontinous spaces" or different "dimensions." "It is in these spaces," writes Minujín, "that various effects of all kinds of possible variabilities would be developed . . . light effects . . . technologies . . . unimaginable sounds . . . temperatures . . . texts . . . films . . . theatrical actions . . . physical sensations . . . drawings . . . paintings . . . people performing singing dancing . . . a live scenography. Menesunda means to begin to live through art."[84] By 1972, the artist was planning a *Menesunda of Arte Argentino*, an environment on a much larger scale than the 1965 version, which would be accessible to one hundred people simultaneously.[85] It was intended to represent all the arts—poetry, theater, drama, visual arts, technological arts, music, lights, [and] sound."[86] "The idea," explains Minujín, "is to exhibit Argentine art through an environment with happenings, that is, actions created by the artists themselves." Live elements were also proposed in this initial outline, including "rock, electronica, poetry recitals, [and] cinema."[87] Although these projects never took place, they show how the concept of *Menesundas* became central to Minujín's thinking about collaborative practice and the creation of environments. These projects indicate that Minujín did in fact see *La Menesunda* as something that could travel across space and time—as a kind of score that could be used to reconstruct a particular situation. As Claire Bishop points out, Allan Kaprow's comparable work *Yard* (1961) was conceived of as a score and thus was able to be recreated *ad infinitum*.[88]

Art historian Irene V. Small observes that artists' embrace of ephemerality and anti-institutionalism "obviates the very notion of the original." Indeed, the ephemerality of *La Menesunda* was part and parcel to its radical proposition.[89] What are we to make of the iterative nature of *La Menesunda*, especially considering its 2019 reconstruction in New York? When the environment was reconstructed for the first time in 2015 in Buenos Aires, it was done with a great deal of fidelity to the original. Scholar Isabel Plante describes this second iteration as an opportunity to experience the celebrated work that "we have read and heard so much about"; however, she also points out that the precise reconstruction of each environment's details was alien to Minujín and Santantonín's practice in that such a fastidious attention to detail was not the point of the original installation, which was characterized by its spontaneity and ephemerality.[90] Interestingly, Plante observes that this exercise in historical curiosity, carried out largely by studying archival photographs, not only faithfully reconstructed the 1965 artwork but also, perhaps unintentionally, reproduced the sensationalism of the 1965 press coverage as well.[91]

What then is the relationship between the "experiences" conceived by the artists of Argentina's *arte nuevo* and the experience economy of the early twenty-first century? If *arte de los medios* questioned the reliability of information, documentation, and history itself, what should we make of artworks reconstructed from mediated memories? Minujín's prescient observation that the media had invaded the customs, perceptions, and behavior of its pliable subjects now, at the beginning of the twenty-first century, speaks to an environment of technological overload far more invasive than that of the nascent technologies of the 1960s. As Daniel R. Quiles suggests, these early works of media art are thus ripe for informational updates from the present.[92] However, like the productive gaps between reality, mediation, and fiction that *arte de los medios* interrogated, scripts or scores for performances are open to interpretation. The faithful reconstruction of an artwork from the past need not preclude the conceptual gains of performing the piece anew in the present. Indeed, a historical understanding of a different moment of technological "invasion" might be useful in a society characterized by a seemingly unprecedented acceleration of spectacle. The concept of *menesunda*—of mess and chaos—as a creative crucible that moves us beyond the circumscribed relationships between media and everyday life is up for grabs in its reinstallation.

I would like to express my gratitude to David Lamelas, Leopoldo Maler, and Marta Minujín for generously sharing their memories of La Menesunda's creation, as well as Helga Christoffersen, Isabel Plante, Daniel R. Quiles, and Irene V. Small for their thoughts and suggestions at different stages of the research for this essay.

1. Elize M. Mazadiego argues that Argentinian artists adopted happenings as a specific response to the particular expression of modernity in Argentina, "actively creating new spaces and experiences by which they could imagine a different nation." See Mazadiego, "Dematerialization in the Argentine Context: Experiments in the Avant-garde in the 1960s" (PhD diss., University of California San Diego, 2015).
2. The exhibition was open from May 18 to June 6, 1965.
3. Jorge Romero Brest, "Letter to Peter Townsend," in *Listen, Here, Now! Argentine Art in the 1960s: Writings of the Avant*-Garde, ed. Inés Katzenstein (New York: Museum of Modern Art, 2004), 133.
4. Argentinian-Italian artist Lucio Fontana proposed the use of television for artistic purposes in the 1952 "Spatialist Manifesto for Television"; however, it is unclear whether the proposal was ever put into practice. As far as I have been able to establish, no other artist had used closed-circuit television in a work before. Warhol's *Outer and Inner Space*, featuring Edie Sedgwick watching a prerecorded videotape of herself, deals with related themes but was not made until 1966. Additionally, Bruce Nauman's closed circuits date to the late '60s and early '70s. See Christine Mehring, "Television Art's Abstract Starts: Europe circa 1944–1969," *October* 125 (Summer 2008): 29–64.
5. The sidelining of Minujín in relation to *arte de los medios* is perhaps due to the great deal of attention she has received more broadly, as well as to differences between the artists that would emerge as *arte de los medios* became more explicitly political over the course of the late 1960s, a shift that was not pursued by Minujín. See, for example, Alexander Alberro, "A Media Art: Conceptualism in Latin America in the 1960s," in *Rewriting Conceptual Art*, ed. Michael Newman and Jon Bird (London: Reaktion Books, 1999), 140–51 and 233–36; and Karen Benezra, "Media Art in Argentina: Ideology and Critique 'Después del Pop,'" *ArtMargins* 1, no. 2–3 (2012): 152–75.
6. In this essay, I use the term *media art* to refer to a broader tendency in Argentinian art, one that includes Minujín, and *arte de los medios* when I am specifically referring to the group formed by Roberto Jacoby, Eduardo Costa, and Raúl Escari.
7. Sofía Dourron, "La Menesunda," in *La Menesunda Según Marta Minujín*, ed. Victoria Noorthoorn, exh. cat. (Buenos Aires: Museo de Arte Moderno de Buenos Aires, 2015), 47.
8. Jorge Romero Brest, Marta Minujín, and Rubén Santantonín, "La Menesunda," exh. pamphlet (Buenos Aires, 1965), reproduced in Katzenstein, *Listen, Here, Now!*, 107.
9. Undated typescript document, Marta Minujín Archive.
10. Ibid.
11. Artists were included in the Di Tella Prize exhibition at the invitation of Jorge Romero Brest and the winners of the national and international prizes were chosen by an international panel of judges. Andrea Giunta, "Rewriting Modernism: Jorge Romero Brest and the Legitimation of Argentine Art," in Katzenstein, *Listen, Here, Now!*, 81.
12. According to Sofía Dourron, *The Woman's Head* was the work of Pablo Suarez, and it is, in fact, highly reminiscent of his work as a solo artist. See Dourron, "La Menesunda," in Noorthoorn, *La Menesunda*, 50.
13. Sofía Dourron et al., "Reconstructing *La Menesunda*," in Noorthoorn, *La Menesunda*, 179.
14. Ibid., 180.
15. The traditional definition of the work of art was first tested in Argentina by the Concretists and the Madí group in the 1940s with the invention of *marco recortado* [cutour canvas], irregularly shaped works that reconceived the artwork as a "concrete," real object and problematized the space beyond the painting. The Concretists also embraced a broad interdisciplinary practice, often including dance, theater, music, and poetry in their exhibitions, events, and publications. However, these artists did not seek a total synthesis of the arts, nor did they ever completely abandon the traditionally conceived notion of the work of art.
16. See John King, *El Di Tella y el desarrollo cultural argentino en la década del sesenta* (Buenos Aires: Asunto Impreso Ediciones, 2007), 80–85.
17. See Andrea Giunta, *Avant-Garde, Internationalism, and Politics: Argentine Art in the 1960s* (Durham: Duke University Press, 2007); and María José Herrera, "En medio de los medios: La experimentación con los medios masivos de comunicación en la Argentina de la década del 60," in *Arte argentino del siglo XX: Premio Telefónica de Argentina a la Investigación en Historia de las Artes Plásticas* (Buenos Aires: Fundación para la Investigación del Arte Argentino, 1997).
18. Greenberg had wanted to award this prize to Emilio Renart. For a full account, see Giunta, "Rewriting Modernism," 82–83; and Giunta, *Avant-Garde, Internationalism, and Politics*, 213–14.
19. David Lamelas in conversation with the author, Los Angeles, March 15, 2019.
20. Dourron, "La Menesunda," 47.
21. Photographs of *La Menesunda* indicate that the refrigerator door bears the "SIAM" marker. According to David Lamelas, his 1967 installation *Situación de tiempo*, which took place in the same space as *La Menesunda*, consisted of seventeen televisions provided by SIAM Di Tella. Lamelas in conversation with the author, 2015.
22. For a full account of this episode, see Ana Longoni and Mario Mestman, "After Pop, We Dematerialize: Oscar Masotta, Happenings, and Media Art at the Beginnings of Conceptualism," in Katzenstein, *Listen, Here, Now!*, 156–72.

23. Minujín was included, for example, in the exhibition "International Pop" organized by the Walker Art Center in 2015, and "The EY Exhibition: The World Goes Pop," organized by Tate Modern in 2015.
24. Noting the status of Pop in Argentinian art, Jorge Romero Brest writes, "Our Pop was initially more like that of Europe than the United States, but the consequences have been different, not only because our creators stopped making Pop art but rather because they moved toward 'arte de los medios' and 'visual experiences.' Neither Marta Minujín, Dalila Puzzovio, Delia Cancela, Pablo Mesejean, Alfredo Rodriguez Arias, nor Juan Stoppani are Pop artists now." See Romero Brest, "Report and Reflection on Pop Art," trans. Gabriel Pérez-Barreiro, in Katzenstein, *Listen, Here, Now!*, 129.
25. Giunta, *Avant-Garde, Internationalism, and Politics*, 158.
26. Marcelo E. Pacheco, "From the Modern to the Contemporary: Shifts in Argentine Art, 1956–1965," in Katzenstein, *Listen, Here, Now!*, 20.
27. Ibid., 16.
28. Catherine Spencer, "Performing Pop: Marta Minujín and the 'Argentine Image-Makers,'" *Tate Papers* 24 (2015), https://www.tate.org.uk/research/publications/tate-papers/24/performing-pop-marta-minujin-and-the-argentine-image-makers.
29. See Jorge Romero Brest and Oscar Masotta, *El 'Pop Art'* (Buenos Aires: Editorial Columba, 1967).
30. Marta Minujín, "Destruction of my works at the Impasse Ronsin, Paris," in Katzenstein, *Listen, Here, Now!*, 59.
31. Ibid., 61.
32. Jorge Romero Brest, "Letter for Buenos Aires," in Katzenstein, *Listen, Here, Now!*, 135.
33. Marta Minujín, "Destruction of my works," 59.
34. Marta Minujín in conversation with the author, March 29, 2019.
35. Fernando Garcia, "Rubén Santantonín: El Fantasma de la Menesunda," *La Nación,* April 3, 2016, https://www.lanacion.com.ar/opinion/ruben-santantonin-el-fantasma-de-la-menesunda-nid1884938.
36. Giunta, *Avant-Garde, Internationalism, and Politics*, 159.
37. According to artist Luis Wells, who belonged to the group of Informalist painters that rose to prominence in the 1950s, the idea for a labyrinth emerged in discussions among the group, most of the members of which were of a slightly older generation than Minujín and included himself, Kenneth Kemble, Emilio Renart, and Santantonín. Wells writes, "The idea of the labyrinth came out of the meetings we had at Kenneth Kemble's home on Martínez, to which only Santantonín came. We took a maquette to Romero Brest and he rejected it because he was supporting the Pop group. A while later we realized that Santantonín was working on *La Menesunda* and we were annoyed with him. But things happened so quickly in 1965 that we soon forgot about it." Wells quoted in Garcia, "El Fantasma de la Menesunda."
38. Rubén Santatonín, "Arte cosa," foreword to *Collages y cosas*, exh. pamphlet (Buenos Aires: Galería Lirolay, 1961).
39. Letter from Rubén Santantonín to Marta Boto, December 1961, cited in Giunta, *Avant-Garde, Internationalism, and Politics*, 158.
40. Leopoldo Maler, email message to author, April 4, 2019.
41. Undated typescript document, Marta Minujín Archive.
42. "La Mene . . . Que?" *Dinamis*, June 17, 1965; "Sinvergüenzas?," *El Eco de Tandil,* December 12, 1965; Daniel Alberto Dessein, "Sobre un Lamentable Espectáculo," *La Gaceta,* Tucumán, June 2, 1965; "'Algo' para locos o tarados," *Careo*, June 2, 1965.
43. David Lamelas in conversation with the author.
44. Statement by Ignacio Pirovano (Buenos Aires, 1965), Marta Minujín Archive.
45. Minujín's friend and role model Alberto Greco had incorporated live animals into his *arte viva: 30 ratas de la nueva generación* [live art: 30 rats from the new generation]. See Victoria Noorthoorn, "The Vertigo of Creation," in *Marta Minujín: Obras 1959–1989*, exh. cat. (Buenos Aires: Museo de Arte Latinoamericano de Buenos Aires, 2010), 245.
46. Longoni and Mestman, "After Pop," 160.
47. Daniel R. Quiles, "Between Code and Message: Argentine Conceptual Art, 1966–1976," (PhD diss., City University of New York, 2010), 51.
48. Marshall McLuhan, *Understanding Media: The Extensions of Man* (New York: Signet, 1964), 272.
49. Jacqueline Barnitz, "A Latin Answer to Pop," in *Readings in Latin American Modern Art*, ed. Patrick Frank (New Haven: Yale, 2004), 199–202.
50. Noorthoorn, "The Vertigo of Creation," 245.
51. "Café Olé," *Revista Metropólis*, August 1983. See also Longoni and Mestman, "After Pop," 160.
52. "Marta y La Menesunda," *La Razón*, May 20, 1965.
53. Giunta, *Avant-Garde, Internationalism, and Politics*, 146.
54. Daniel R. Quiles, "Dead Boars, Viruses, and Zombies: Roberto Jacoby's Art History," *Art Journal* 72, no. 3 (fall 2014): 73, 38–55, 41.
55. Ibid., 42.
56. Dourron, "La Menesunda," 49.
57. Ibid., 53, 178. The televisions were manufactured in Argentina on behalf of the US company DuMont for a short time. See Gonzalo Aguilar, "Televisión y la vida privada," in Fernando Devoto and Marta Madero, *História de la vida privada en la Argentina* (Buenos Aires: Taurus, 2000).
58. Marta Minujín in conversation with the author. See also Aguilar, "Televisión," 6.

59. Ibid.,
60. Jorge Romero Brest, "'Awareness of Image' and 'Awareness of Imagination' in the Process of Argentine Art," in Katzenstein, *Listen, Here, Now!*, 116.
61. Cristina de Irala, "La Diosa de La Menesunda," *Gente*, July 25, 1968.
62. Ana María del Valle, "Marta Minujin reunió personalidades en un inquietante 'happening.'" *Revista Gente* 2, no. 67 (November 1966), unpaginated.
63. Nadja Rottner, "Marta Minujín and the Performance of Softness," *Konsthistorisk tidskrift/Journal of Art History* 83, no. 2 (2014): 110–28.
64. Oscar Masotta, *Happenings* (Buenos Aires: Editorial Jorge Álvarez, 1967), 9.
65. Daniel R. Quiles, "Mediate Media: Buenos Aires Conceptualism," in "Transmissions in art from Eastern Europe & Latin America, 1960–1980: Research Files," ed. Zanna Gilbert and Magdalena Moskalewicz, *post: Notes on Modern and Contemporary Art from Around the Globe*, February 16, 2016, https://post.at.moma.org/content_items/755-mediate-media-buenos-aires-conceptualism.
66. Roberto Jacoby, "Desmaterialización, diseminación, intertextualidad," in *Deseo nace del derrumbe: Roberto Jacoby acciones, conceptos, escritos*, ed. Ana Longoni (Madrid: La Central/Museo Reina Sofía, 2011), 35.
67. According to Jacoby, Barthes and Saussure had a significant impact, and particularly Barthes's 1957 *Mythologies*. See Claire Bishop, *Artificial Hells* (New York: Verso, 2012), 107, 313.
68. Roberto Jacoby, Eduardo Costa, and Raúl Escari, "An Art of Communications Media," in Katzenstein, *Listen, Here, Now!*, 223.
69. Eduardo E. Eichelbaum, "Happening para un jabalí difunto," *El Mundo*, August 21, 1966.
70. Bishop, *Artificial Hells*, 107.
71. *Michael Kirby*, "Marta Minujín's '*Simultaneity* in *Simultaneity*,'" *Drama Review* 12, no. 3 (Spring 1968): 148–52.
72. "Happening using mass media communications," undated typescript document, Marta Minujín Archive.
73. Ibid.
74. Ibid.
75. Ibid.
76. Rodrigo Alonso, "On Technological Tactics," *11e Biennale de l'Image en Mouvement*, exh. cat. (Geneva: Centre pour l'Image Contemporaine Genève, 2005), http://www.roalonso.net/en/pdf/videoarte/tacticas_ing.pdf.
77. Leopoldo Maler, email message to author, April 21, 2019.
78. Ibid.
79. Peter Sachs Collopy, "The Revolution Will Be Videotaped: Making a Technology of Consciousness in the Long 1960s" (PhD diss., University of Pennsylvania, 2015).
80. Ibid., 11.
81. Ibid., 10.
82. Oscar Masotta, "After Pop: We Materialize," trans. Eileen Brockbank, in Katzenstein, *Listen, Here, Now!*, 213.
83. Noorthoorn, "The Vertigo of Creation," 275.
84. Undated typescript document (ca. 1966), Marta Minujín Archive.
85. Ibid.
86. Ibid.
87. Ibid.
88. Claire Bishop, "Reconstruction Era: The Anachronic Time(s) of Installation Art," in *When Attitudes Become Form. Bern 1969/Venice 2013*, ed. Germano Celant (Milan: Fondazione Prada, 2013), 430.
89. Irene V. Small, "Material Remains: Irene V. Small on the Afterlife of Hélio Oiticica's Work," *Artforum* 48, no. 6 (February 2010): 96.
90. Isabel Plante, "Reseña exposición: La Menesunda según Marta Minujín," *TAREA* 3, no. 3 (September 2016): 299. Translated by the author.
91. Ibid., 301.
92. Quiles, "Mediate Media," 4.

Marta Minujín in Conversation with Helga Christoffersen and Massimiliano Gioni

Massimiliano Gioni: Can you talk a little bit about what you were doing before you made *La Menesunda* in 1965. When did you go to Paris?

Marta Minujín: I was in Paris from 1961 to '64, but I always went back to Buenos Aires for the winter. I received three grants during that time, which always paid my ticket. So I went back and forth, back and forth, back and forth, and I was mostly working with mattresses.

But then, when I got back to Argentina, I did an exhibition that was more political because there was a fight with the military. Argentina would have two or three years of democracy and then the military would take over. At this time, there were "the blues" [*azules*] and "the reds" [*colorados*]—the military blues against the military reds. The exhibition was at Lirolay Gallery, and I showed mattresses with cardboard rifles, military hats, and military boots. I also went to a factory where those supplies were produced and collected the military's waste. I invited the blues and reds to the opening, and it was almost like a happening.

Back in Paris, I was collecting old mattresses from outside the hospital.

All those mattresses were dirty and infected, so I would disinfect them and bring them up to my studio, where I was living without gas or heat. It was crazy! I would get infections, come back to Argentina, get healthy, and go back to Paris. There, I participated in happenings with Jean-Jacques Lebel, Daniel Pommereulle, and all those people.

MG: So, when you went to Paris in '61, you were already an artist?

MM: Yeah! I was nineteen years old when I went to Paris. I arrived and started working with the mattresses. The first mattress works I did were in Buenos Aires, but I became very famous in Paris because of what I was doing with all those mattresses. There were also other artists from Argentina there, like Alberto Greco.

I was doing happenings where there were no spectators and everyone was immersed in the act of creation, improvisation, and surprise.

I was doing these happenings with big, big, big mattresses, which people could go inside of and feel protected. I realized that fifty percent of a person's life is lived on a mattress—I had also visited a hospital where people were dying on mattresses—so I wanted to work with something that was alive, and a mattress *is* alive. These were my first environments.

After that, I did another piece called *Chambre d'amour* [Room of Love] (1963–64) with a Dutch artist named Mark Brusse, where you entered through a vagina to find a bed inside. When people sat on the bed, everything moved. When I came back to Buenos Aires after Paris, I was crazed over happenings and I did my biggest one yet with a helicopter, chickens, and everything.

MG: How did you connect with all those artists in Paris?

MM: La Coupole, the famous Brasserie in Montparnasse, became my studio. I spent hours and hours there and I invited everybody to come. I met all those artists, and then invited them to participate in *La destrucción* [The Destruction] (1963). For that work, I went to see Niki de Saint Phalle and Jean Tinguely. At the time, I was painting the old mattresses, which were like trash, and Niki said, "Why don't you do your own mattresses?" So I started to make them myself.

MG: And whom did you have a close dialogue with in Paris?

MM: Christo and Lourdes Castro and René Bértholo, who were both from Portugal and great friends of Christo.

MG: Did you also know Pierre Restany?

MM: Yeah, I love Pierre Restany! I met him in Paris with Daniel Spoerri, Robert Filliou, Mimmo Rotella, all of them.

MG: When you returned from Paris in 1964, you exhibited the work *Eróticos en technicolor* [Erotic Works in Technicolor] (1964). Can you tell us a little bit about it?

MM: It's four mattresses, hung by their coils and contorted into very abstract shapes—like penises and vaginas—which connect and enter into each other.

MG: What about *¡Revuélquese y viva!* [Wallow Around and Live!] (1964–85)?

MM: That was the big house. I won a prize for *Eróticos en Technicolor*, and also for *¡Revuélquese y viva!* The sponsor of the prize, Instituto Torcuato Di Tella, was very energetic. All the winners were about twenty to twenty-four years old—these artists completely changed the institution, which was only showing paintings until then. I said, "No. People have to react more!" I wanted to create more reactions. Instituto Torcuato Di Tella was a unique place in the world. It was run by Jorge Romero Brest, who was just so audacious and intelligent. He saw that a new group of very young people was breaking the rules, and he gave us money to create something crazy. That is how *La Menesunda* came about. Jorge believed in me so much. I was only twenty-four years old. He could believe in me, while I could not yet believe in myself.

The prize also included a trip to New York, but I immediately began working on *La Menesunda*, and I didn't go to New York until later in 1965 because I was pregnant. My child was born just as *La Menesunda* opened.

Helga Christoffersen: How did your collaboration with Rubén Santantonín come about? Since he and you developed *La Menesunda* together, I wonder how you knew him and how the vision for the project came together.

MM: At that time, Rubén Santantonín was making *cosas*, as he called them, or "things." These were not sculptures or environments, but *things*, very much in line with the philosophy of Robert Filliou and the Fluxus group, who asserted that things talk to us—not that we talk to things *but that things talk to us*.

I met Santantonín because he was a very popular person in the scene. I was sophisticated because I studied art, earned a four-year degree, and I came from a middle-class family. My father was a doctor. Rubén came from a working-class family—a real working family—and was doing things with bras, which were fantastic! We became good friends. Every day, we would walk through the streets, which inspired our ideas. He was twenty-five years older than I was but he was still like a child—maybe because we never considered ourselves as being of any age. We started to create gigantic environments where people would react to different situations, as if they were living in the art.

This theory has followed me all my life: that everybody is a creator, just by being a human. Just by talking, you are creating, because language is immediate creation.

HC: How did *La Menesunda* specifically come about?

MM: With *La Menesunda*, I wanted to see what would happen when we reproduced the city of Buenos Aires, but in an abstract way. That's why you enter the neon tunnel through a doorway shaped like a human figure—it's like seeing yourself entering into yourself, and then discovering that you are inside a city. Immediately, you feel like you're in the middle of Times Square, but like a Buenos Aires Times Square. It's meant to inspire pride.

The idea was to completely surprise people. First, they would enter the neon tunnel and go upstairs, where they'd see themselves on TV, then, suddenly, they would find themselves in a bedroom where real people were lying in bed. Visitors were completely astonished, they could not believe it! Some people would run away, some people would talk to the couple, and some people would even try to get into bed with them. That was a very interesting reaction.

After that, visitors would reenter *La Menesunda* from another entryway, because we wanted to confuse people—instead, they would enter through the head of the woman. At that time, I thought that fifty percent of women's lives were spent buying makeup, doing makeup, trying makeup, and seeing themselves with makeup. So, that's why the inside of *The Woman's Head* is filled only with makeup.

HC: At the time, was that a commentary on or a critique of women?

MM: My mother and grandmother never worked and, in 1965, most women in Argentina did not work. They were housewives. I hated housewives. I wanted to tell them that all they had in their heads was makeup.

When you entered the carousel, it would go around, leading you either to an exit through the intestine or *la ciénaga* [the swamp]. Many people never made it to the intestine—the best room—because they never saw the entrance. Instead, they would go through the swamp, and then say, "What!? I did not see the intestine!"

HC: Was it intentional that some rooms could be missed entirely? I imagine there would often be confusion when some people would come out of *La Menesunda* and say, "Did I see it all?"

MM: They would go crazy! They wanted to go back in and they couldn't.

HC: You wanted to make it difficult?

MM: Yes. I always liked the idea that something is missing. For instance, I am very famous in Argentina, so I signed a dollar with the statement: "Take me, I am yours." People would then have to think about whether they wanted to sell the dollar with my signature on it, or use it. It's like if you found a dollar bill signed by Andy Warhol in New York, would you sell it, keep it to sell it later, or spend it? I always want to create that kind of situation. That's what I like about art: to wake up senses and ideas, to wake people up from their everyday lives, to wake up feelings they've never felt before.

MG: Another piece I remember seeing in Buenos Aires was a sculpture that resembles a nest.

MM: *Comunicando con tierra* [Communicating with Earth] (1976). That was later.

MG: Oh, yes. Speaking of the '70s, can you talk about *La Academia del Fracaso* [Academy of Failure] (1975)? I love the title.

MM: Yeah, it's a university where you learn how to fail. When you enter, a nurse vaccinates you against triumphalism. It was a kind of performance. People would come to talk about how many times they had failed, even if they were very successful. The students, who were there every day, had to wear a crown of thorns.

MG: Were you the director of the Academy?

MM: I was.

MG: Could you talk about how *Minuphone* (1967) and *Minucode* (1968), two legendary pieces of yours, developed?

MM: I did *Minuphone* in 1967. At the time, I was working with the idea of mass media and I was crazy over Marshall McLuhan, so I went to see him at Fordham University.

MG: Were you able to just approach him?

MM: No, what happened was that after I did *Three Country Happening* (1966) with Allan Kaprow and Wolf Vostell, it was featured in the *New York Times*. It was all about media, and so McLuhan knew me from that. I was also very famous here in the '60s. I couldn't walk down the street because I was always on television. I worked with Andy Warhol all the time. Then I became like a crazy Pop artist.

Mass media influenced me so much, and *Minucode* developed when the Center for Inter-American Relations in New York invited me to do something. I got a grant from the Rockefeller Foundation and I spent all the money publishing questionnaires in New York newspapers.

The responses were selected by a computer, and then eighty economists were invited to a room where there were three waiters with champagne. As they talked, they were filmed with six cameras fixed on tripods—capturing the entire conversation in one giant picture, stretching from the ceiling to the floor.

The next day, I invited only politicians, and the day after, people in the fashion industry. On the last day, only artists came. Every group was totally different in how they moved and what they did. One week later, I projected the films. It was not immediately after the event because I had to go get the 16mm film developed. When it was shown, it was like a social environment, and that was fantastic.

MG: Could you also talk about how *El Batacazo* [The Long Shot] (1966) came about?

MM: After *La Menesunda*, I was selected for the Instituto Torcuato Di Tella International Prize . . .

MG: For someone who invented an *Academy of Failure*, you won lots of prizes.

MM: [Laughter] Yeah, it's true. I won all the prizes. I won seventy grants.

MG: Seventy!

MM: That's why I never sold a piece of art until I was forty years old. Because I didn't want to sell. I was against galleries and against museums. I hated museums, but Instituto Torcuato Di Tella was not a museum. At the time, I would say, "Death to the museums. Kill the museums. Kill the art galleries. Don't sell any art." I didn't believe in selling. I created and destroyed all my work because I believed that art was not objects, it was life.

But, you see, even though I got grants, I was always very poor. The only good one was from the Guggenheim. That grant is now $40,000;

that's a lot! At the time, it was $8,000. I used $6,000 to make *Minuphone*, and I lived on $2,000 for a year. I always spent all my money on my work, and I usually didn't have anything left to live on.

You know how long *La Menesunda* lasted? Fifteen days—because another exhibition was coming. But Rubén Santantonín and I worked on it for three months.

MG: I've always been interested in that aspect of the history of art. "This is Tomorrow"—the legendary 1956 show at the Whitechapel Art Gallery, traditionally recognized as the birthplace of Pop art—lasted only a few weeks in the month of August, a time slot that nobody would want. It's amazing how short some of the most legendary shows were.

MM: Yeah, *La Menesunda* lasted fifteen days—nothing! Many people in the papers wrote that Santantonín and I were crazy, that we were idiots, that we were silly, and that we should go to jail. *La Menesunda* may have been open for just fifteen days, but it lasted in the memory of the people for fifty years! What's amazing is that people went crazy. They would wait eight hours to go inside *La Menesunda* for just ten or fifteen minutes.

I believe this idea was more important than anything else: an environment with different situations was a way of living differently, *a way of living art differently*; whereas a painting might only reflect something inside you, *La Menesunda* forced you to enter the scene, and you could not go back, even if you wanted to. There was claustrophobia. Everything was a surprise. Nobody could really tell what would happen in the next room or how long they would remain inside. For that reason, we didn't want to reveal too much about what was going on in *La Menesunda* and we didn't want the press to write too much about it either.

HC: The work seems very specific to Buenos Aires, from the neon lights to the smells of the street; however, I know that at that time, you were in dialogue with many other artists from many other places outside

Buenos Aires. I wonder how *La Menesunda* was influenced not only by Buenos Aires but also by these conversations with international artists?

MM: I never saw anyone do anything similar. Niki de Saint Phalle and Jean Tinguely did that big "nana" [*Hon—en katedral* [She—a Cathedral] (1966)], but that was after *La Menesunda*.

HC: Exactly. It was done a year after *La Menesunda,* from June to September 1966, at the Moderna Museet in Stockholm.

MM: I was already working with Santantonín, and he was doing things very similar to Robert Filliou. The idea was to create things, to break what art was. That was the concept, to change things completely. Christo, for instance, is still the only artist whose work can be compared to what I do, because he does fantastic, gigantic things, and I also like to do gigantic things.

What was good about *La Menesunda* was that it was real; it was Buenos Aires in the '60s. It's a work of art that breaks all the rules, but most people would say, "No, it's not art. It's something else." *Menesunda* is *Lunfardo*, or Argentinian slang, for a difficult, awkward, or embarrassing situation.

In *La Menesunda*, there are two situations that are very much Buenos Aires: the neon tunnel—which also smelled of fried food—and the octagonal mirror room. You see yourself in the mirrors, it still smells of fried food; you see all the confetti, like the lights of Lavalle Street, which were much more like Times Square than they are now. At that time, every person walked in Buenos Aires with their books; now they walk with cellphones. There were many intellectuals in Buenos Aires, which is why I knew about Marshall McLuhan. When I got the Di Tella Prize, I stayed in Buenos Aires, after having traveled to Paris, to produce *La Menesunda* and *El Batacazo*—and then went to New York, where I stayed. There, I became much more involved with art and technology and that's how I created works like *Minucode*. I imported all the hippie culture from New York; I was a hippie, completely. It was amazing because everyone became a hippie in Buenos Aires.

MG: What was *El Batacazo*?

MM: *El Batacazo* was a big pentagon with plants, and inside there were four situations. You could not see the entirety of *La Menesunda* from outside, but with *El Batacazo*, you could see everything from the outside. First of all, you enter by foot and you see lots of rabbits, all of which are alive. You then encounter a sculpture of a football player in position. You arrive at a slide, which you go down, and land among sculptures depicting the faces of women. It was actually the face of Virna Lisi. The women were gigantic, like twenty-four feet long and pink. Then you had to walk back and enter the world of the astronaut. Everything was made of vinyl and sewn by both hand and machine. Eventually, you would exit through a tunnel with bees.

MG: With bees?

MM: Yeah. Inside transparent glass, there were many, many bees, as we are synchronous with animals. With the Di Tella Prize, I brought the entire installation to New York. It was crazy. I knew Leo Castelli because he had visited Buenos Aires for an international prize. I took half of my grant money from the fellowship to get to New York, without knowing any English, without knowing where I wanted to live, without knowing anyone. I went by boat and when I arrived, I went to meet Señor Castelli. I got very lucky.

MG: You showed *El Batacazo* at Bianchini Gallery in New York. Sturtevant had her first show there in 1965. Did you know her?

MM: Yeah, I knew her!

MG: So, you were saying that you brought *El Batacazo* to New York . . .

MM: Well, I went to see Castelli and I said, "This piece is arriving by boat tomorrow. What can I do?" and he said, "Okay, talk to Bianchini," since he was a friend of Castelli's. And he said okay. So, when *El Batacazo* arrived in the port, it went directly to the gallery, where it was shown for only one week, because the rabbits died.

They also used flies instead of bees, and the flies kept escaping from the glass.

It was very successful. There were reviews in the *New York Times* and all the magazines, but animal rights activists closed it down. So, I gave it back to the Santini Brothers, who were the transporters, and they destroyed the whole thing because I didn't have the money to store it or send it back. I spent all my grant money bringing that work to New York and then just threw it away. Crazy, but I would do it again.

Later, I met Andy Warhol, who was very poor, and Lichtenstein, who was also very poor. Everyone was poor. But we were happy because we were crashing all the parties with the Velvet Underground and Nico. It was another New York, one that was also very dangerous. A friend of mine was killed in the street because somebody hit her. Now it's different, but it was a fantastic time.

I would hang out at the Cedar Tavern, which is where I met Carolee Schneemann. She was my best friend. With her, I met Al Hansen, Dick Higgins, and Claes Oldenburg. I was not making technological art yet, but I talked with Allan Kaprow and Wolf Vostell and we invented *Three Country Happening*. Around the same time, Rauschenberg was doing the *9 Evenings* series with Experiments in Art and Technology, but I was back in Argentina at the time. In Buenos Aires, the mass-media expert Oscar Masotta, who was a kind of philosopher and psychoanalyst, was talking with me about how our work was becoming media. So I went back to New York and did *Three Country Happening* with Kaprow and Vostell.

But I took too much LSD. I threw everything out, and it was three or four years until I did another performance. At that time, Timothy Leary, Allen Ginsberg, and all those people were doing "freak-outs" and I didn't want to be an artist, I wanted to enjoy life. That's all. I just wanted to live. I went to San Francisco. I went to Mexico. I went to live on a commune. Then, finally, I went back to Buenos Aires.

The problem was that I was so famous by the time I was twenty-two years old that I could not even walk down the street. Then the military took over in Argentina and people forgot the whole thing. Many people disappeared. Things got bad. But, at a certain point, I was hugely popular—like Britney Spears. Our generation was born under a special star; Mick Jagger is my age—though it seems like just yesterday that he was twenty-five. We were born under a special star because we were all the same. We were all the same, this generation from the '60s. In New York, I was with Jimi Hendrix and Janis Joplin, and then everybody started dying. It was very freaky—it went *boom*. Carolee Schneemann, like me, was a survivor. She was a survivor because she never had success at that time, perhaps because she was a woman. Now, however, she's recognized.

HC: Did you feel marginalized yourself, as a woman?

MM: The thing is that I have a very, very big ego. I always believed that I was a genius, so that allowed me to do so many things. But, at the same time, no museums in Buenos Aires own my work. I have work in the collections of the Tate, MoMA, everywhere, but not here in Argentina, because they believed that I was crazy, or that I was *estrafalario* [eccentric]. They never believed that I was a big artist, but I always thought that I was a genius, so I didn't care.

HC: Do you feel that it took longer for you to be recognized, as was the case with Carolee Schneemann?

MM: I didn't have any problems as a woman, perhaps because I was so bougie. For instance, Billy Klüver, from Experiments in Art and Technology, never helped me, but I knew how to create and exhibit at galleries, so it didn't matter.

I also really believed that I was a genius, like everyone else. I was with Salvador Dalí every day at the St. Regis Hotel because we were both geniuses. Andy Warhol believed he was a genius. Charlotte Moorman, Nam June Paik, everyone believed they were a genius. Who cares if the others don't believe you, too bad for them!

HC: Did you think of your own work as resisting or even fighting patriarchy or the notion that artistic genius—at that time and in the environments you were part of—was often defined by men?

MM: No, no, no. I believed that art doesn't have a gender. I didn't even believe that I was a woman—it doesn't matter.

HC: So you didn't work from a gendered perspective, let's say . . .

MM: No, I never thought that way.

HG: Your work was not intended as criticism or to resist what you saw around you?

MM: It can be critical, but not from a specific, gendered perspective, just as a human being. I believe that art is at the top of everything. It's a very crazy idea, but I believe that art is bigger than politics, bigger than religion, bigger than energy. Tracey Emin said that art protects you. After I had my daughter, I never went to the doctor anymore, not even to have my vagina looked at—nothing [laughs]. Nevermore! Nothing's happened to me, because art protects me. Many of us believe that—because if not, how can you explain Mick Jagger jumping around on stage at his age? Ours is such a crazy generation. But many died—many, many, many died. All my friends died. And all my friends here in Argentina, they all died.

HC: Do you think you had an awareness of how to take part in everything without going too far?

MM: Oh, with the drugs?

HC: Yes, for example.

MM: Well, I probably lost like ten or fifteen years of my life because I was so involved with drugs. The only way to stop me was when they put me in jail. I was also an alcoholic, and I stopped that too. But I believe it was very good that I did everything. I am a survivor. Remember.

MG: Did you meet Marcel Duchamp?

MM: No.

MG: He famously said—and he was probably referring to Oldenburg—that happenings made boredom interesting. But your happenings were never boring, were they?

MM: No! They were all funny.

MG: Did you think of your happenings or environments as a form of entertainment?

MM: No. I just wanted people to *live* in art. And a way of doing that is to go inside, laugh, see something new, and react to it. I was always interested in participation, but it didn't always have to be funny. *Academy of Failure,* for example, was not that funny.

MG: Were you interested in the idea of the spectacle, or the way that the media was making everything spectacular? *Minucode* is very much about the spectacularization of identity.

MM: But it's not a spectacle, no! I was interested in the four hundred people that took part in *Minucode*, how they looked at themselves, and how they behaved. It's always about the people. I was interested in the people. I wanted to see how they behaved when, for example, they were surrounded by economists. It was about observing and being observed.

MG: This brings me to another question. Some of your environments remind me a bit of a rat maze, you know?

MM: No!

MG: Did you ever think of them as experiments with people?

MM: No, I didn't like art experts or elitists. I just wanted to reach the people. My art was going directly to the people. The small videos that I now do all the time on Instagram are about the same thing. They are not meant to be intellectual, even if I am an intellectual.

MG: Since you mentioned Instagram, are you aware of this phenomenon of pop-up museums—like the Museum of Ice Cream, for example— which are basically just backgrounds for selfies? These places offer immersive experiences, as they call them. In a sense, *La Menesunda* could be seen as a predecessor to this kind of Instagram museum.

MM: Well, Epcot copied *La Menesunda*. There was a room that was exactly like the last room of *La Menesunda*: the pentagon with confetti. It was exactly the same.

MG: How do you feel now that something that was somewhat avant-garde is being recycled for popular entertainment?

MM: I don't know.

MG: Are you excited by it? Are you opposed to it? Do you feel it's something your work anticipated?

MM: Because I'm always working on the next thing, I don't really register things like that.

MG: I have two further questions. From New York, you went to Washington, DC, and then eventually back to Buenos Aires. What made you leave New York and, eventually, the US?

MM: My husband began working at the Organization of American States. He was an economist. He came to New York with me for one or two years and studied at Columbia University, but we went back to Buenos Aires because our son was there, being cared for by my father. We didn't have any money, and New York was already too expensive.

In New York—and really everywhere—I was interested in the underground. Sex workers interested me a lot. I became friends with a sex worker who I'd visit all the time and she would always be dressed up in her apartment. They would pay her $500 to go to Chicago, be with a man, and come back. She was very famous, and from Argentina, too. I started looking into porn shops. I was interested in the power of sex in relationships. That's why I started those paintings of penises and vaginas in the *Erótica* series. Then I had a show in Washington where I did *Soft Gallery* (1973). I also did some pieces of theater with puppets—gigantic things made from papier-mâché—and then I went back to Buenos Aires and started the *Academy of Failure*.

MG: My last question has to do with your image. When did you start thinking that your own image could become a medium for your art? When did you become an image, so to speak?

MM: It was very slow, because when I arrived back in Argentina around 1969, I started getting death threats.

MG: From whom?

MM: From military groups.

MG: Was that in reaction to any specific artwork?

MM: No, no. First, they closed the Instituto Torcuato Di Tella. Then a terrible right-wing group called Tacuara would say, "We're going to kill your son with knives, slowly," and would threaten to kill me too. So, I started to resist. I was a hippie and I dressed like a hippie, but then I changed completely and started wearing suits like a man. I was always wearing a suit. And then, slowly, with the happenings and other things that I did in Washington, DC, I connected with some people from the Bread and Puppet Theater in New York. After that, I started dressing like a general, using masks and everything. Then, slowly, I continued to invent.

MG: You slowly became Marta Minujín.

MM: Yeah.

MG: In a way, it was a defense mechanism. It was both an act of resistance and an act of aggression.

MM: Yeah.

MINUYORK: Marta Minujín in the USA

—

Aimé Iglesias Lukin

THE ROAD TO NEW YORK

Marta Minujín's geographical itinerary is symptomatic of a significant power shift in the postwar art world: at a very young age, she traveled from Argentina to Paris, first in 1961; but in the mid '60s, left the old city for New York, the new preferred destination of artists in search of career advancement. This new inclination among young creatives was not simply a matter of preference but was, in part, the result of a program of cultural diplomacy hatched in the midst of the Cold War that was meant to enhance interhemispheric relations by fostering alliances between institutions in the United States and Latin America. Among them, the Instituto Torcuato Di Tella was perhaps the most active in supporting and promoting avant-garde visual arts in Argentina and abroad; and Minujín happened to be one of the favorites of the Director of the Di Tella's Centro de Artes Visuales [Center for Visual Arts], or CAV, Jorge Romero Brest.[1] As we will see, although Minujín quickly assimilated into the New York art scene—working with some of the most important artists and curators of the late 1960s neo-avant-garde—she always maintained a critical intellectual distance from the city that allowed her to analyze American culture as only a migrant artist—at once both insider and outsider—could.[2]

Before traveling to New York for the first time in late 1965, her art had already been exhibited in the United States in two exhibitions showcasing avant-garde Argentinian art. First, Minujín was included in the traveling exhibition "New Art of Argentina," curated by Jan Van der Marck and coproduced by the Di Tella's CAV and the Walker Art Center in Minneapolis, where it would open in 1964.[3] There, Minujín exhibited *La Batalla* [The Battle] (1962), a piece of wood and cardboard, and *Homenaje a la almohada* [Homage to the Pillow] (1962), made from cardboard, wool, and fabric. And second, in 1965, Minujín was included in "Buenos Aires 64," an exhibition curated by Hugo Parpagnoli at the Pepsi-Cola Hall in New York.

THE FIRST HAPPENINGS

After the tremendously successful installation of *La Menesunda* at the Di Tella, which lasted from May 18 to June 6, 1965, Minujín participated in the Di Tella International Prize exhibition—after having already won the national edition of the prize the previous year—along with Pol Bury, Sven Lukin, James Rosenquist, and Frank Stella, among other invited artists. Minujín showed *El Batacazo* [The Long Shot], her second environmental happening. The prize, which brought many international artists to Buenos Aires, was one of the many strategies through which the institute fostered exchange with the United States.

El Batacazo consisted of a hexahedron-shaped structure with two stories. The interior was divided by panels, creating a circuit in which visitors would be constantly stimulated as they moved through it. The walls were made of glass, allowing visitors to see one another as they interacted with the piece, thus incorporating them into the spectacle. An audio recording invited visitors to remove their shoes and enter the structure, which contained four main "situations." First, visitors would walk through a tunnel referred to as the *Space of Sports*, where neon silhouettes of rugby and soccer players flashed on and off, creating the illusion of movement. After climbing up some stairs, visitors would find the *Ecological Section*, complete with caged rabbits. Visitors would then move on to the *Playboy Section*, an attempt to embarrass the public, who had to go down a slide that landed them on the head of a seventeen-foot-tall inflatable naked doll—inspired by Italian actress Virna Lisi—that emitted erotic sounds when stepped on. The *Space Section* followed and included several rubber figures of astronauts on the floor and ceiling, alluding to that era's expectation of finally sending men to the moon. To exit the piece, visitors would have to walk through a nerve-racking hallway, surrounded by thousands of bees trapped behind glass panels, with flashing neon lights embedded in the floor. As in *La Menesunda*, Minujín chose to title the piece with a *Lunfardo* [slang] term, *batacazo*, meaning a fall or bump, or more figuratively, an unexpected and fortunate triumph or success.

El Batacazo addressed many of the period's concerns. The effects of the boom of mass media and spectacle on social understandings of the body were evoked by the physical interaction between visitors and the figures of athletes and movie stars; but were also formally alluded to in the use of new materials like neon, plastic inflatables, and rubber. The section dedicated to the space race simultaneously conjured both the optimism associated with new technologies and the pessimism inherent in the competitive world views that characterized the Cold War era. *El Batacazo* offered a reflection on natural systems of communication and community-building with the inclusion of the beehive, while at the same time, it demonstrated a formalist approach to nature with the inclusion of the rabbits, which Minujín referred to as "soft shapes in movement."[4] In sum, the participatory nature and ludic tone of the environment gave the piece a sense of apparent naïveté, while simultaneously maintaining its serious political implications.

Given the success of her environments, Brest and van der Marck put Minujín in contact with Leo Castelli, who was a partner in Bianchini Gallery at the time, and he invited her to present the piece there. Using the remaining funds from her 1964 Di Tella Prize to finance the trip, Minujín installed a second version of *El Batacazo* at Bianchini, which opened to the public on February 8, 1966.[5]

For the New York presentation of *El Batacazo*, the title was translated as "The Long Shot," slightly nudging the implications of the term toward a more explicit sense of both odds and optimism. Minujín had to make a few adjustments for this version, including the replacement of the bees with flies due to safety concerns.[6] The piece was well received by critics and had many visitors, but was forced to close just a week after its opening due to the demands of the ASPCA (The American Society for the Prevention of Cruelty to Animals), which cited the death of some of the rabbits and expressed concern about the hundreds of flies that had escaped the enclosures and roamed freely through the gallery space.[7]

Despite its brevity, the exhibition nonetheless cemented Minujín's place in the New York art world. The secretary at Bianchini gallery was married to Roy Lichtenstein, and she helped Minujín connect with the artists of the New York Pop art scene. Among them was Andy Warhol, who had heard of Minujín's work through Allan Kaprow and welcomed her into his inner circle. During that time, she also became good friends with Al Hansen, who organized collective happenings in his loft, many of which she participated in. As a result of *El Batacazo* and the contacts she established during that time, Minujín received the Guggenheim fellowship, which allowed her to return to New York in late 1966.

COMMUNICATION TECHNOLOGIES

Planning her return to Buenos Aires after *El Batacazo*, Minujín coordinated an international happening with Allan Kaprow and Wolf Vostell, scheduled for October 1966. Titled *Three Country Happening*, the work involved a series of events that would take place simultaneously in each artist's city of origin: Buenos Aires, New York, and Berlin. Minujín's took up the theme of concurrency with her contribution to the piece, titled *Simultaneidad en Simultaneidad* [Simultaneity in Simultaneity], which consisted of a two-part happening that took place in multiple locations: at the Di Tella's CAV and, aiming for the participation of the general public, in the circuits of the mass media.

One of the parts, titled *Enveloping Simultaneity*, occurred in two phases. On October 13, 1966, Minujín gathered sixty distinguished personalities of different disciplines to be filmed, photographed, and recorded while a closed-circuit television system transmitted the footage live. And then, a little over a week later, on October 24—at the same time that Kaprow and Vostell did their performances—the guests were invited back to the Di Tella to observe themselves on TV and hear their voices on the radio. The other part, titled *Instantaneous Invasion*, also took place on October 24. Minujín bombarded 120 people in their homes—in which they had been (consensually) filmed, photographed, and recorded during the week prior—by telephone calls and telegrams. All this was broadcast that night at midnight on TV, along with instructions from Minujín, transmitted via radio, for the audience to participate remotely. On the radio, Minujín declared: "Now me, Marta Minujín, I am invading you." Additionally, five hundred people received telephone calls and telegrams with the message: "You are a creator."[8]

Simultaneidad en Simultaneidad marks a new stage in Minujín's career, in which media theory and technology became central to her work. The piece takes up the proliferation of live television and closed circuits to address the political potential of mass media; and in a sense, it anticipated the complexities of image construction in the digital era. The piece also speaks to her international ambitions and the important role of collaborations and networks would play in her practice.

Thanks to the Guggenheim fellowship, Minujín arrived back in New York in late 1966, and given the intensification of her work's engagement with ideas about communication and technology, she arranged to meet Canadian media theorist Marshall McLuhan, who had influenced her work deeply. Soon thereafter, on April 28, 1967, she created *Circuit Super-Heterodyne*, "an incursion into mass media" presented at the Pavilion de la Jeunese at Expo 67 in Montreal. Expanding on the themes and format of *Simultaneidad*, Minujín invited people to complete a questionnaire published in the newspaper, after which an electronic calculator would select and organize participants, grouping them according to certain physical characteristics or personality traits. On the day of the performance, one group would go to a café in the pavilion, the second to a theater, and the third would stand in line near the entrance. Those in the theater would see clips from films such as *Citizen Kane*—which addresses similar themes of both media and power—a live feed of themselves captured through a closed-circuit television, and a live feed of the group in the café. The spectators were thus faced with images of the past (in the film), of their own present (in the closed-circuit televisions), and of what awaited them outside in the future (in the footage of the café). The groups would then rotate. On top of all this, four helicopters transmitted images of the pavilion from above so that the audience was aware of their physical location in the general area. To this already intense exchange of information, Minujín incorporated Polaroids of the audience and reproductions of their silhouettes with photosensitive paper and stroboscopic light. The visitors' voices were recorded and projected over the pavilion's amplifiers. Additionally, using a teletype machine, visitors could send invented news to a newspaper to be published in the its afternoon edition. In tandem, radio stations transmitted a live recording of the event mixed with fake information mixed in with comments from participants. As related by art critic Luc Perrault, Minujín's goal was to "drown participants in audiovisual information and to instantly fabricate stories about the participants to invert roles [of the spectacle and the spectator]." "Technology," Perrault continues, "has invaded our lives. An experience such as the one that Marta Minujín plans to carry out should once and for all convince us of the need to seriously consider the consequences of this."[9] By turning communication into noise, Minujín offers an explicitly critical view of the social role of mass media and the potential of art to denaturalize the effects of technology in our everyday lives.

In a similar vein, for her Guggenheim fellowship, Minujín proposed a technological sculpture that would take the form of an everyday object: a phone booth. To create it, she connected with E.A.T. (Experiments in Art and Technology), a group that promoted collaborations between artists and engineers, and was founded by Robert Rauschenberg, Billy Klüver, Robert Whitman, and Fred Waldhauer. Through them, she met Per Biorn, an electrical engineer working at Bell Labs who would help her fabricate the piece, titled *Minuphone* (1967)—a portmanteau incorporating her name as a kind of signature that confirmed the object's status as a work of art.

The work consisted of a telephone booth—of the same size and format as the ones installed on the streets of New York—altered to facilitate psychedelic experiences and a general dislocation of sensations. When the visitor entered the booth, they could see their own image on a screen embedded in the floor. Depending on the buttons pressed, dialing a number would unleash one of a series of aleatory effects, which included: green and black liquids streaming down the side panels, partially obscuring the visitor's ability to see; green fog filling up the cabin; a photosensitive paper that used a UV light to print the silhouette of the visitor; and a sequence of lights—referred to by Minujín as the “color organ”—that changed according to the pitch of the user’s voice. There was also a recording of the visitor’s voice that would be played back on a speaker with an echo effect. Finally, at the end of the experience, visitors would receive a Polaroid of themselves.[10]

Minuphone was exhibited at Howard Wise Gallery, opening on June 27, 1967, and continuing through the rest of the summer. It had taken weekly sessions over the course of eight months for Minujín and Biorn to build it, which they did at Biorn’s home in New Jersey. Minujín claims that the idea to make a telephone booth came from observing the alienation and anxiety of people trying to use them in public spaces.[11] With the stimuli offered by *Minuphone*, visitors experienced a profound disconnection from their mundane day-to-day interactions with technology.

Proving herself a natural addition to the New York milieu, in February 1968, Minujín was invited to be a guest lecturer at New York University’s School of Continuing Education’s seminar Adventures in New Media, along with Tony Conrad, Chryssa, Terry Riley, Robert Rauschenberg, Robert Whitman, La Monte Young, and others. She also participated in the workshop Mass Media Scenes, a part of the Eighth International Artists’ Seminar at Farleigh Dickinson University in Madison, Wisconsin, along with artists Luis Camnitzer, Michael Snow, Marvin Goldstein, Luis Felipe Noé, Nancy Graves, and Ay-O.

In 1968, Minujín produced *Minucode*, which comprised an event held at the Center for Inter-American Relations in New York, and is perhaps the pinnacle of the experiments in technology and communication she began with *Simultaneidad*. For *Minucode*, Minujín announced four cocktail parties, each dedicated to a particular category of guests—businessmen, politicians, fashion-industry workers, and art world habitués.

Minujín recorded and edited footage of the events, and then invited the guests to a gallery space where the resulting films were screened.[12]

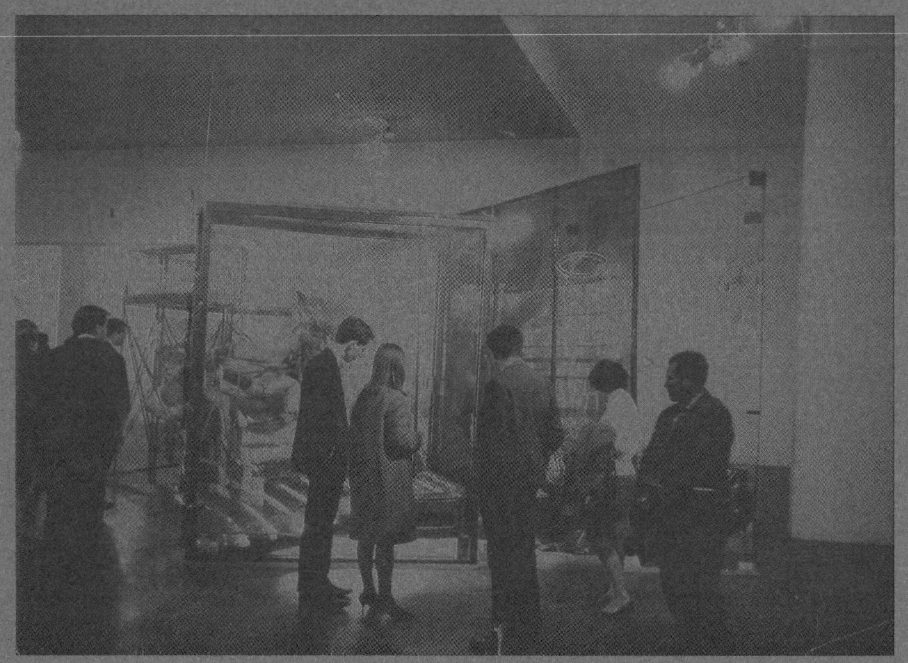

Marta Minujín, *El Batacazo* [The Long Shot], 1965–66. Installation view: Bianchini Gallery, New York

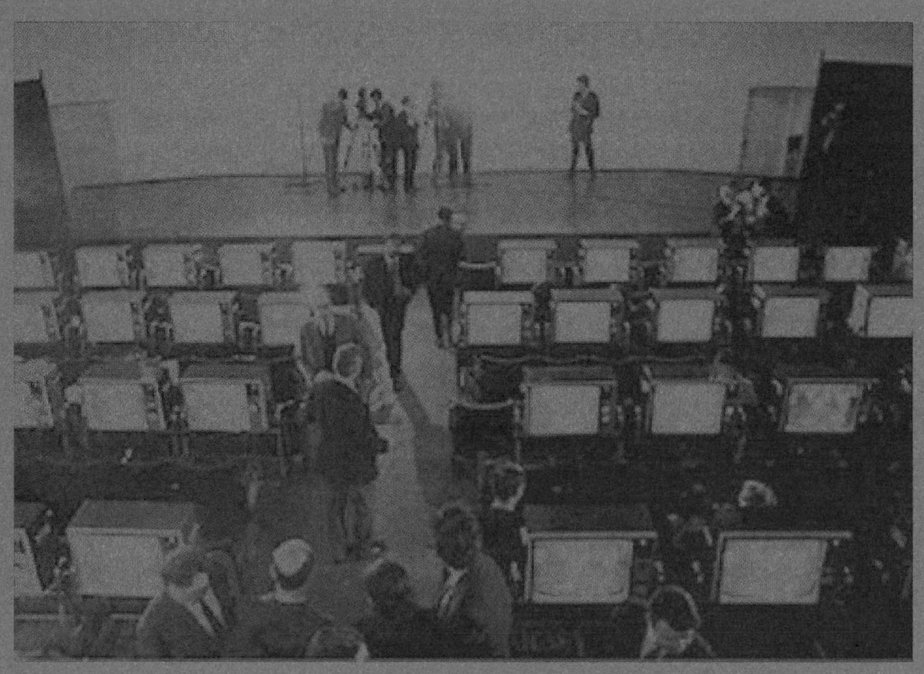

Marta Minujín, *Circuit Super-Heterodyne*, 1967. Installation view: Expo 67, Montreal

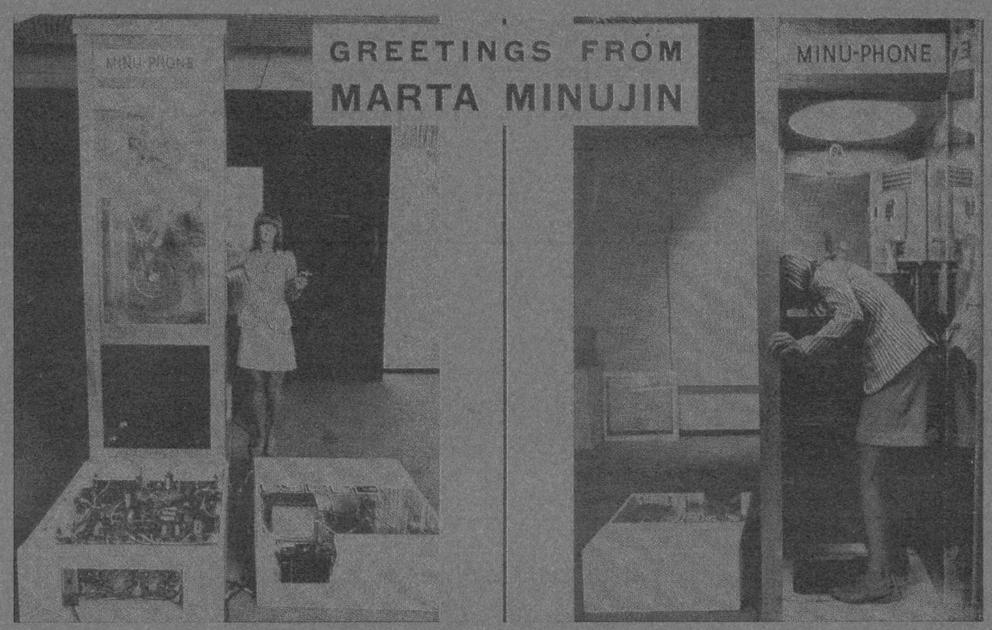

Promotional postcard for *Minuphone* (1967), presented at Howard Wise Gallery, New York, 1967

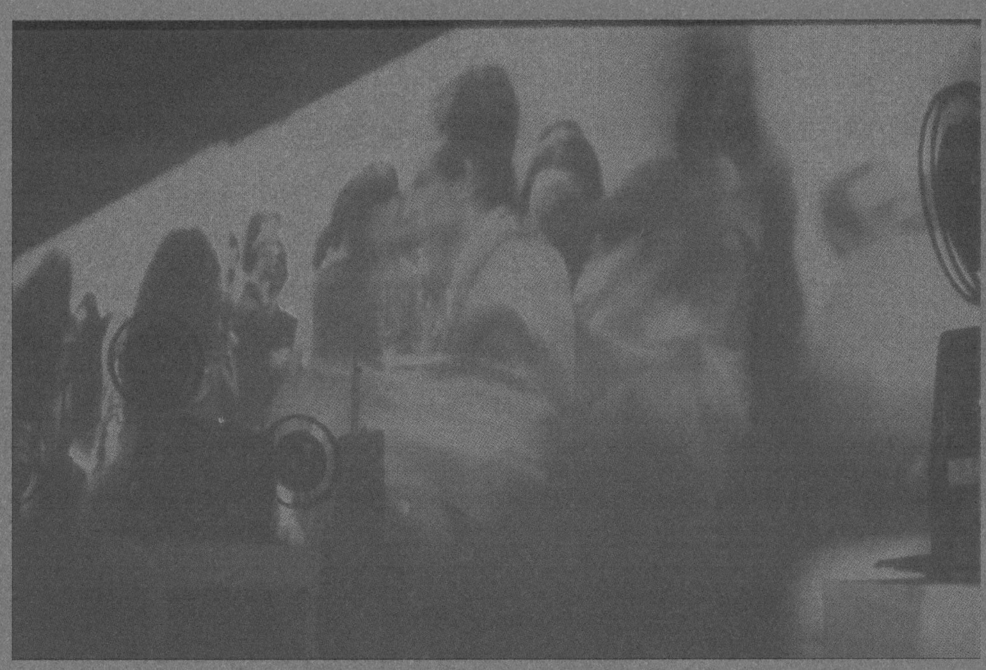

Marta Minujín, *Minucode*, 1968. Installation view: Center for Inter-American Relations, New York

According to Alexander Alberro, "At one level, then, *Minucode* functioned as a 'social-scientific environment.'. . . On another, the content of *Minucode* was the medium. Information was brushed against information."[13] Minujín thus challenged the role of the institution and its social dynamics not only by hosting the parties but also by arranging them into a mirror-like configuration in which people could see reflections of themselves.[14] Still, as pointed out by Gabriela Rangel, the work cannot only be read as institutional critique, but also as alerting more broadly to the new value of images and the role that media plays in society. As Rangel argues, "Minujín carried out a *détournement* of the perceptual patters that shape the mass communications and information media in the construction of both social and individual identity."[15]

HIPPIE CULTURE, CULTURAL EXCHANGE

Immediately after *Minucode*, Minujín returned to Buenos Aires to make a work that is, perhaps counterintuitively, very telling of her relationship with the United States. For *Importación-Exportación* [*Import/Export*], presented in July 1968 at Di Tella, Minujín literally imported to Buenos Aires the hippie culture and psychedelic aesthetics she experienced while living in New York City and visiting San Francisco. As written on the poster, interspersed with commercial trade jargon: "Information makes us adopt facts, ideas, trends, no matter their origin. The economic factor—country of origin—does not confer nationality to the product. Import is an interpretation of the materiality of information." As such, the exhibition space was dressed as a "hippie temple" using items she brought from the United States—such as clothing, perfumes, and posters—and featured a slide projection of psychedelic designs, the smell of incense, and light shows tuned to the rhythm of rock and roll and Hare Krishna music.[16] The fact that the export part of the project—in which she would export Argentinian culture to New York—was never accomplished can be understood as a kind of latent metaphor for the power imbalance between the United States and Latin America, which Minujín was well aware of. She would address this imbalance directly in her last New York piece, *Payment of the Argentine Foreign Debt to Andy Warhol with Corn, The Latin American Gold* (1985), which we will return to later on.

Minujín was charmed by the creative liberty she observed in hippie culture. In March of 1969, she filmed several scenes of hippie life in Central Park in preparation for a film that was ultimately never finished, but clips of which would be shown in Buenos Aires the following year. She also traveled to San Francisco, where she experimented with the perception-widening effects of LSD, and to Mexico, where, influenced by the writings of Carlos Castaneda, she would try psychedelic mushrooms.

Around that time, Kynaston McShine invited Minujín to participate in "Information," his iconic 1970 exhibition at MoMA. Had her project not been canceled due to budget restrictions, it would have included a rented aerostatic glove and five pounds of flowers, the petals of which would have been thrown from the sky. She is however still included in the exhibition catalogue, which published reproductions of her works *Minuphone* and *Minucode*.[17]

THE *–PPENING* SERIES[18]

Soon thereafter, Minujín would begin a series of participatory public actions titled with a portmanteau of a describing word and the word "happening." As previously mentioned, Minujín had, since 1965, defined her participatory environments as *happenings*, some of which were devised in collaboration with Kaprow, who had coined the term in 1959.[19] Theorist and fellow Argentine Oscar Masotta criticized the overuse of the term in contemporary art at that time but, interestingly, noted Minujín as an exception because her work was in constant flux and refused to follow the norms of what a happening should be.[20]

The first event of the *–ppening* series, *Buenos Aires, hoy ya! (Filmpenning)*, took place in September 1971 at the art school Escuela Panamericana de Arte and brought together movies, music, poetry, and the "theater of life." *Filmpenning* was quickly followed by *Interpenning*, a collaboration with artist and actor Richard Squire for Corcoran Gallery in Washington, DC, that was staged in different locations throughout 1972. When she was invited to participate in

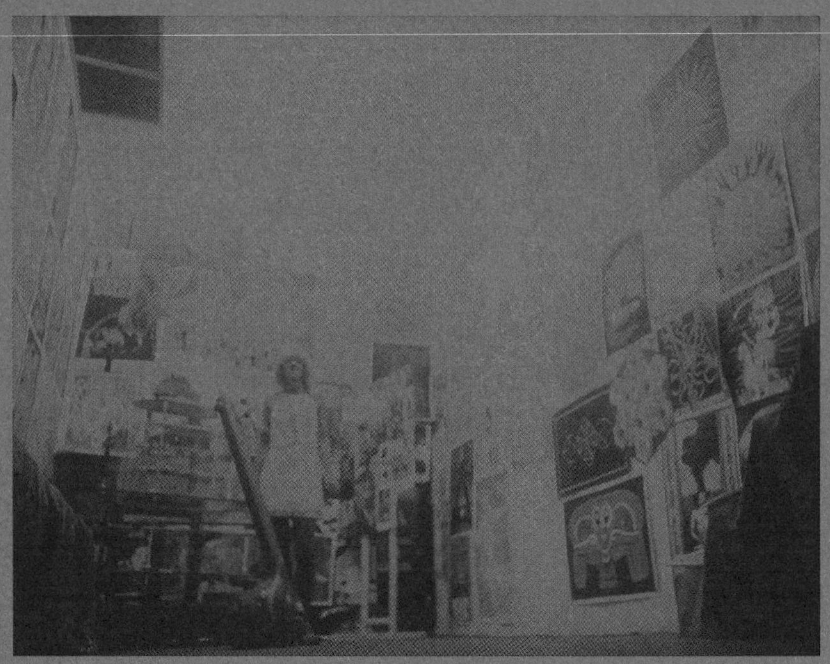

Marta Minujín, *Importación-Exportación* [Import/Export], 1968. Installation view: Instituto Torcuato Di Tella, Buenos Aires, 1968

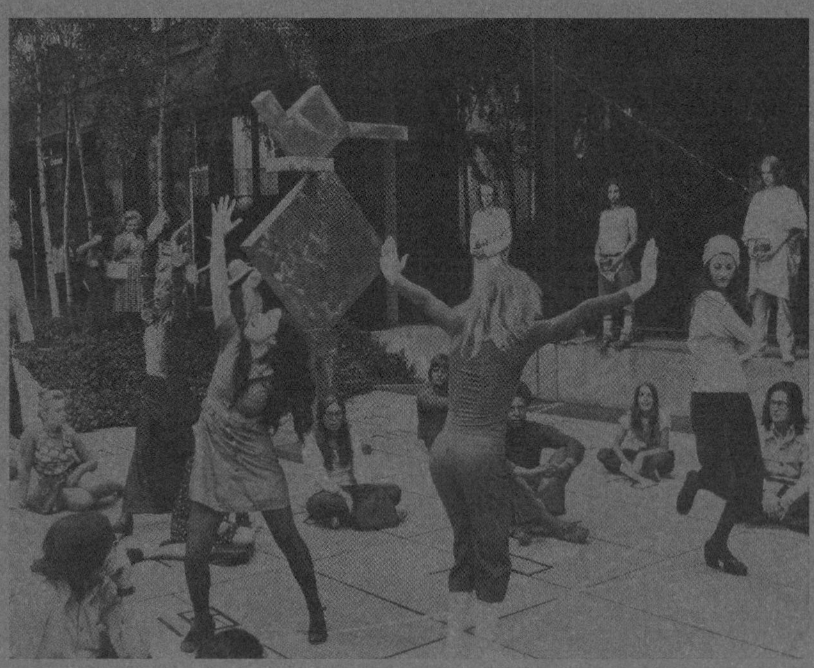

Marta Minujín, *Interpenning*, 1972. Performance: Museum of Modern Art, New York

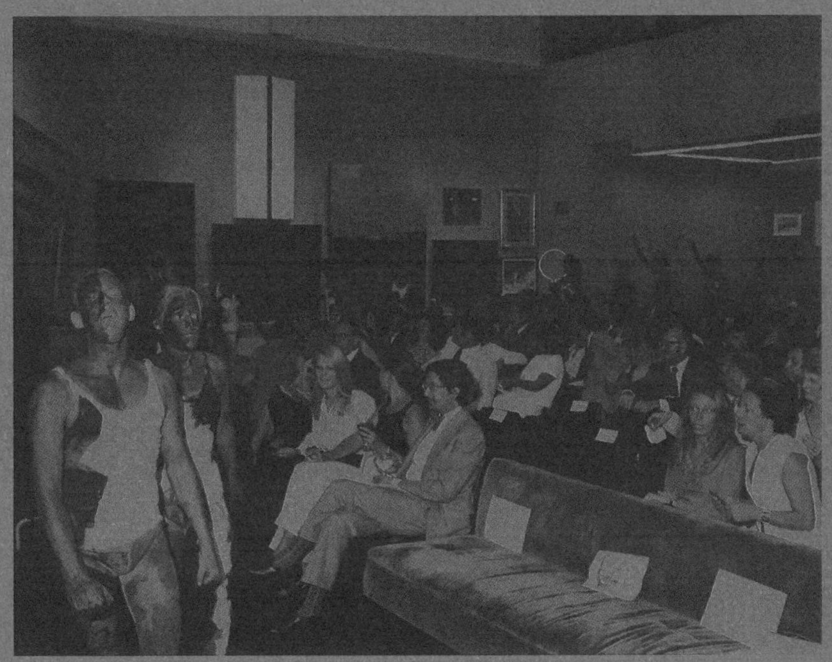

Marta Minujín, *Nicappening*, 1973. Performance: Sotheby's Parke-Bernet, New York

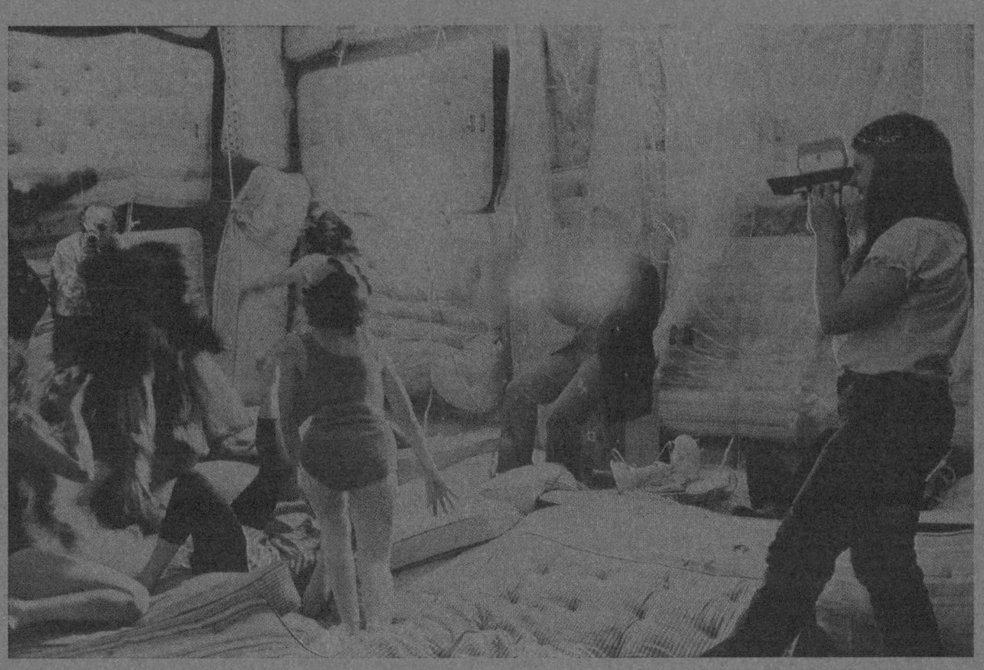

Marta Minujín, *The Soft Gallery*, 1973. Installation view: Harold Rivkin Gallery, Washington, DC

MoMA's Summergarden program for the first time in August of that same year, Minujín decided to restage *Interpenning* in collaboration with Chilean artist Juan Downey, who installed a labyrinth made of ultrasonic waves—an "invisible architecture" meant to "break the patterns and rules of an existing social situation and to create new patterns of interaction in which people participate more actively and more consciously."[21] *Interpenning* was also performed at the New York Avant Garde Festival, which was organized by Charlotte Moorman and took place aboard the steamboat *Alexander Hamilton* on October 28, 1972.

In June 1973, Minujín organized *Nicappening* at Sotheby's Parke-Bernet benefit auction for survivors of an earthquake that had recently occurred in Nicaragua. Attempting to raise social consciousness, the performers interrupted the institutional setting by screaming, "Have you realized what happened?" at the audience.

The final work in this series, and probably the most accomplished, took place during MoMA's Summergarden program in 1973. Minujín orchestrated an "opera-cantata-happening," titled *Kidnappening*, with the help of Gary Glover.[22] The event, which began at 8:00 pm, was an homage to the recently deceased Pablo Picasso, and more than forty performers, their faces painted with Cubist compositions, were contracted to participate. The choreography included an "alphabet of [forty-four] movements . . . derived from the poses used in Picasso's art," with performers acting out the sharp lines and angles characteristic of Cubism.[23] While dancing, the performers sang soliloquys citing modern artists, philosophers, politicians, and poets. The lyrics, which were both sung and screamed by the performers, were selected by Minujín with the help of Claudio Bedel, a Chilean poet living in New York City. In addition to the many quotes from Picasso, there were some from Cézanne, Renoir, Matisse, Derain, Braque, Brancusi, Duchamp, and Filippo Tommaso Marinetti's "Manifesto of Futurism." The performers also recited lines from thinkers such as Plato and Mao Zedong.[24]

The main act took place around 10:00 pm, when the performers suddenly began to surround the audience. While chanting the word "kidnappening," they grabbed fifteen spectators—most of whom had previously agreed to participate in the action—and took them from the event without further explanation. Those “kidnapped” were blindfolded and taken to different locations around the city, including a concert, an apartment on the Upper East Side, the French Consulate, a barbershop, and the Brooklyn Bridge.

Kidnappening was the fourth and final work in the *–ppening* series, and it can be understood as the dialectical synthesis of Minujín’s experiments with interruption, participation, and institutional critique. However, the synthesis offered in *Kidnappening* is not resolute but rather messy and complex. Moreover, due to the performative nature of the work—which now exists only as folder of documents labeled “Kidnappening”—it can only be understood using the records held in both Minujín’s and MoMA’s archives, which together comprise a fairly complete account of the event, including photographs, participant testimonies, and other forms of documentation.

Minujín’s preparatory notes indicate that she had originally planned to title the event either *Picappening* or *Picassening*. As she recalls: “Picasso had died, and I was impacted and wanted to pay homage to him. . . . I started flipping through the pages of a book with Picasso’s works. . . . I remember it was very late at night, and the characters that would come to make up the show I was imagining started to take shape and to sing the words once spoken by Picasso. And I decided to make an Opera-Happening.”[25]

Only later did Minujín decide that the kidnappings would be the performance’s central focus. This decision might have been made on a whim, or perhaps it was intended as a publicity stunt; in any case, we must acknowledge the conceptual shift that it entails. Minujín paid homage to the master of modern painting with a performance exemplifying the era’s broader aesthetic shift away from painting and toward the body and action.

As Minujín states: “Picasso represents the freedom, the euphoria, and the desperation to create and unroll the Ariadne’s thread that we all have inside ourselves. He is the greatest example for artists of the

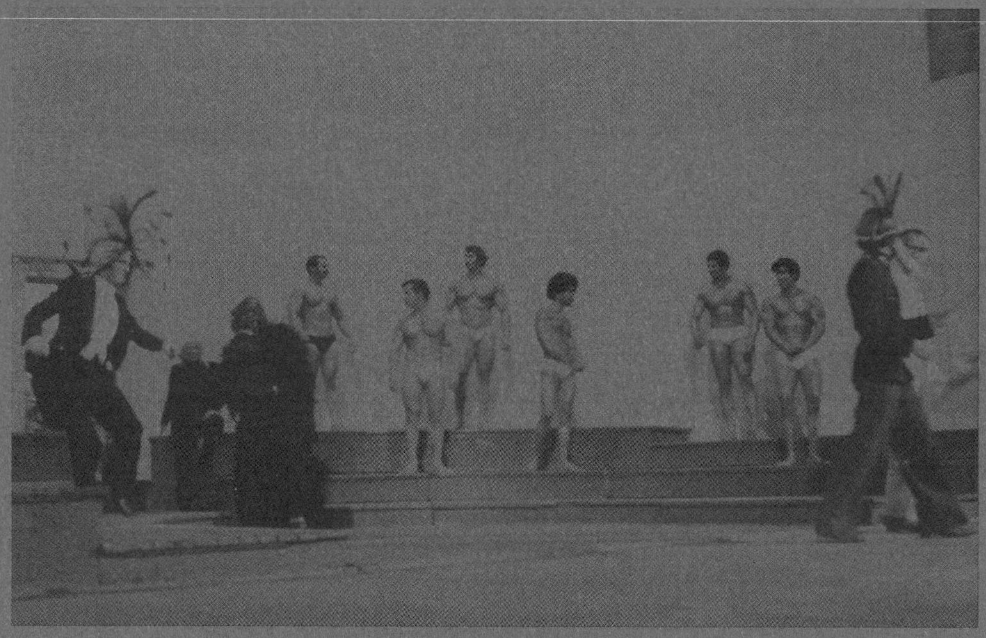

Marta Minujín, *Imago Flowing*, 1974. Performance: the Naumburg Bandshell, Central Park, New York

STEFANOTTY

FOUR PRESENTS: Time aesthetically registered

A video piece created by Marta Minujin and Juliam Cairol-
Running time- 60 minutes

At Stefanotty Gallery, 50 West 57 Street, Tuesday, October 8th, at 9 p.m., Marta Minujin and Julian Cairol and the audience will explore the labyrinths of time following its course which, like that of a river, runs from the past to the present and from the present to the future, in an attempt to unveil the aesthetic nature of that perpetual present where everything is at the condition of not being.

He who knows the forms of the present, knows all: the things that took place in the inscrutable past, and those that will take place in the future. A century, a year, a night, an hour that contains the whole history where, it is said, all the presents are present.

Black tie.

For further information, please call Stefanotty Gallery (586-5252)

50 WEST 57 NYC 10019 TEL 586-5252

Invitation for Marta Minujín and Julián Cairol's exhibition "Four Presents: Time Aesthetically Registered" (1974), at Stefanotty Gallery, New York

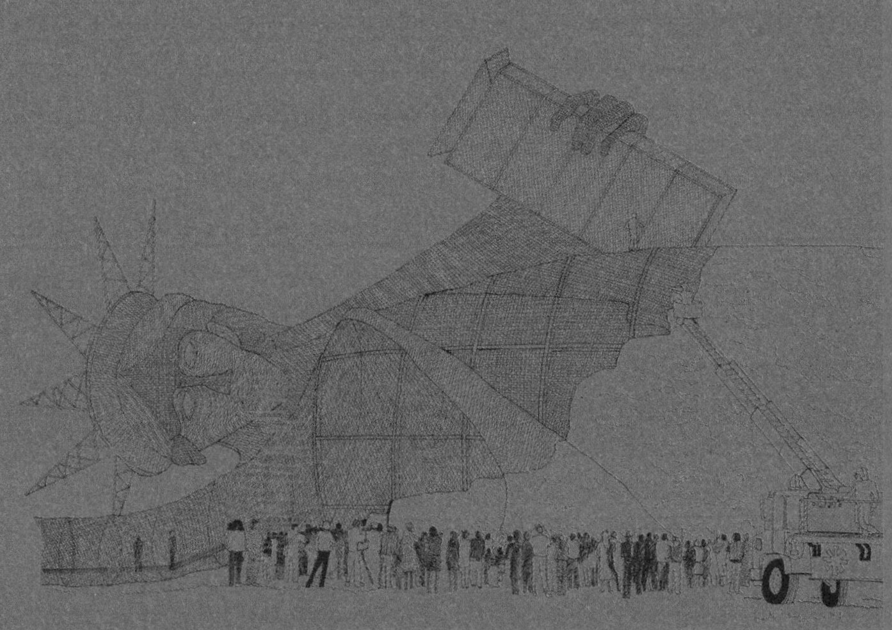

Marta Minujín, *Statue of Liberty Covered in Hamburgers*, 1979, Ink on paper vellum, 31 ½ × 43 ½ in (80 × 110.5 cm)

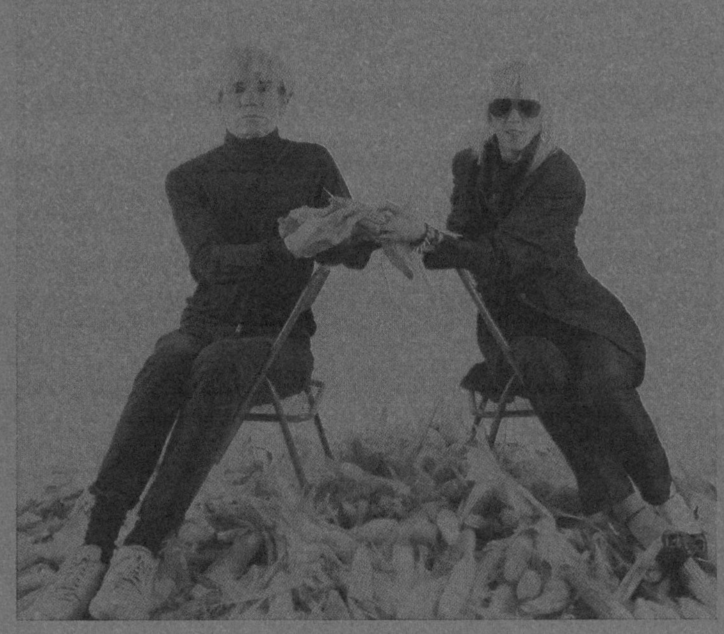

Marta Minujín, P*ayment of the Argentine Foreign Debt to Andy Warhol with Corn, The Latin American Gold*, 1985 (detail). Six c-prints, 38 ⅜ × 39 ¼ in (92.4 × 99.7 cm)

twentieth century, the innovator who created more shock, [only] to later see these shocks of his turned into canons."[26] With *Kidnappening*, Minujín attempts to recover Picasso's original shock value by literally bringing his work to life and transgressing the boundaries of the picture frame as well as those of the institution itself. The Museum of Modern Art, after all, is not just a museum but the very cathedral of modern art's canonization. Minujín's work thus denounces the sterilization of the historical avant-garde by institutions like MoMA. Perhaps then, as Minujín's creative process advanced, she realized that the greatest homage she could pay to Picasso was not to simply bring his cubist characters to life but rather to honor the king by laying siege to his castle—that is, the museum.

Many kidnapped participants were taken to the apartments and studios of Minujín's friends, who had prepared dinners and decorated especially for the occasion.[27] One destination was Max's Kansas City, the iconic restaurant and bar that had been an underground art hub since the 1950s. Participants' testimonies indicate that many, after being "abducted" and taken to a second location, eventually ended up at Max's Kansas City to celebrate. This points to another interpretation of *Kidnappening* as an experiment in trust and circles of belonging.[28] In this sense, *Kidnappening* relates to *Simultaneidad en Simultaneidad* and *Minucode*, which also took on community and self-image as their main themes.

Both *Minucode* and *Kidnappening* straddled the line between the inside and the outside of the art institution, introducing strong critiques of the traditional division between art and life by refusing to distinguish between them. The participatory aspect of the performances highlighted this critique, emphasizing the role of social interaction in the politics of the art world politics. An interesting inversion emerges: In *Minucode*, the outside world is incorporated into the museum, while, in *Kidnappening*, the museum is expanded into the outside world.

In addition to its layered critique of art world politics, it is impossible to not read *Kidnappening* as a playful yet dead-serious reference to the real kidnappings then being carried out by paramilitary forces across

Latin America, as well as to the infamous kidnappings of Patty Hearst and others in the United States. As one participant noted: "Since the Sixties [we have] witness[ed] a wave of hijackings . . . kidnappings of ambassadors, 'states of siege,' airline terminal snipers, Munich."[29] Thus, the institutional critique in *Kidnappening* must be understood as a more expansive political commentary on normativity, violence, and the possibility of art as escape, even if this exit must take the form of violence. The work deals with the politics of the art world, while simultaneously invoking political events from the real world, bringing them both into the museum context.[30] We must also consider the more cynical implications of staging a violent action at such an upscale event. As noted by the same participant, the work plays with "a psychology that sought excitement and novelty without any real threat of danger . . . the chic mentality seeks to cash in on such vicarious danger without any real threat."[31]

Critical while at the same time intentionally shallow, *Kidnappening* forced participants to experience social and institutional violence in a playful yet highly acute simulacrum. Interestingly, it was only at a significant distance from her home country, and in experimenting with the social and physical boundaries of the New York art world, that Minujín could offer such a prophetic and incisive work about the violence then roiling the American continent.

BETWEEN THE CENTER OF POLITICS AND THE CENTER OF ART

Minujín's works from the 1970s are barely studied, as critics have demonstrated a clear preference for her pioneering role in the happenings and technology-based artwork that emerged in the mid-to-late 1960s. The former works are, however, some of her most interesting, epitomizing the shift her practice would take toward public space and mass participation, as demonstrated by the *–penning* series.

Compared to the technological complexity of works like *Circuit Super-Heterodyne* and *Minucode*, Minujín's 1972 piece *Sound Happening* appears simple, but is perhaps the most poetic of her works inciting sensorial dislocation. With the assistance of Carl Colby, Minujín recorded sounds from nature—birds, rain, and the ocean—which played over speakers installed in Washington, DC's Rock Creek Park. Organized by the Art Barn, the experience was designed to alter perception, creating the illusion that birds were coming from the floor and water was pouring down from trees. As the poster states: "It's a happening because the rules of nature are reversed through the use of technology."[32]

The setting for her next piece in DC was Harold Rivkin Gallery, a cube-shaped cement room, measuring sixteen feet on each side. Invited to collaborate with Richard Squire, Minujín wanted to invert the rough materiality of the space by creating a gallery where people could "experience art in a soft manner."[33] For that purpose, they rented two hundred mattresses from the recently closed Cairo Hotel. The hotel had been an important place for the political elite, but had, in recent years, become a hub for crime, and was ultimately closed by the police after three homicides took place there. Minujín and Squire paid the doorman in charge of the building one dollar per mattress, tossing them onto the street from the hotel windows so that they could be transported to the gallery, where they would be tied to the walls, ceiling, and floor with ropes.

For the twenty days that *Soft Gallery* was open, several artists were invited to intervene in the space with works of their own. Squire was in charge of the first ten days— from April 17 to 27—during which he presented his piece *It's a Dog's Life*, and solicited participation from Claudio Badal, The Continental Drifters, Jean Dupuy, Tom Green, David Mcintosh, Caroll Sockwell, and Norman Yeh. Minujín had the following ten days of programming, inviting Mike Breed, Juan Downey, Ray Johnson, and Charlotte Moorman—who performed with a cello made of ice—to participate. She also facilitated a screening of works by Simon English, Al Hansen, and Carolee Schneemann, along with documentation of a performance created especially for the event, titled *How to Be in a Movie*—in which participants were filmed imitating their favorite movie stars—and footage of *Nicappening*. Participants testified that La Monte Young instructed a group of 150 people to jump on the mattresses during the exhibition's opening, and that the artists invited the audience to untie the mattresses and deinstall the gallery for the closing event.[34] *Soft Gallery* signals Minujín's increasing interest in participatory and collaborative art, at the same time that it recuperates the formal interest in malleability versus rigidity present in some of her earliest works.

This interest in the tension of materials would take a new turn the following year with the exhibition "Frozen Sex," which was open from May 20 to June 5, 1974, at Hard Art Gallery in DC.[35] The show comprised a series of paintings depicting penises and vaginas—the only works on canvas that Minujín made between the mid '60s and the '80s. The paintings were composed of adjacent curvy surfaces in hues of pink. At first glace, the pieces resembled frozen food, but upon closer inspection, were clearly representations of sexual acts. As Julián Cairol writes in the exhibition poster's text: "through this conceptual process, Marta Minujín unveils the empirical instrument upon which eroticism was built, depicting [the penises and vaginas] as anonymous objects of consumption. Sex no longer belongs to the individual, but to culture."[36] For the opening event, a female and a male dancer did a striptease with their bodies painted pink. A week later, Minujín, along with a group of participants, did an action in which they went to the Washington Monument, distracted the guards, and added pink filters to the lights, briefly transforming the obelisk into a colossal phallus.

The works had been painted the previous year in Minujín's DC studio, during which time she also conducted a kind of ethnographic survey—visiting porno cinemas, cabarets, and sex shops to study the new tendencies of sexual freedom, and their relationship to consumption and pop culture. The series involved a moral provocation but also one of legality: shown for the first time in Buenos Aires in November 1973 at Galería Arte Nuevo, Minujín's exhibition was closed by the police only three hours after it opened. For Minujín—a woman—to present erotic art within the tense social and political climate of Argentina in late 1973 involved a double risk.[37] In this sense, *Frozen Sex* prefigures the important role Minujín would play in Argentina upon her return to the country in the second half of the 1970s, when, in the midst of censorship and mass murders committed by the dictatorial government, her works would become surreptitiously more political, proposing a democratization of space through public participation in seemingly playful and conceptual performances.[38]

In 1974, while back in New York, Minujín received a grant for $1,000 from the Menil Foundation to develop *Imago Flowing*, an event that would take place on September 24 of that year at the Naumburg Bandshell in Central Park. Presented on the park's stage, the piece was an opera-happening in four acts, the first of which featured twenty bodybuilders covered in blue-tinted Vaseline posing in positions typical of athletic competitions. Then, one actress and twelve actors dressed as angels danced and sang lyrics written by Minujín and inspired by the Greek philosopher Heraclitus. In the third act, a Russian dancer dressed in feathers performed alongside the famous drag queen Alexis del Lago, who arrived dressed as King Kong, changed into Marlene Dietrich, and then finally into Greta Garbo. For the fourth and final act, Minujín took the stage to light the torches held by the some sixty performers, who descended into the space of the audience to grab the preselected participants, who were dressed in black, and led them in a procession to the final, private event. The dinner-art action that followed was titled *The Dramatization of Eating in an Aesthetic Act*, and invitees included Michael Kirby, Susan Sontag, and Taylor Smith. Only black foods—caviar and dyed bread, butter, and champagne—were served in a black-clad room in a restaurant. In stark contrast with the rest of this black banquet, the white angels murmured and sang into the ears of the guests.

The last work Minujín made in New York before moving permanently back to Argentina in 1975 was *Four Presents: Time Aesthetically Registered*, a collaboration with her friend Julián Cairol, presented on October 8, 1974, at Stefanotty Gallery in New York. The sixty-minute-long "video-spectacle" consisted of a conference for fifty spectators, all of whom were required to attend in black-tie attire. Upon entering, they were asked to sit in chairs arranged in a chess-like configuration. In the center, a TV played a previously recorded video, referring to the past. On the sides, two other TVs showed the present through a closed-circuit feed of the conference, and the future was presented with a plaque reading "Future tense." The conference was interrupted by an opera singer, a surprise speech by an actor who accused the creators of being "Latin American artists," a couple having a loud argument, a fake burglar, and then finally by the appearance of a fake newspaper proclaiming the death of Henry Kissinger. The interruptions themselves were indeed the real spectacle; the idea being to raise consciousness on the subjective nature of temporal perception.

In this work, we see similar topics as those addressed in *Cha/Cha/Cha*, a magazine created that same year by Minujín, Cairol, and Downey. Though it was never published in any official capacity, circulating around New York's underground as a typewritten document, *Cha/Cha/Cha* gained a mythical status, and remains a testament to the consciousness shared by these migrant artists in their search for strategies of insertion into this new culture. In the magazine's press release, the editors identified one of the main problems for Latin Americans living in New York: that their work "remain[ed] unknown to the[ir] countries of origin." For that reason, the magazine aimed to "restore this cultural patrimony and make it known in all Latin America and within the Latin community [*comunidad latina*] in [the US]," as well as to disseminate "material concerning the artistic activities taking place in Latin American countries and Europe."[39] While this exchange of information was their immediate objective, the authors had an even more ambitious one: to redefine regional culture as a "critical document for the investigation of the significance of Latin American artistic production."[40] Thus, *Cha/Cha/Cha* identified how the metropolitan scenery of New York offered an alternative space where identity formation and regional political awareness could overlap. In this context, the artists' struggle for visibility altered traditional attachments to the nation-state, and in its place they proposed a Pan-American consciousness.

After finally settling down in Buenos Aires in 1975, Minujín continued to explore her Latin Americanisms with works like *Comunicado con Tierra* [Communication with Earth] (1976), a giant bird's nest built with soil brought from Machu Picchu, and *Arte Agrícola en Acción* [Agricultural Art in Action] (1977–79), a performance that furthered Minujín's engagement with issues of commercial trade and of geopolitical power imbalances that had initially been explored in *Importación-Exportación* and would crystallize with *The Payment of the Foreign Debt to Andy Warhol in Corn, The Latin American Gold.*

As previously mentioned, many of Minujín's works from the late 1970s challenged ideas of authority and vigilance in the midst of one of the world's most repressive dictatorial regimes. In particular, the *Monuments* series, enacted a real democratization of public symbols of power through audience participation. The series began with *El obelisco acostado* [The Obelisk Lying Down], presented in the First Latin American Biennial of São Paulo in 1978. By tilting a hollow wooden obelisk on its side, allowing visitors to enter the structure through the bottom, Minujín inverted the phallic symbol of Buenos Aires, demonstrating the necessity of considerations of gender in any real critique of power. In this sense, she continued what she had begun in 1974, when she covered the Washington monument in pink light. The next step for Minujín was to make these monuments edible—escalating the public's participation to a more active form of physical intervention. After *El Obelisco de pan dulce* [The Panettonne Obelisk] (1979) in Buenos Aires, she made *The James Joyce Tower in Bread* in Dublin for the festival Rosc '80: The Poetry of Vision. The piece paid homage to Downes, the bread maker in James Joyce's *Dubliners*. In all these cases, the monuments were laid down with the help of cranes and then covered with food. Intended as part of this series, in 1979, Minujín conceived—but has not yet managed to produce—*The Statue of Liberty Covered in Hamburgers.* The sketches, however, propose a life-size mesh replica of Lady Liberty that would be toppled down and covered with burger patties, perhaps the most popular—Pop—American food. Cooked by firemen with flamethrowers, the patties would then be placed in buns and given to the audience. In her tackling of two such iconic symbols of Western culture, Minujín insists that the *idea* of liberty is not enough, but that we must occupy it, distribute it, and embody it in order to achieve real democracy.[41]

During a visit to New York in 1985, Minujín created a piece that, in some ways, concludes of her exploration of cultural trade and hemispheric relations by addressing the subject of national debt—the main tool for the United States' dominance of Latin America since the region's slow return to democracy in the 1980s. *Payment of the Argentine Foreign Debt to Andy Warhol with Corn, The Latin American Gold* is comprised of twelve photographs depicting a performance Minujín did with Warhol at The Factory in September 1985. Minujín bought hundreds of ears of corn at a Puerto Rican market, which she then spray-painted gold and piled on the floor of Warhol's studio. The photographs show the artists seated back to back amid the pile of corn, then slowly turning toward the camera until Marta offers the corn to Warhol and he accepts. After the performance, both artists went to the Empire State Building and handed the corn out to passersby. Marta was, in a sense, also paying debt to Warhol for his profound influence on her work. Both artists dealt in similar themes of pop culture, mass media, celebrity, and image; while they had, in part, arrived at these topics from different paths, Warhol and Minujín shared a critical and ironic view of systems of belonging in the art world.

With pieces like *Statue of Liberty* and *Payment of the Foreign Debt*, we can see that Minujín's relationship with the United States was neither passive nor submissive, but that she was highly aware of the systems of dominance that dictate foreign policy and her position in relation to those systems as they play out in the international art arena as well.[42]

To end on a positive note, we must highlight Minujín's recent recognition in this international arena. For the 2017 documenta 14 in Kassel, Germany, Minujín was invited to recreate her iconic 1983 work

El Partenón de libros [The Parthenon of Books], the most important of her participatory monument interventions: a life-size replica of the Greek Parthenon covered with books that had been forbidden by totalitarian regimes, which was originally created to celebrate Argentina's return to democracy. The work was a celebration of the commonality of knowledge and of participatory and shareable liberty, posing a challenge to censorship that is as valid today as it was at the time of its conception.

SEAMS OF POWER

Looking at Minujín's works from her time in New York, we begin to see a more complex image of the artist—clearly just as intent on achieving an expansion of media as she was on reflecting on ideas of power and belonging. She landed in New York with *El Batacazo*, a work that critically engaged the culture of spectacle that dominated the 1960s by complicating and expanding the definition of the work of art with a combination of Pop aesthetics and audience participation. She also continued the exploration of mass media with participatory, technology-based works that she had initiated with *Simultaneidad* and brought to synthetic apex with *Minucode*.

Throughout the 1970s, Minujín's interest in psychedelia and hippie culture led her to emphasize the sensorial aspects of her work, while also allowing her to reflect on cultural exchange in works such as *Importación-Exportación*. Her work cannot be understood as a simple observation on, or perhaps indictment of, the role of mass media in identity construction but rather as critically engaged with the power imbalance that defines the relationship between the US and Latin America. Using irony to bring this imbalance to the fore, her work *Payment of the Foreign Debt*, was as much a commentary on Latin American impoverishment as it was a condemnation of the United States' economic stranglehold on the region. During the second half of the '70s, after having returned to an Argentina that was enduring one of the most violently oppressive dictatorial regimes in the continent, Minujín became more overtly political. With the

Monuments series, she used public participation to tackle the ideas of both memory and democracy, proposing a revision to the social contract in which power is distributed to and incorporated by all.

Throughout this arc, we see a truly innovative artist who executed some of the most advanced artistic experiments in media and technology of her time; and, in her merging of art and life, expanded our understandings not only of spectatorship but also of the relationship between art, media, and society more generally. With her dynamic works that incite as much fun as they do critical reflection, Minujín offers a unique perspective on Western culture and the seams of power that hold it together.

1. See Serge Guilbaut, *How New York Stole the Idea of Modern Art: Abstract Expressionism, Freedom, and the Cold War* (Chicago: University of Chicago Press, 1995); Claire F. Fox, *Making Art Panamerican: Cultural Policy and the Cold War* (Minneapolis: University of Minnesota Press, 2013); Andrea Giunta, *Avant-Garde, Internationalism, and Politics: Argentine Art in the Sixties*, trans. Peter Kahn (Durham: Duke University Press, 2007); Rodrigo Alonso, *Imán, Nueva York: Arte argentino de los años 60* (Buenos Aires: Fundación Proa, 2010); and Aimé Iglesias Lukin, "Contrabienal: Redefining Latin American Art and Identity in 1970s New York," *ICAA Documents Project Working Papers* 4 (November 2016): 4–17.
2. This essay is indebted to the research published in Victoria Noorthoorn, ed., *Marta Minujín: Obras 1959–1989* (Buenos Aires: Malba-Fundación Constantini, 2010); particularly to the extensive chronology compiled therein by Javier Villa.
3. The show traveled to the Akron Institute in Akron, Ohio, in October, to the Atlanta Art Association in December 1965, and finally to The University Art Museum at the University of Texas at Austin in February 1966.
4. Noorthoorn, *Marta Minujín: Obras*, 70.
5. French dealer Paul Bianchini was a leading figure in the promotion of Pop art in the United States and Europe. His gallery gained notoriety with its 1964 exhibition "American Supermarket," which included works by Jasper Johns, Roy Lichtenstein, Claes Oldenburg, and Andy Warhol. See Noorthoorn, *Marta Minujín: Obras*, 141. See also, Ana Longoni, Alejandrina D'Elía, and Fernanda Carvajal, eds., *Minuphone*, 1967–2010 (Buenos Aires: Espacio Fundación Telefónica: Fundación Espigas, 2010)
6. See Ana Longoni, D'Elía, and Fernanda Carvajal, *Minuphone, 196*
7. Grace Glueck, "Art Notes; Safari to Senegal CHECK, MATE? INNER EXPERIENCE RESHAPING THE TATE," *New York Times*, February 6, 1966.
8. See Michael Kirby, "Marta Minujin's 'Simultaneity in Simultaneity,'" *Drama Review* 12, no. 3 (1968): 149–52; and Noorthoorn, *Marta Minujín: Obras*, 74.
9. Luc Perrault, "Circuit," in *Marta Minujín: Minucodes*, ed. Gabriela Rangel, Alexander Alberro, and Inés Katzenstein (New York: Americas Society, 2015), 130–145.
10. For a detailed account of the work, see Longoni, D'Elía, and Carvajal, *Minuphone*.
11. "I would be in Times Square and people would be talking on the phone, but with all that was going on in Times Square, speaking on the phone was almost impossible." "Marta Minujín in conversation with Ana Longoni and Fernanda Carvajal," in Longoni, D'Elía, and Carvajal, *Minuphone*, 113.
12. For a detailed account of this work, see Alexander Alberro, "Media, Sculpture, Myth," in *A Principality of Its Own: 40 Years of Visual Arts at the Americas Society*, ed. José Luis Falconi and Gabriela Rangel (New York: Americas Society, 2006), 160–77. See also, Alberro, Katzenstein, and Rangel, *Minucodes*.
13. Alberro, "Media, Sculpture, Myth," in Falconi and Rangel, *A Principality of Its Own*, 165.
14. The instructions sent to participants read: "From the moment you enter the cocktail party, you become a part of the 'invisible' environment that is being filmed in order to become 'visible.' When you see the replay of your cocktail party, you will find that you are not part, but rather the sub-plot, of the social environment." Marta Minujín, "Statement from Marta Minujín and the administration of the Center for Inter-American Relations Art Gallery to all participants in *Minucode*," in Alberro, Katzenstein, and Rangel, *Minucodes*, 52.
15. Gabriela Rangel, "May 1968 à la Minujín," in Rangel, Alberro, and Katzenstein, *Minucodes*, 11.
16. See Noorthoorn, *Marta Minujín: Obras*, 82. See also Marta Minujín, *Marta Minujin: los años psicodélicos, edición facsimilar completa de Lo inadvertido, diario underground de 1969* (Buenos Aires: Mansalva, 2015)
17. Marta Minujín, correspondence with Kynaston McShine, September 18, 1970, The Museum of Modern Art Archives, New York. MoMA Exhibitions, Series 934, Folder 33.
18. A version of my research on *Kidnappening* was presented at the 2017 Institute of Fine Arts / Frick Symposium on the History of Art. See Aimé Iglesias Lukin, "A Hostage Situation at the Museum of Modern Art: Marta Minujín's 1973 *Kidnappening*," MoMA, *Post: Notes of Modern and Contemporary Art Around the Globe*, November 22, 2017, https://post.at.moma.org/content_items/1074-a-hostage-situation-at-the-museum-of-modern-art-marta-minujin-s-1973-kidnappening.
19. The term was first used by Kaprow in the title of his 1959 work *18 Happenings in 6 Parts*, which took place from October 4 to 10, at the Reuben Gallery in New York. See Christopher W. Bigsby, *A Critical Introduction to Twentieth-Century American Drama*, vol. 3, *Beyond Broadway* (Cambridge: Cambridge University Press, 1985), 45.
20. For more on Minujín's place between categories and Masotta's reading of her work, see Catherine Spencer, "Performing Pop: Marta Minujín and the 'Argentine Image-Makers,'" *Tate Papers* 2 (Autumn 2015), http://www.tate.org.uk/research/publications/tate-papers/24/performing-pop-marta-minujín-and-the-argentine-image-makers, accessed April 18, 2017.
21. "Art Event Staged by Marta Minujín in Museum Garden," press release no. 96 (August 1972), The Museum of Modern Art Press Release Archives, New York, https://www.moma.org/momaorg/shared/pdfs/docs/press_archives/4877/releases/MOMA_1972_0106_96.pdf?2010, accessed September 10, 2017.
22. The Summergarden program was sponsored by Mobil, and beginning in 1971, offered free late-night events on weekends during the summer featuing a wide range of performances. According to MoMA's records, that summer the program received a daily attendance of 1,200 people, with a season total of 56,000. For her performances on August 3 and 4, Minujín received a budget of $400, with the rest left to "the impossible or the miraculous." Marta Minujín, "Kidnappening," in "Kidnappening Folder," Marta Minuín Archive. Courtesy the artist and Henrique Faria Fine Art. Translated from Spanish by the author.

23. Marta Minujín, "Picappening, Picassening, Picassonning," in Minujín, "Kidnappening Folder," Marta Minuín Archives.
24. From Mao, Minujín included: "When you do anything, unless you understand its actual circumstances, its nature, and its relations to other things, you will not know the laws governing it, or know how to do it, or be able to do it well." Interestingly, something similar could be said of *Kidnappening* itself, in that the work cannot be understood without paying attention to its actual circumstances—i.e. the museum setting—or to "its relations to other things," such as the rampant kidnappings in Latin America and elsewhere. Mao Zedong, "Problems of Strategy in China's Revolutionary War," in *The Wisdom of Mao* (New York: Citadel Press/Kensington, 2002), 13.
25. As Minujín detailed in a manuscript written shortly after the performance, the work would be an "opera because in some moments arias would be sung, [a] cantata because there would be many choruses, and [a] happening because at the end something really unexpected would happen, an overflow of incidentals." In *Interpenning*, the use of intermission, and interruption was taken even further, rendering the entire event as a disruption. Marta Minujín, "Kidnappening," in "Kidnappening Folder," Marta Minujín Archive, Buenos Aires.
26. Marta Minujín quoted in *Marta Minujín: Happenings y Performances* (Buenos Aires: Ministerio de Cultura del Gobierno de la Ciudad Autónoma de Buenos Aires, 2015), 120. Translated by the author.
27. Some spectators were taken by surprise. As Ty Castellan noted in his written testimony: "The event being somewhat dis-organized [*sic*] and crowded, [some of the hostages] were chosen randomly [and at the last minute] from the audience. This created greater confrontation possibilities, another desirable element in the piece." In Minujín, "Kidnappening," in "Kidnappening Folder," Marta Minujín Archive, Buenos Aires.
28. Probably the most beautiful story shared—and perhaps invented—by Minujín in her memoir was that of a young art student who, visiting New York from Chicago for the weekend, heard on TV about the performance and decided to attend. Curious but with no expectations, she happened to be among those kidnapped. She was taken to the photographer Anton Pelli's studio, and the two fell in love at first sight and married soon after. Her testimony, as transcribed by Minujín, concludes romantically, "I wish all artists in the world were dedicated to crossing people's destinies." Minujín, "Kidnappening," in "Kidnappening Folder," Marta Minujín Archive, Buenos Aires.
29. "Participant Linda's Testimony," in "Kidnappening Folder," Marta Minujín Archive, Buenos Aires.
30. In this regard, one could compare Minujín's works with Graciela Carnevale's *Acción del encierro* [Confinement Action], in which the artist locked visitors inside a gallery, forcing them to acknowledge and challenge their oppression by breaking their way out. This action was part of the exhibition series Ciclo de Arte Experimental [Experimental Practices of Art Series], organized by the Grupo de Arte de Vanguardia de Rosario in October 1968. Similarly, in July of that same year, the Rosario group assaulted and interrupted a lecture by Jorge Romero Brest. For more information on these experimental actions, see Ana Longoni and Mariano Mestman, *Del Di Tella a "Tucumán Arde": vanguardia artística y política en el 68 argentino* (Buenos Aires: Eudeba, 2008); Longoni, *Vanguardia y revolución: arte e izquierdas en la Argentina de los sesenta-setenta* (Buenos Aires: Ariel, 2014); and Giunta, *Avant-Garde, Internationalism, and Politics*.
31. "Participant Linda's Testimony," in "Kidnappening Kidnappening Folder."
32. Noorthoorn, *Marta Minujín: Obras*, 84.
33. Marta Minujín quoted in ibid., 92.
34. Ibid., 92–3.
35. Located on 15th street in what was then a marginal area of the capital city, Hard Art Gallery was an alternative space that, just a few years later, would become a hub for DC's nascent punk scene.
36. Reproduced in Noorthoorn, *Marta Minujín: Obras*, 149. See also Francisco Lemus, "Frozen Sex," ex. brochure (New York: Herlitzka + Faria, May 15–July 4, 2018), http://www.henriquefaria-ba.com/en/exhibiciones/frozen-sex/acerca_de.
37. In October of 1973, Juan Domingo Perón assumed his third democratic presidency. Very shortly after, the stability of the country was challenged by right-wing paramilitary groups, initiating a bloody period of dictatorship that would last until 1984.
38. See, in particular, Minujín's works *Academia del Fracaso* [Academy of Failure] (1975), *Espi-Art* (1977), and *El obelisco acostado* [The Obelisk Lying Down] (1978) described in Noorthoorn, *Marta Minujín: Obras*, 98–101, 110–11.
39. For more information on the magazine and its role in the community of Latin American artists in New York, see Aimé Iglesias Lukin, "Cha/Cha/Cha: A Latin American Twist to 1970s New York," Cite, Site, Sights, Colección Patricia Phelps de Cisneros, Art and Ideas from Latin America, April 23, 2018, https://www.coleccioncisneros.org/editorial/statements/chachacha-latin-american-twist-1970s-new-york.
40. "*Cha/Cha/Cha* was a Magazine of Art Criticism Dedicated to the Investigation of the Latin-American Artistic Production," undated and unpaginated document, "Cha Cha Cha Folder," Marta Minujín Archive, Buenos Aires.
41. Noorthoorn, *Marta Minujín: Obras*, 110–23.
42. Ibid., 108.

Forget Paris: An Interview with Christo

Massimiliano Gioni: Do you remember how you met Marta Minujín in Paris at the beginning of the 1960s?

Christo: That was a long time ago, but I will try to remember. I could barely speak French. I never formally studied French or English; I learned in the streets. I didn't have the money to study and, at that time, I had to do odd jobs to make a living. I met Marta in the early '60s. In Paris at the time, there were two groups of Spanish, Portuguese, and Latin American artists, which is how I got to know her. I was friends with a group of Portuguese artists producing this very nice handmade journal called *KWY*. It was published in an edition of three hundred, about one hundred of which were signed by each contributor in a special edition for subscribers. It was very precious. Marta was affiliated with that group of Spanish- and Portuguese-speaking artists, and she was friends with an Argentinian artist named Alberto Greco. That's how I met her.

MG: What do you remember about her?

C: She was just as she is now. Marta was very flamboyant. She was also very active—doing all these temporary installations and performances. I remember the destruction of the mattresses [*La destrucción* [The Destruction] (1963)] of course, which was just one of her many actions but ultimately became her best-known. It must have been 1963. Marta organized a happening where she destroyed and burned several sculptures made out of cardboard and mattresses in an empty lot on the Impasse Ronsin in Paris, where many other artists had studios.

MG: Marta says you wrapped her up at the end of the happening. She even has a photograph in which she looks almost like one of your packages.

C: I don't remember that. There were so many people, but it was a special thing. I remember where it happened and I remember that it wasn't really about objects—it was an action. Mainly, I remember Marta, because she was, as she still is, very lively, very present. She knew everybody.

MG: Was your studio on the Impasse Ronsin at that time? Jean Tinguely and Niki de Saint Phalle had their studios there, as did Yves Klein, and, famously, Constantin Brancusi was there until his death in 1957.

C: No, no, no. I had only a *chambre de bonne*, a bedroom where I did my small packages, and a garage in Arcueil—which is in the south of Paris—where I made my barrels and other large pieces.

MG: At this point, had you already been involved with the *Nouveau réalisme* movement?

C: You are an art historian so I should tell you this: I have never been involved with *Nouveau réalisme*. Even if I would have liked to, they refused me. That group was very strictly regulated, almost orthodox; nobody could join except the people who had signed the original 1960 manifesto.

MG: Weren't you among the signatories of the manifesto?

C: I would have been very happy to sign it, but I was not accepted because I was criticized for my work being too "intervention" and not enough Dada.

MG: That's interesting. So, at the beginning, it was just Arman, François Dufrene, Raymond Hains, Yves Klein, Daniel Spoerri, Jean Tinguely, and Jacques Villeglé, and later, César Baldaccini, Gérard Deschamps, Niki De Saint Phalle, and Mimmo Rotella also joined . . .

C: Of course, yes, many other people joined or started being identified with *Nouveau réalisme* later on. I think the first manifesto was published in late 1960, but at that time, there was already a larger interest across Europe and the Americas in the idea of new realism and the use of objects and popular culture. The biggest champion of this broader movement was the New York art dealer Sidney Janis, who mounted the exhibition "The International Exhibition of the New Realists" in 1962.

MG: In his gallery at 15 East 57th Street?

C: Yes. Janis was already mounting exhibitions with artists from all over the world—English, Italian, and French artists—even before the terms *Pop* or *realism* became very common. The artists associated with *Nouveau réalisme* showed in his gallery. For me, around that time, everything in life was so complicated. I was a refugee, nobody liked me, nobody was interested in my work, and I was prevented from even approaching Sidney Janis, but Janis succeeded in contacting me and I lent him two packages for the landmark "New Realists" exhibition, for which poet John Ashbery wrote the catalogue text. This is technically why I am associated with *Nouveau réalisme*. At that time, I was not yet in America, but as a consequence of the Sidney Janis show, *Nouveau réalisme* became a much looser category that included many more artists.

MG: Would you say that artists from Latin America or even from Spain, Portugal, or, like you, Bulgaria were systematically ostracized at that time?

C: Yeah, it was very normal. Europe and France in particular were much more guarded. Artists like Yves Klein and Jean Tinguely would decide who could join their movement and sign their manifestos.

MG: Would you say that movements like *Nouveau réalisme* or even Pop were nationalistic?

C: I don't know if I can say that they were exactly nationalistic, but they certainly had a local flavor and a local quality.

MG: Did you feel a closer affinity with international artists? Is that how you met people like Minujín?

C: I was very young at that point, and I tried to have an affinity with everybody in order to exhibit my work. If you want to make art and have shows, you can't care too much about idealistic or ideological affinities. When you're very young, you need to make your work visible, because if it's not visible, the work does not exist. The work also needs to be sold. When it's sold, the work goes out of your studio and it works *for* you. People see it on the wall of a gallery or somebody's house and it doesn't matter whether they think it's terrible or beautiful because, at that point, the work is already working for you.

MG: Many of your works from that time—and Minujín's installations, such as *La Menesunda*—are often read in relation to the new kind of consumerism that completely transformed the culture of the 1960s. Did you see your work, or the work of artists like Minujín, in relation to those changes?

C: I don't think so. I have never considered my packages, for example, in relation to consumer culture, because they were miserable, idealistic works. I was a political refugee who had escaped by walking in the woods like the refugees you see today, with no family, without even knowing how to speak any foreign languages. My packages were very poor, miserable objects. They didn't have anything to do with industrial packaging. They were very humble things—not very nice—very old things, and, of course, they were very far from the concept of consumerism or even Pop art imagery.

MG: What role did the city of Paris, or dialogues with other artists like Minujín, play in the creation of your work?

C: You should understand that we are talking about a very loose period. I can't speak specifically for Marta, but it's not that all the young artists of the moment were interested in consumerism or Pop. There was a much more free—more anarchistic—attitude at that time. When I was working with my materials, the packages, and the objects, I wasn't really thinking of products.

MG: What about the storefronts you did early on? Were they more explicitly connected to commercial culture? Did you feel that these early environments like yours, or like Minujín's, were directly inspired by the experience of shopping in cities or the department stores of the postwar period?

C: For me, the storefronts are really about architecture. That's when I started to think about approaching the work in a different way. The way we do our projects involves so much planning, it's like building a building: we work with professional workers, not with performers. There is no improvisation. We hire heavy-duty ironworkers and consultants: it's like building bridges or skyscrapers. I don't know if Marta thinks that way too. Maybe she does. It's not about consumption but rather about the demands and processes of industrial work.

For both of us, and for many international artists in the 1960s, Paris was very exciting but also very tough. I don't know if you ever lived in Paris, but even today, if you don't speak French very well, they're nice to you, but they're also very dismissive. There is no way to make your way in Paris if you can't articulate yourself in proper French—it's just impossible. The intellectualism of French culture is so powerful. All of us international artists—the Germans, the Portuguese, and the South Americans—we were all challenged in similar ways by French culture and conformism, and maybe that's why we gravitated toward each other.

MG: How different was New York in this sense?

C: I spoke neither French nor English. I learned English in the streets, like Jeanne-Claude did. When I came to America, I had a lot of luck in my life. I met Leo Castelli in 1959. He had seen some of my packages and installations and he told me that if I had the money to come to New York, he would put me in a group show. Imagine that. In late 1963, I was in a group show in Paris that Leo saw, and two months later, in February and March of 1964, I did the storefronts, got a room at the Chelsea hotel, and was part of a group show at Leo's gallery—which was at 4 East 77th Street—with Richard Artschwager, Robert Watts, and Alex Hay. That is why we stayed here, because I had never would have dreamed of having this type of exhibition in a gallery in Paris.

MG: Did you meet Marta again in New York in the 1960s?

C: I probably met her later. One person in New York I knew very well, whom I had met in Germany at my first exhibition in 1961, was Nam June Paik. He became one of my oldest friends, even before Jeanne-Claude. Of course, I met Marta many times in New York, nearly every time she came to town. But what I remember best is her energy, her loveliness, and her craziness in Central Park—though I cannot tell you precisely what happened. Everyone was very young and everybody was trying to show his or her work.

MG: Have you ever had any big projects in Argentina or South America?

C: That is a very good question. I have been working for over fifty or sixty years at this point. Jeanne-Claude was so forceful and open, but we had a simple system: we would do projects where people would buy our work. If people in a certain country don't buy your work, why should you do a project there? I am not Australian, but Australian people bought my work, so we did a few projects there. I am not Japanese, but Japanese people bought my work, so we worked there. I am not German, but I have done many projects in Germany because many Germans have bought my work. Most projects came about because collectors had a lot of affection for and interest in my work and would help make the projects happen. That is why I have so many friends and gallery connections in Italy, and why we did many projects there—from the Spoleto Festival to the pieces in Milan to the Porta Pinciana in Rome and Lake Iseo. It was a very natural thing. It is the same thing with Switzerland: I lived in Switzerland before coming to Paris and I have many friends there. The first public building I wrapped was the Kunsthalle in Bern, after I met Harald Szeemann.

MG: So you never saw any of Minujín's major pieces in Argentina, like her *El Partenón de libros* [The Parthenon of Books] (1983) or *El obelisco acostado* [The Obelisk Lying Down] (1978)?

C: No, I never saw them in person, but I have heard about them and seen pictures. I have never been to Argentina. At my age—I am eighty-three—I only want to go where they want me. I have no time to go to other places, unfortunately.

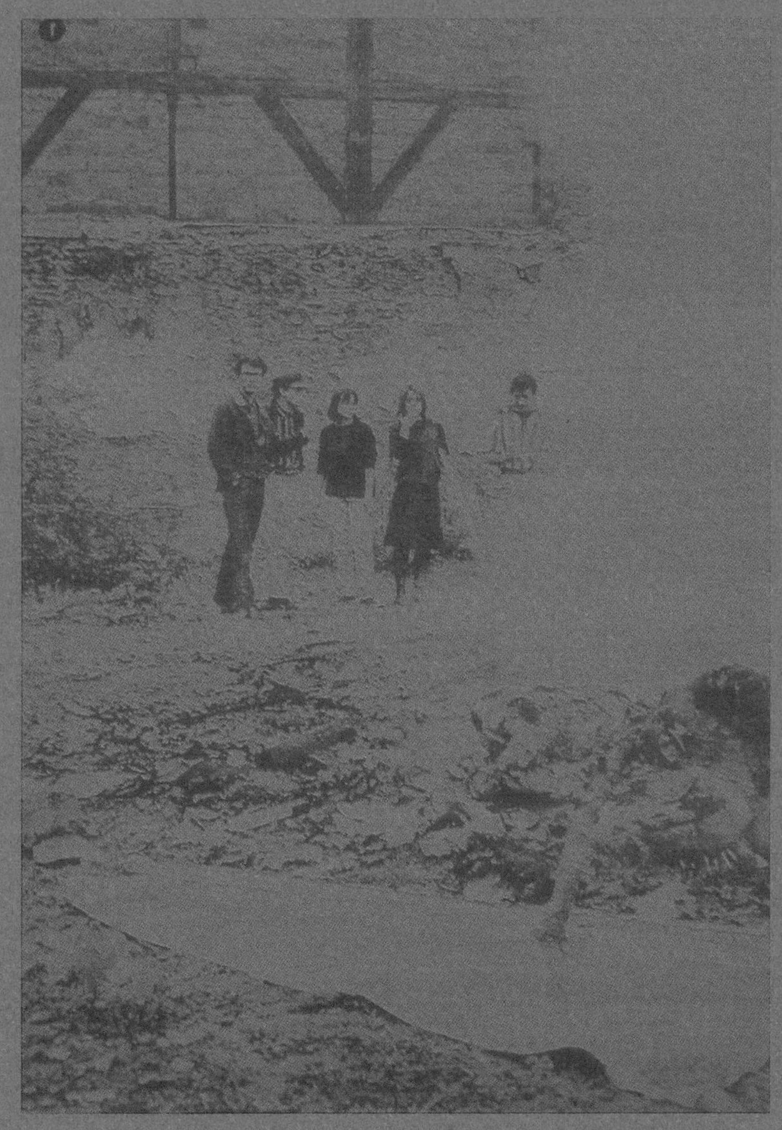

Christo, first from left, and Marta Minujín second from right, at Marta Minujín's *La destrucción* [The Destruction], 1963. Impasse Ronsin, Paris

The following pages present documentation of the legendary environment *La Menesunda*, which Marta Minujín devised with Rubén Santantonín at the Instituto Torcuato Di Tella in Buenos Aires in 1965.

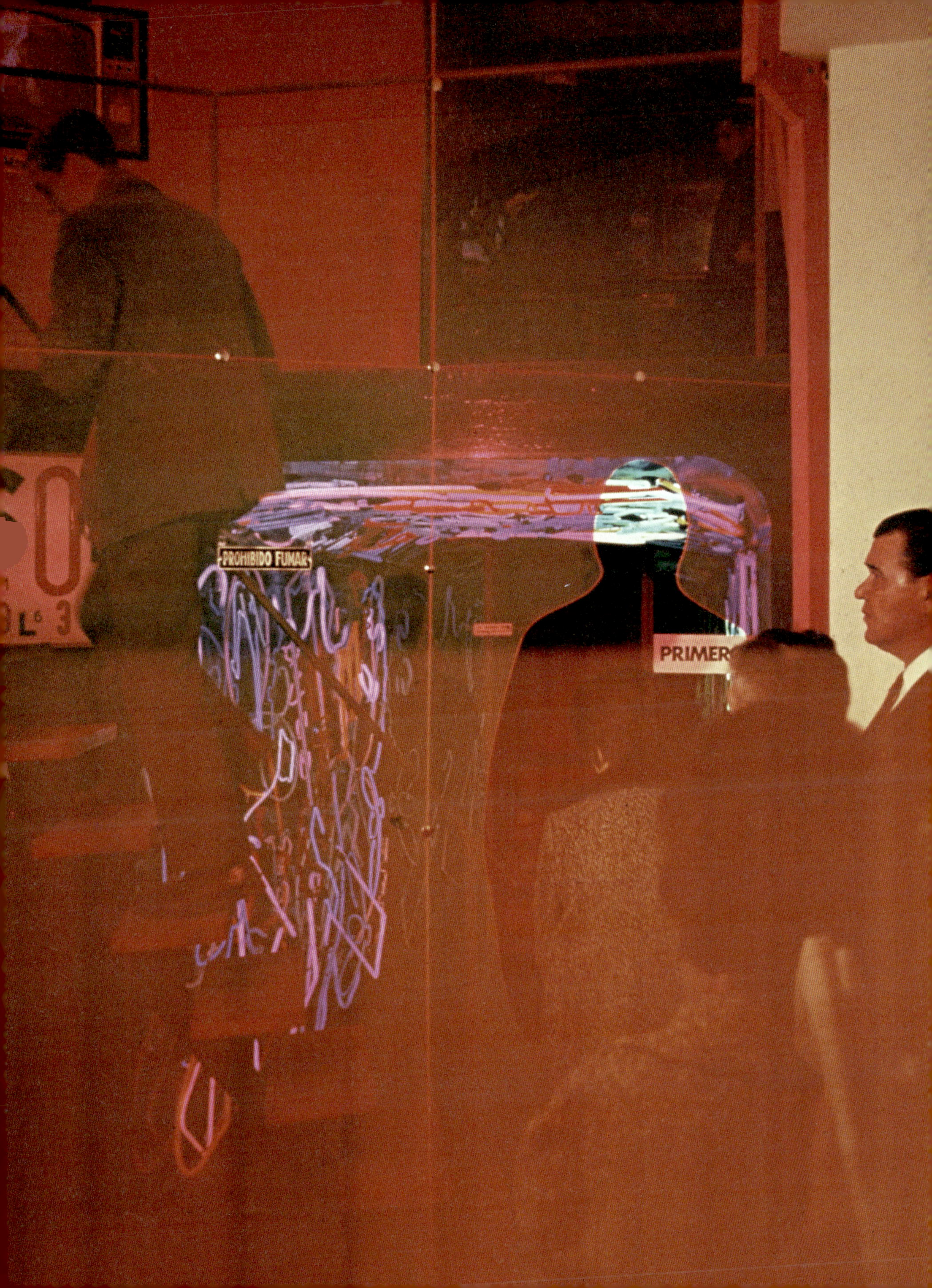
PROHIBIDO FUMAR
PRIMER

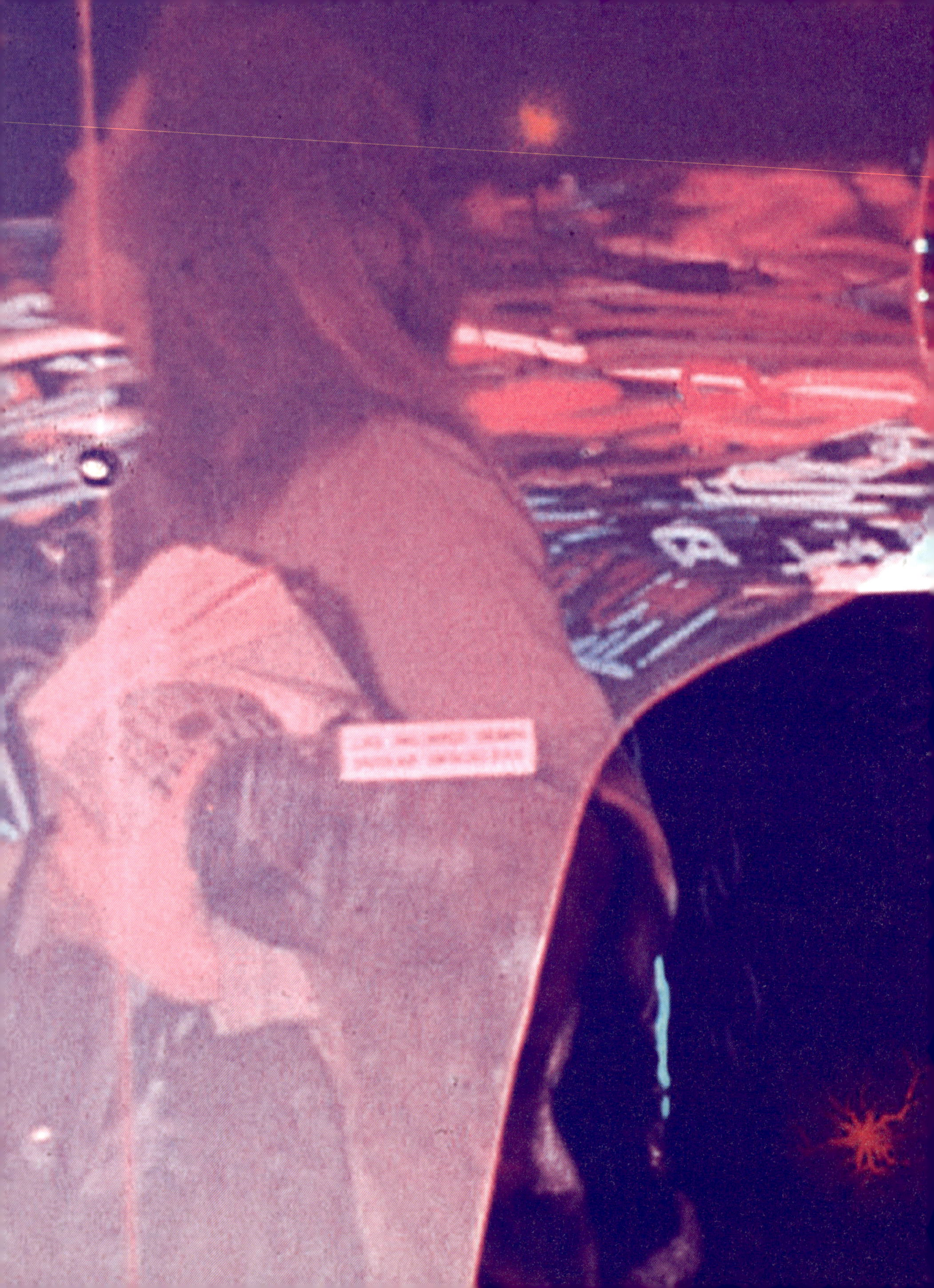

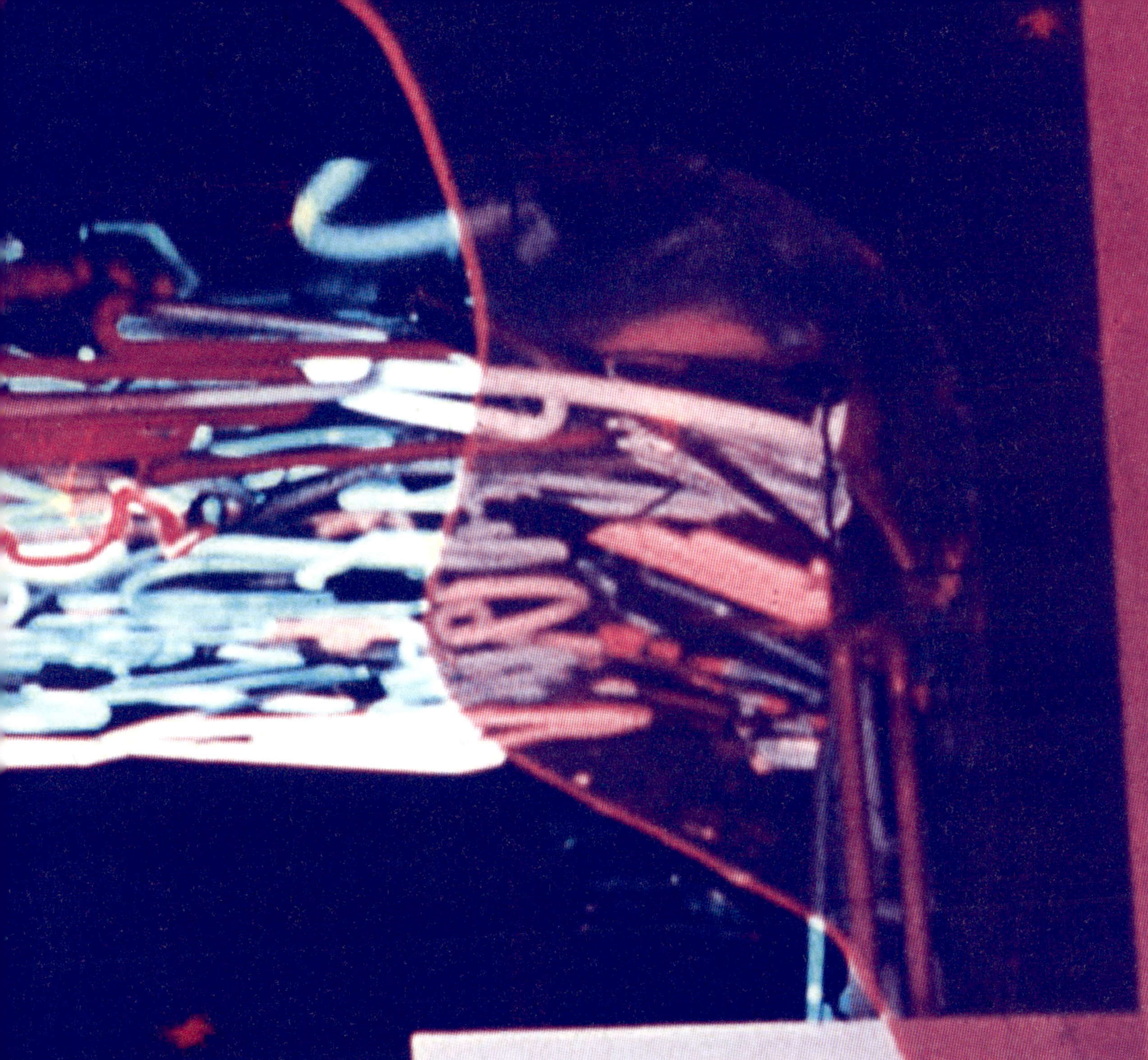

PRIMERO SUB

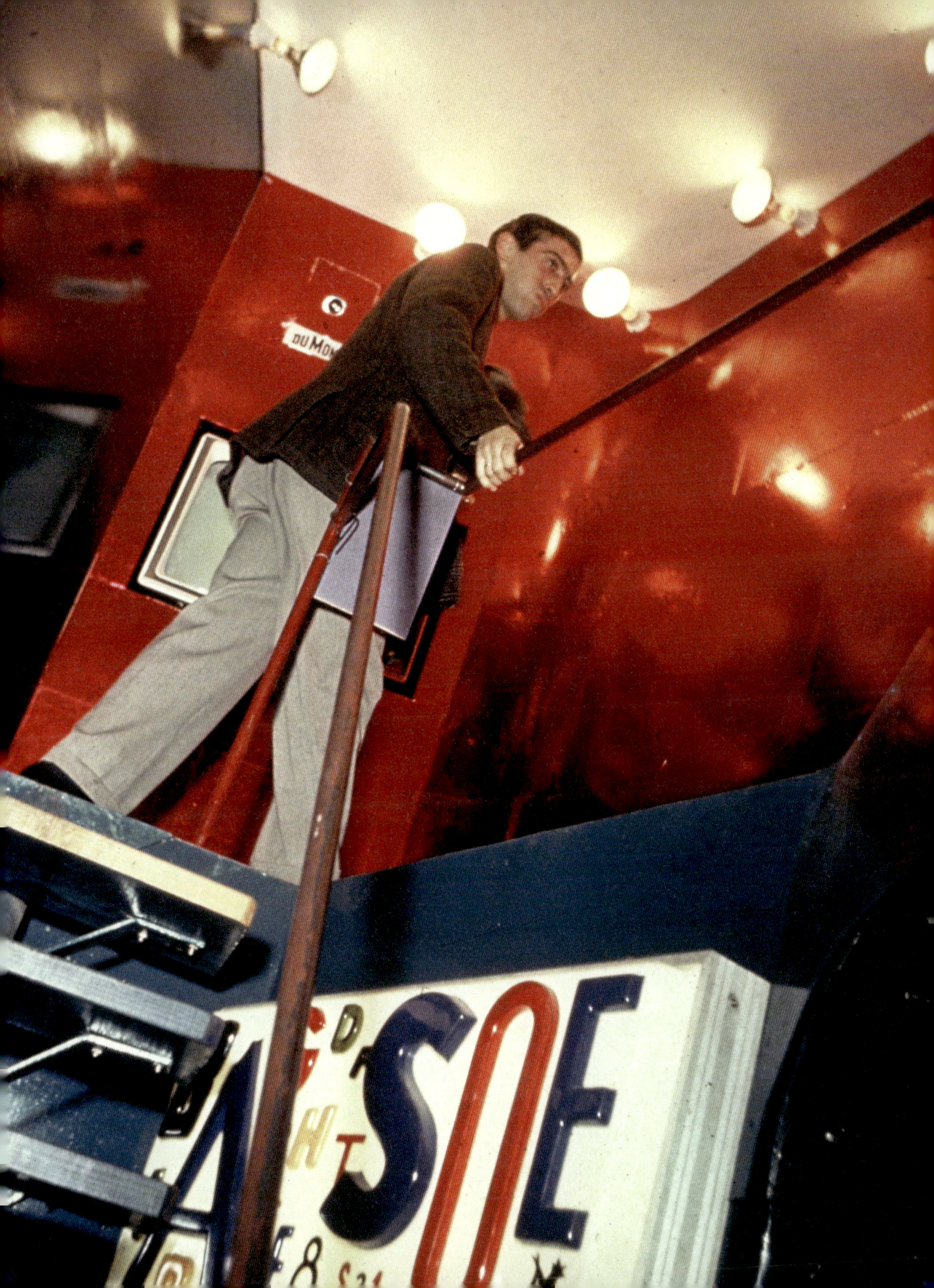

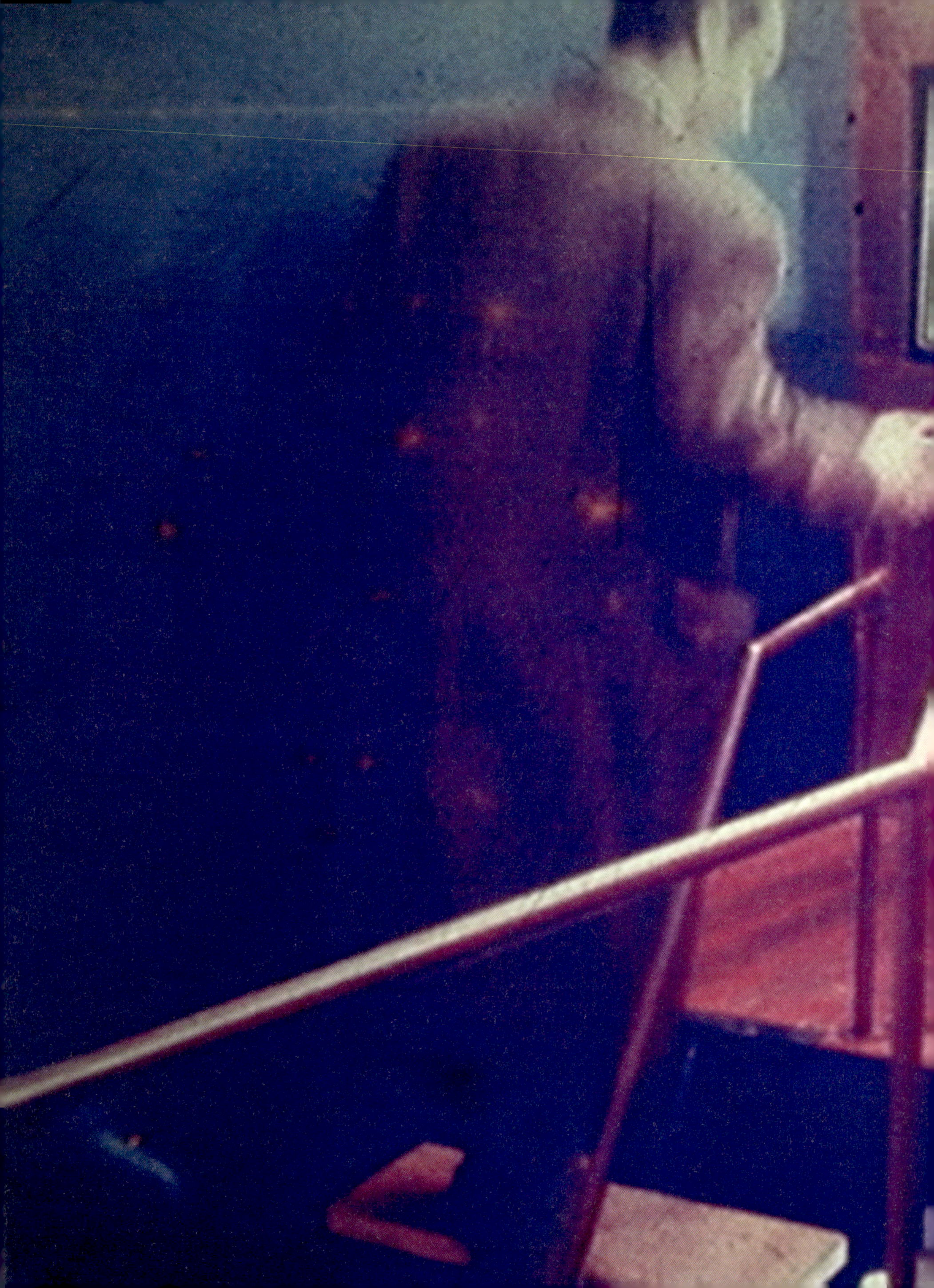

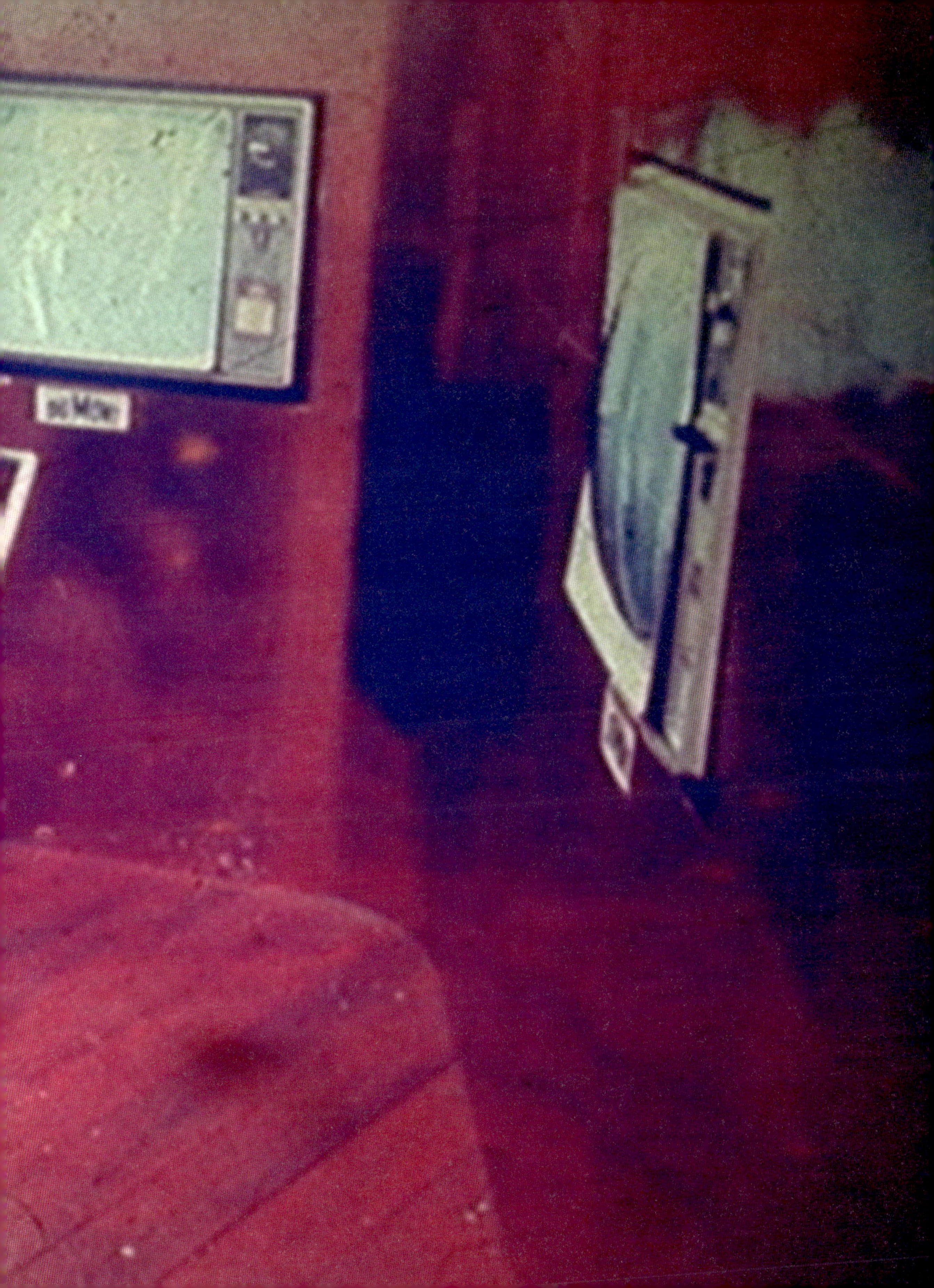

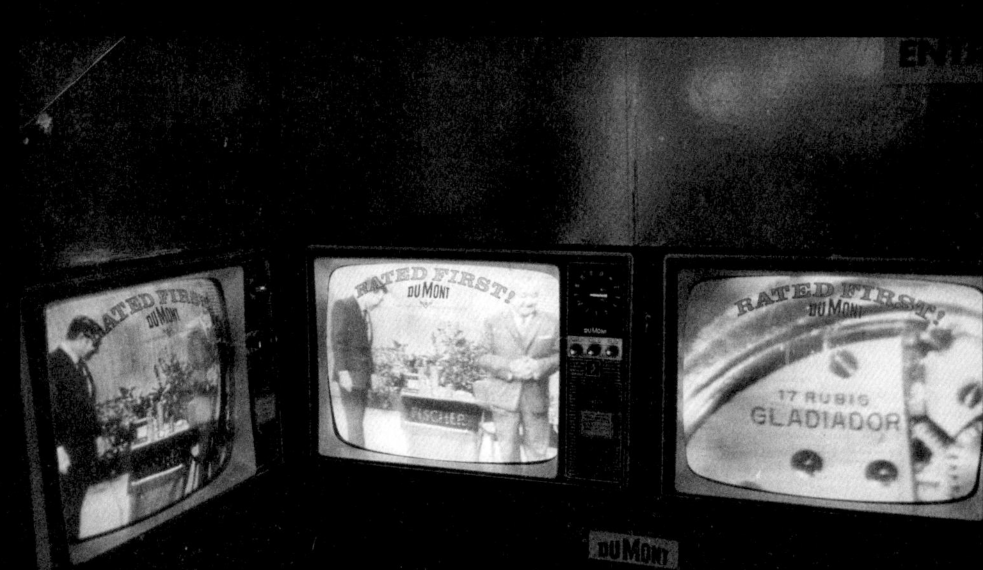
RATED FIRST!
DU MONT
RATED FIRST!
DU MONT
17 RUBIS
GLADIADOR
DU MONT

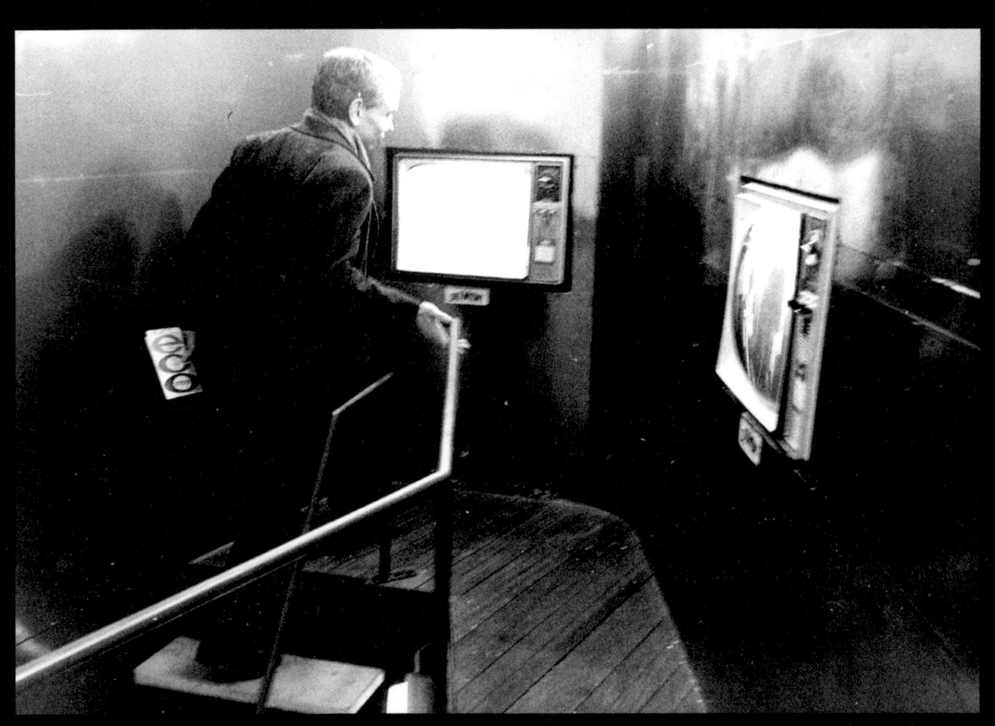
eco

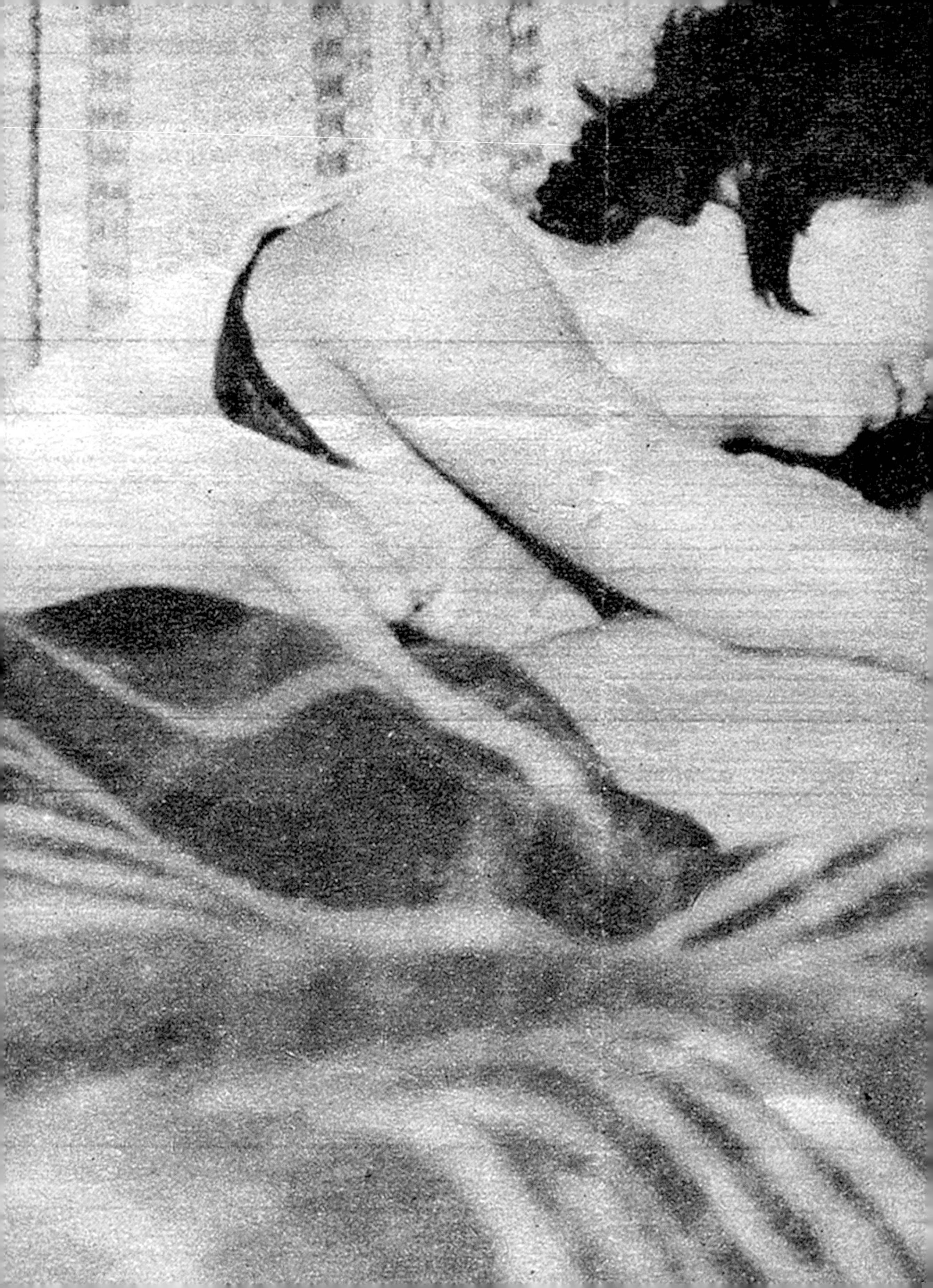

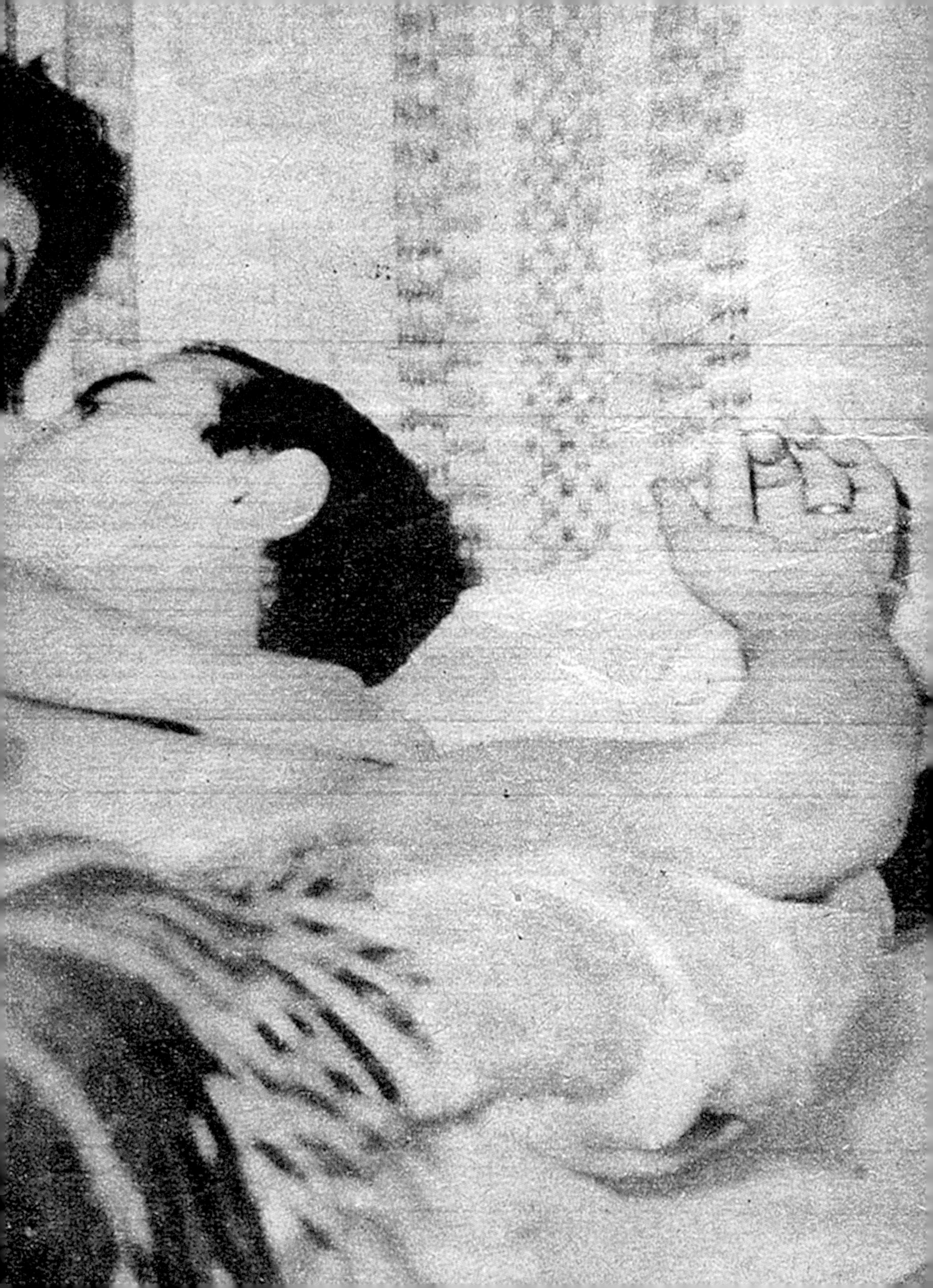

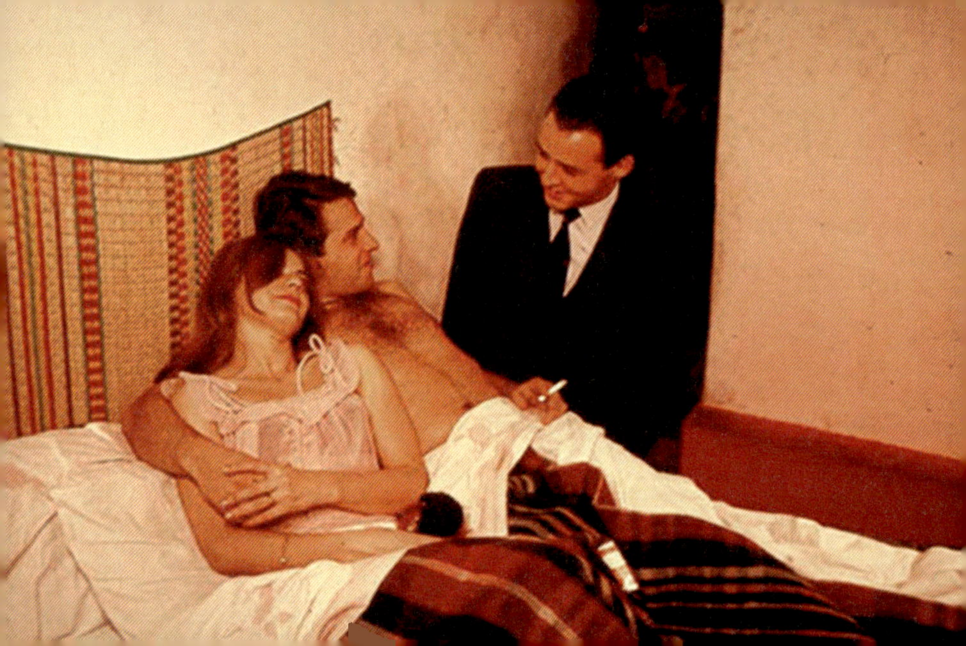

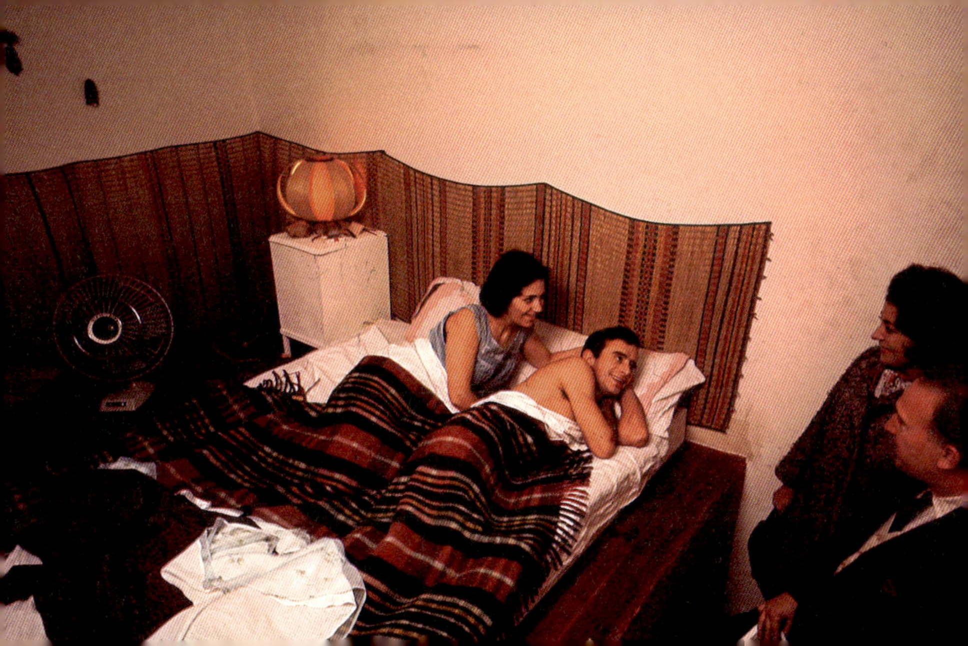

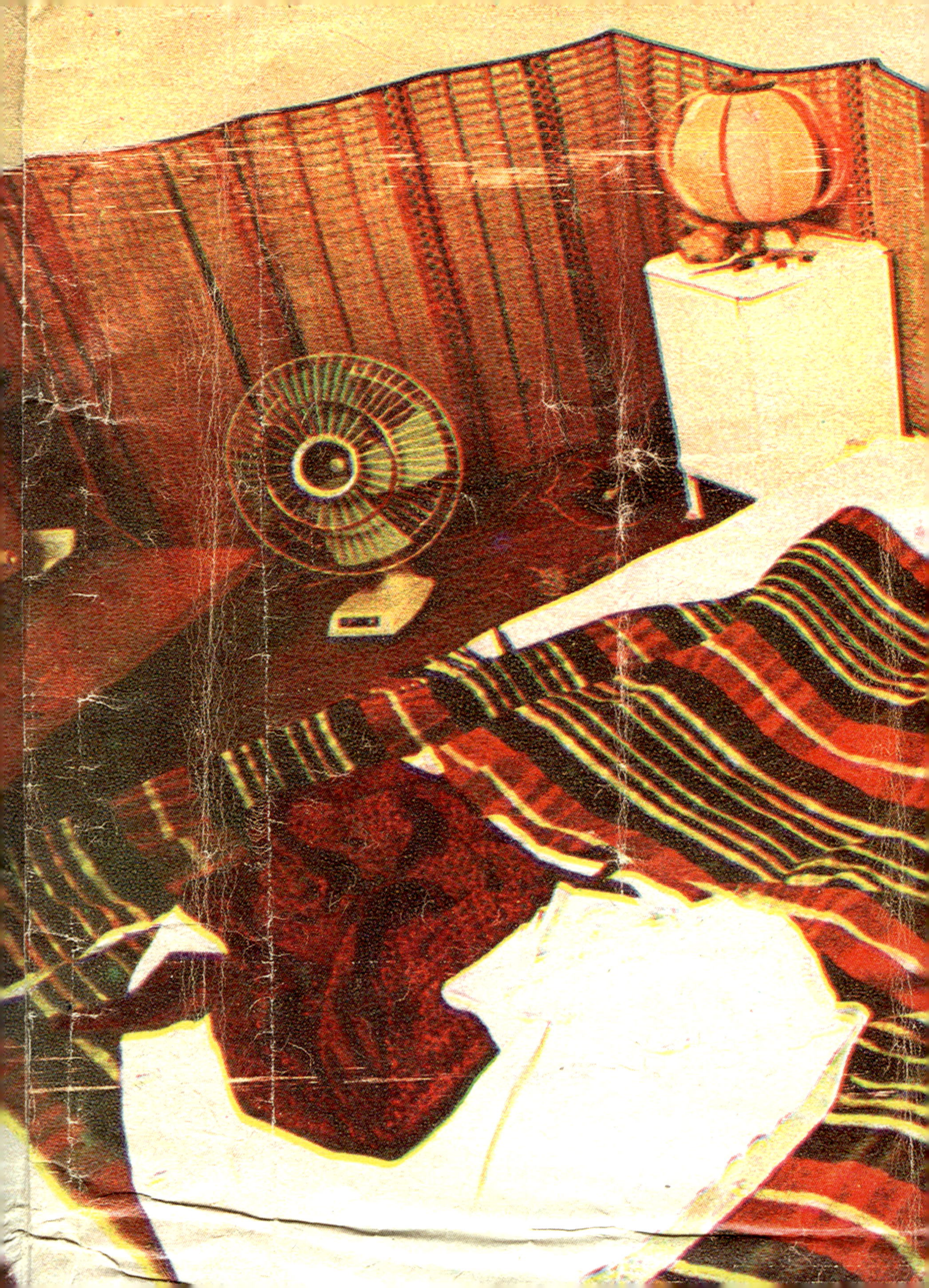

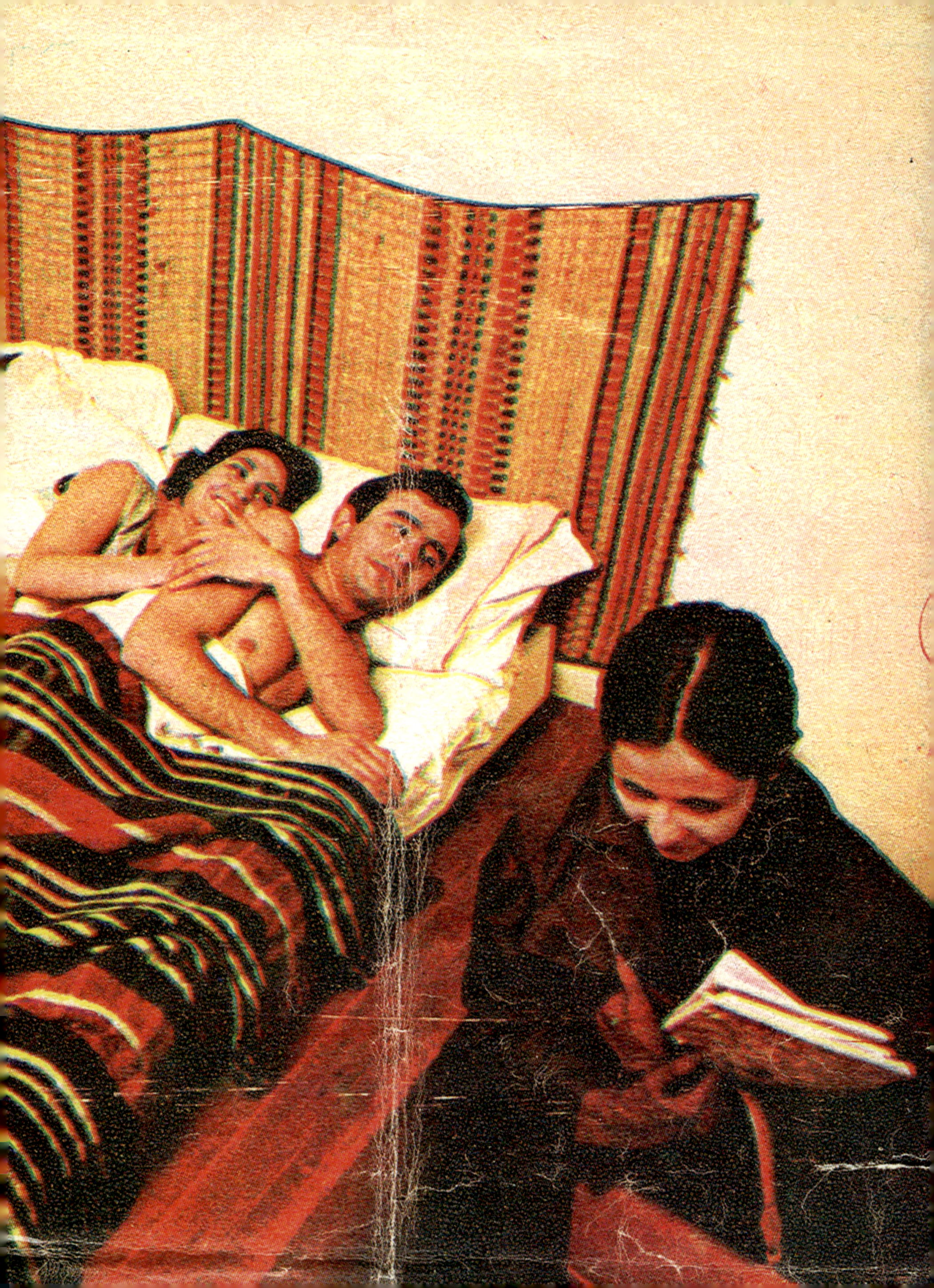

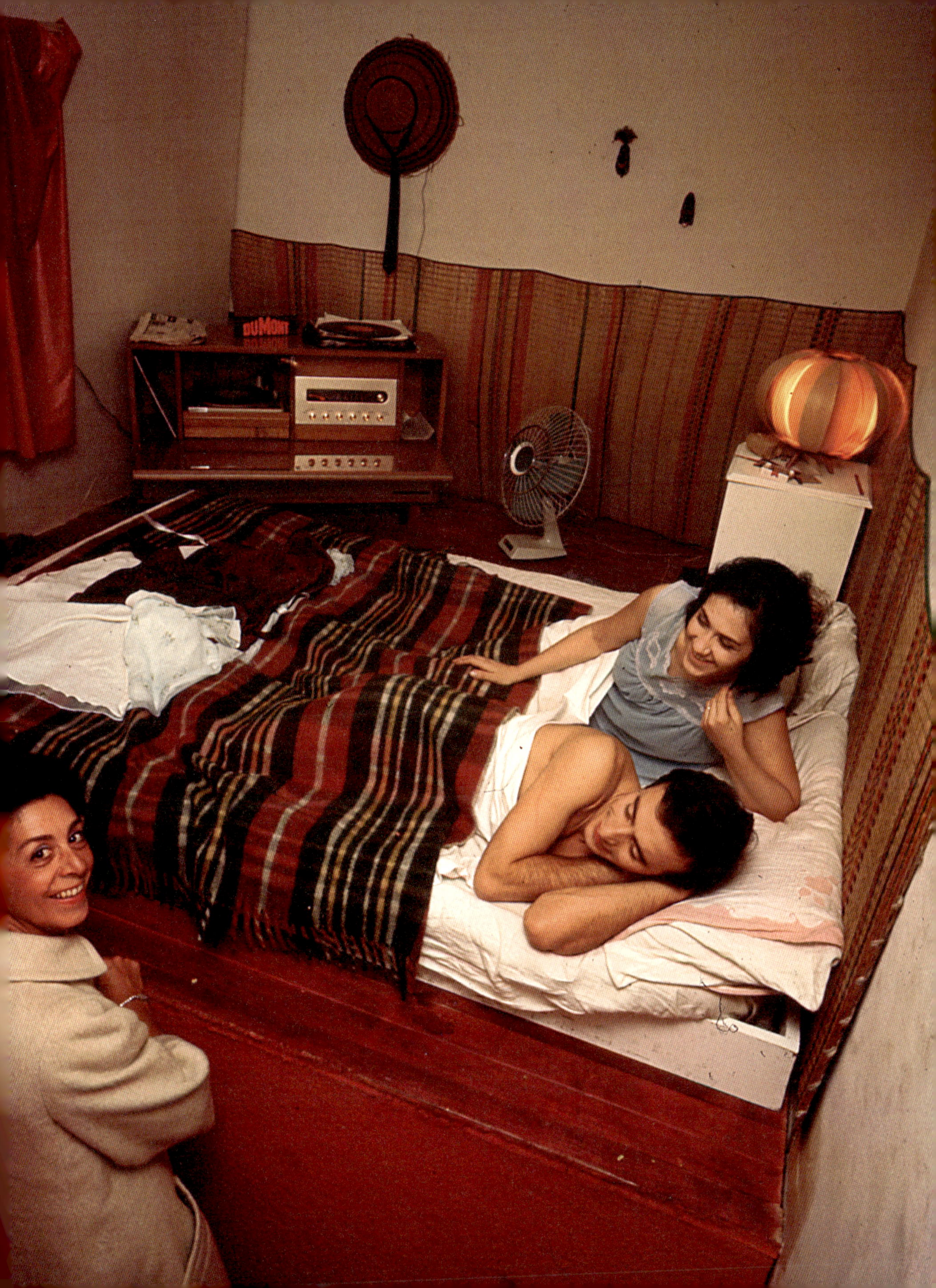
DUMONT

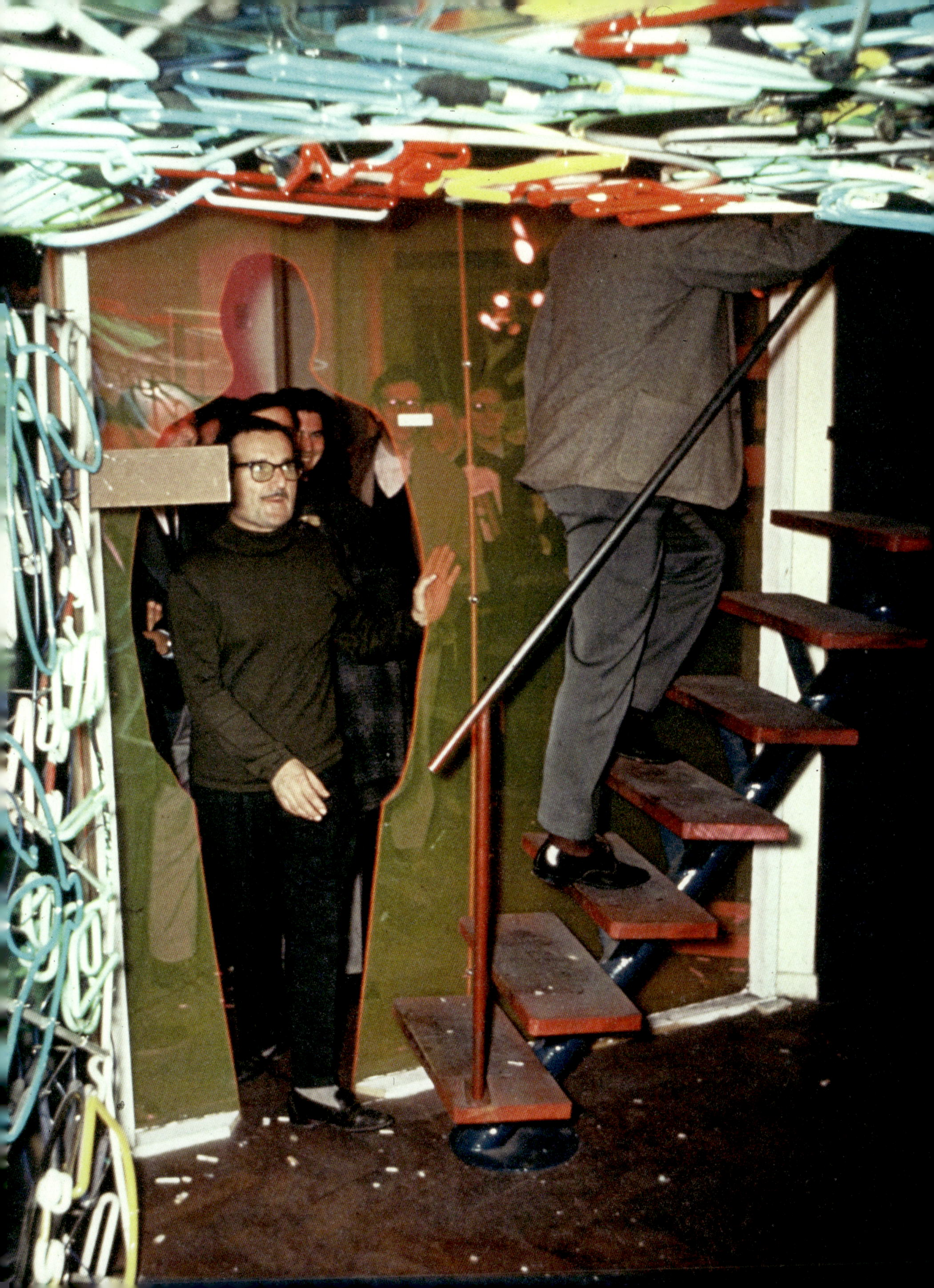

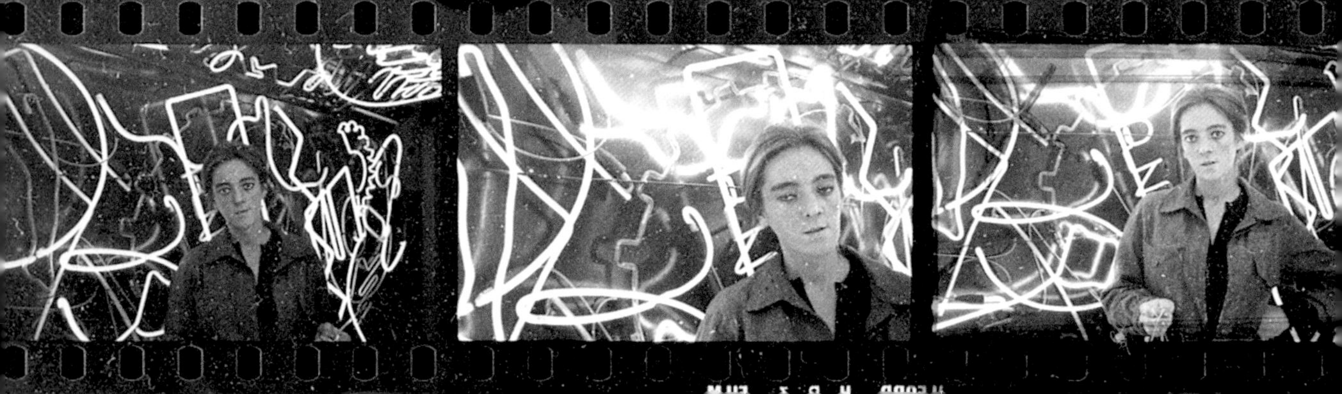

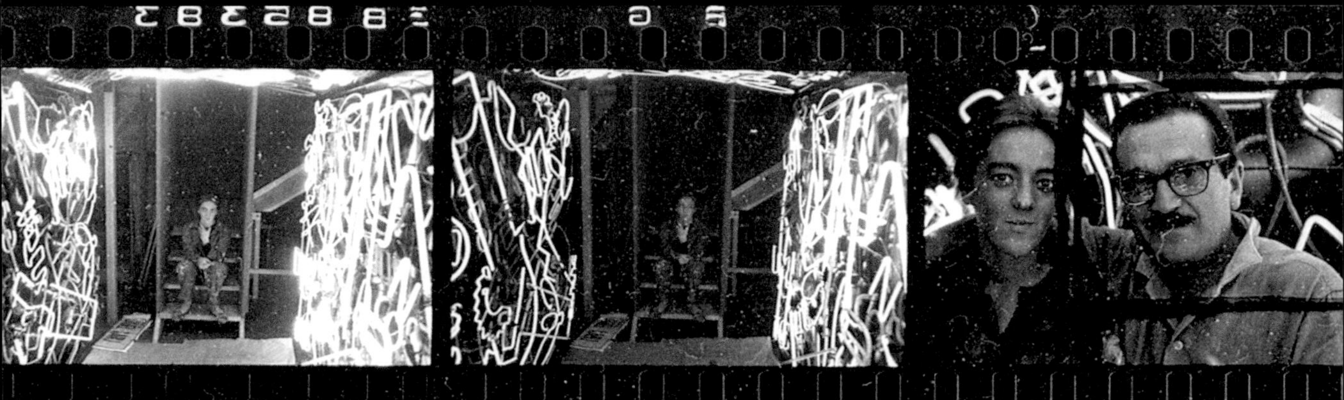

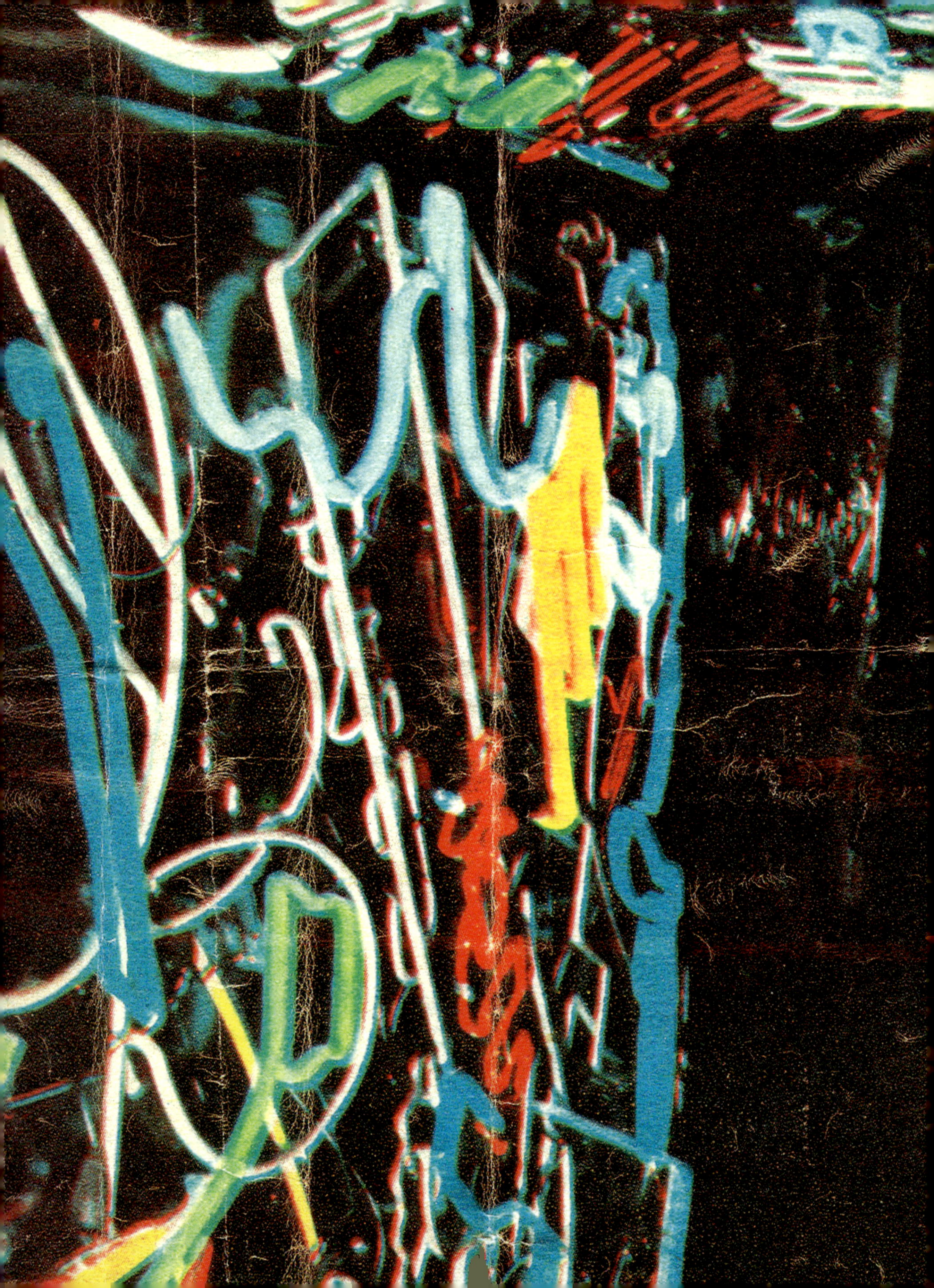

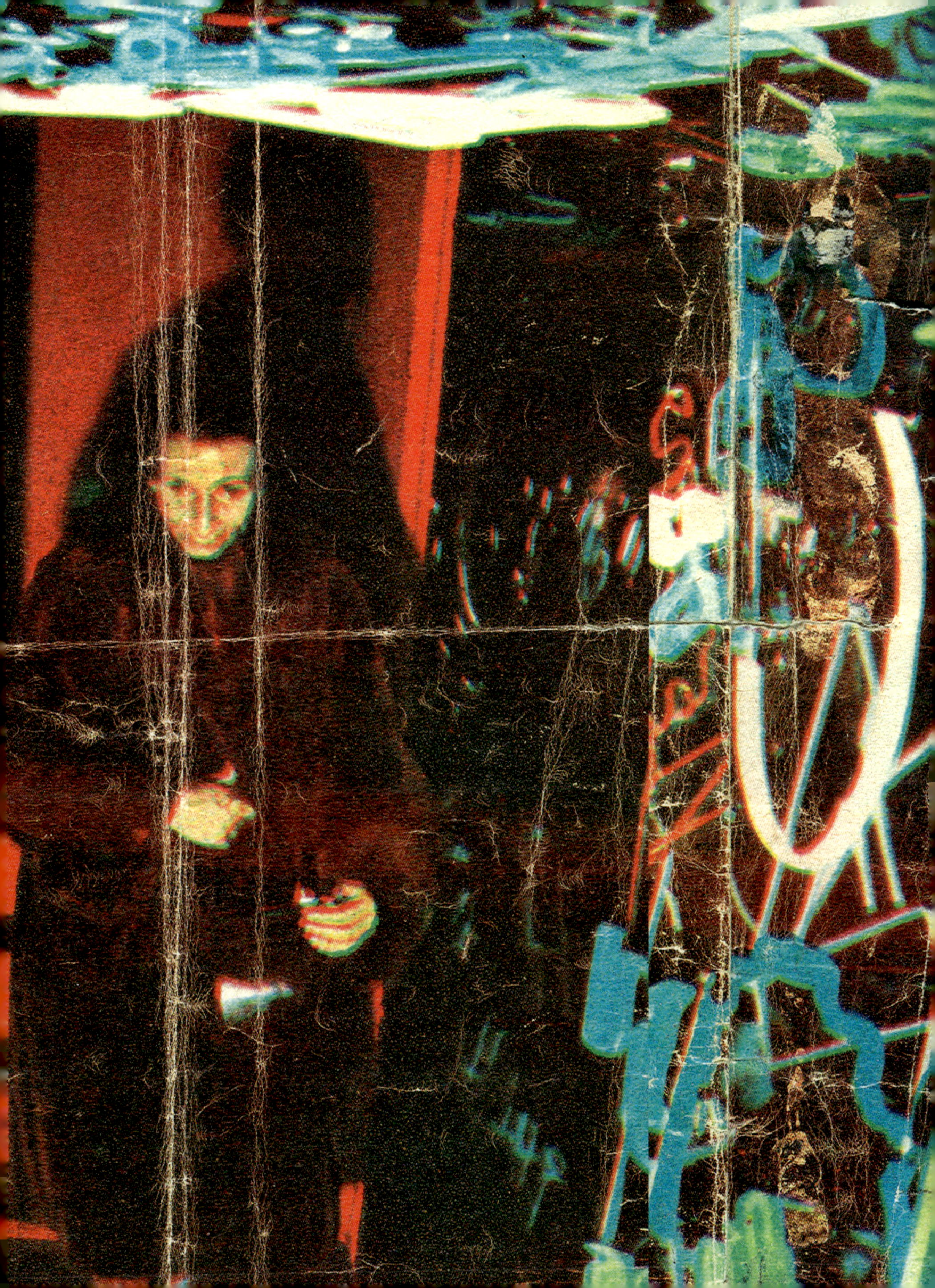

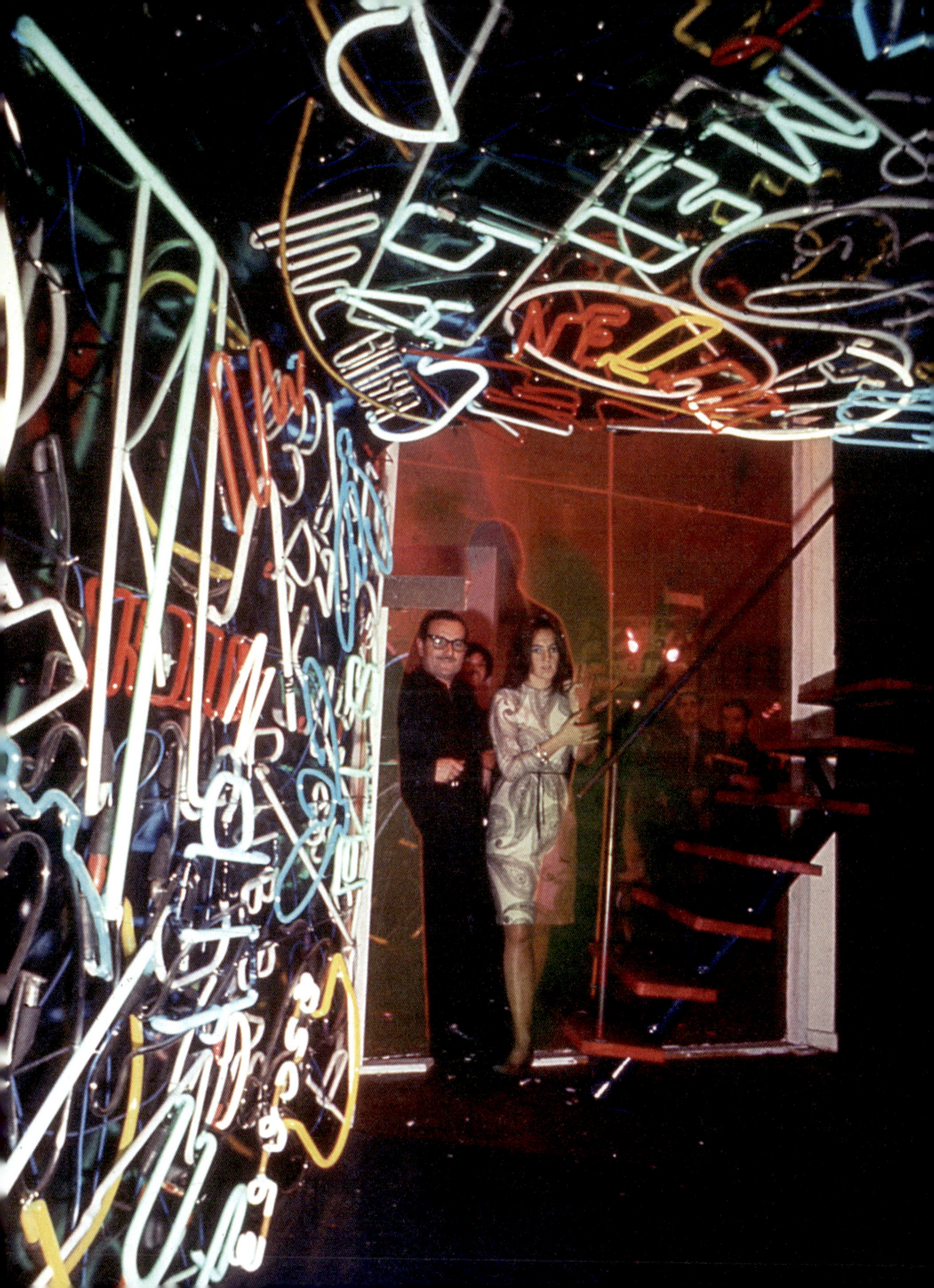

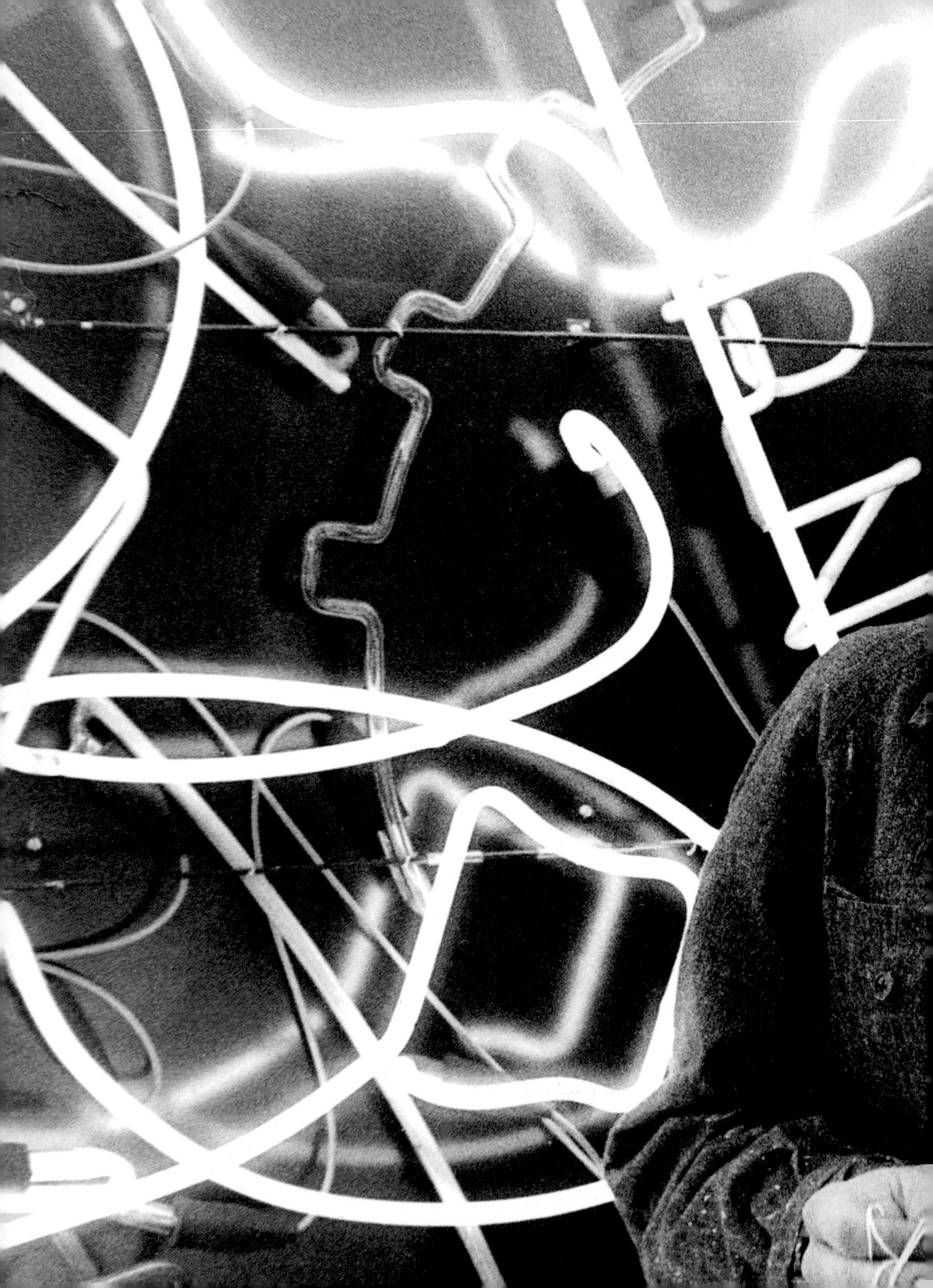

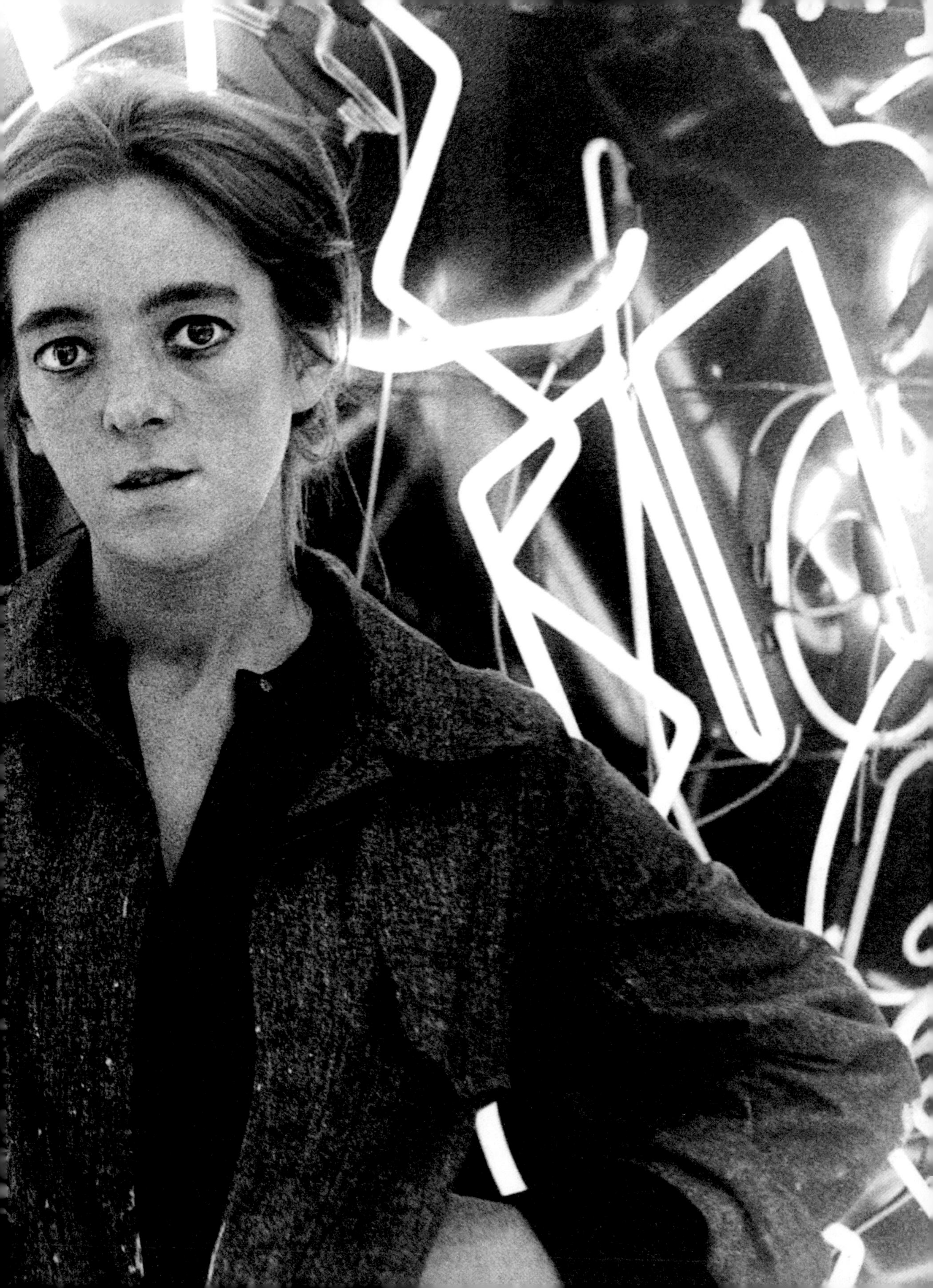

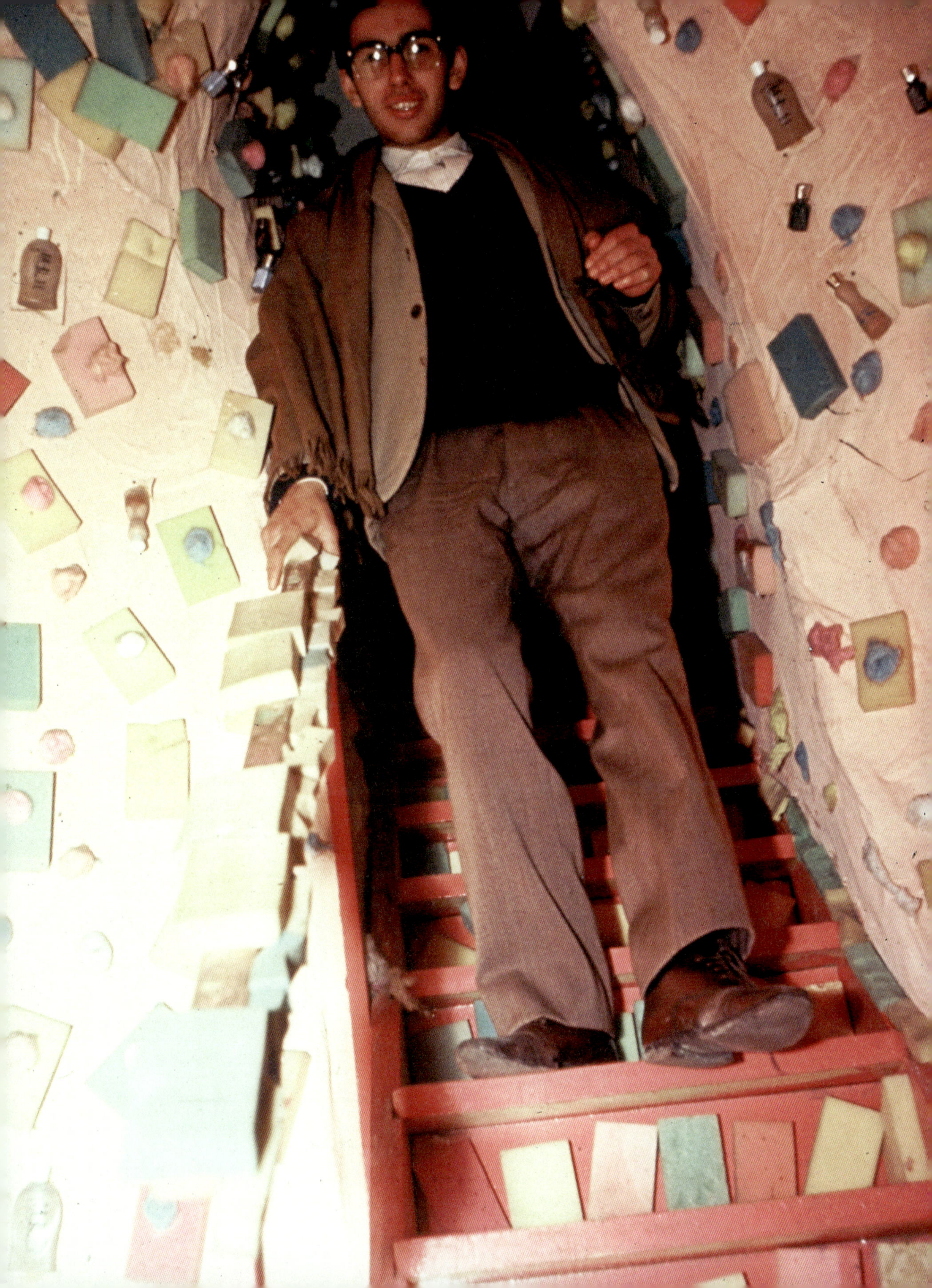

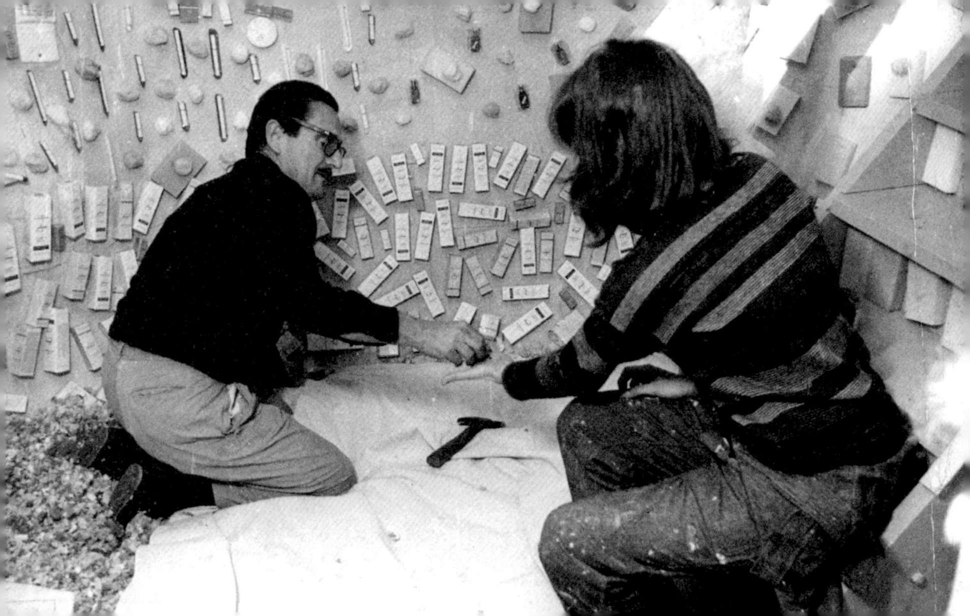

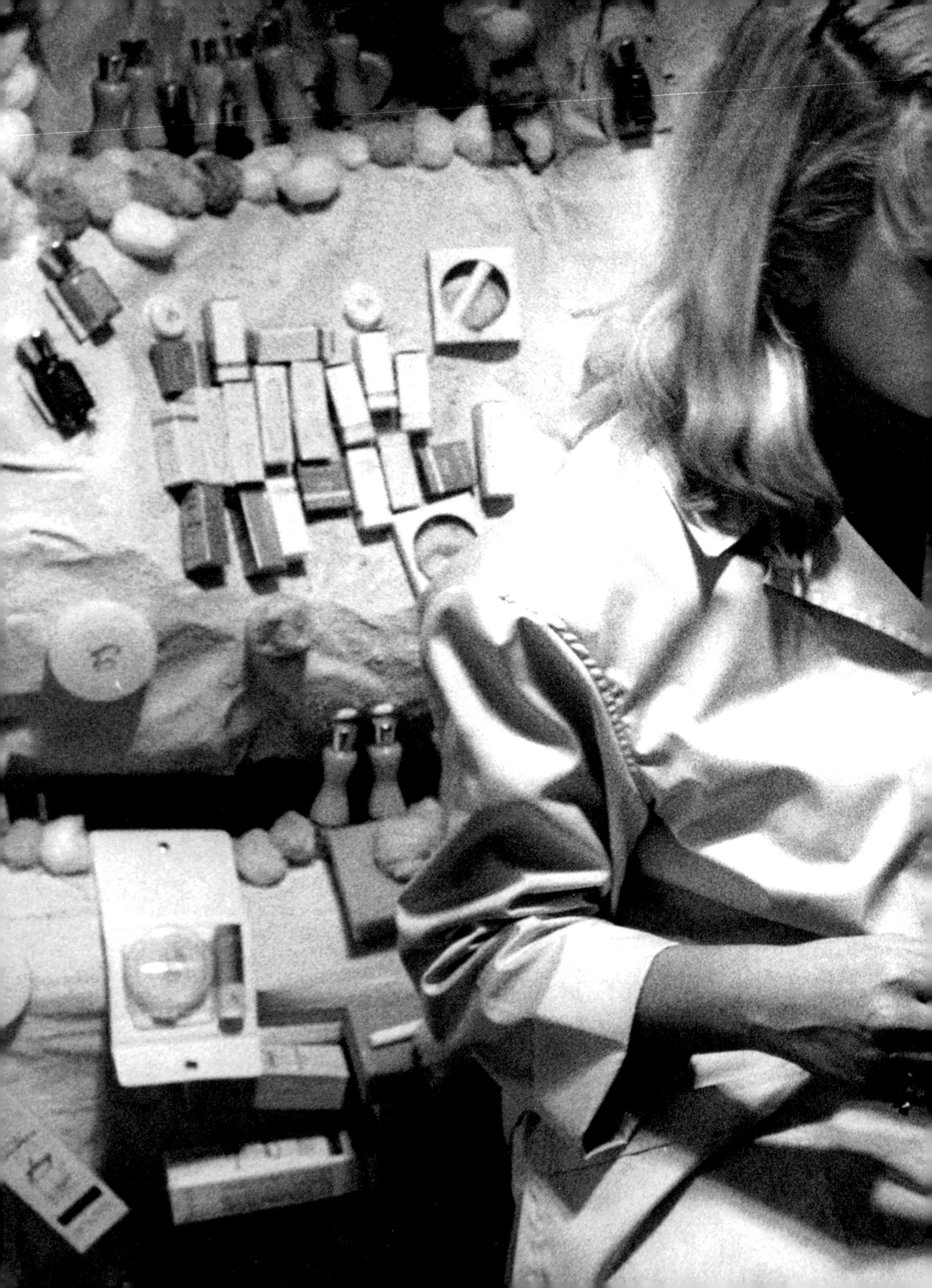

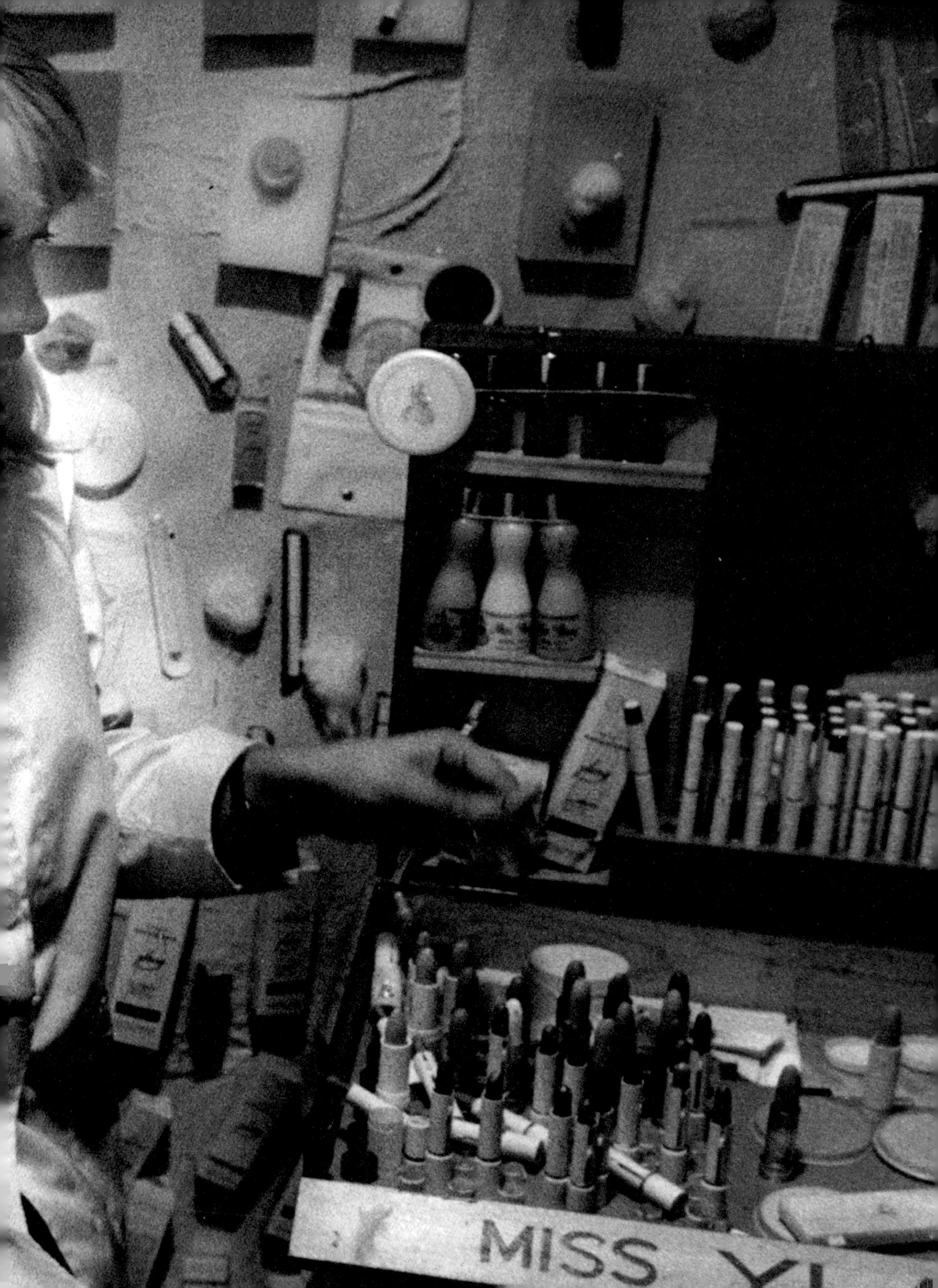
MISS

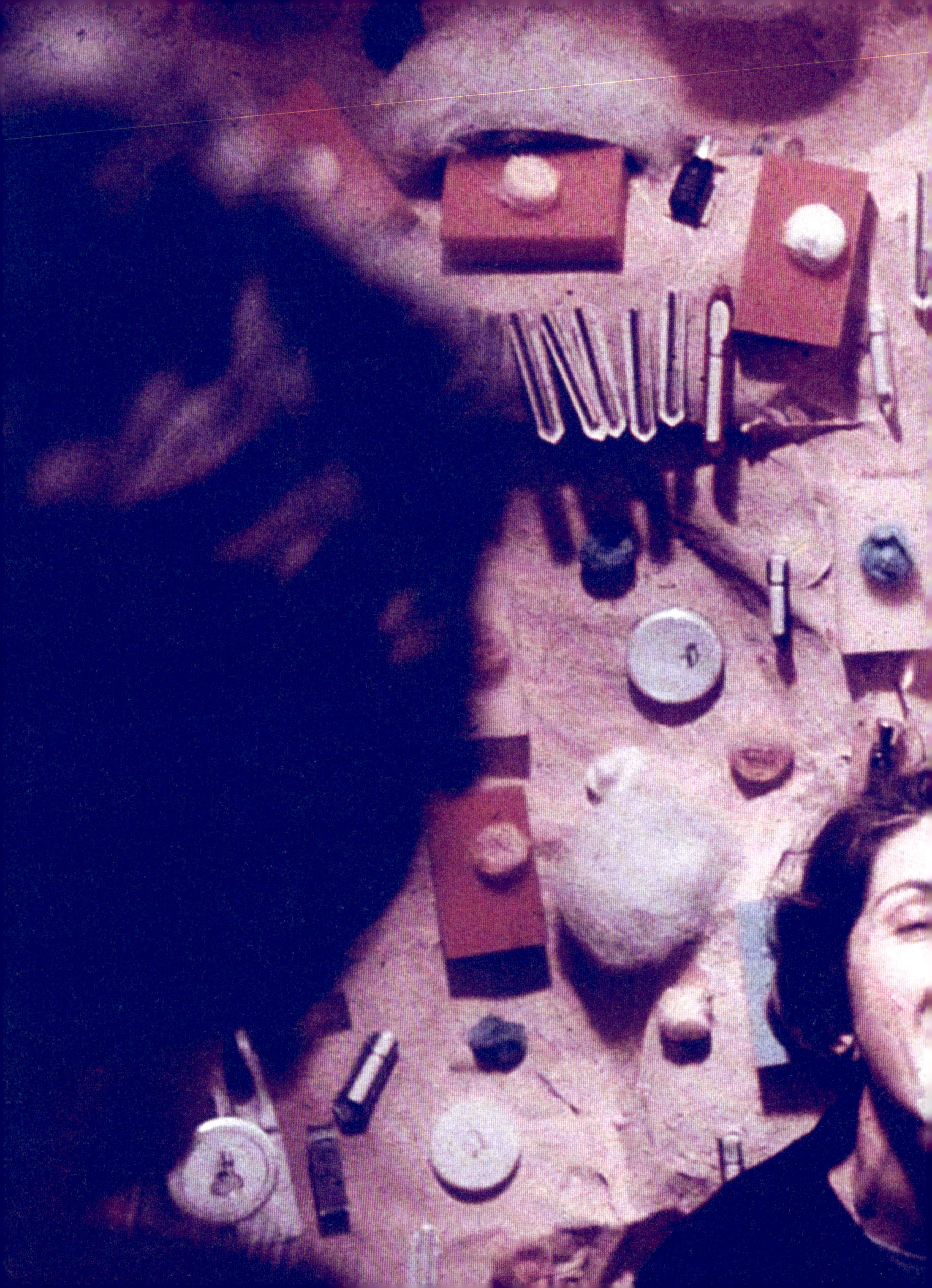

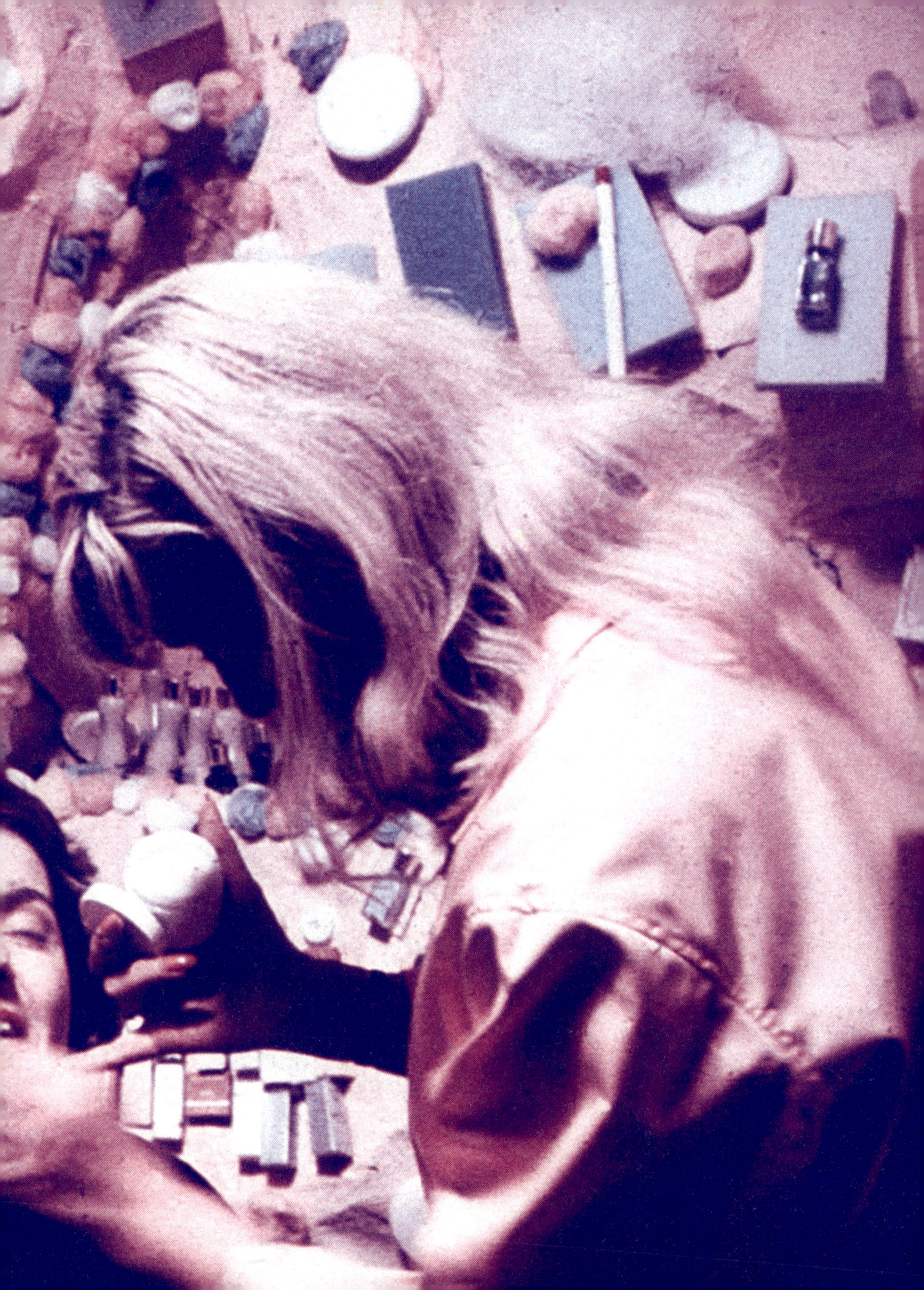

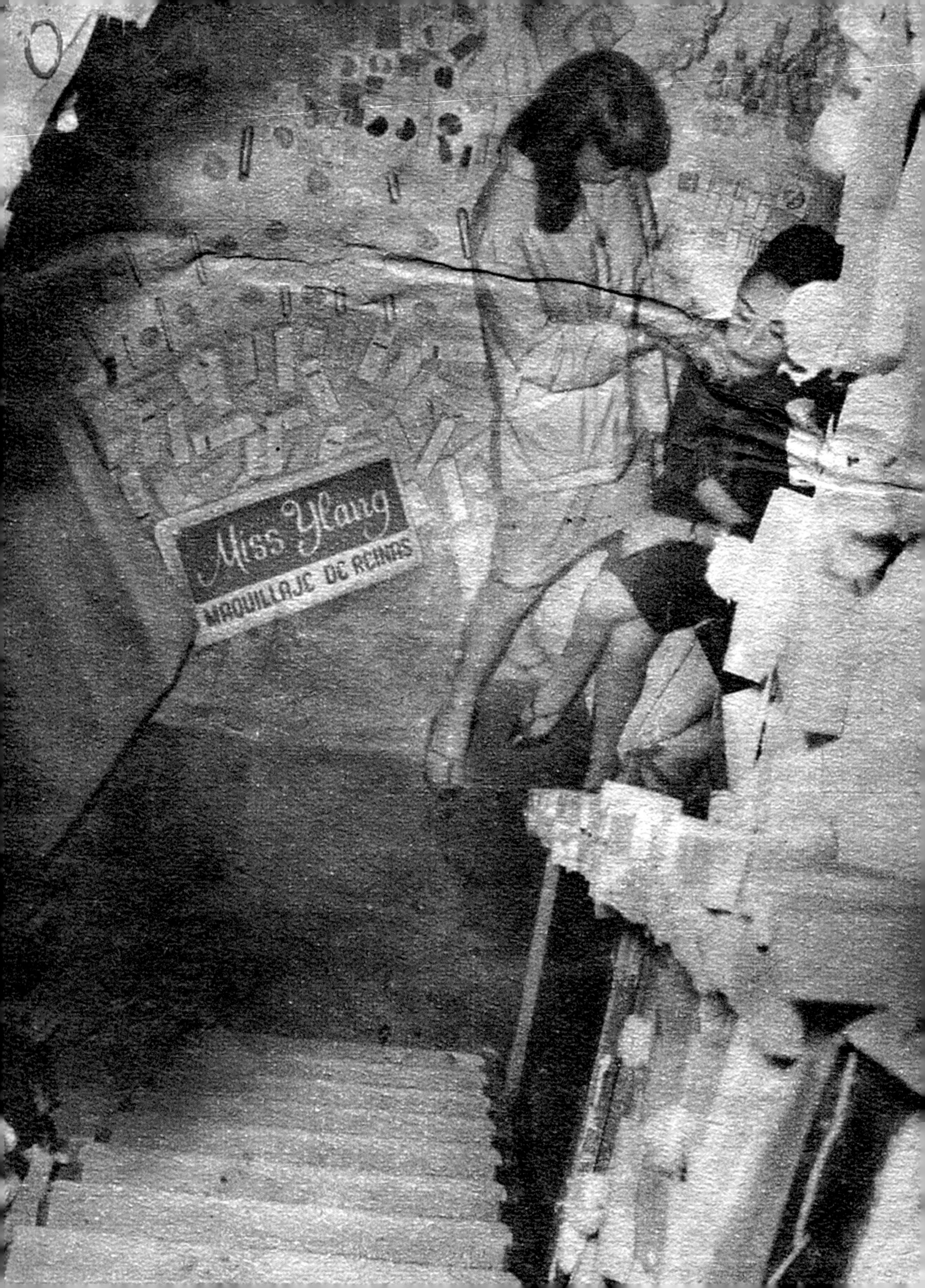
Miss Ylang
MAQUILLAJE DE REINAS

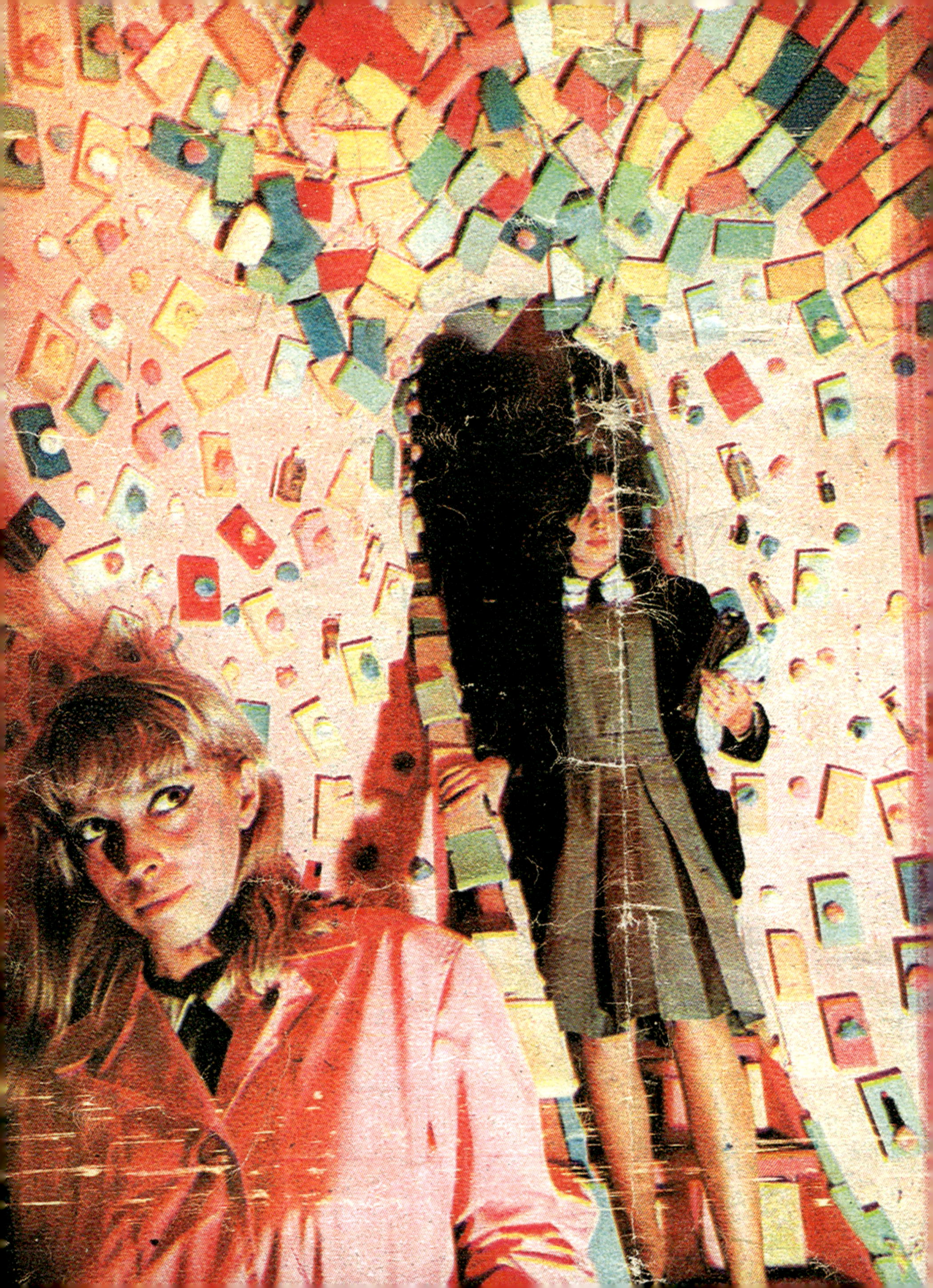

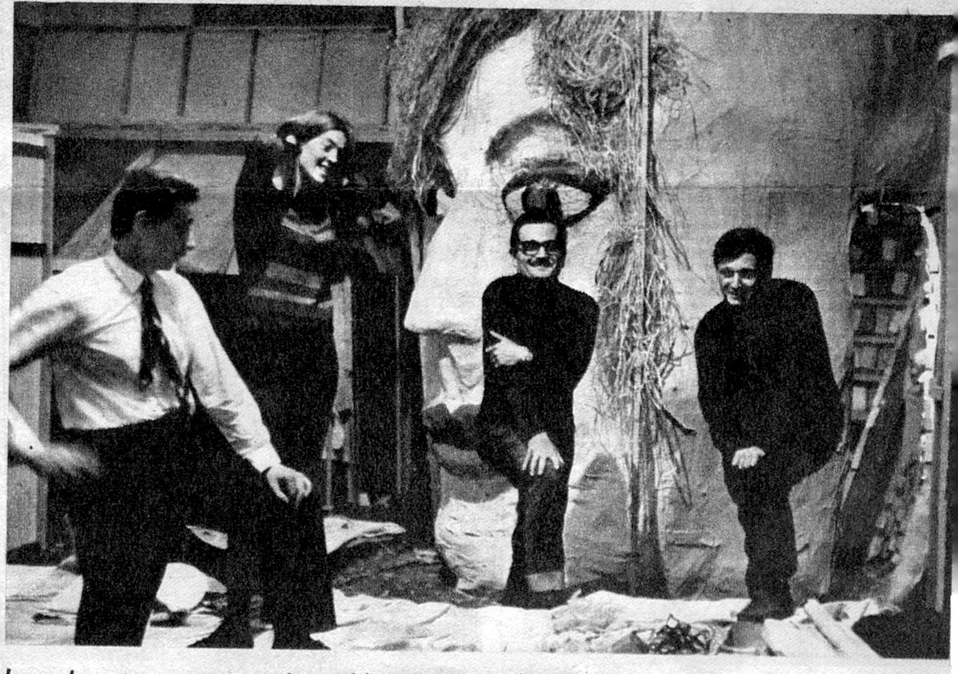

La cabezota corona una increíble "Menesunda" que costó dos millones. "Capricho o disparate, pero muy serio", dicen sus ingenieros, arquitectos y decoradores

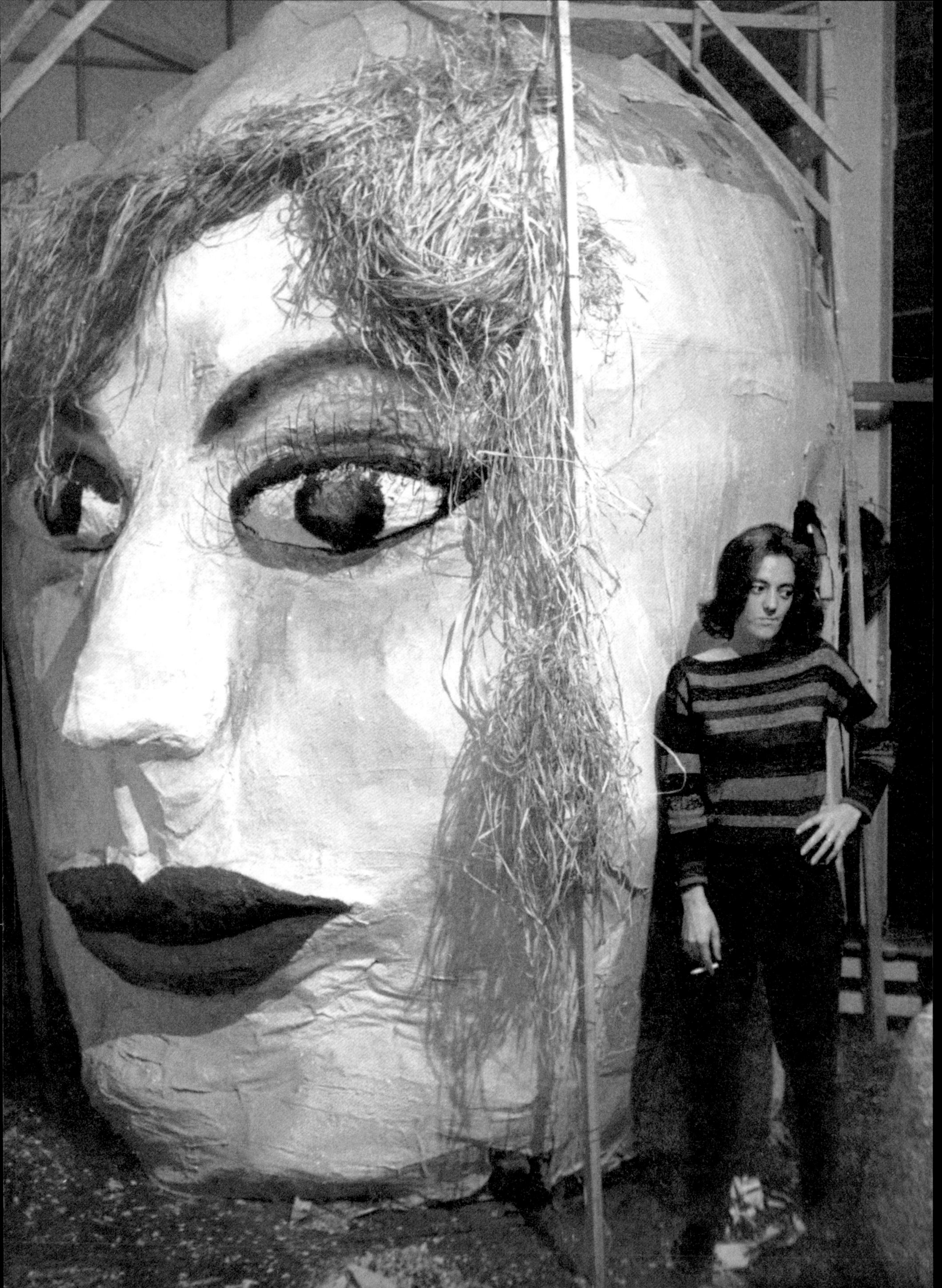

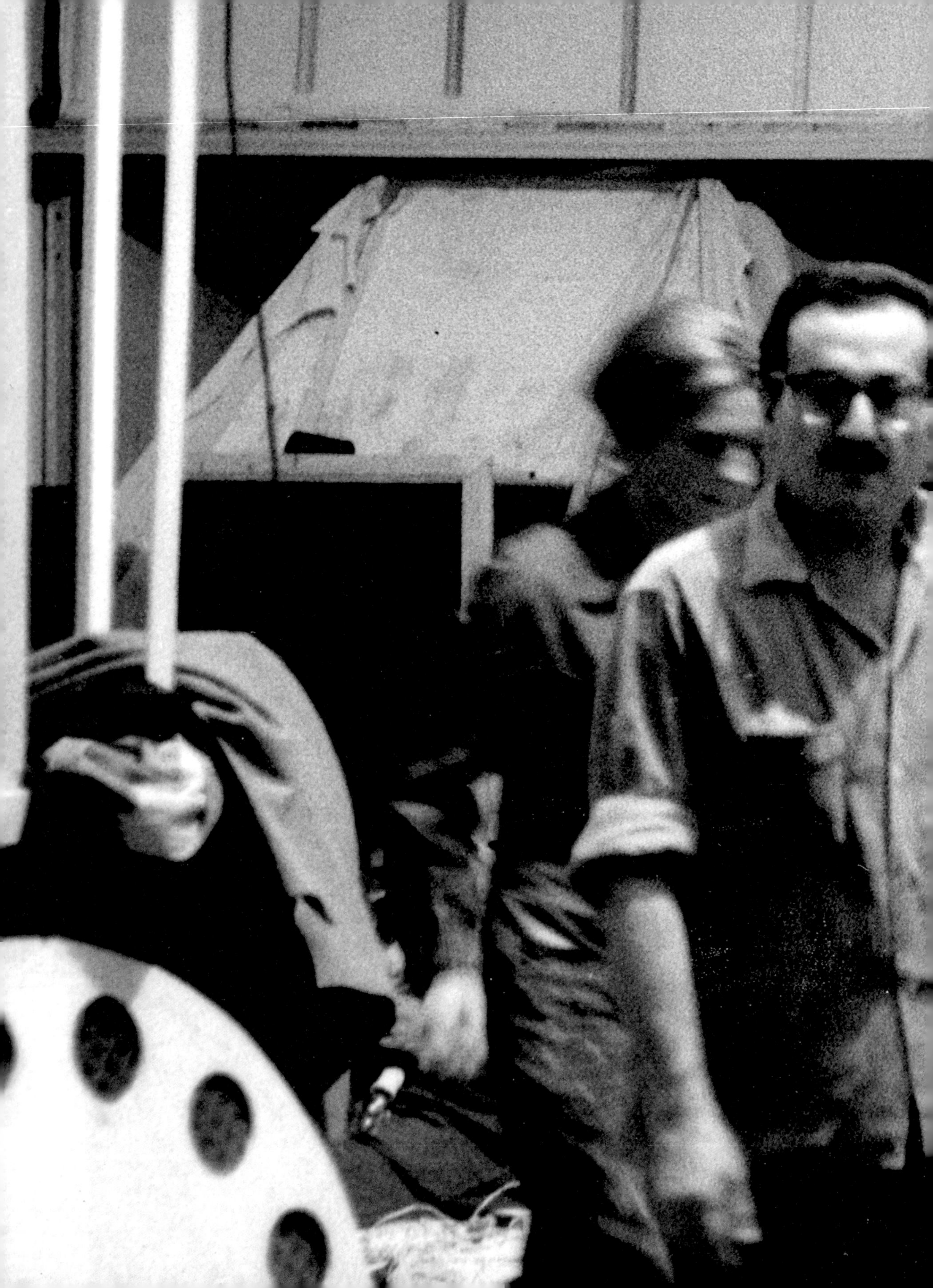

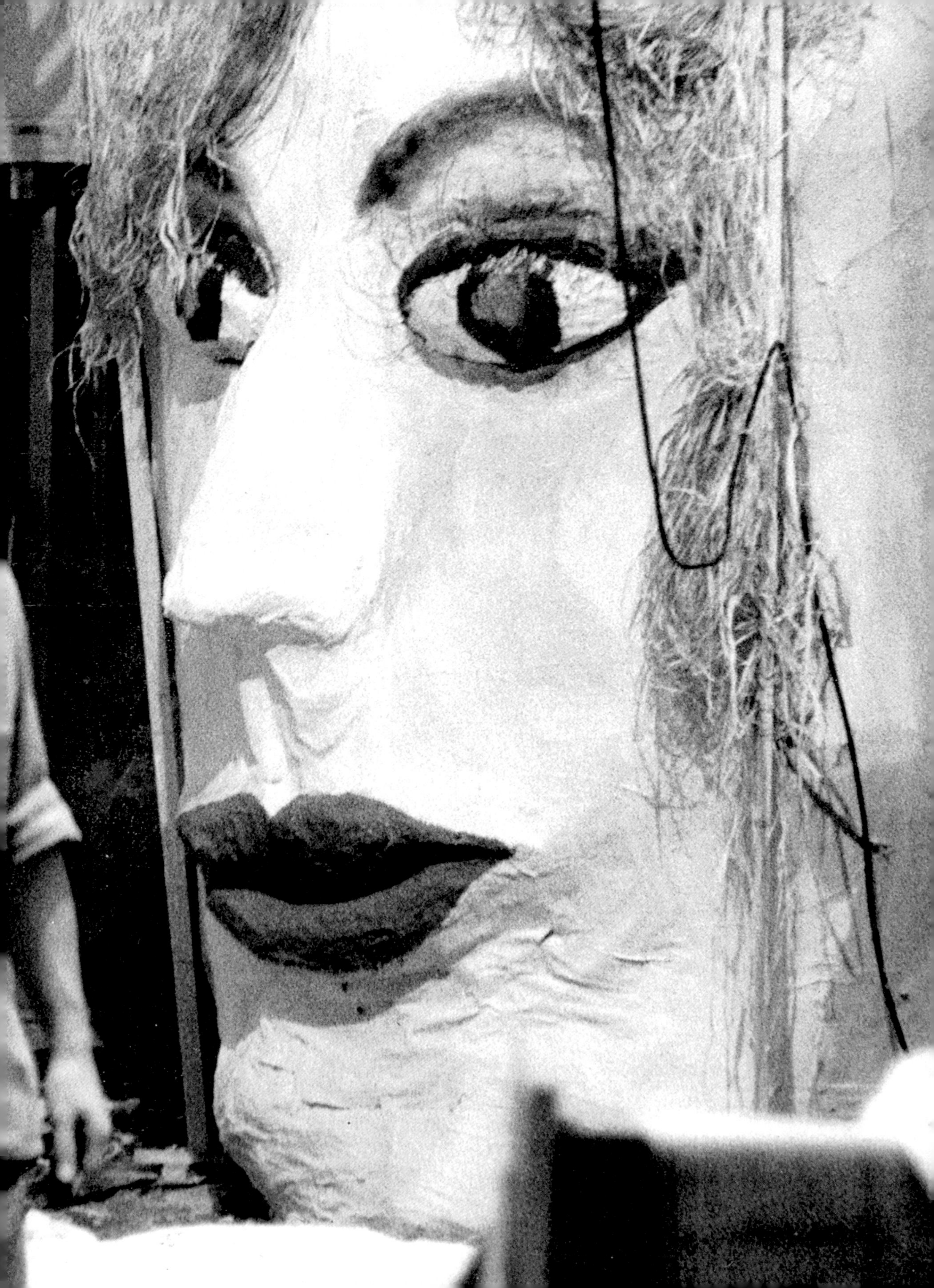

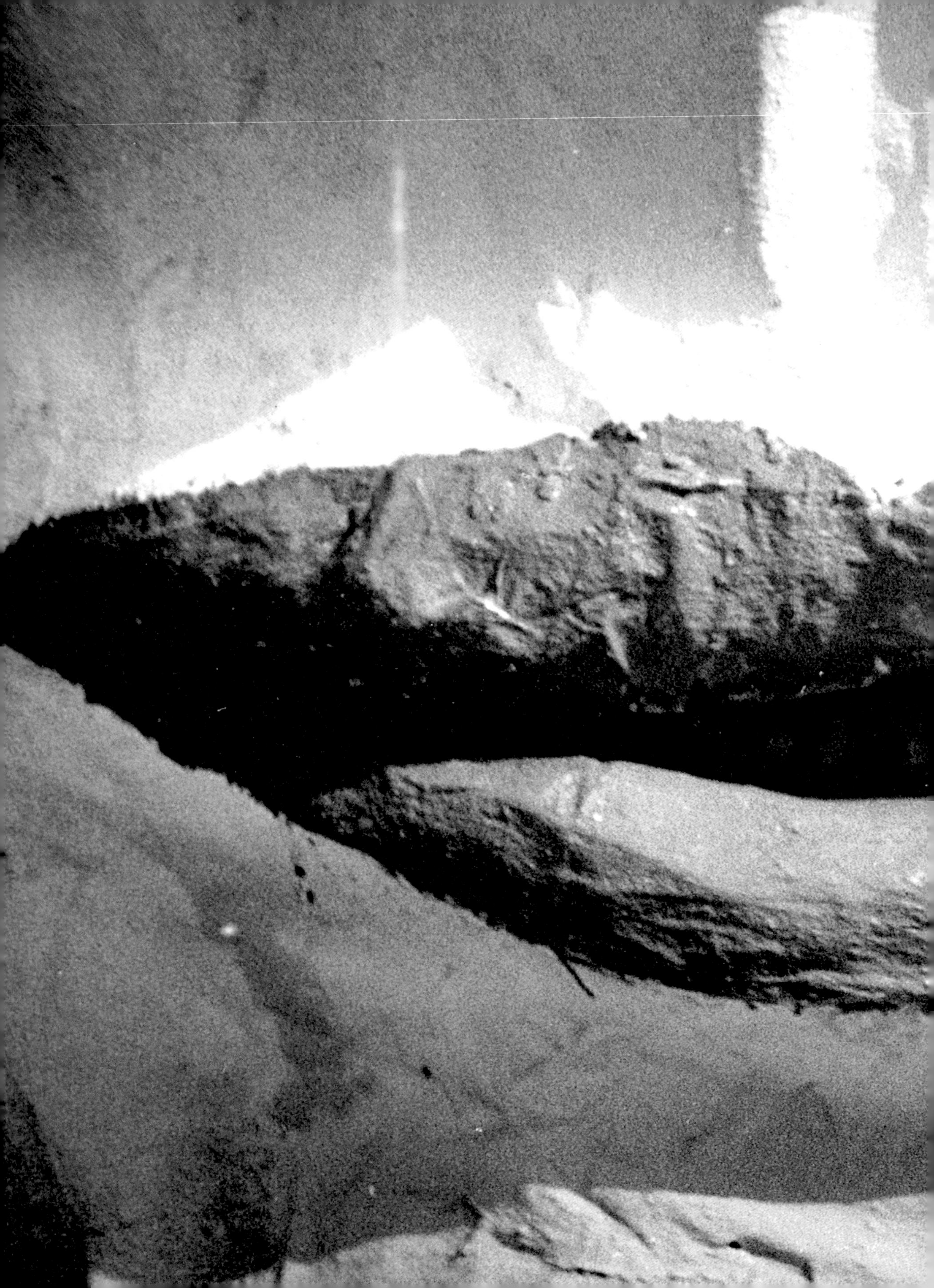

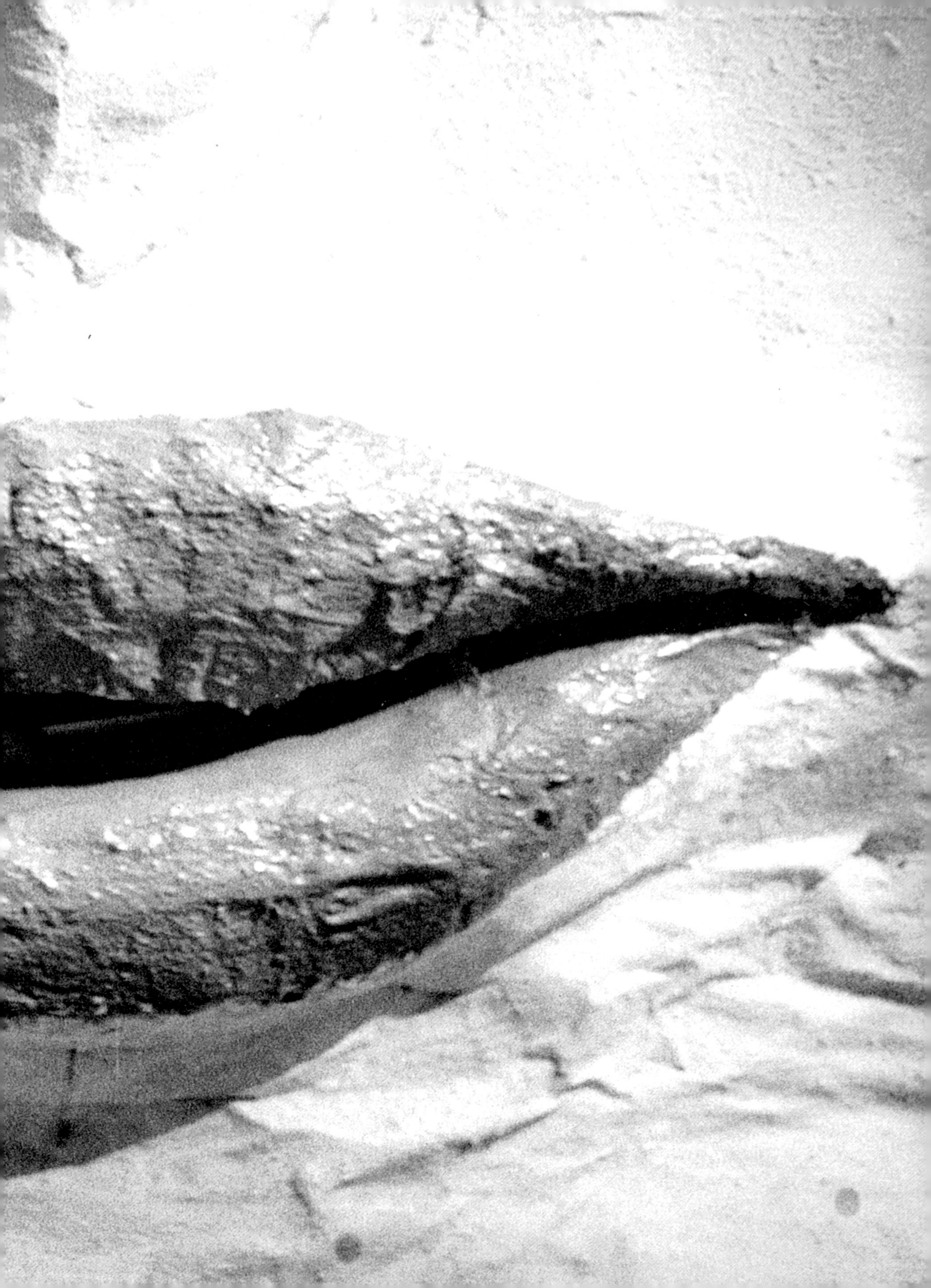

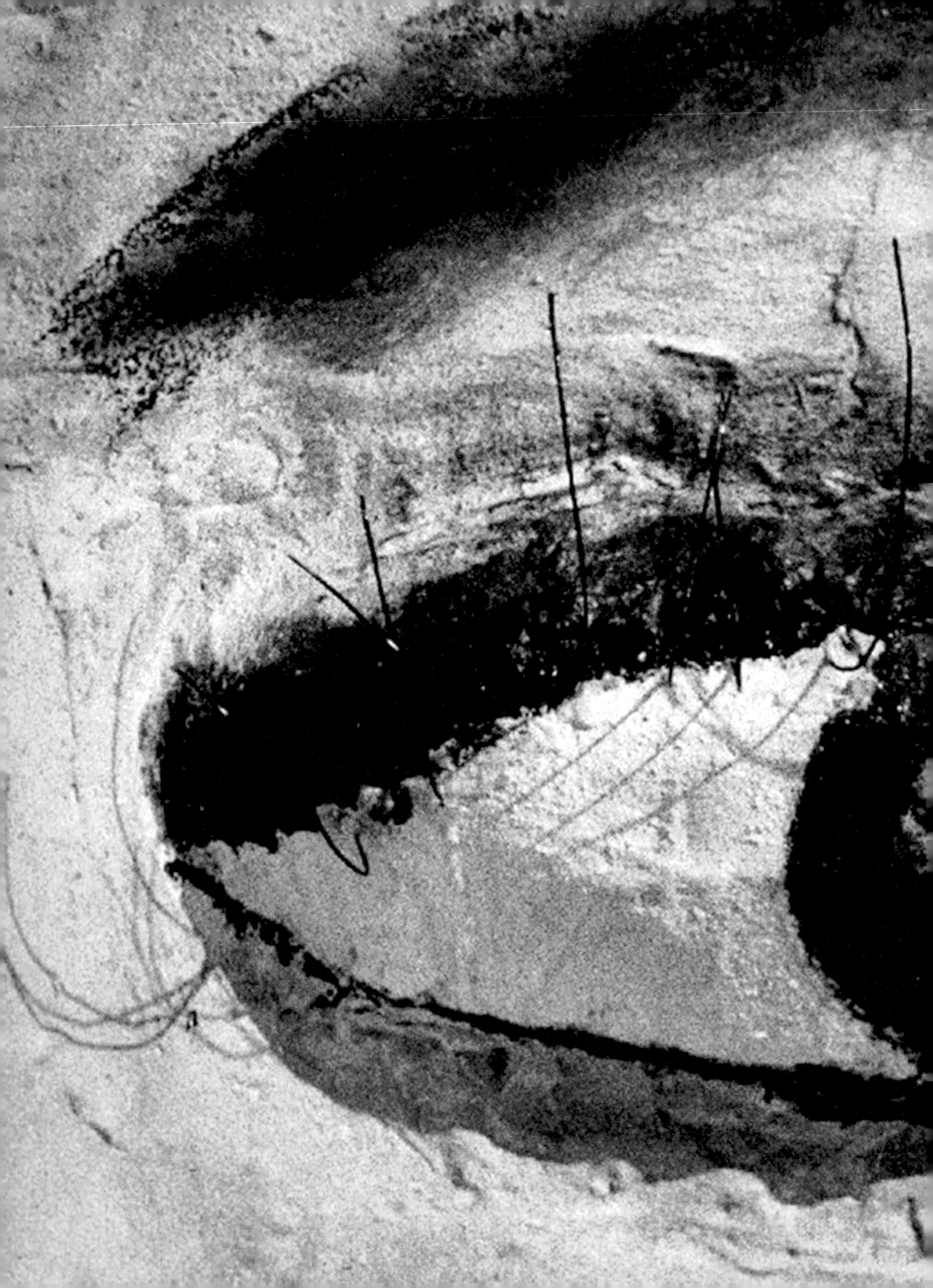

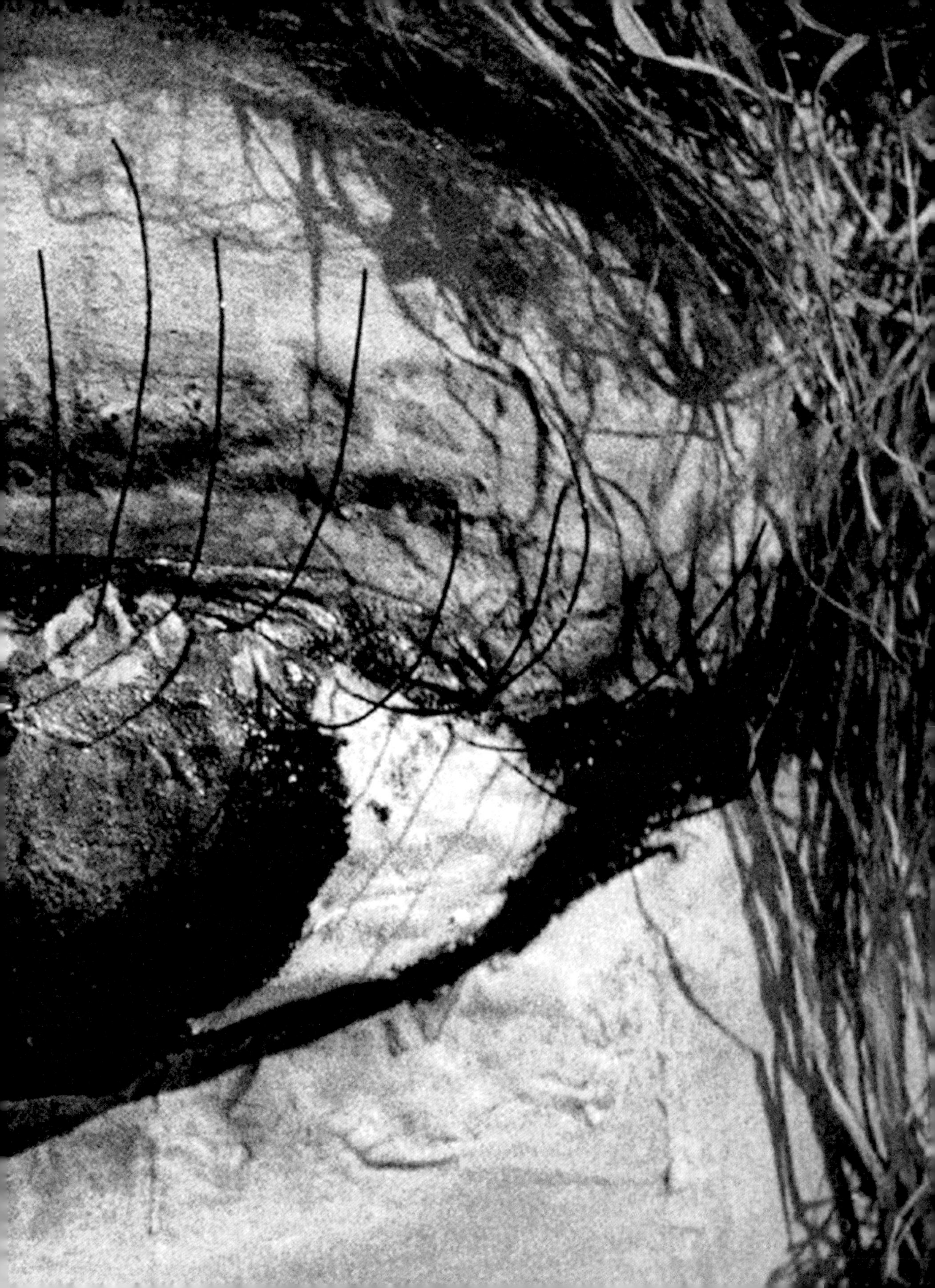

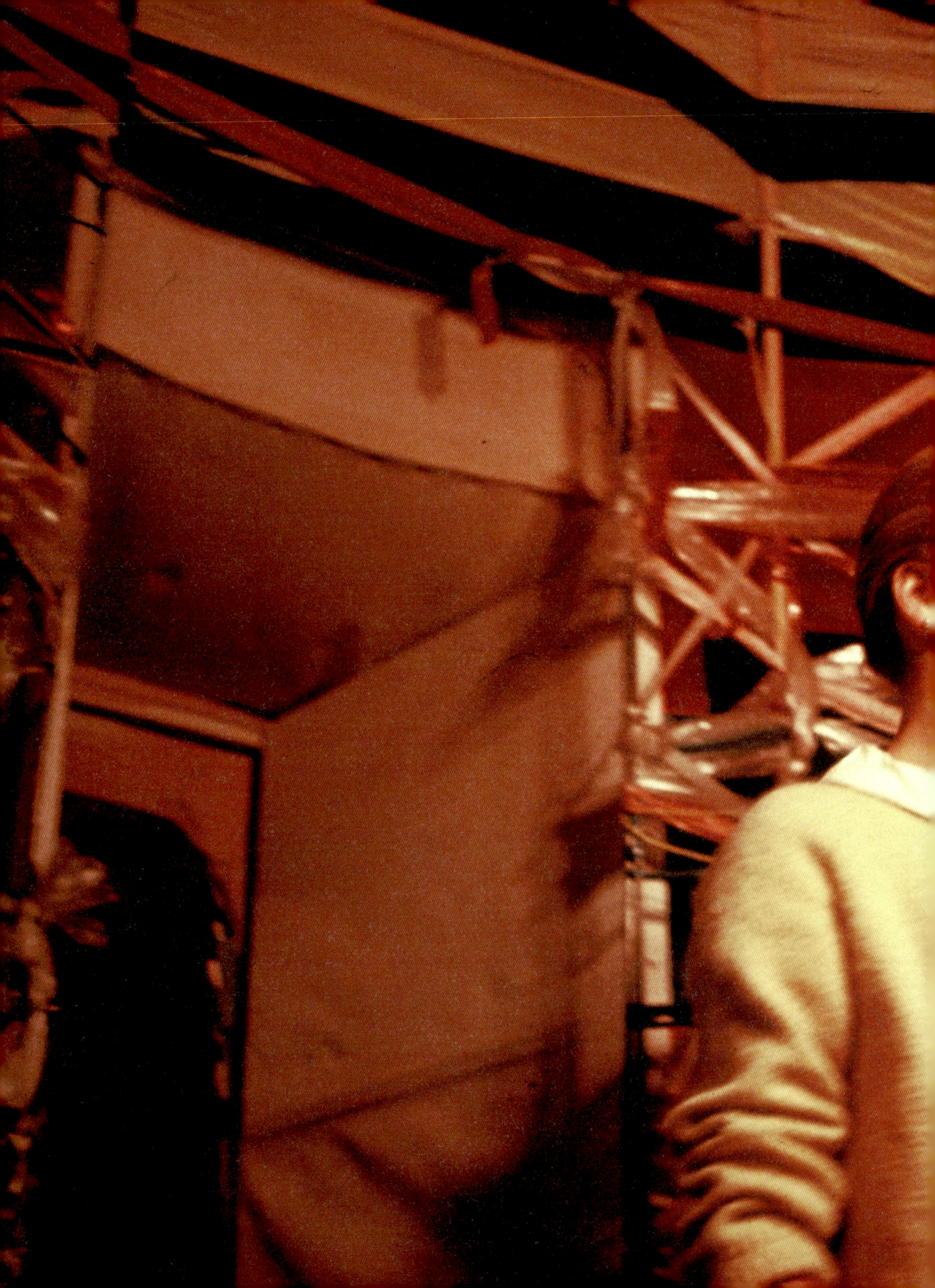

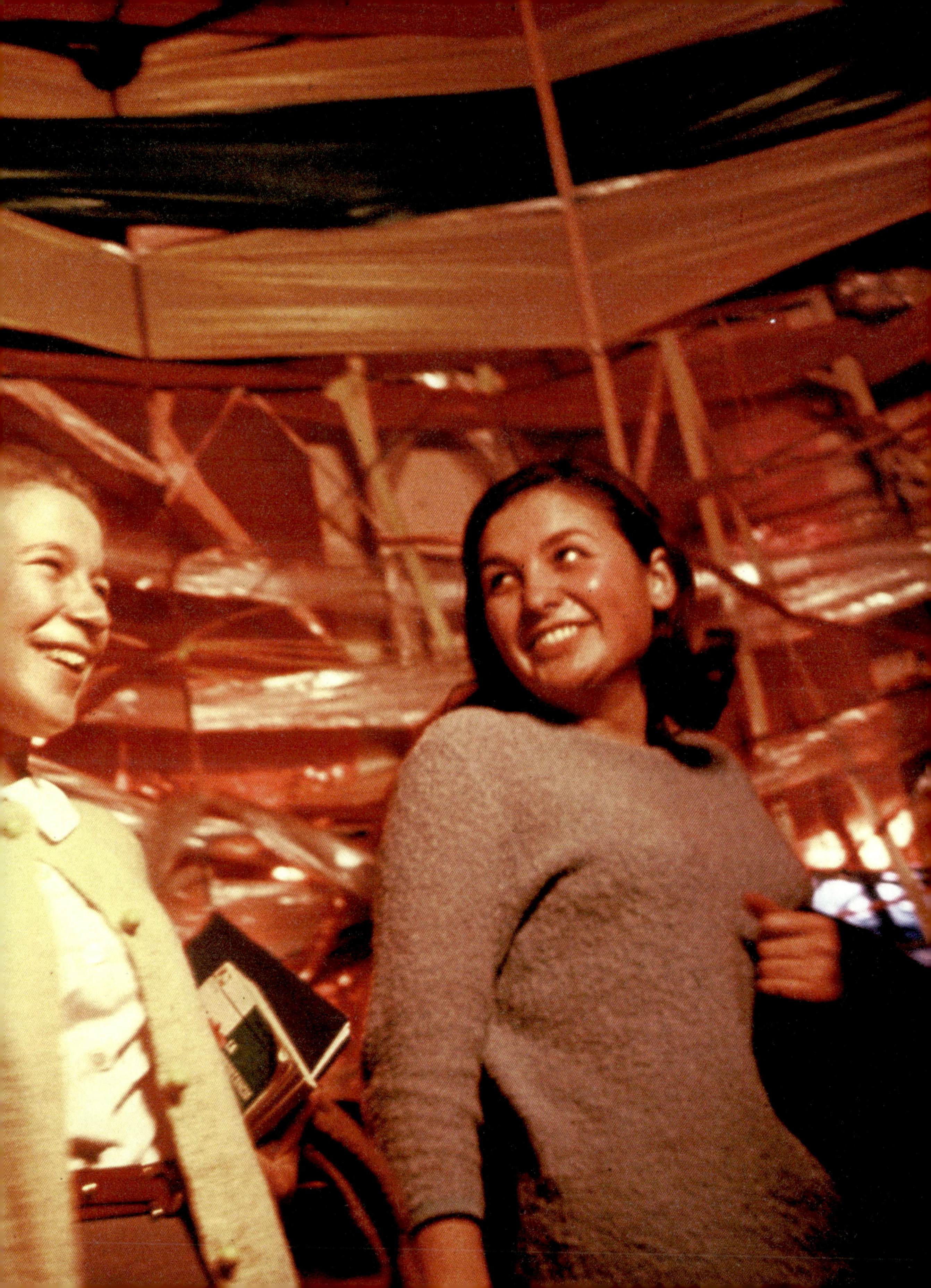

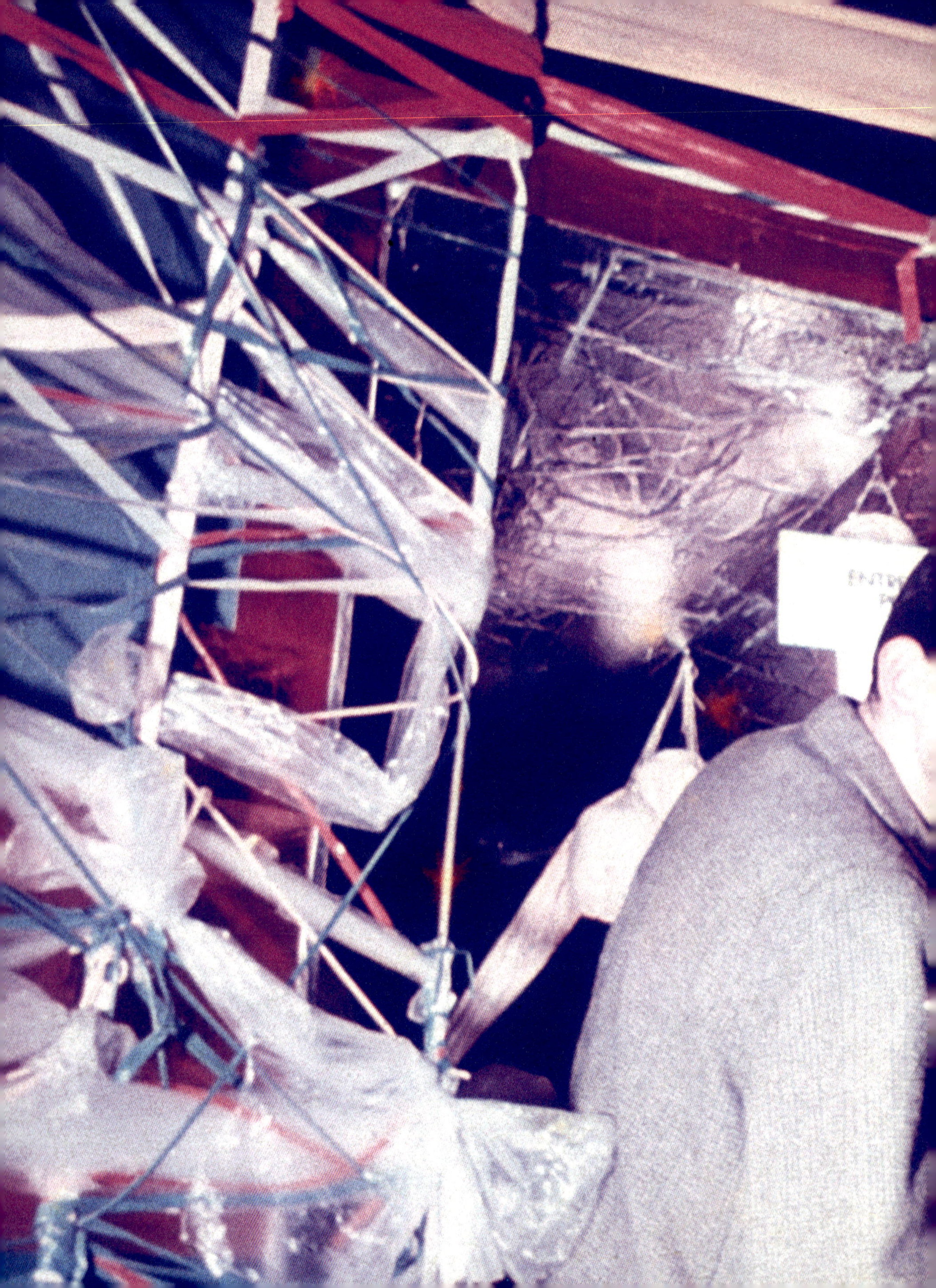

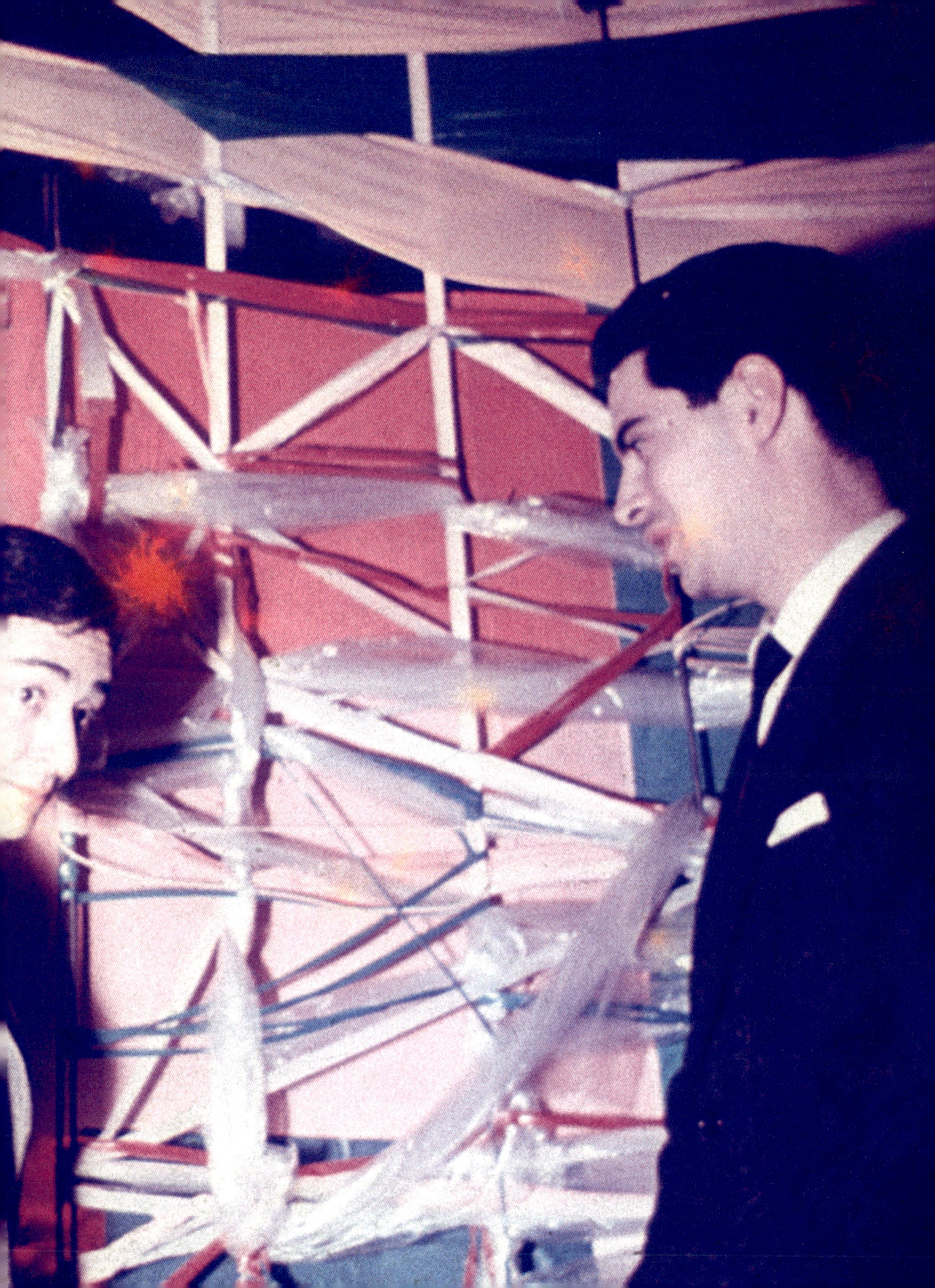

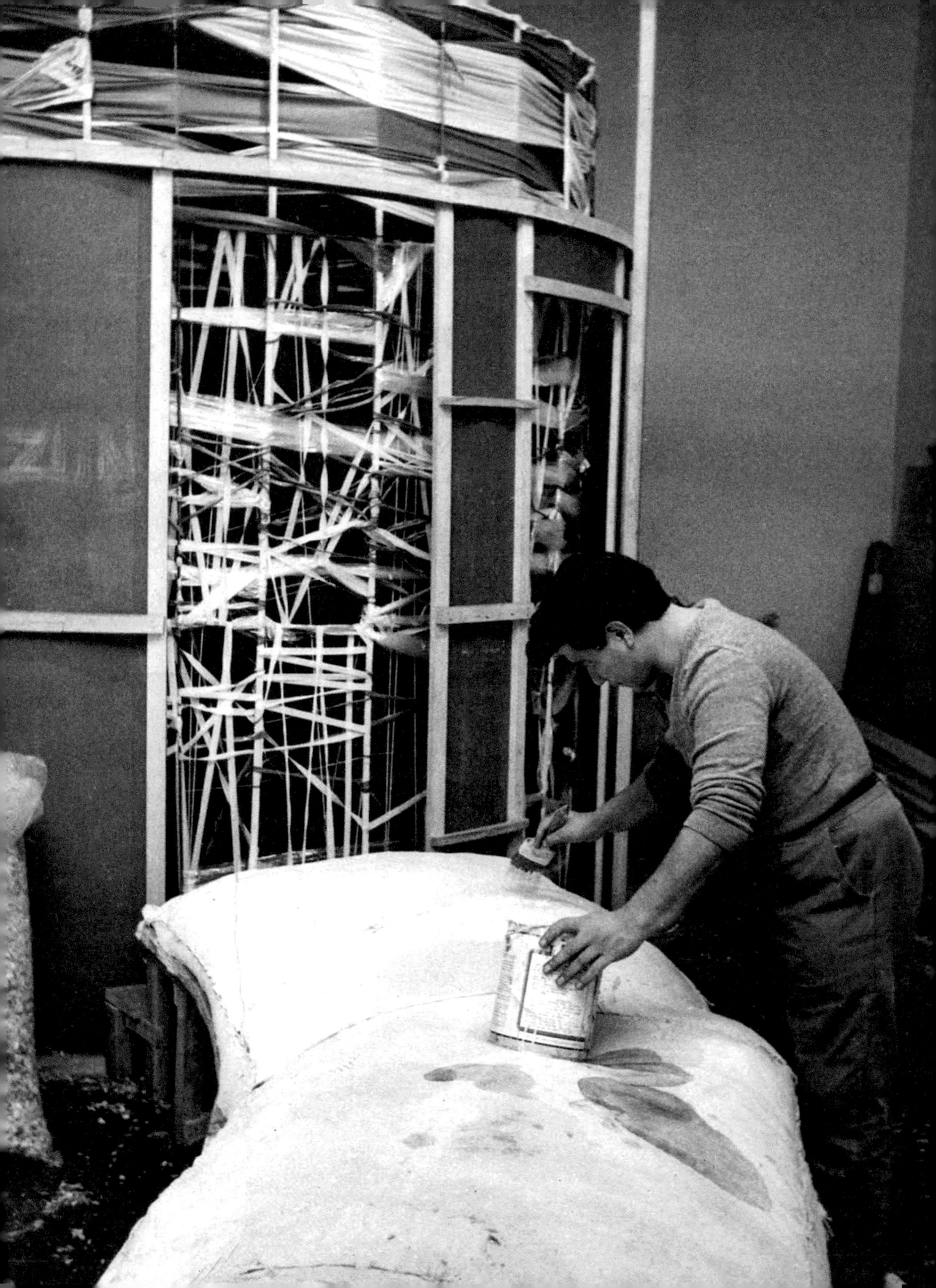

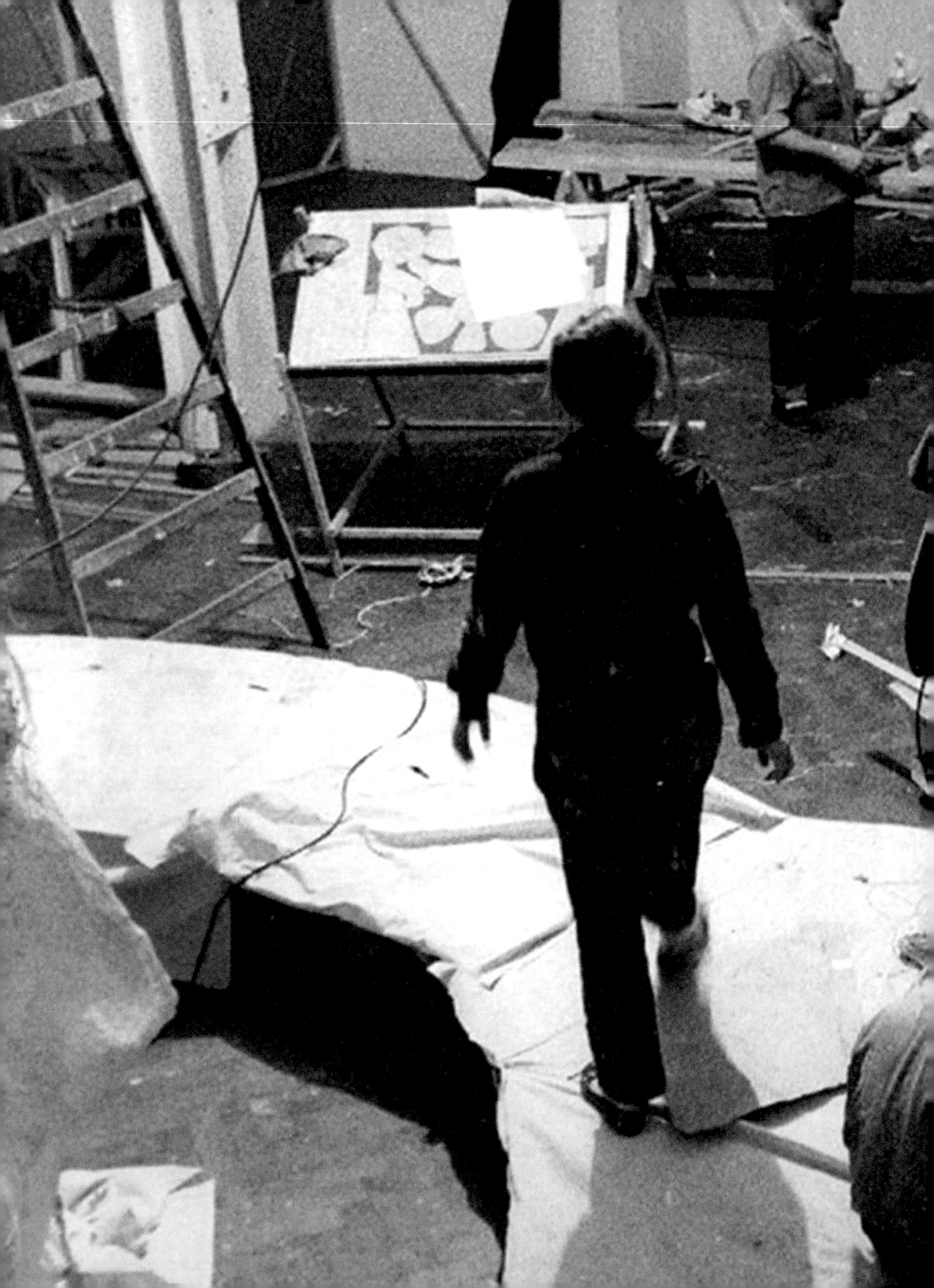

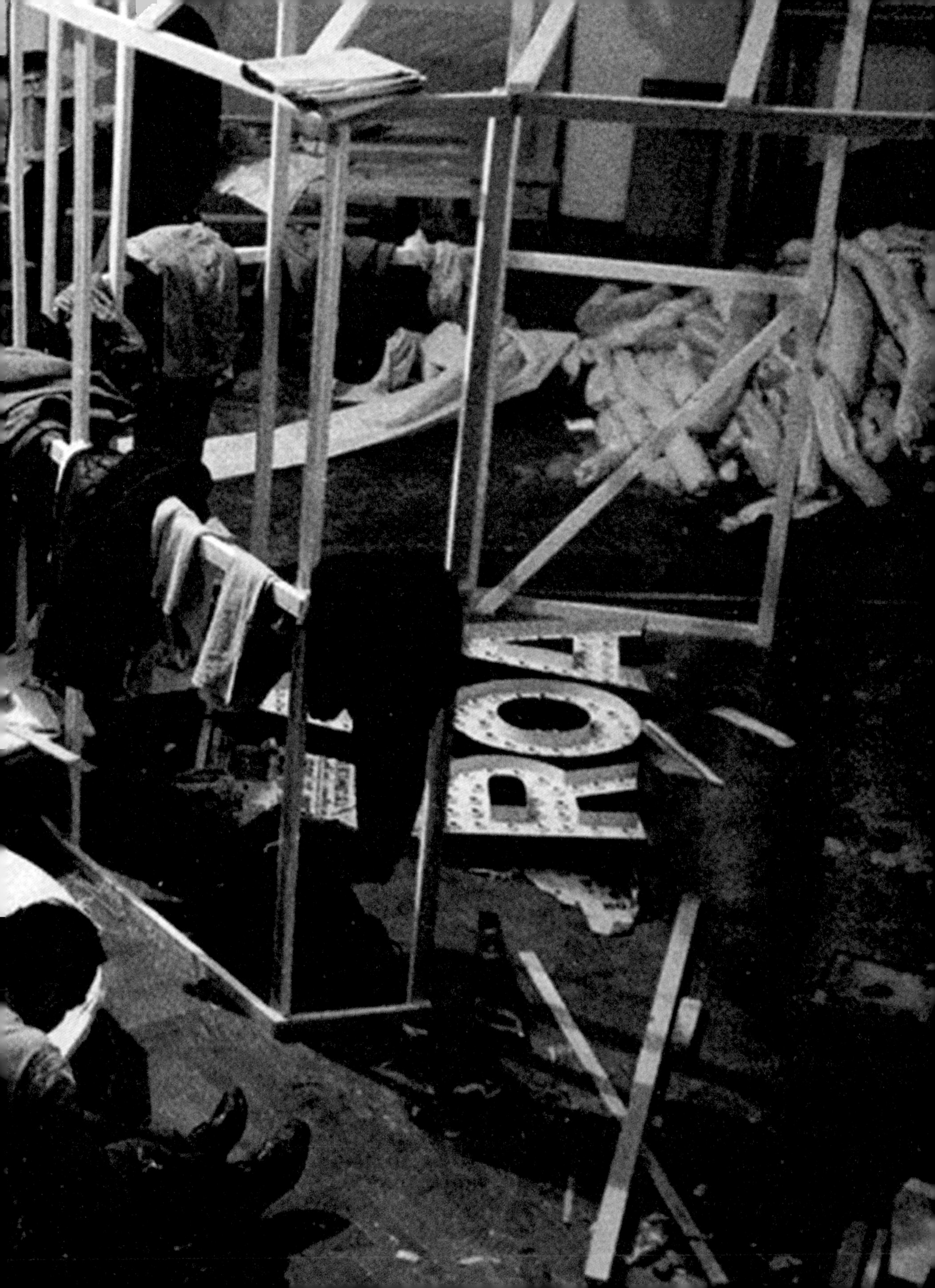
ROA

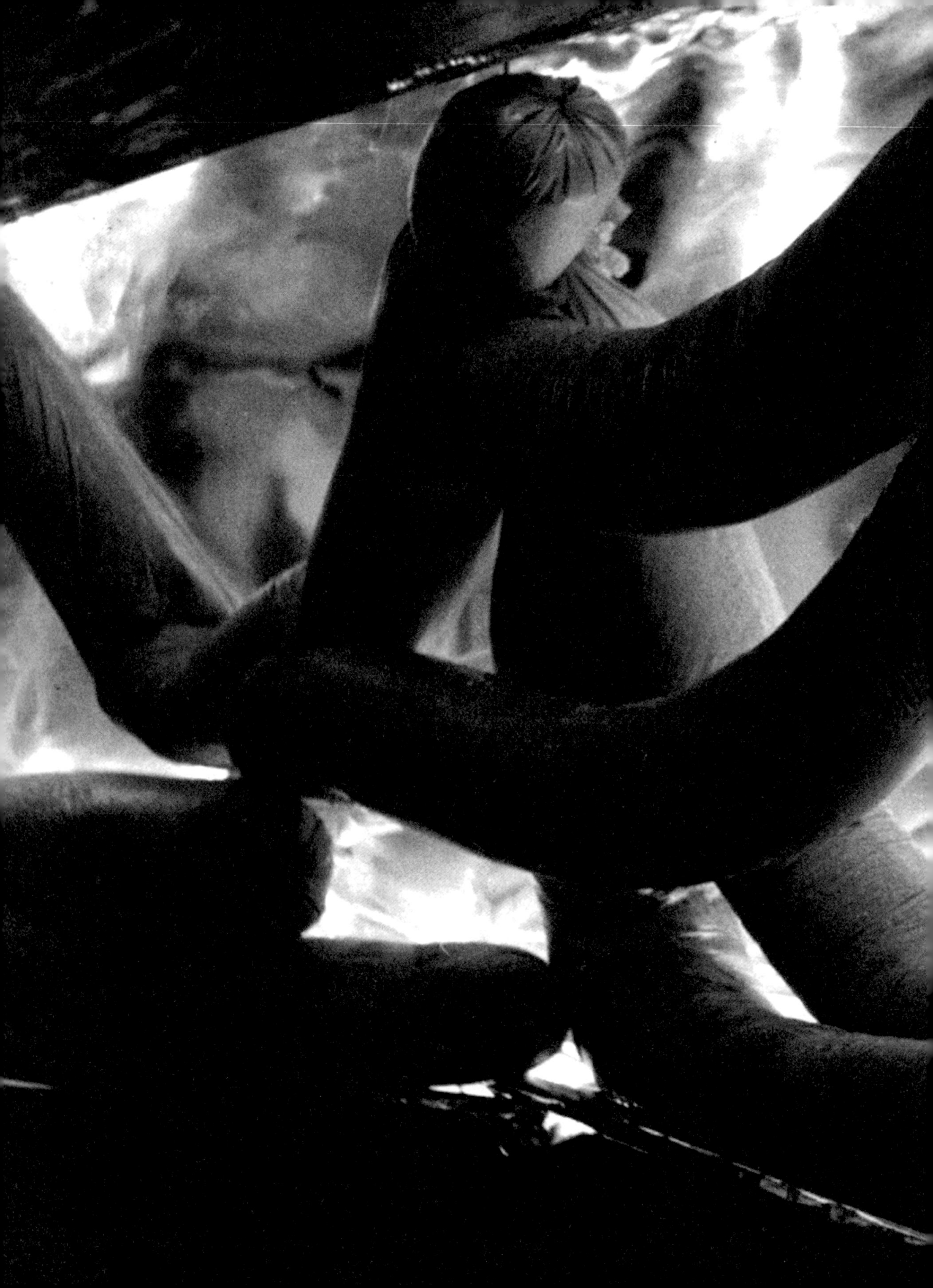

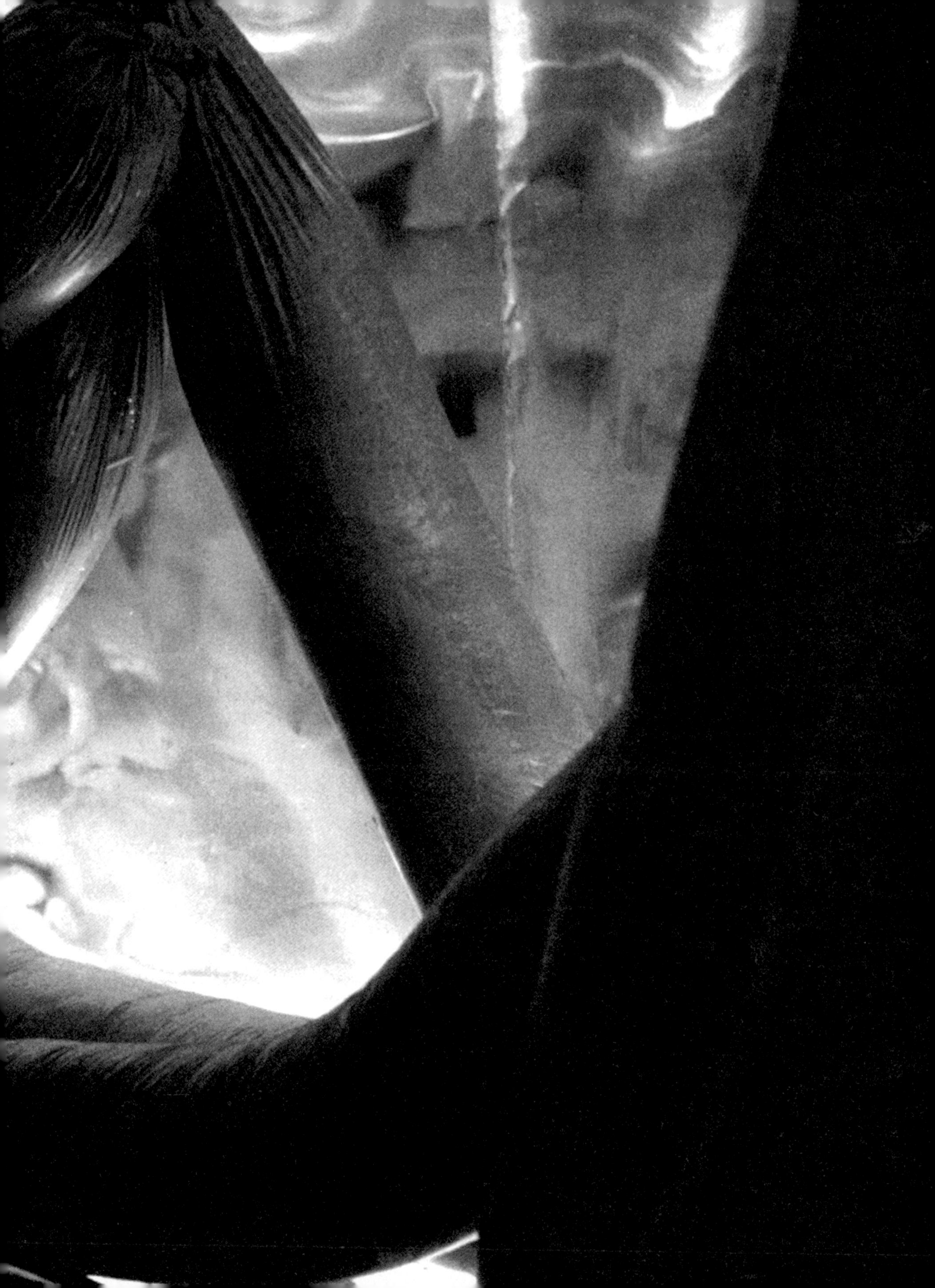

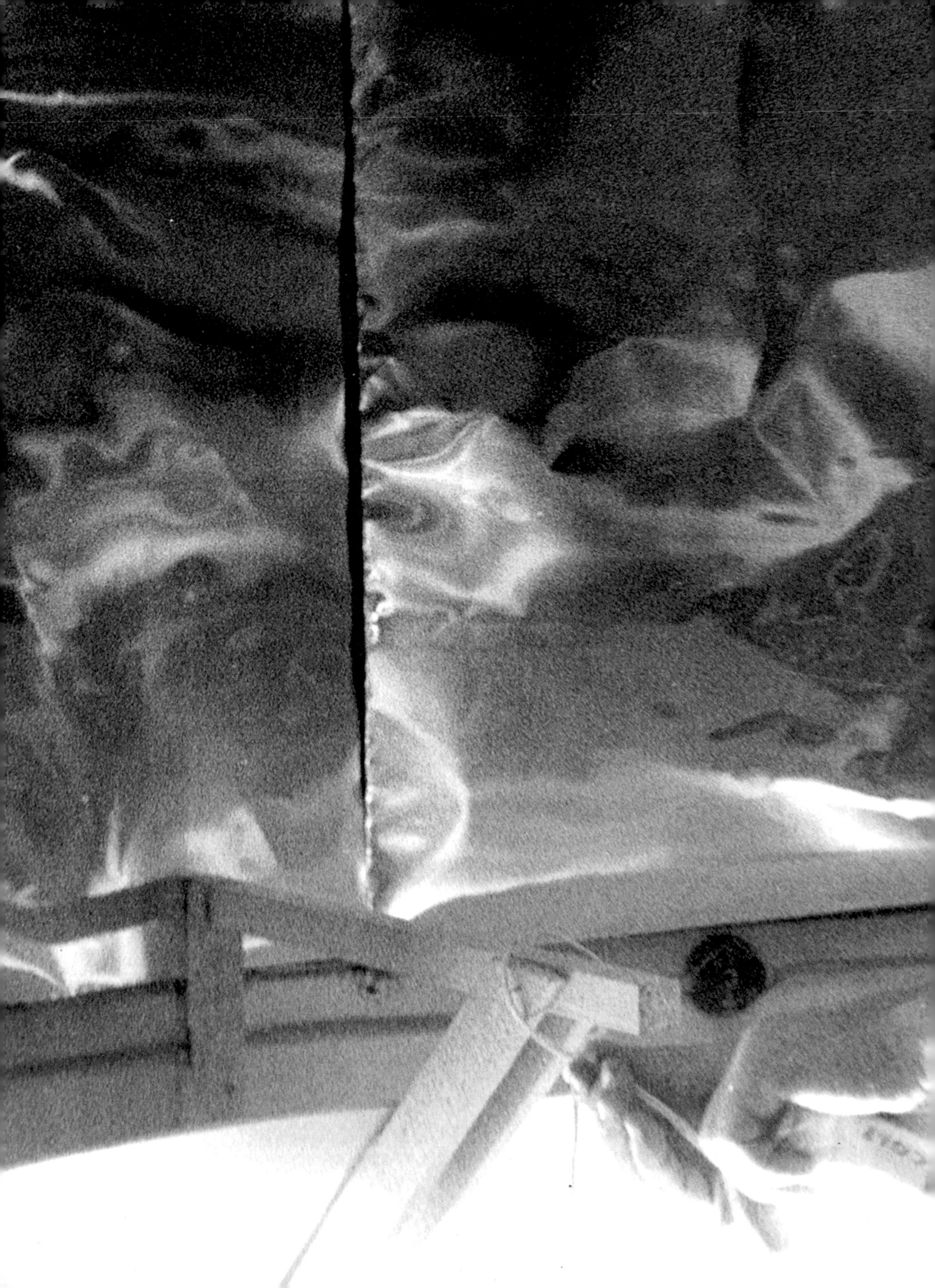

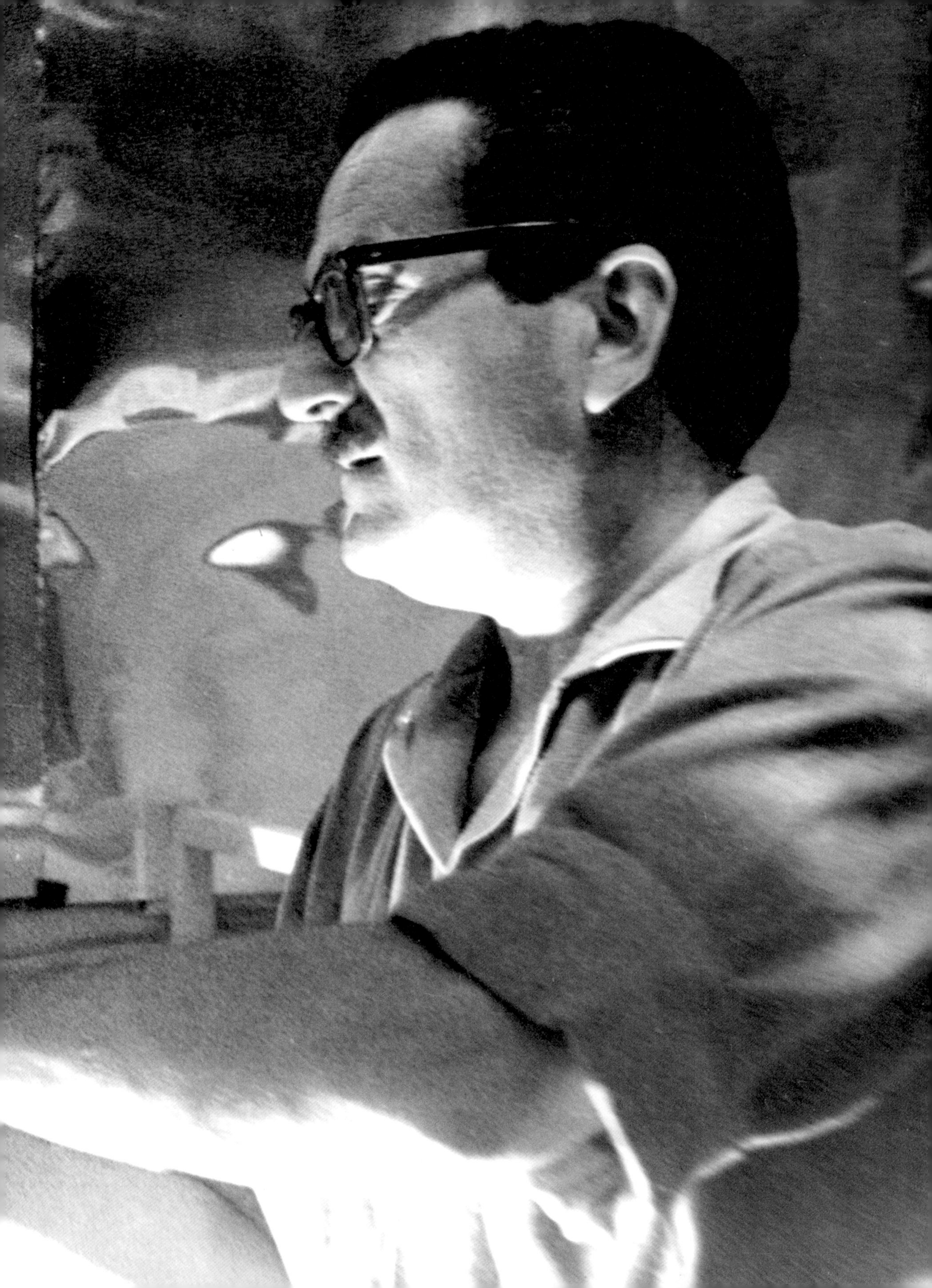

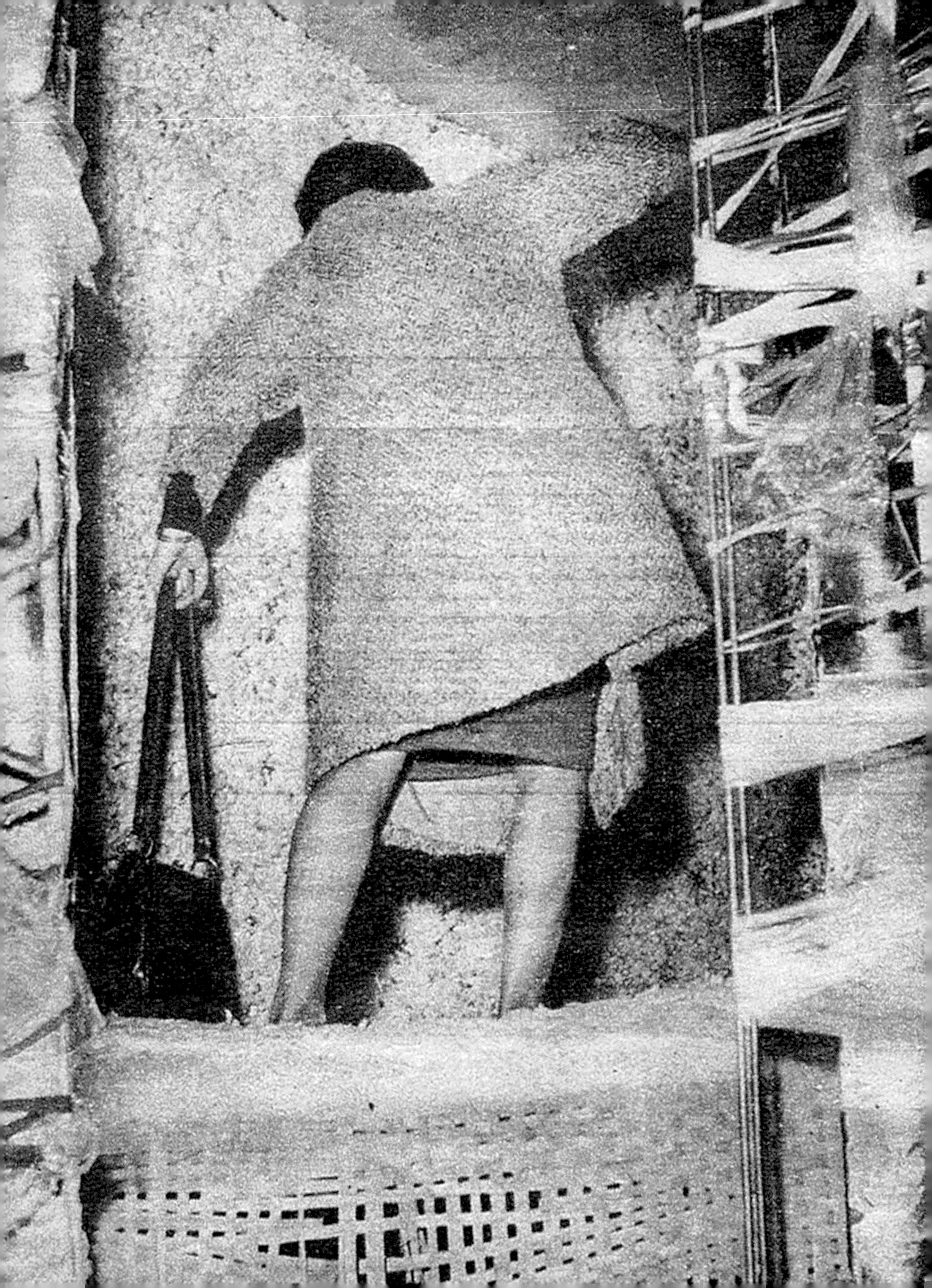

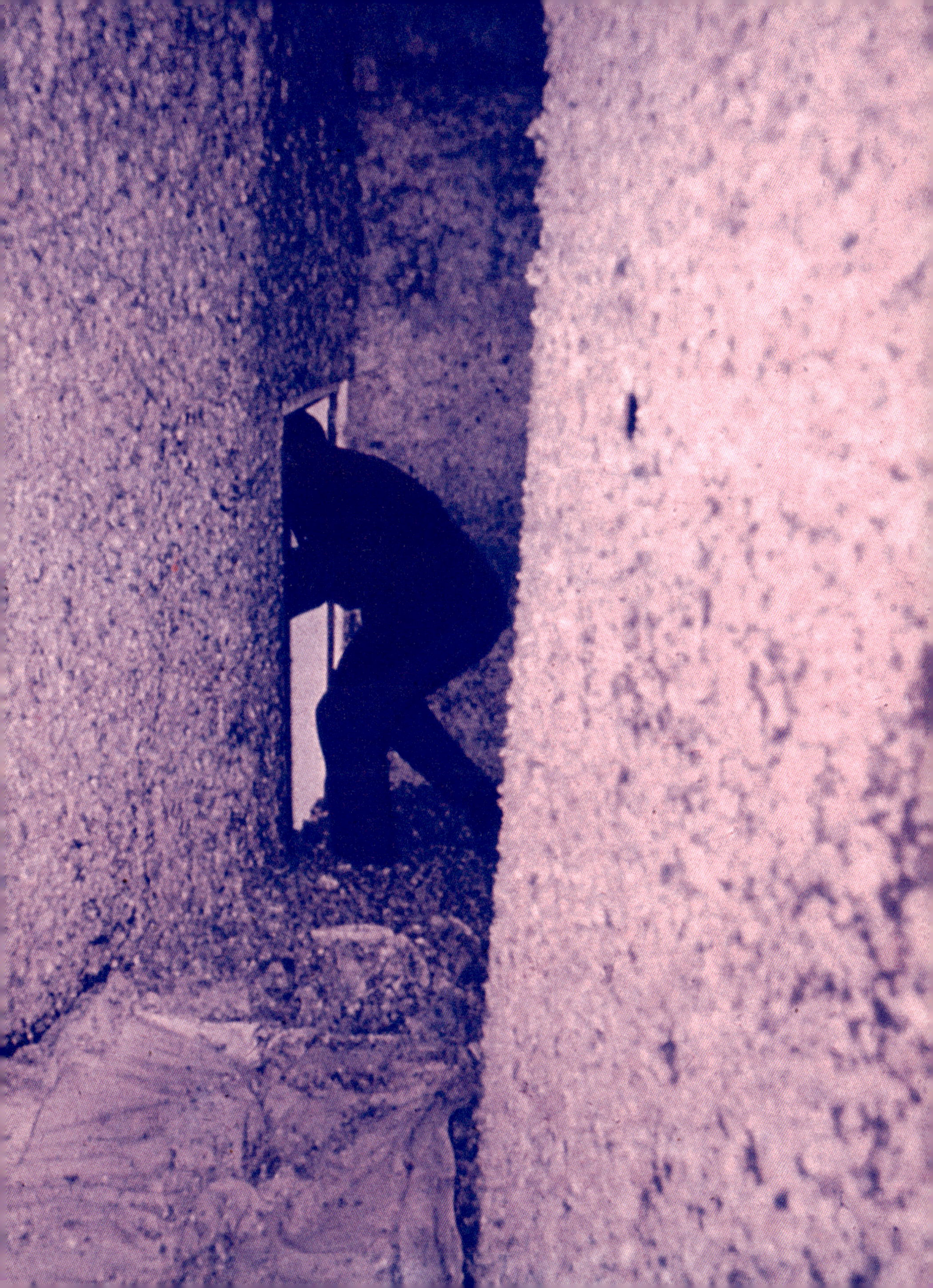

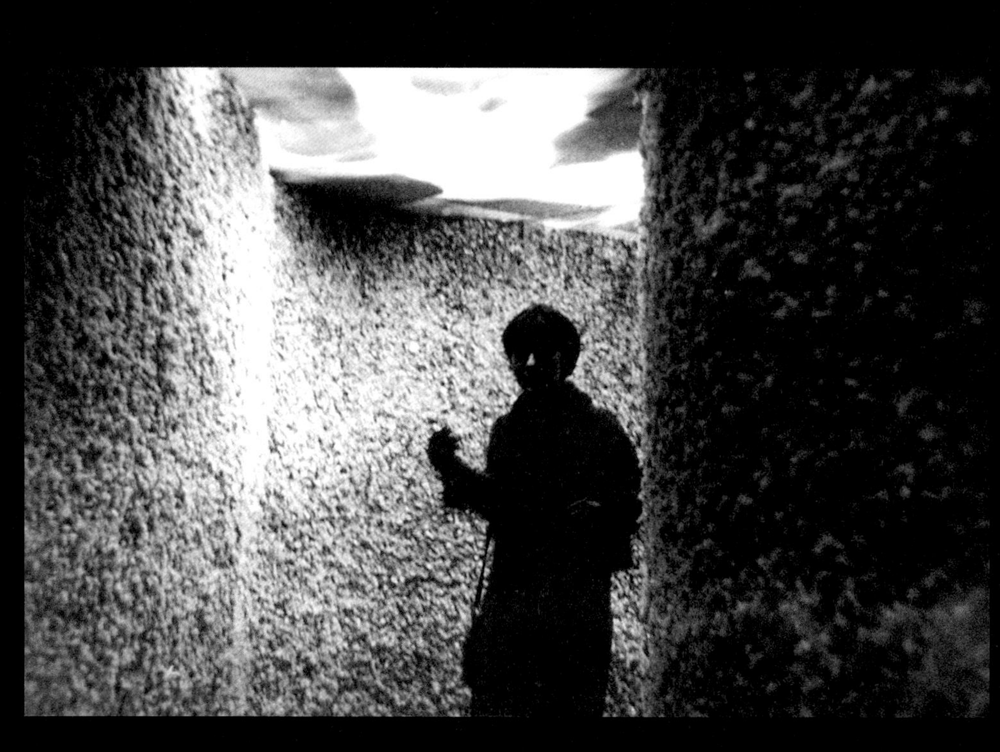

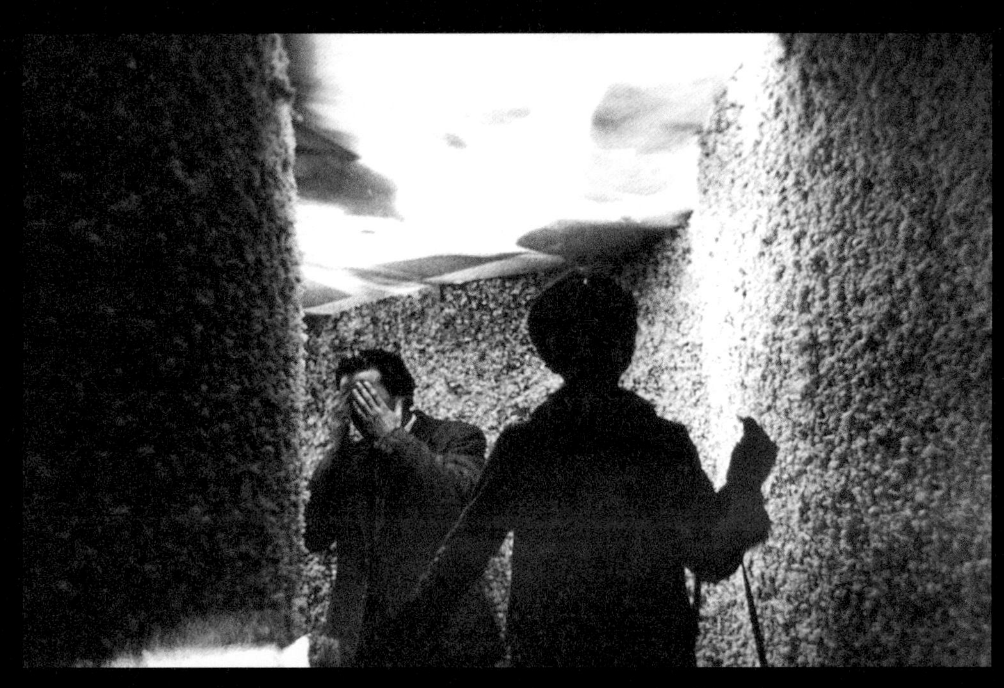

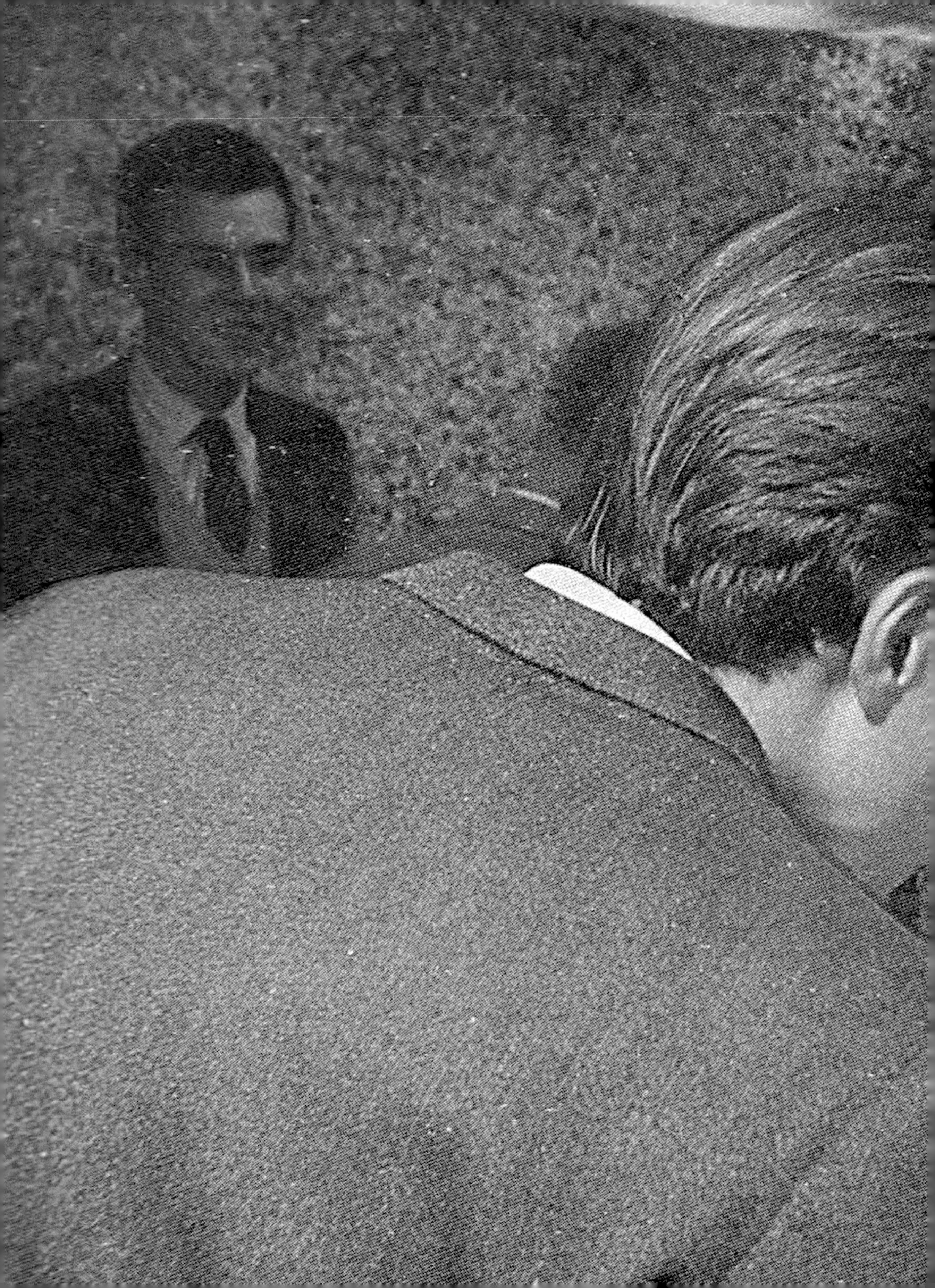

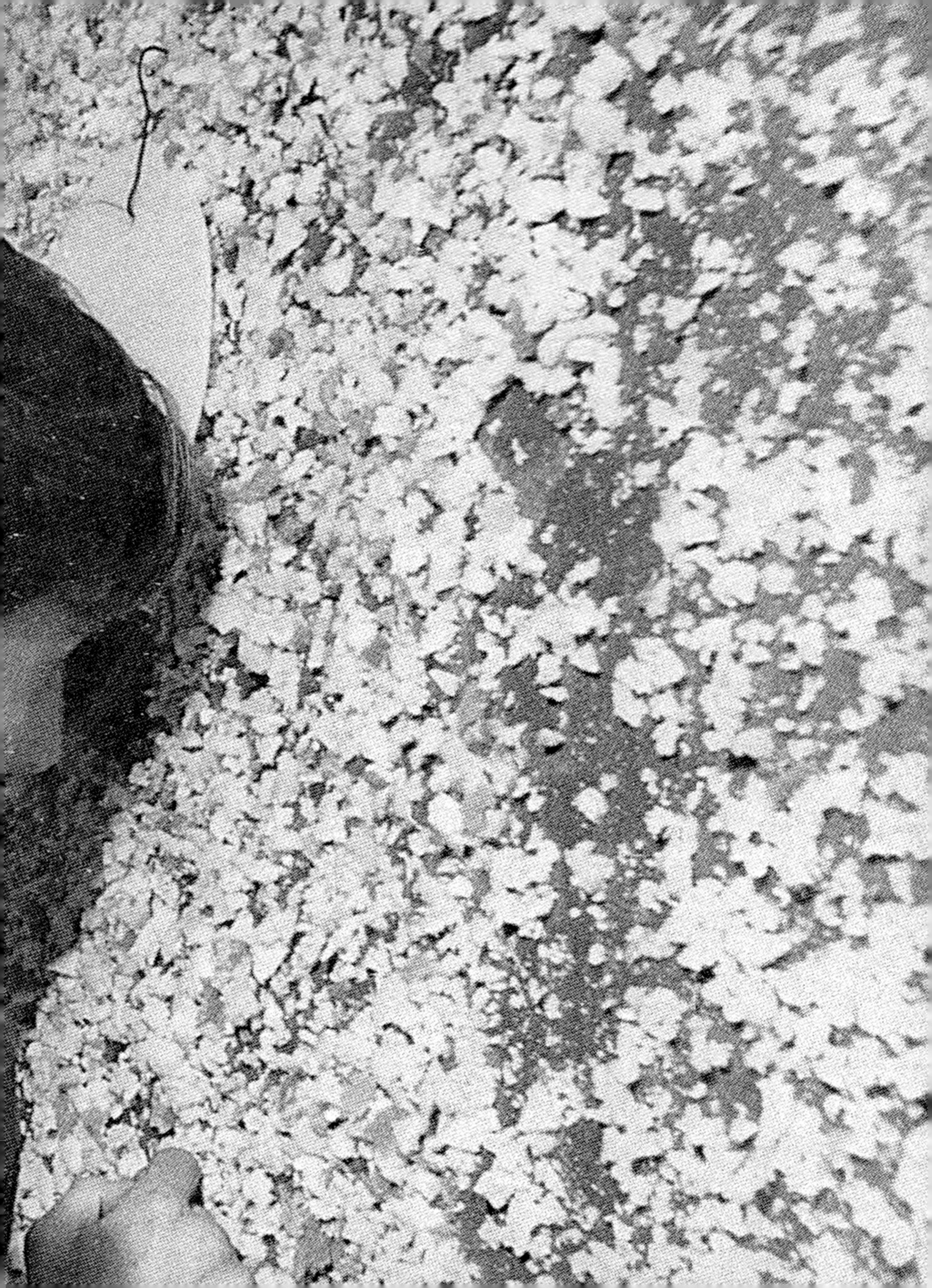

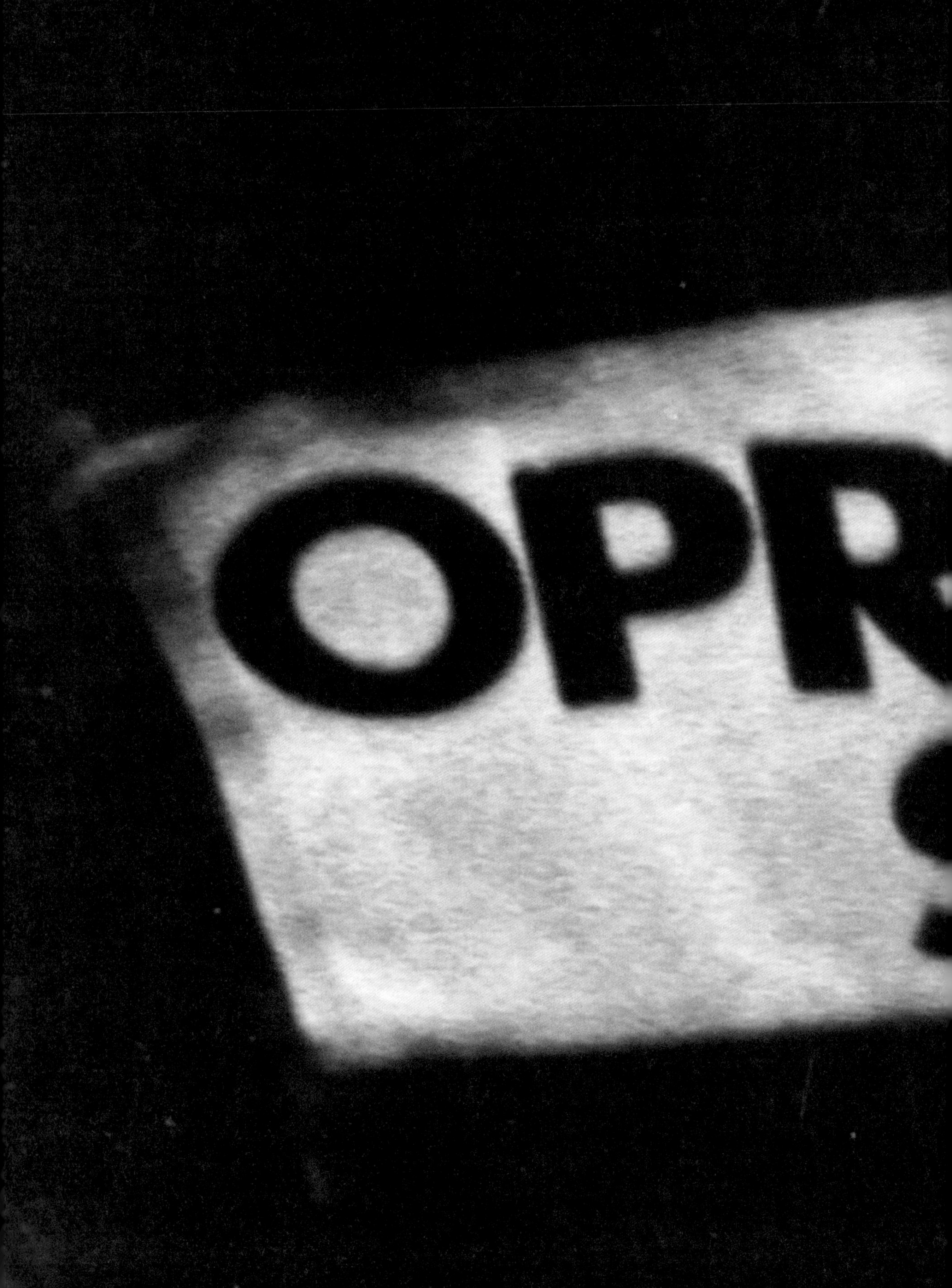
OPR

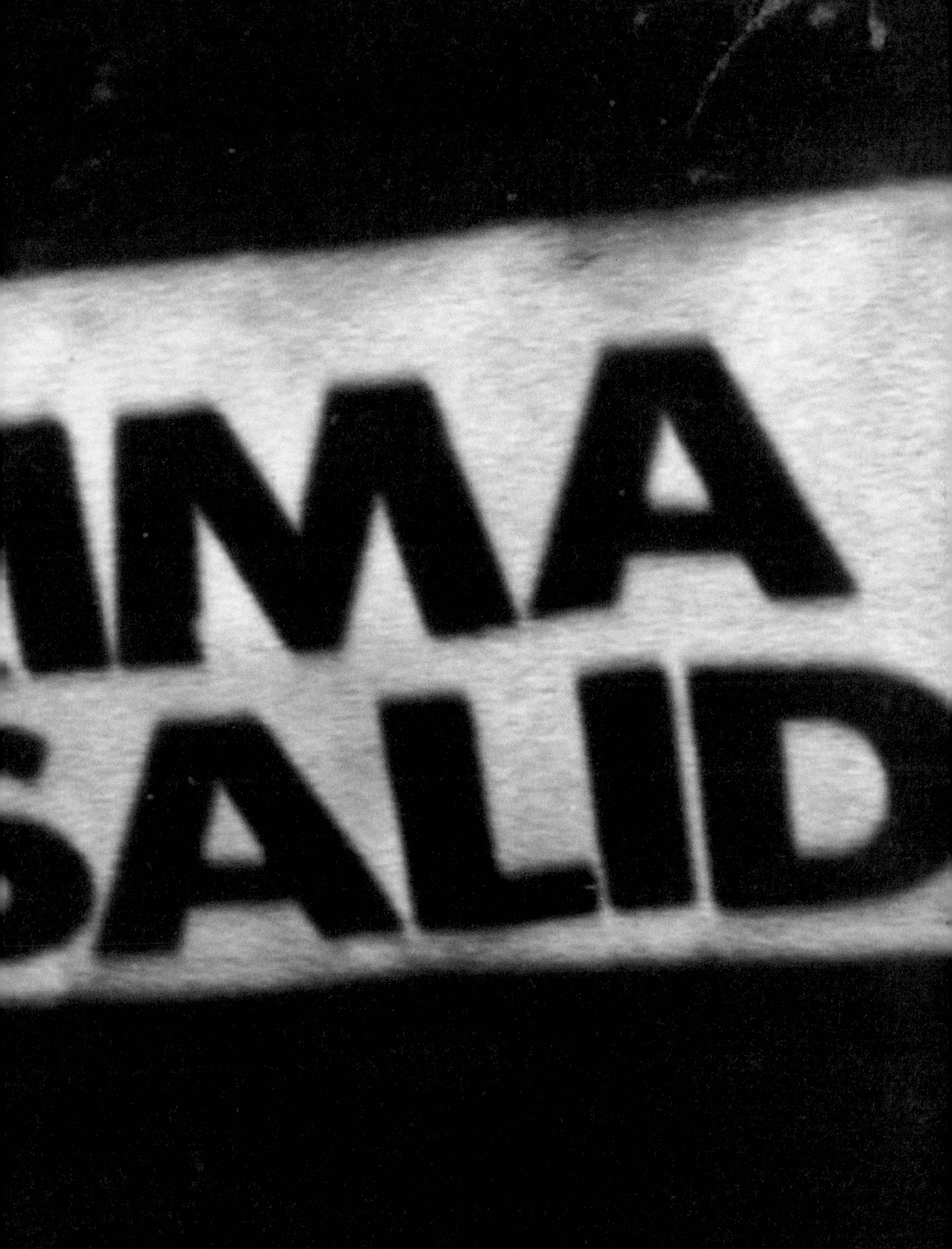
IMA
SALID

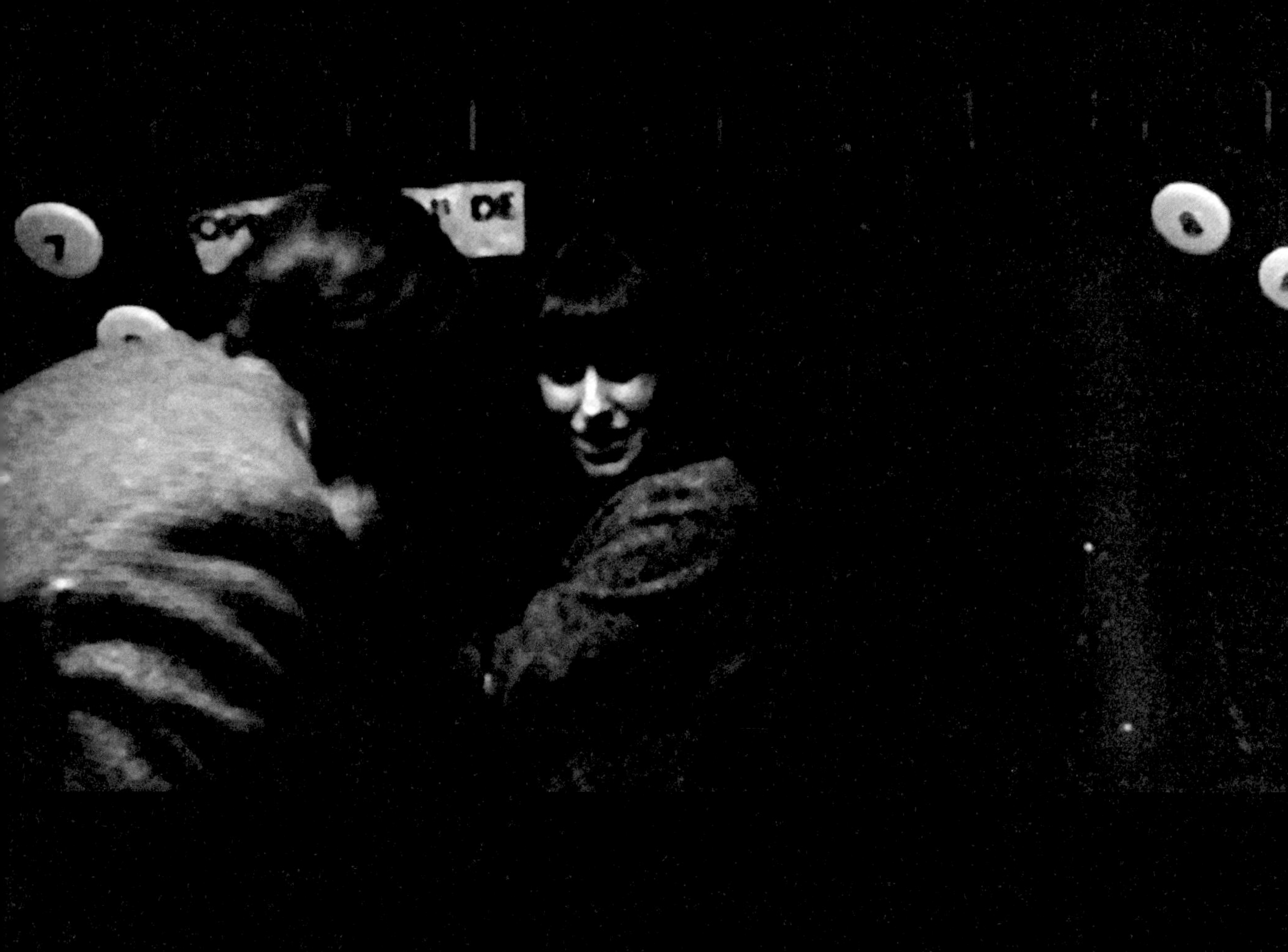

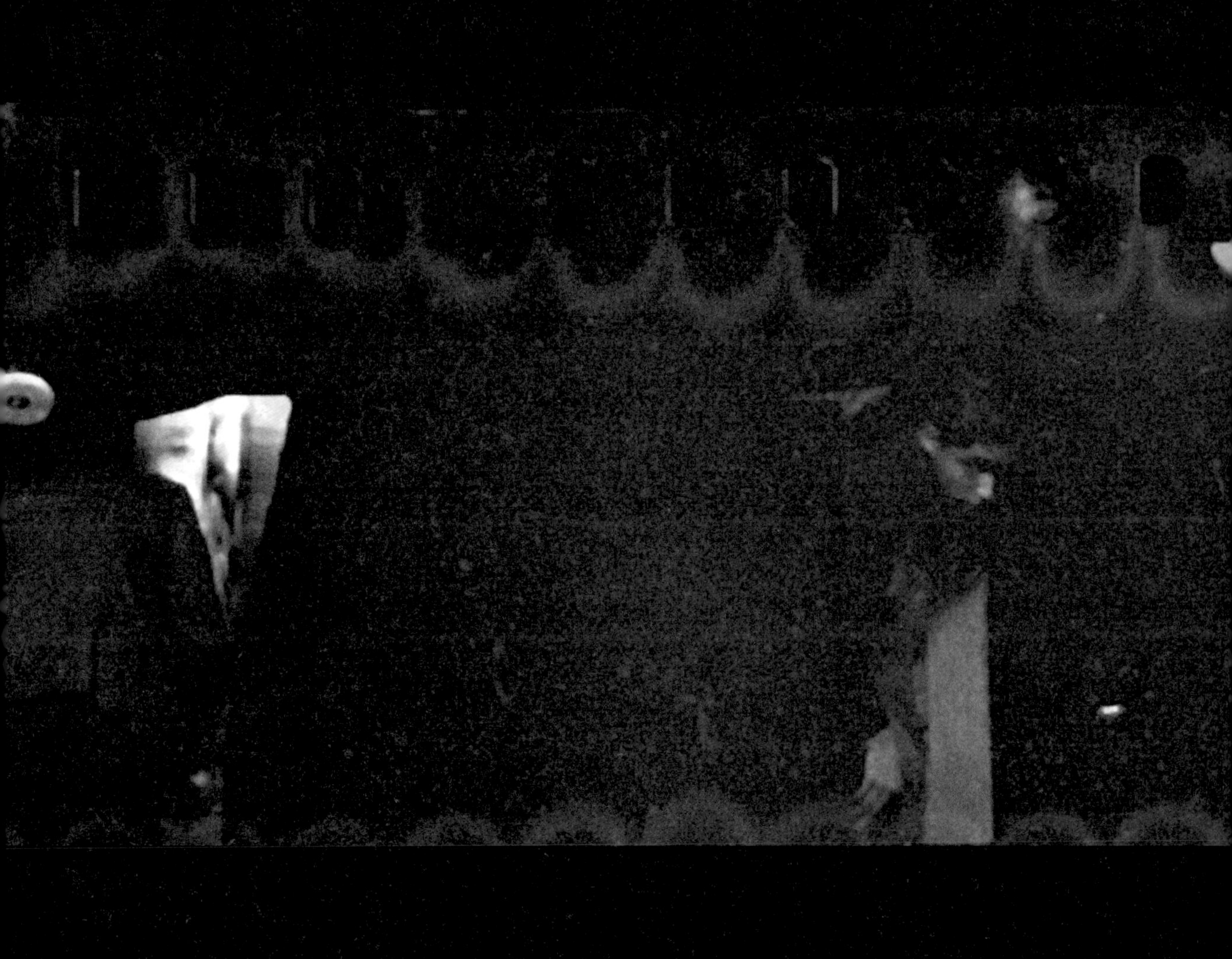

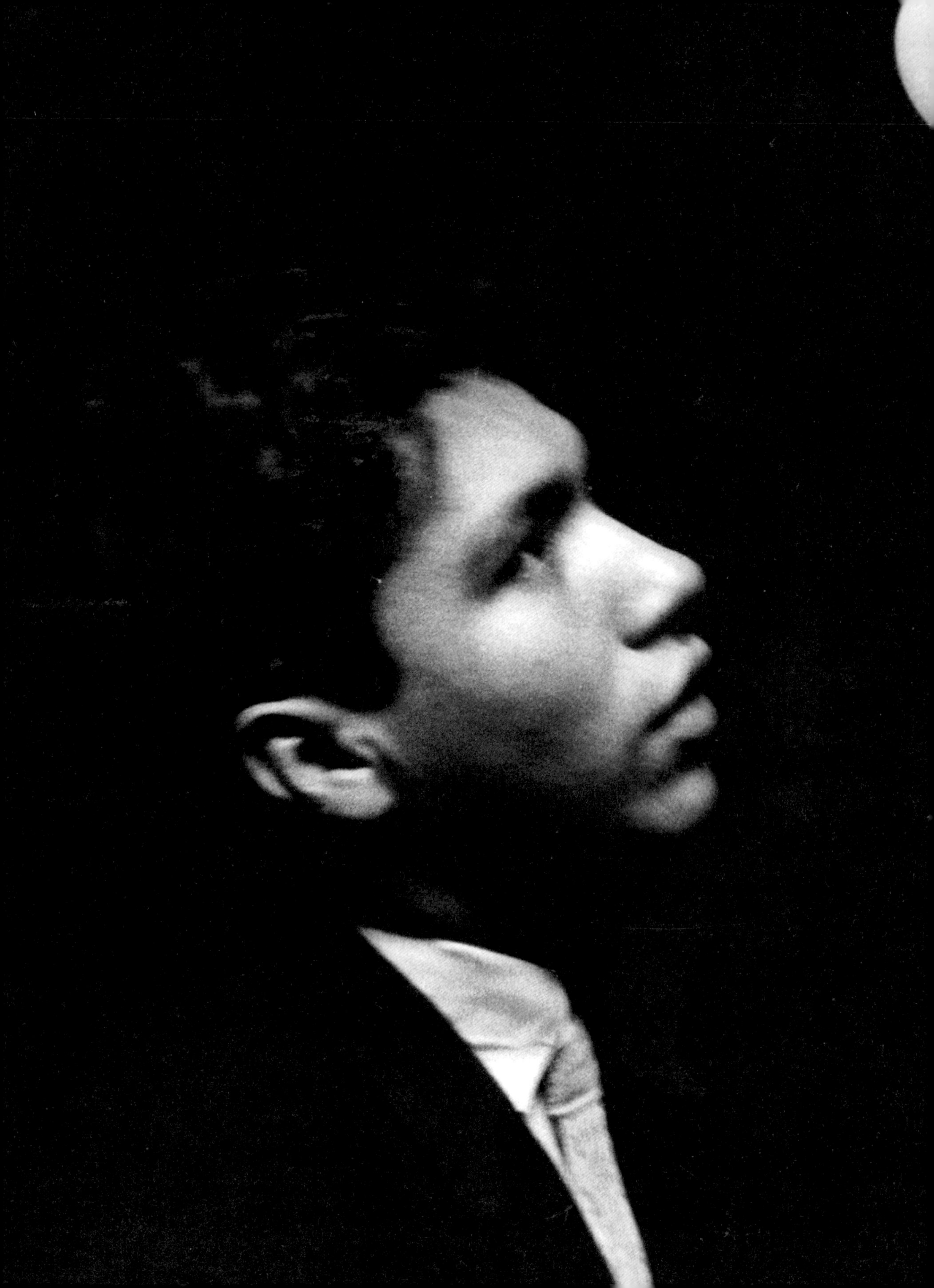

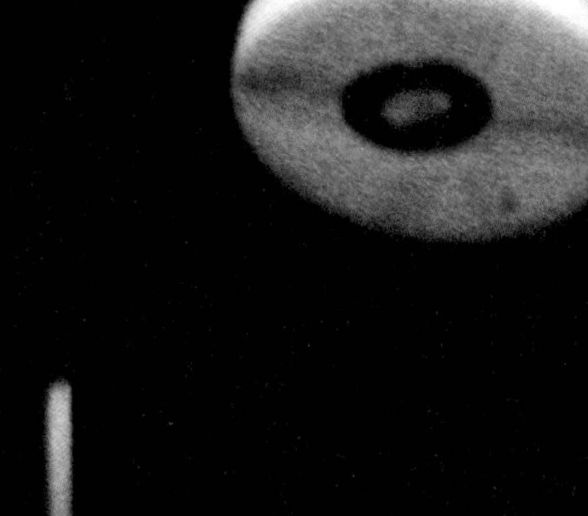
OPRIMA
SALID

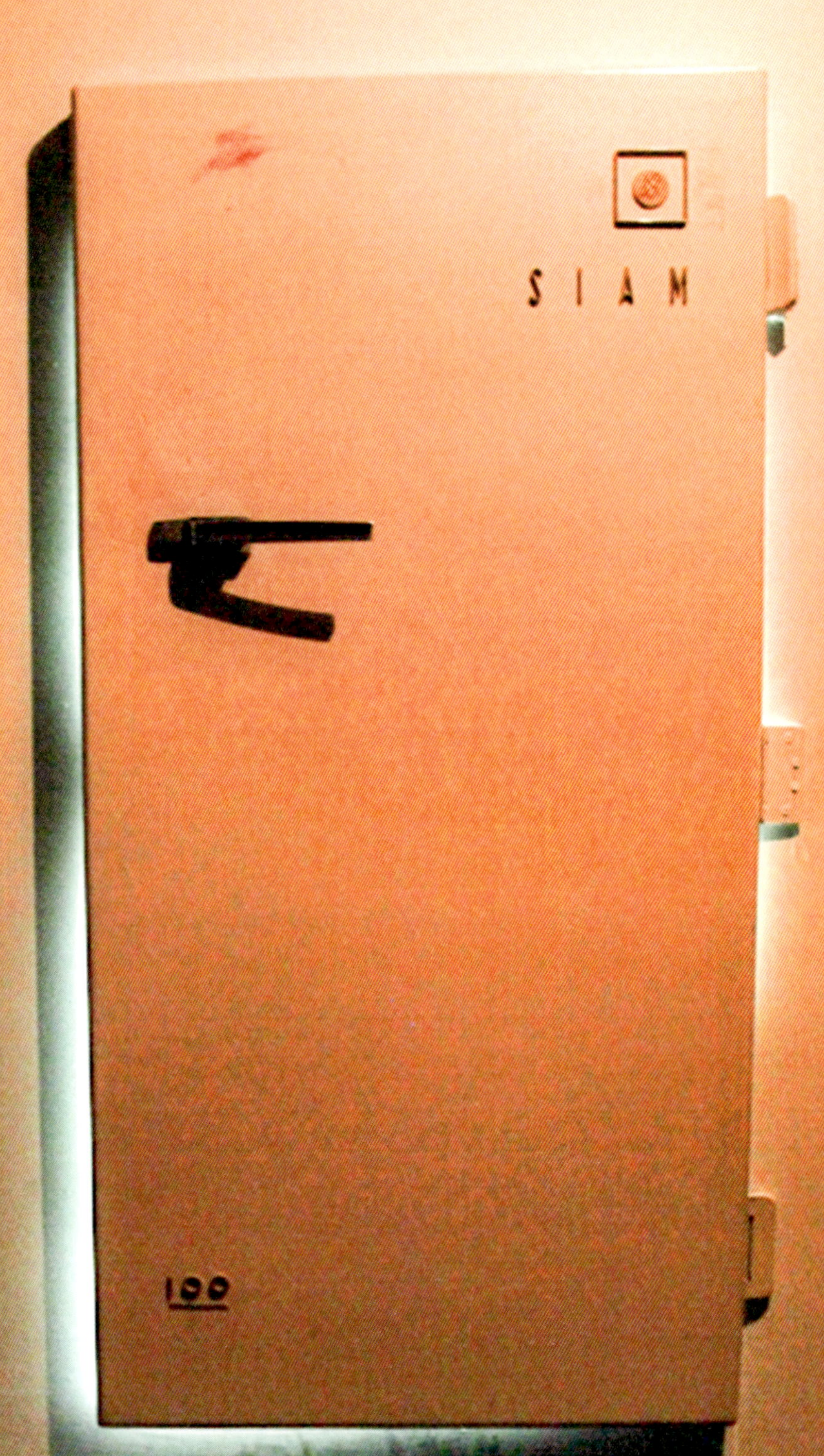
SIAM
100

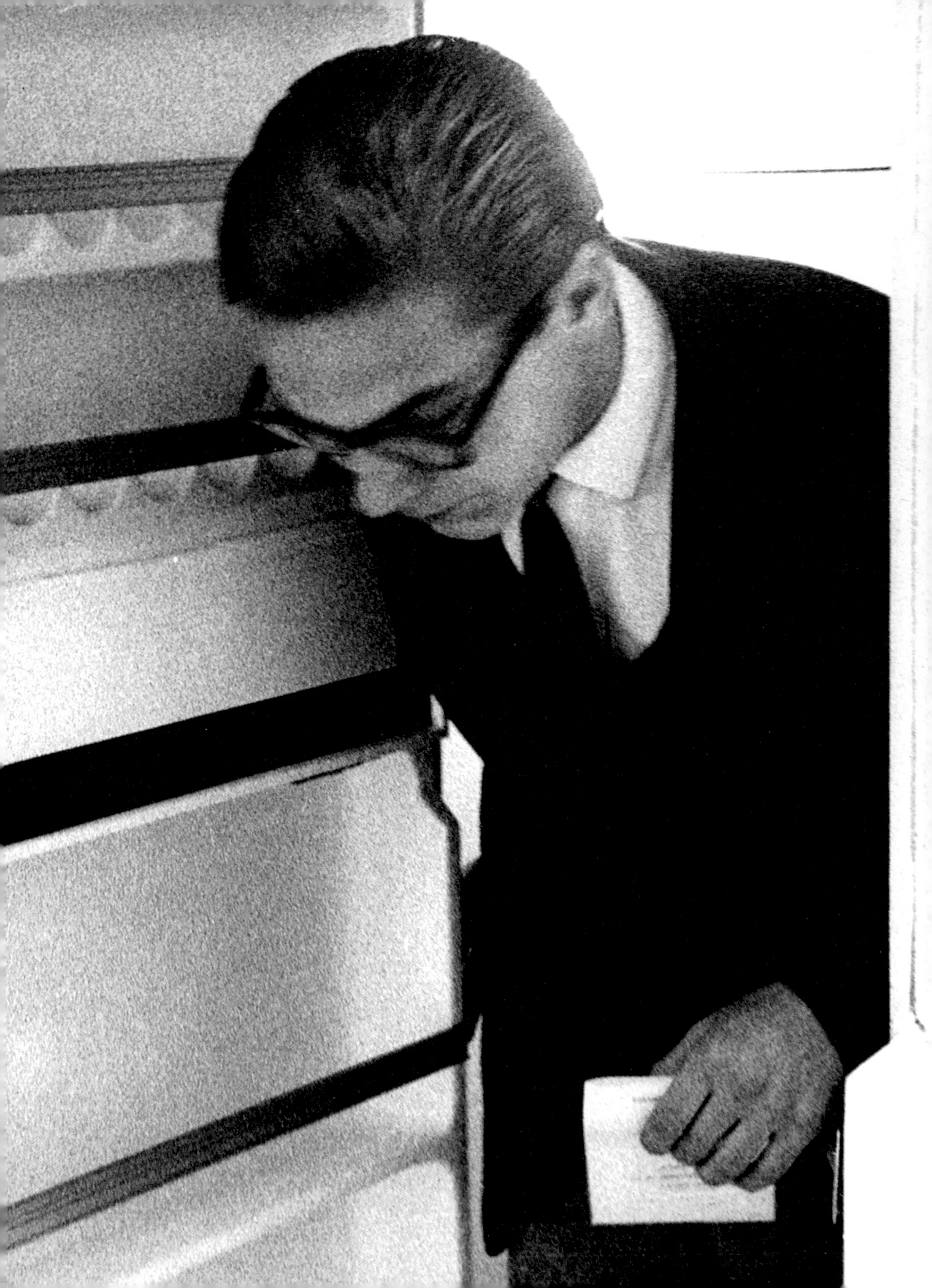

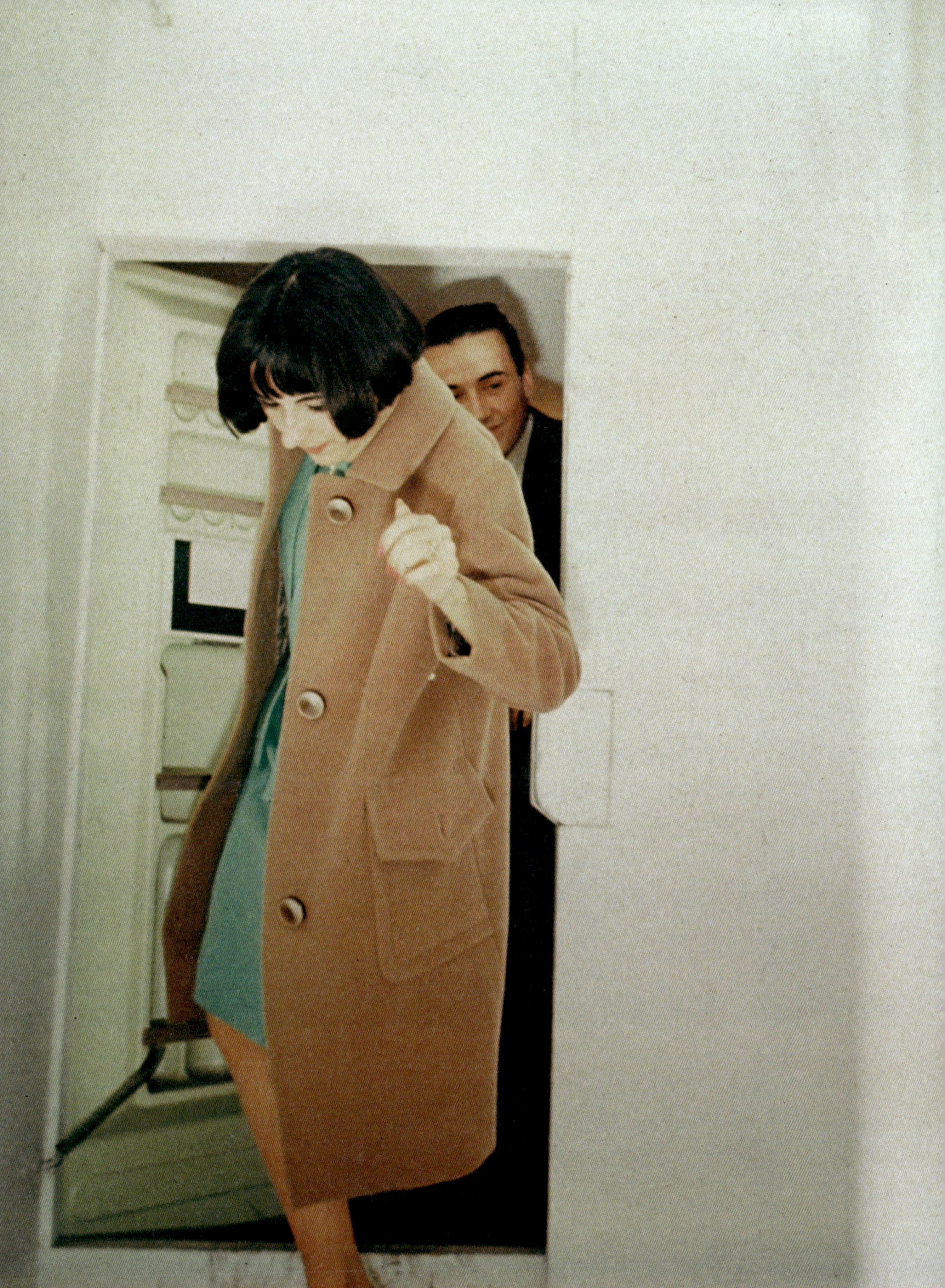

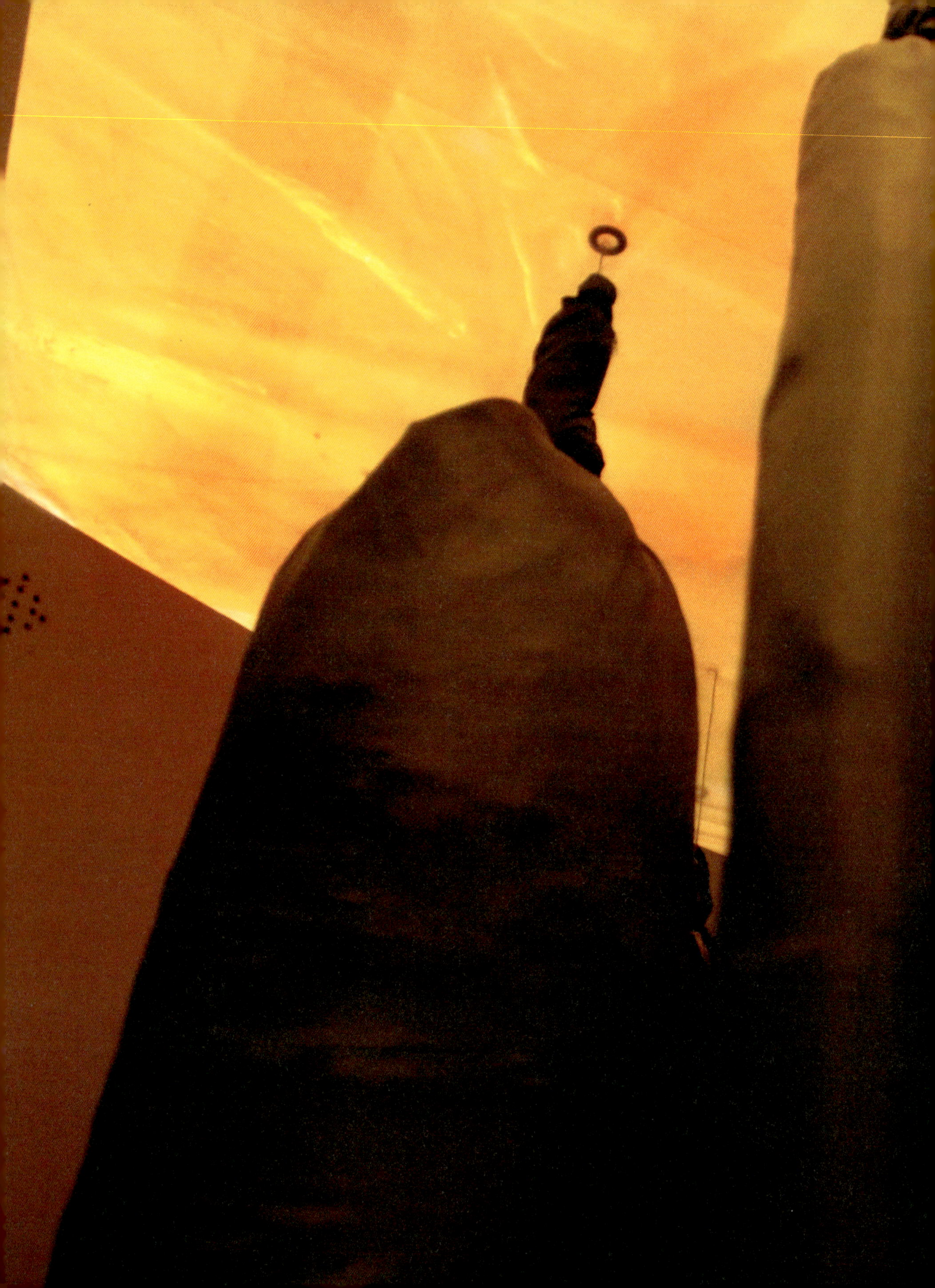

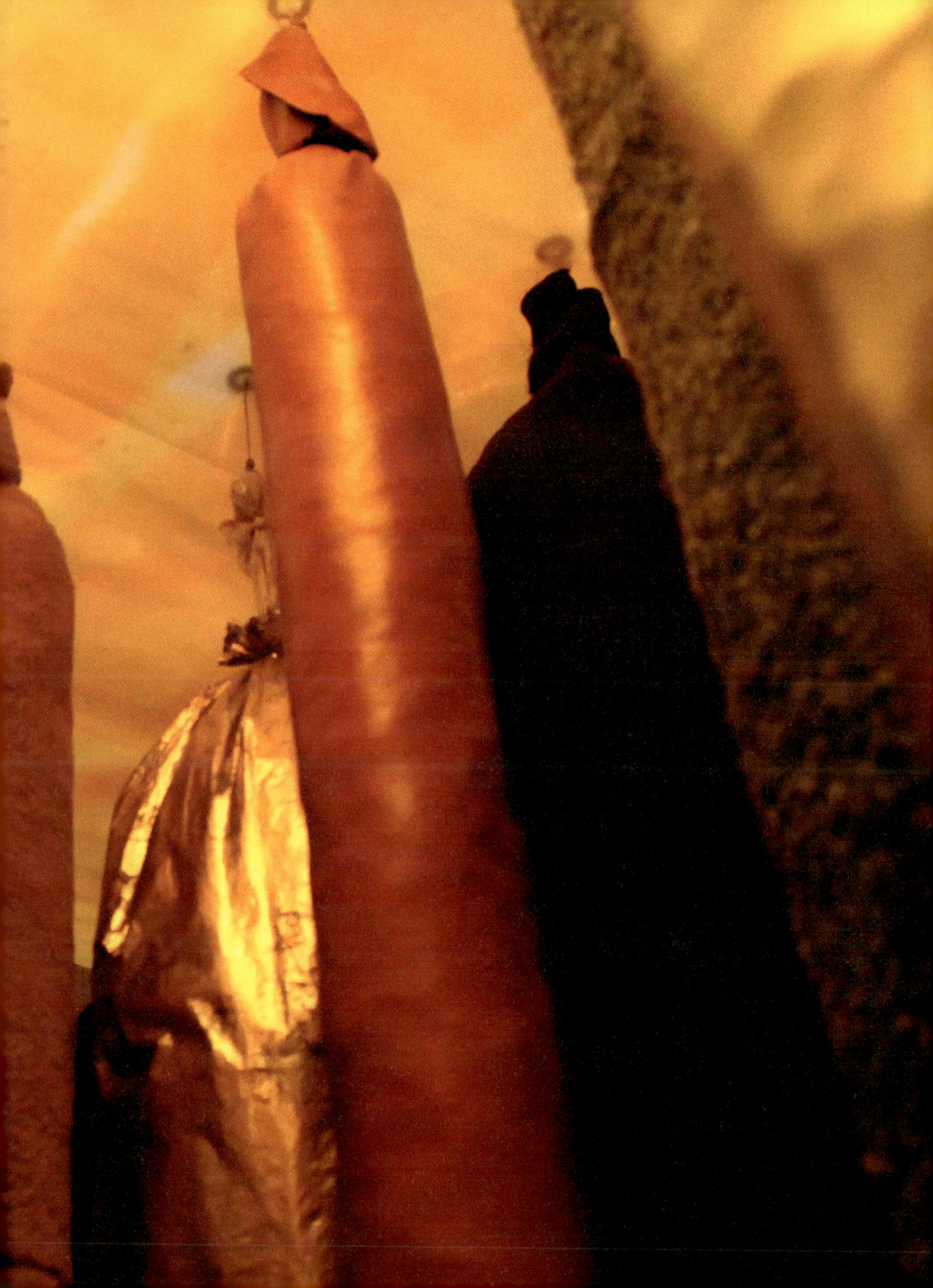

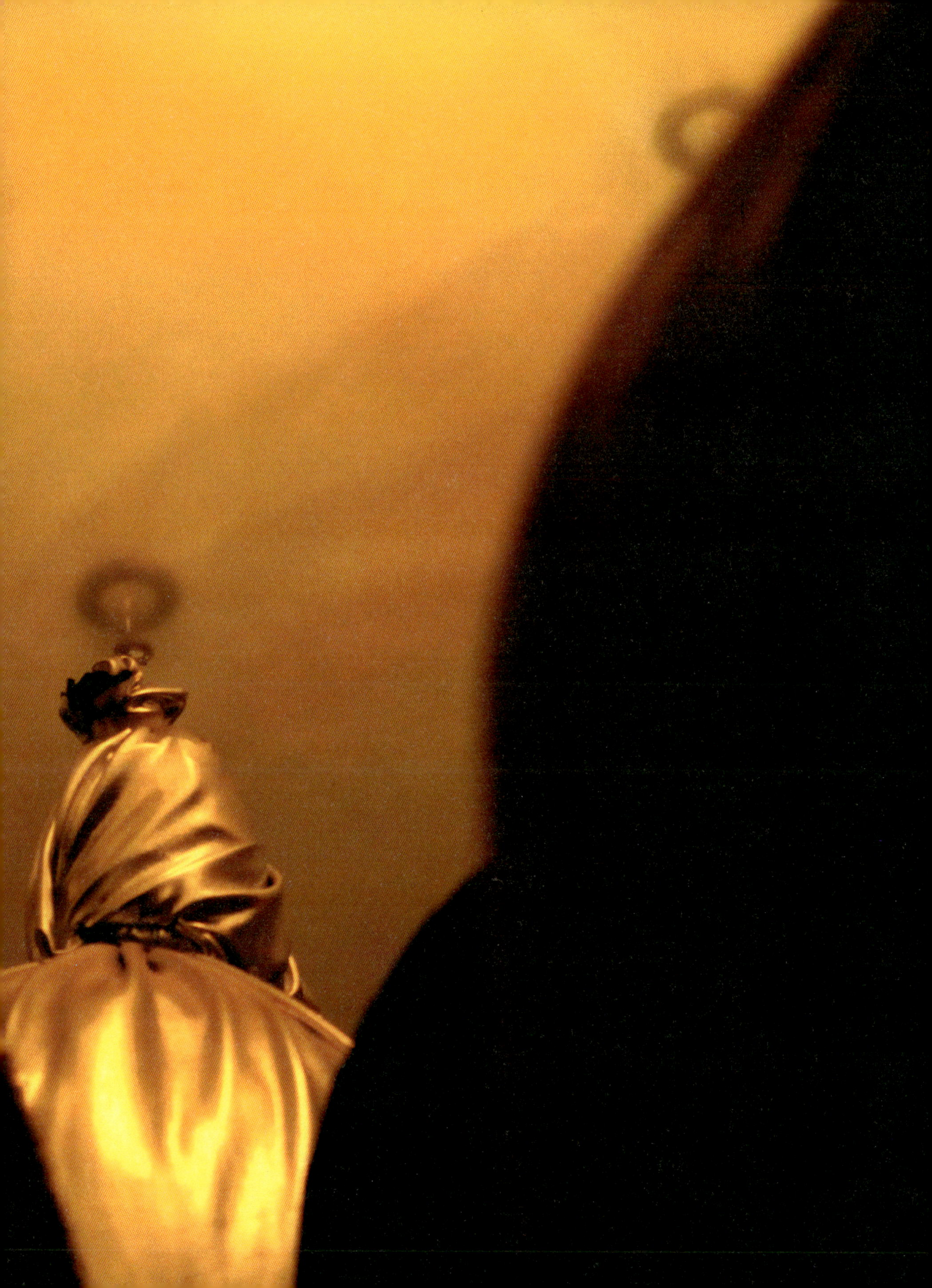

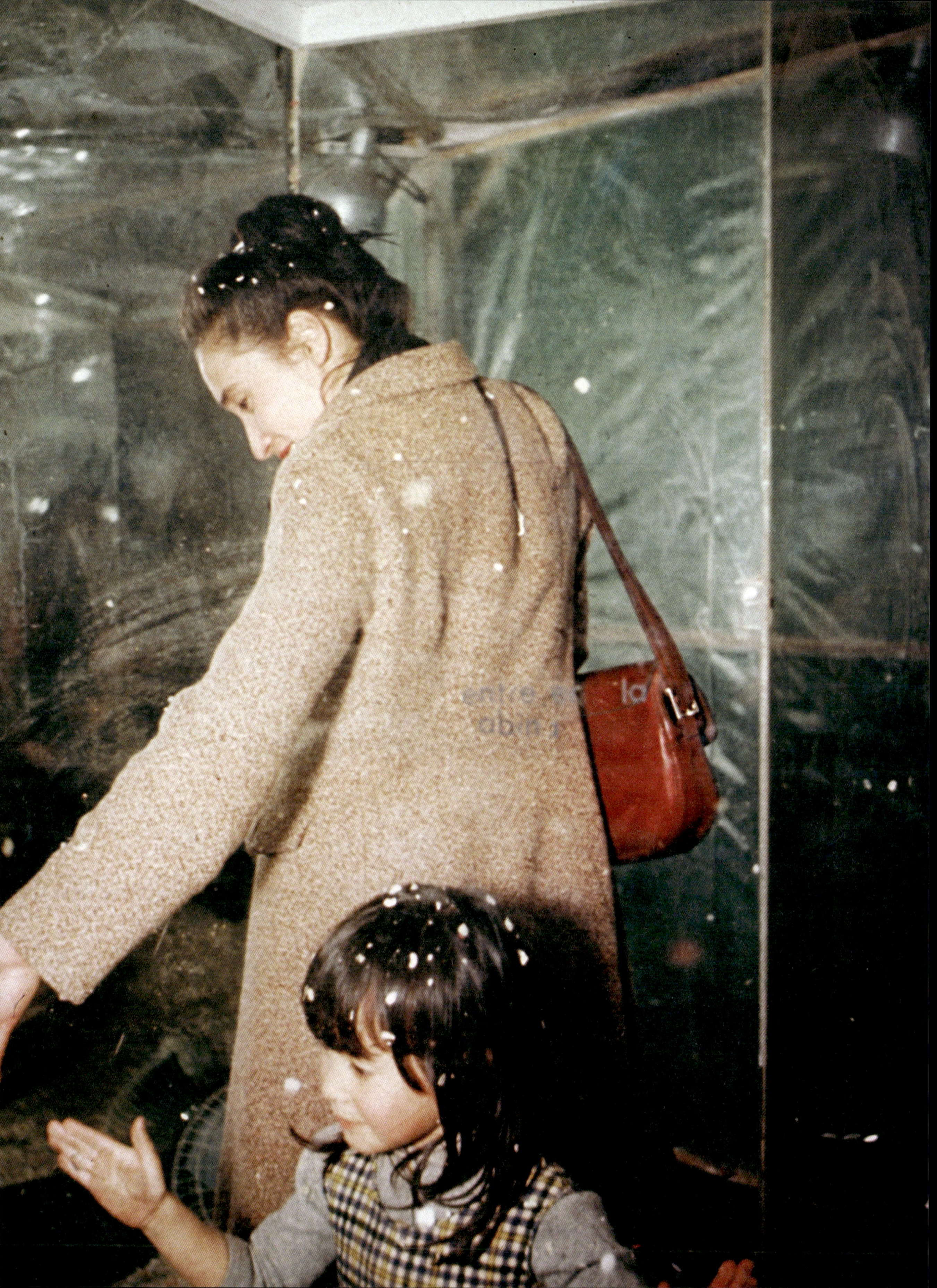

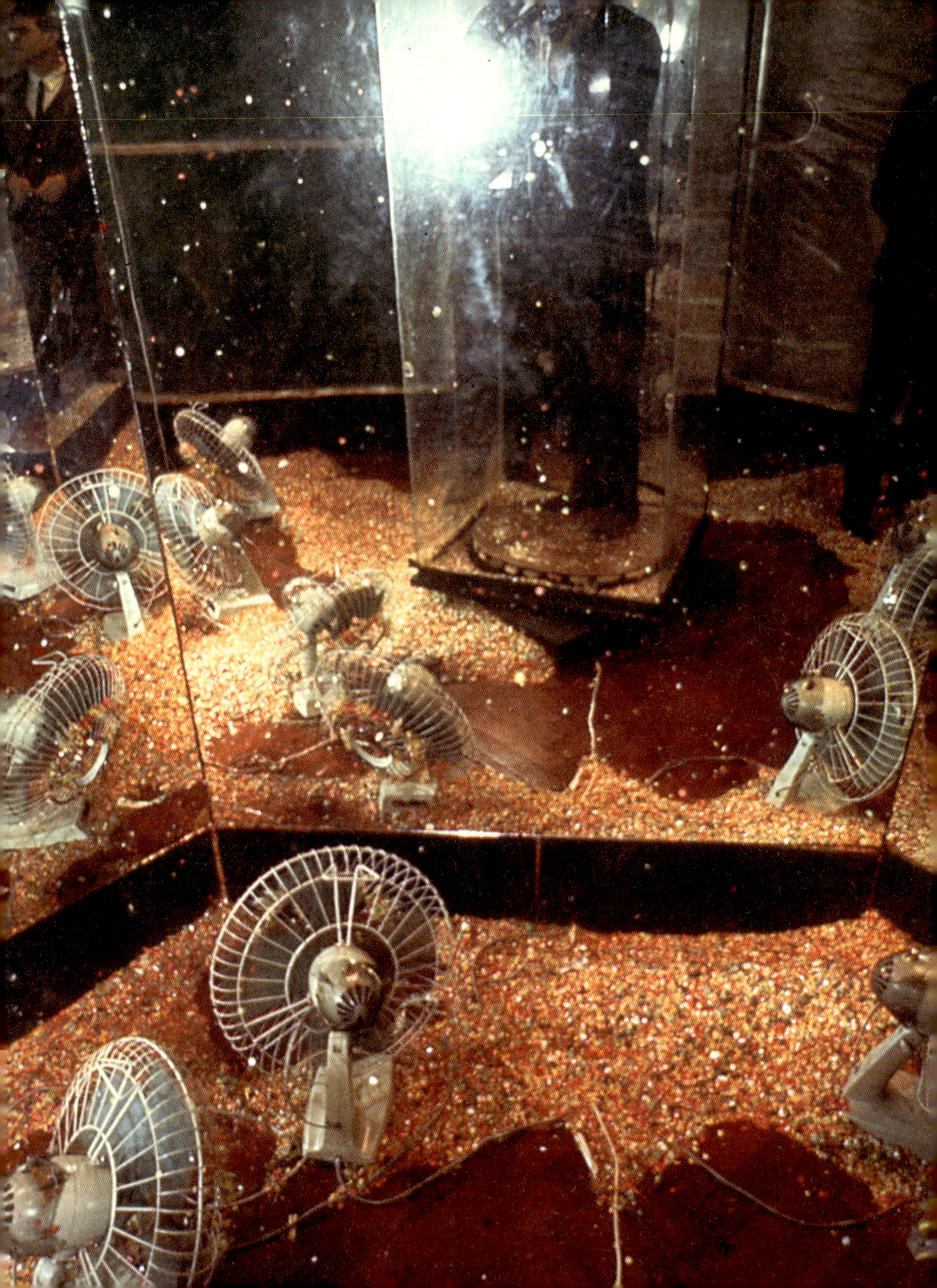

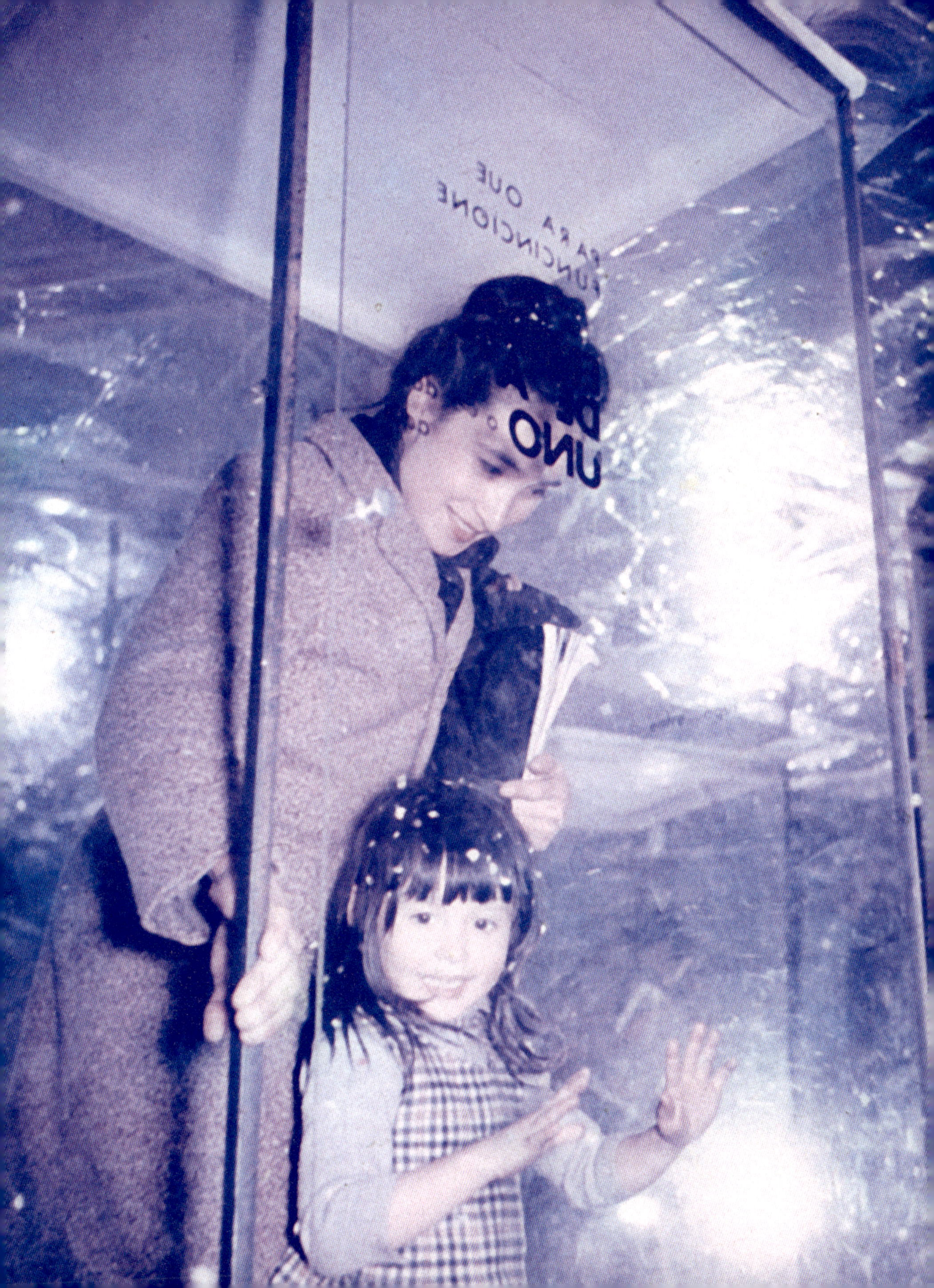

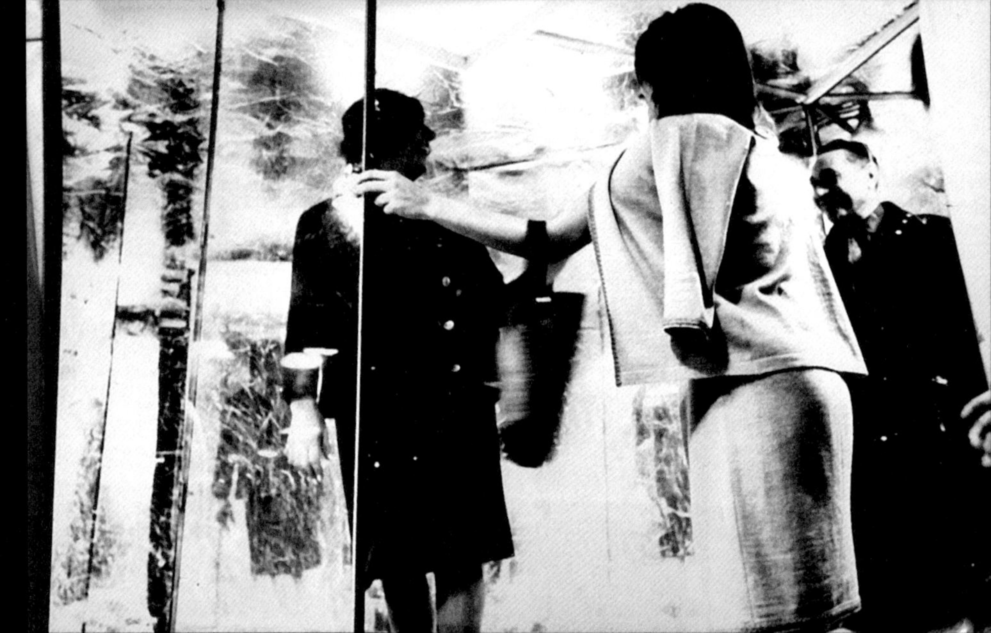

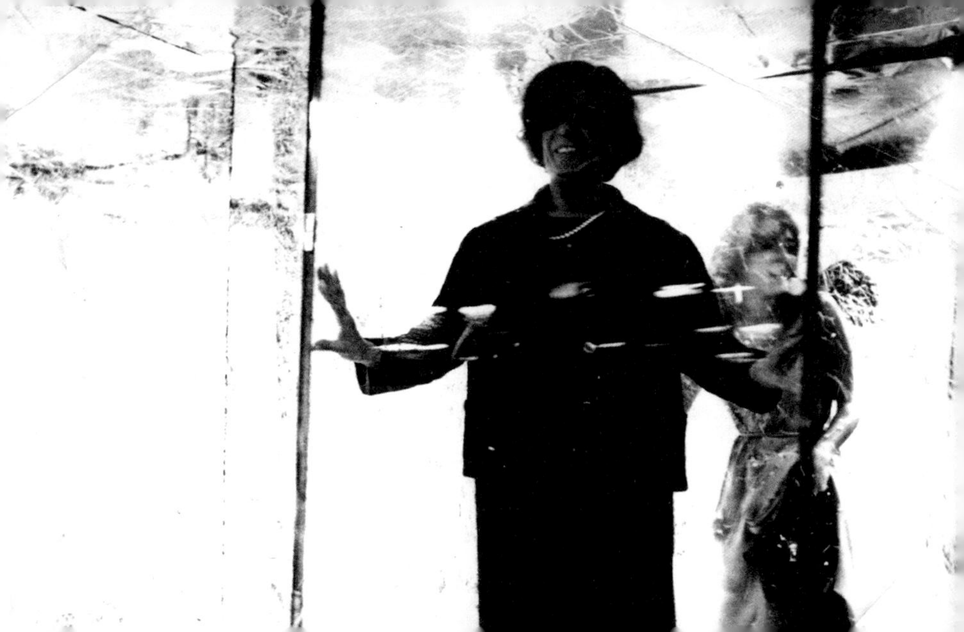

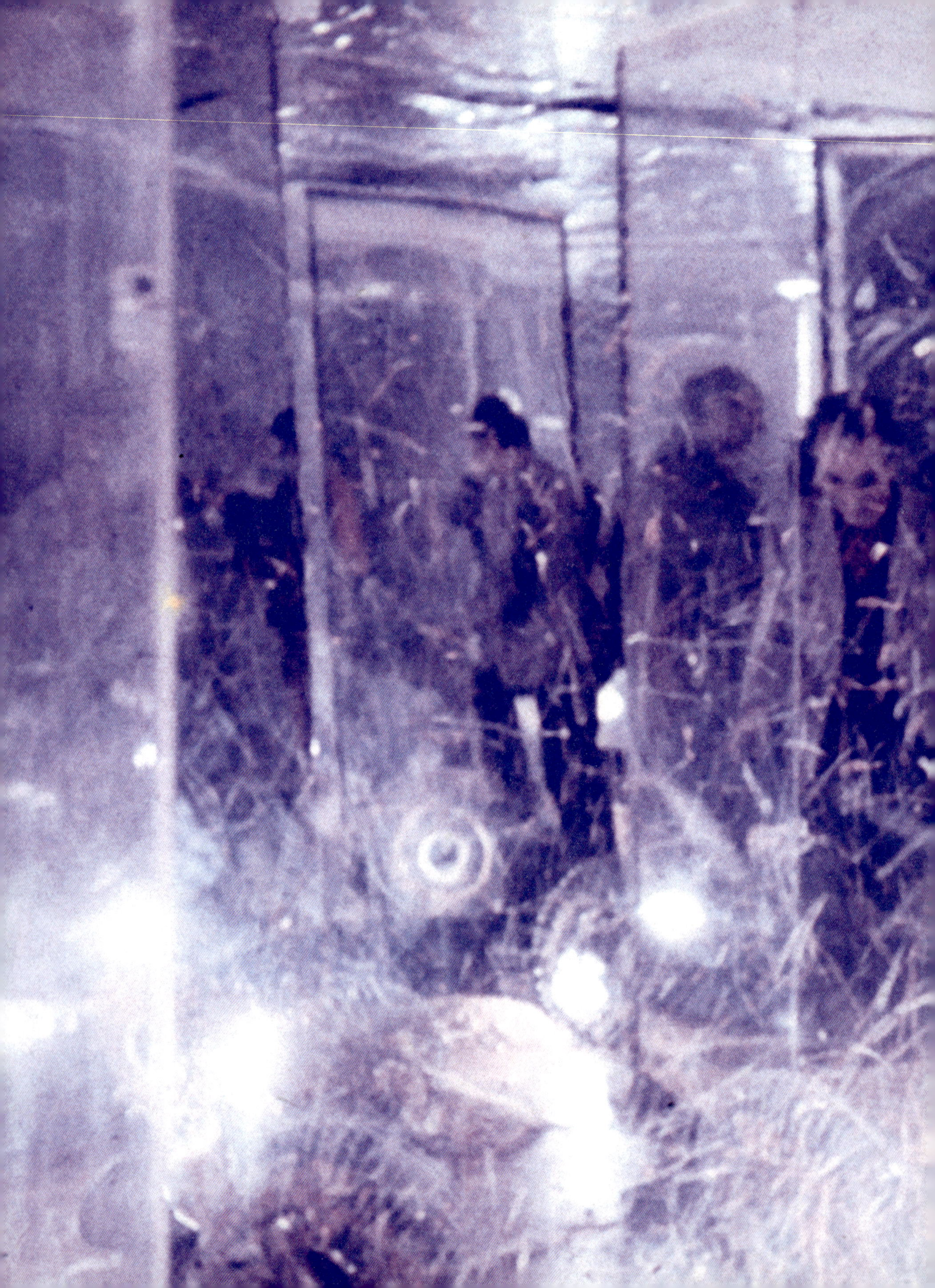

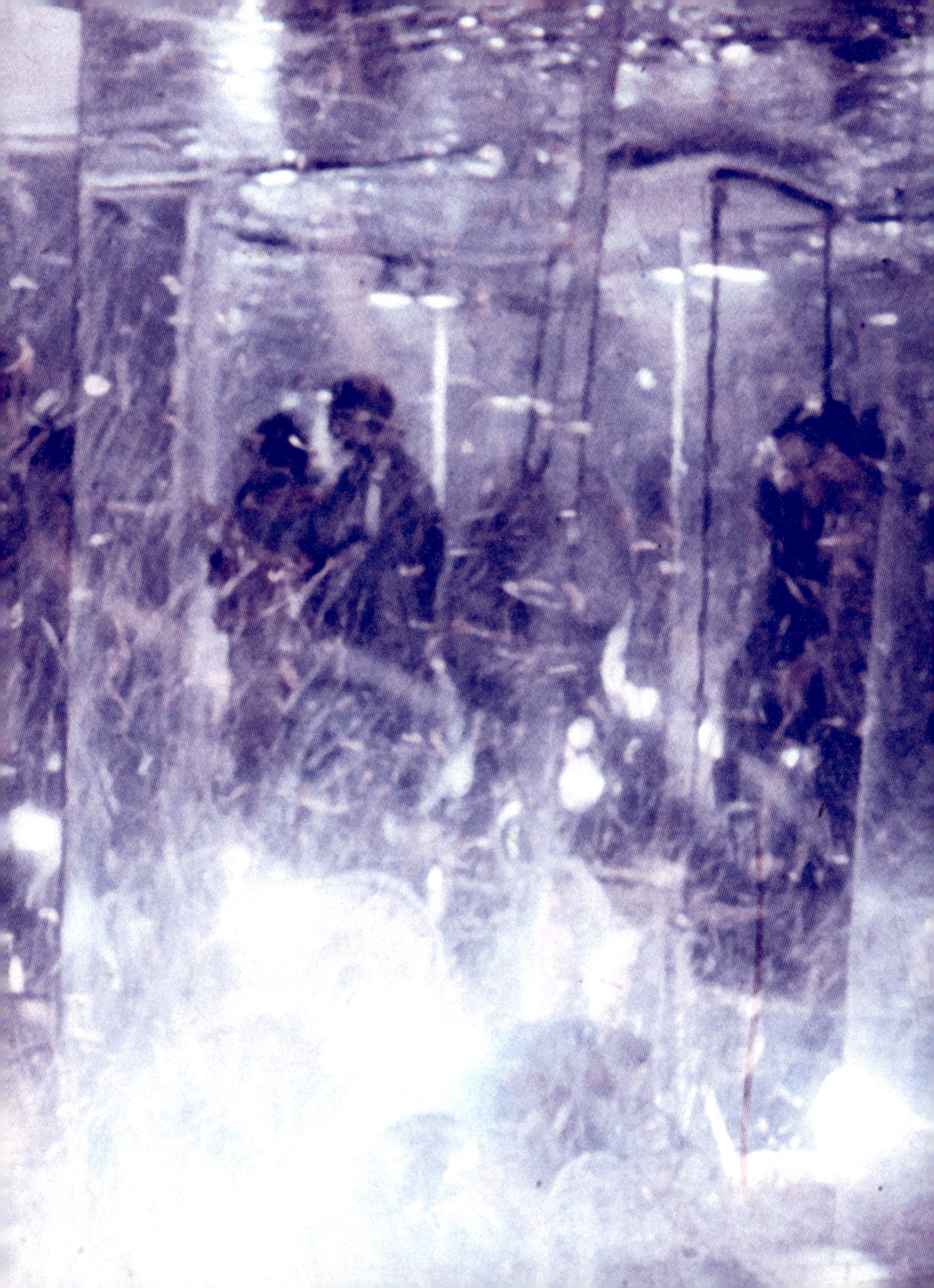

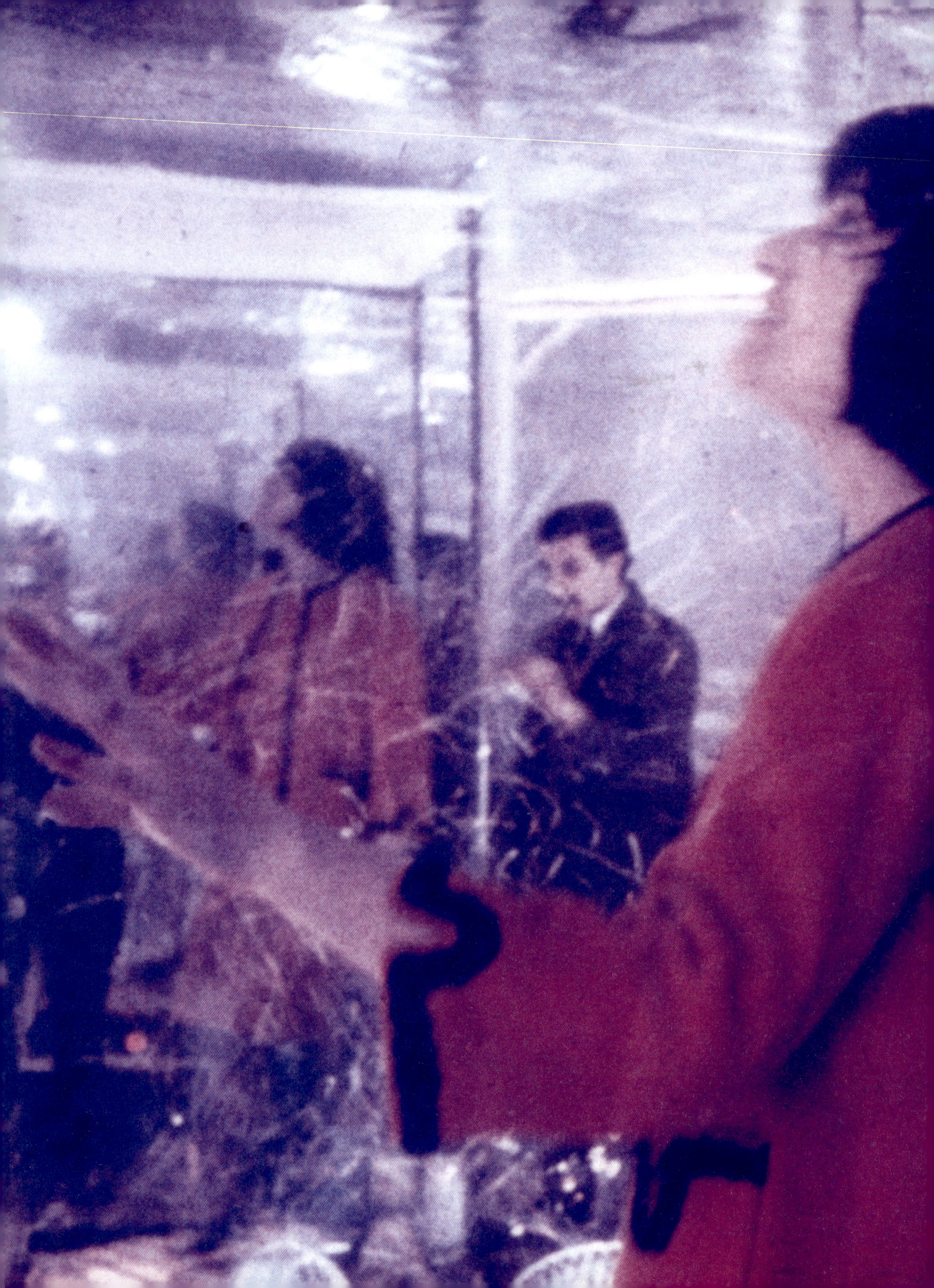

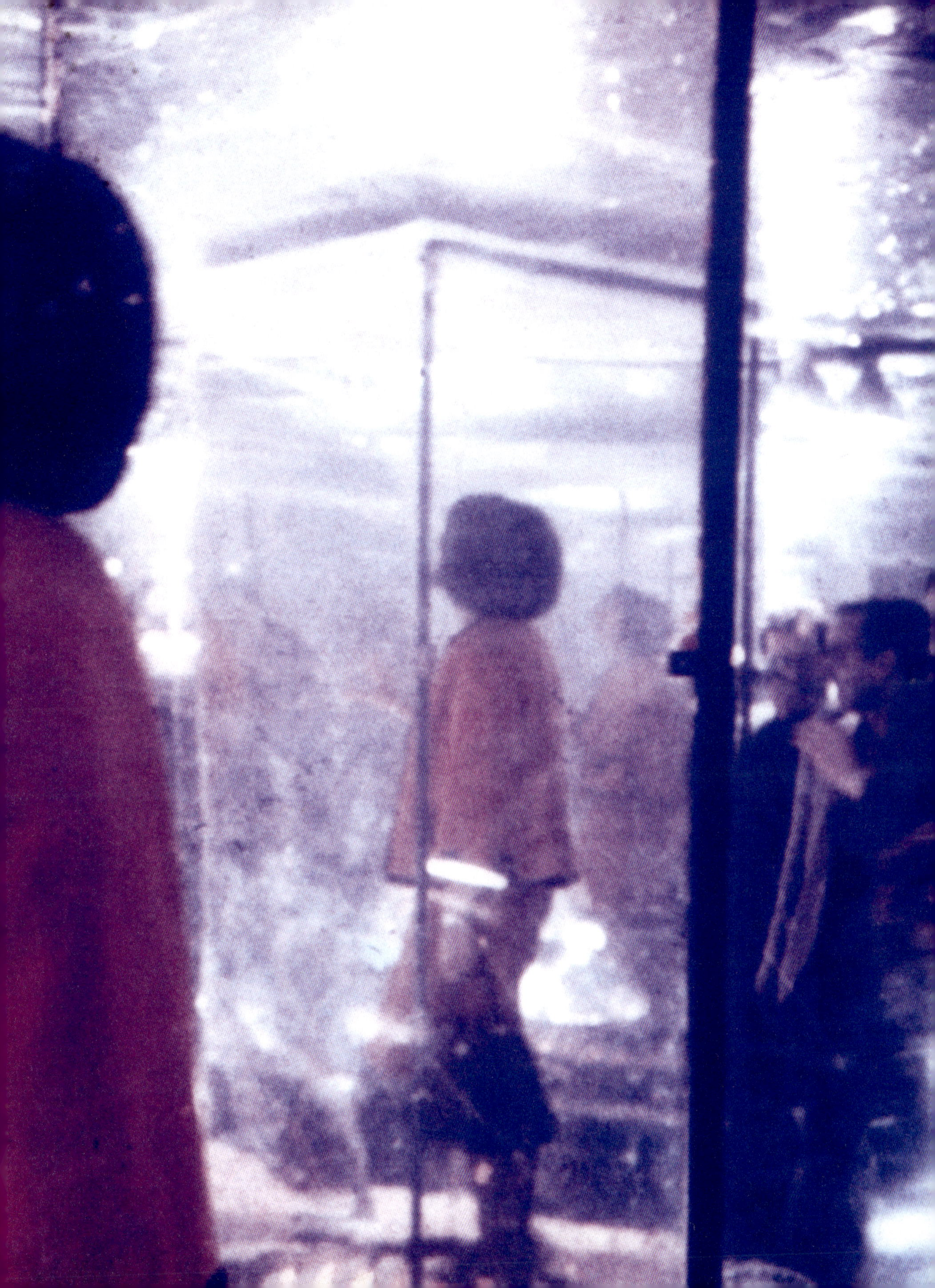

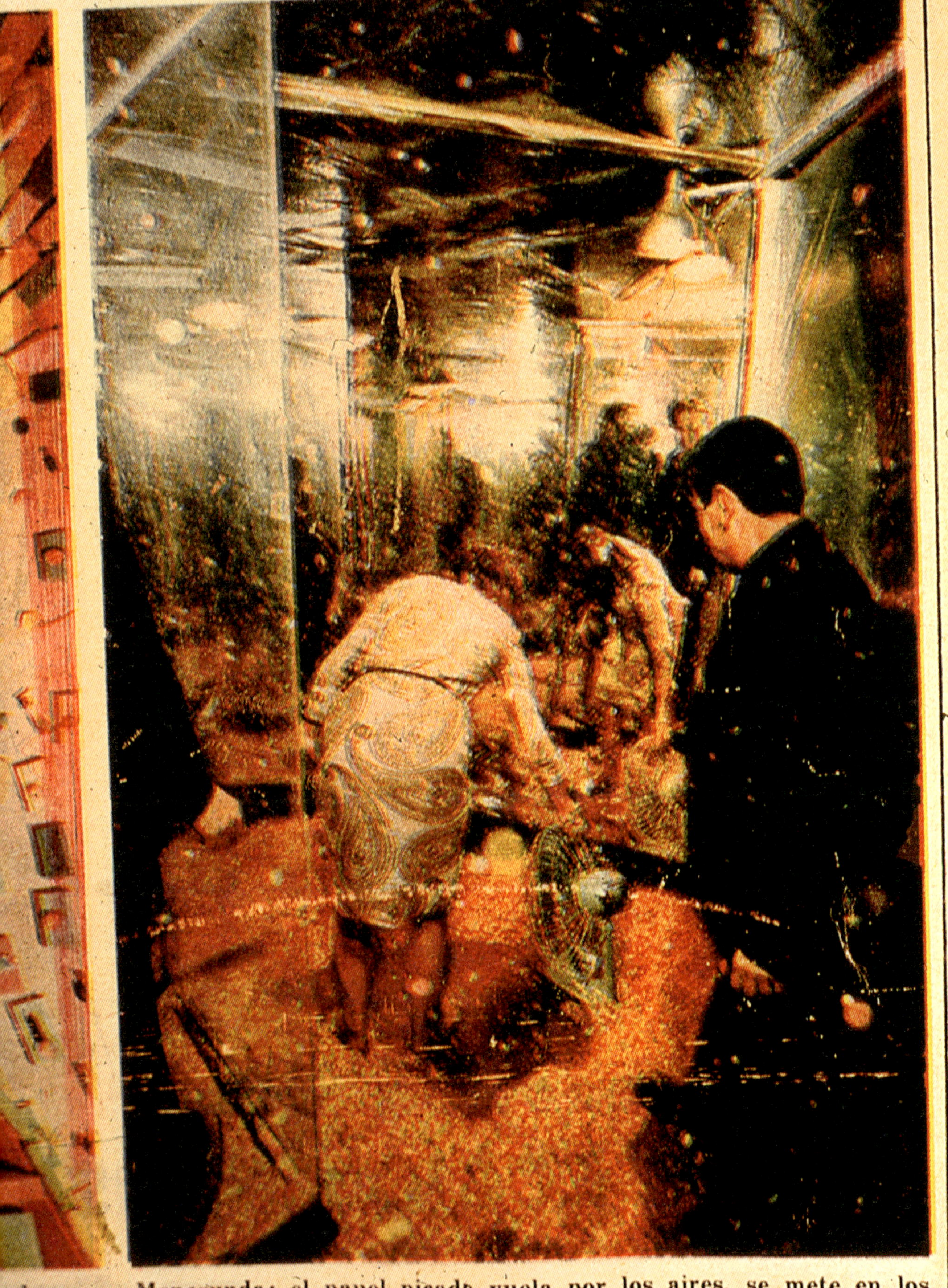

ada por
·n todo".

Menesunda: el papel picado vuela por los aires, se mete en los ojos y el pelo, ahoga a las señoras y produce atroces espasmos.

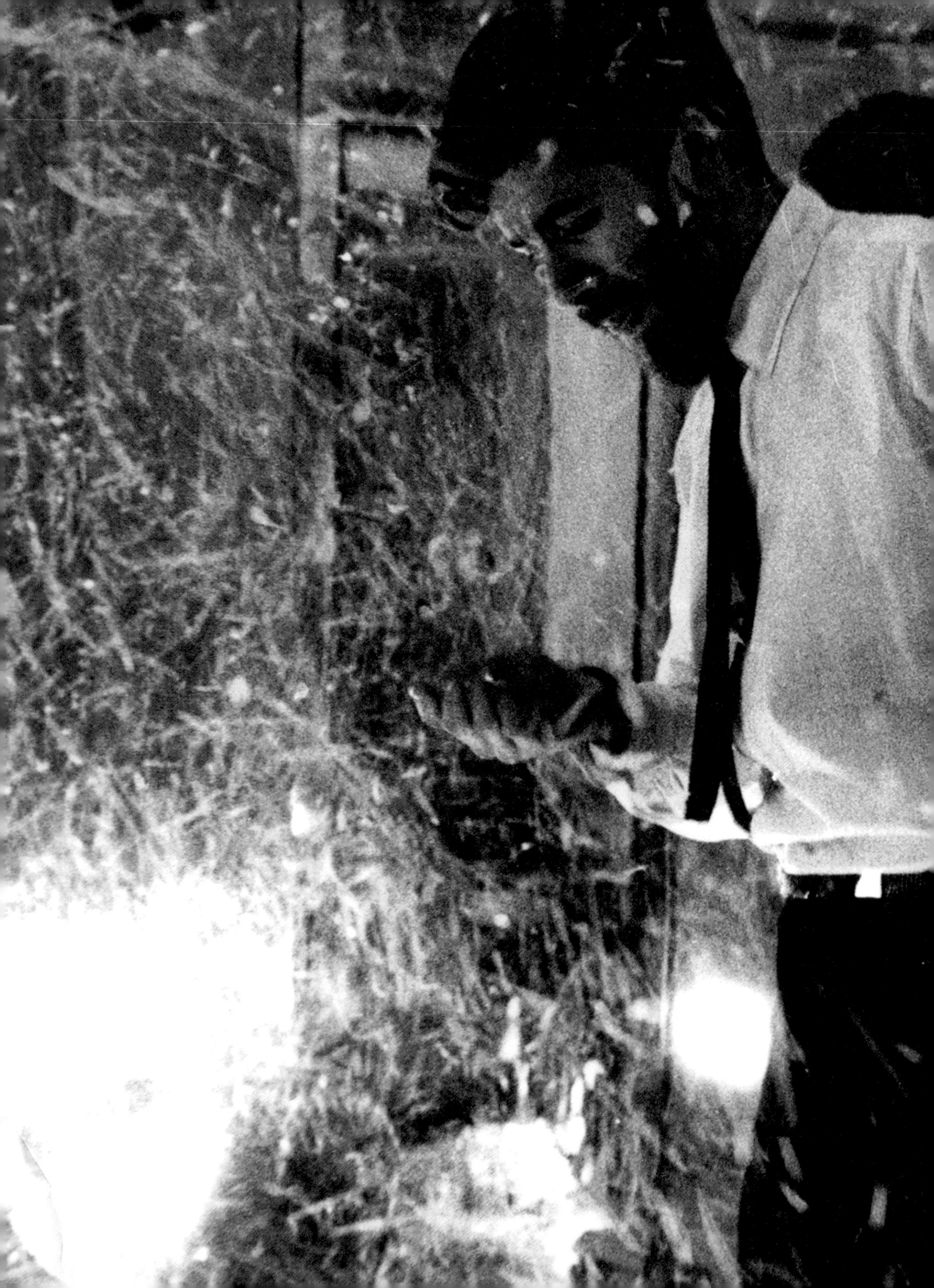

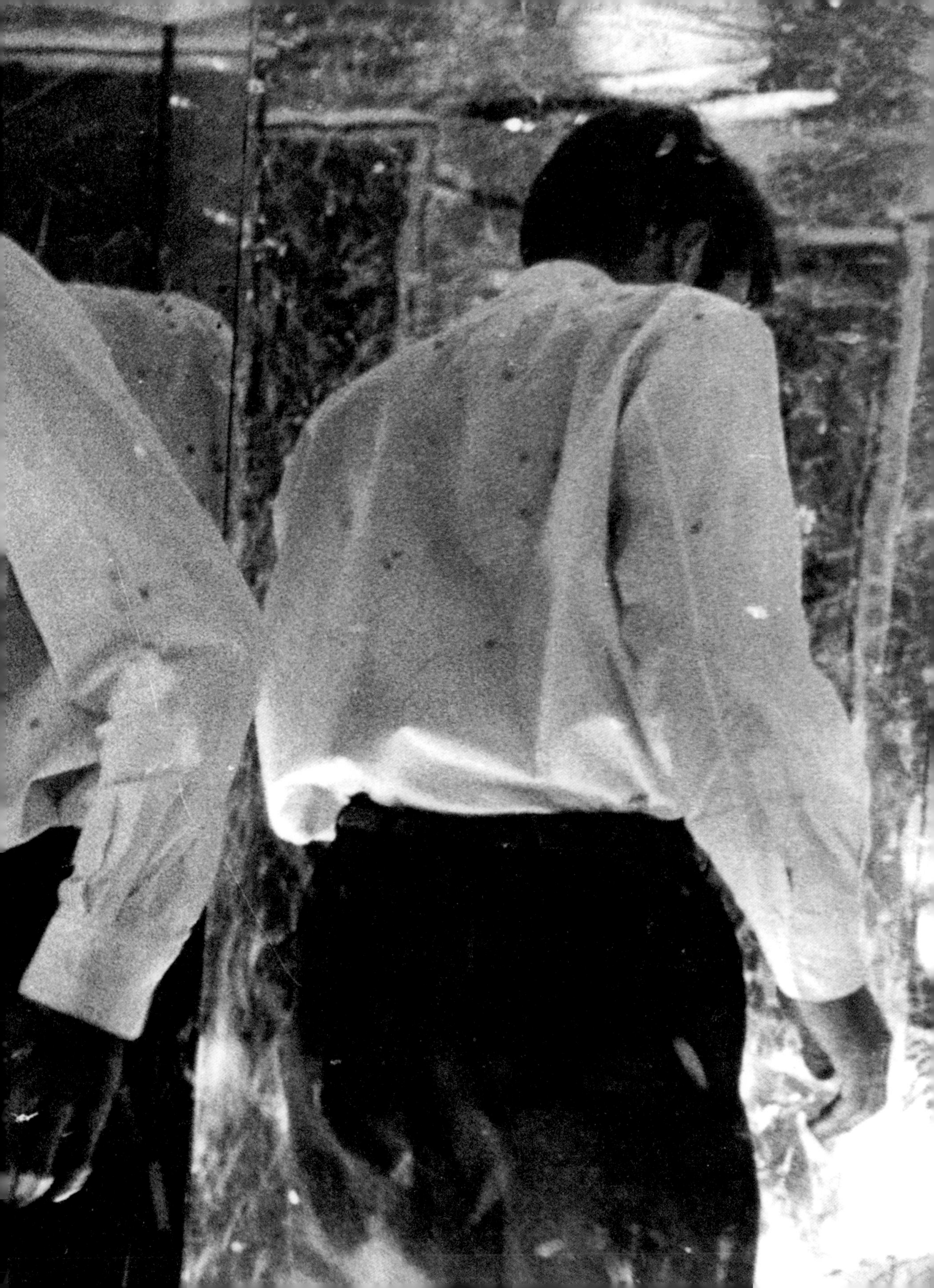

Creación

de

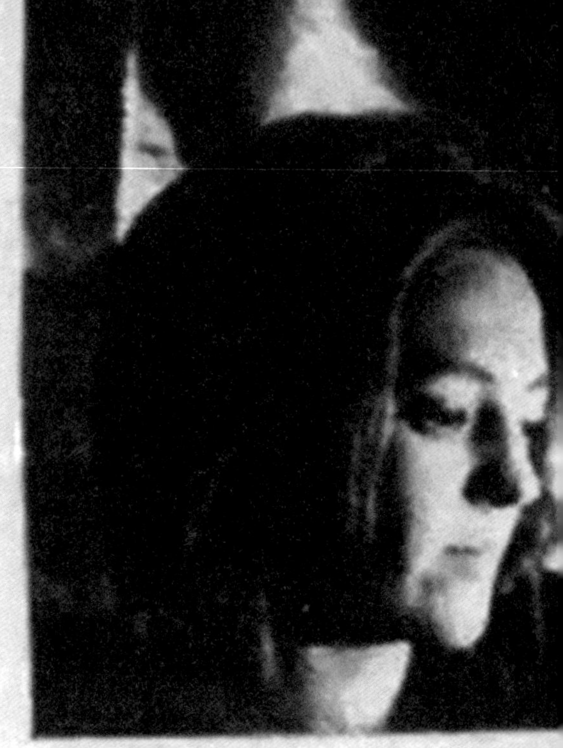

Marta Minujin

LA MENE

BUENOS AIRES, 2

Colaboración

de

Floreal Amor
David Lamelas
Leopoldo Maler
Rodolfo Prayon
Pablo Suarez

REALIZAD
INSTITUTO
POR SUGER
JORGE ROM

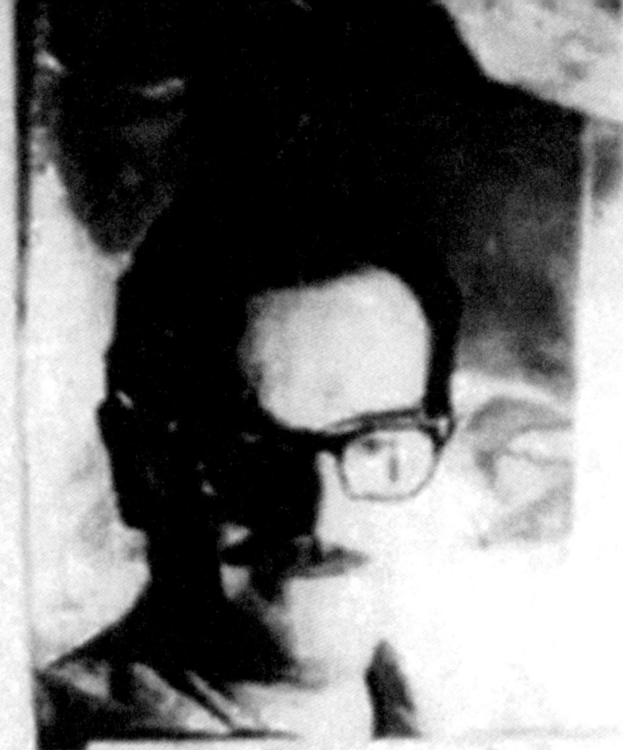

Rubén Santantonín

ESUNDA

MAYO DE 1965

EN EL
DI TELLA
NCIA DE
RO BREST

Alquileres: Mañana

POR SUGERE
JORGE ROME

o Herrer
de las
nidad de
fluidez d
del munc
vivió de
España y
el report

edad y
útbol, dan
lteras, aun
s convien-

como la
rlo en las
delantera,
nasé atrás,
era.... Ca
de Casa
e ser muy
os, un com
habré re
nces, pre

la historia
nio Herre-
traten de
ta. Se tra-
ndial esta-
nales: D.T.
uicio sobre
a sus pa-

r materia
a prima u
amente. Y
ara como

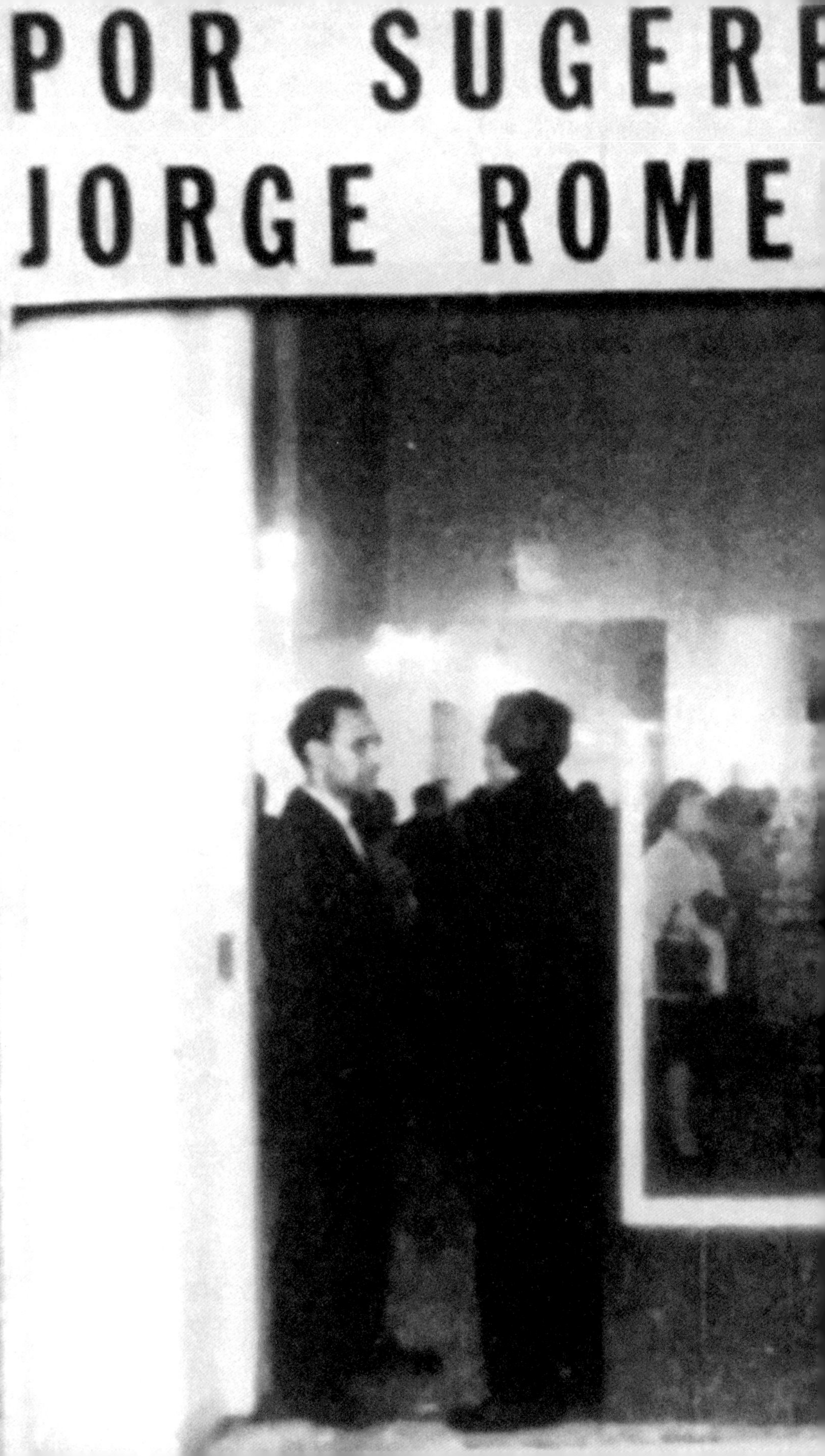

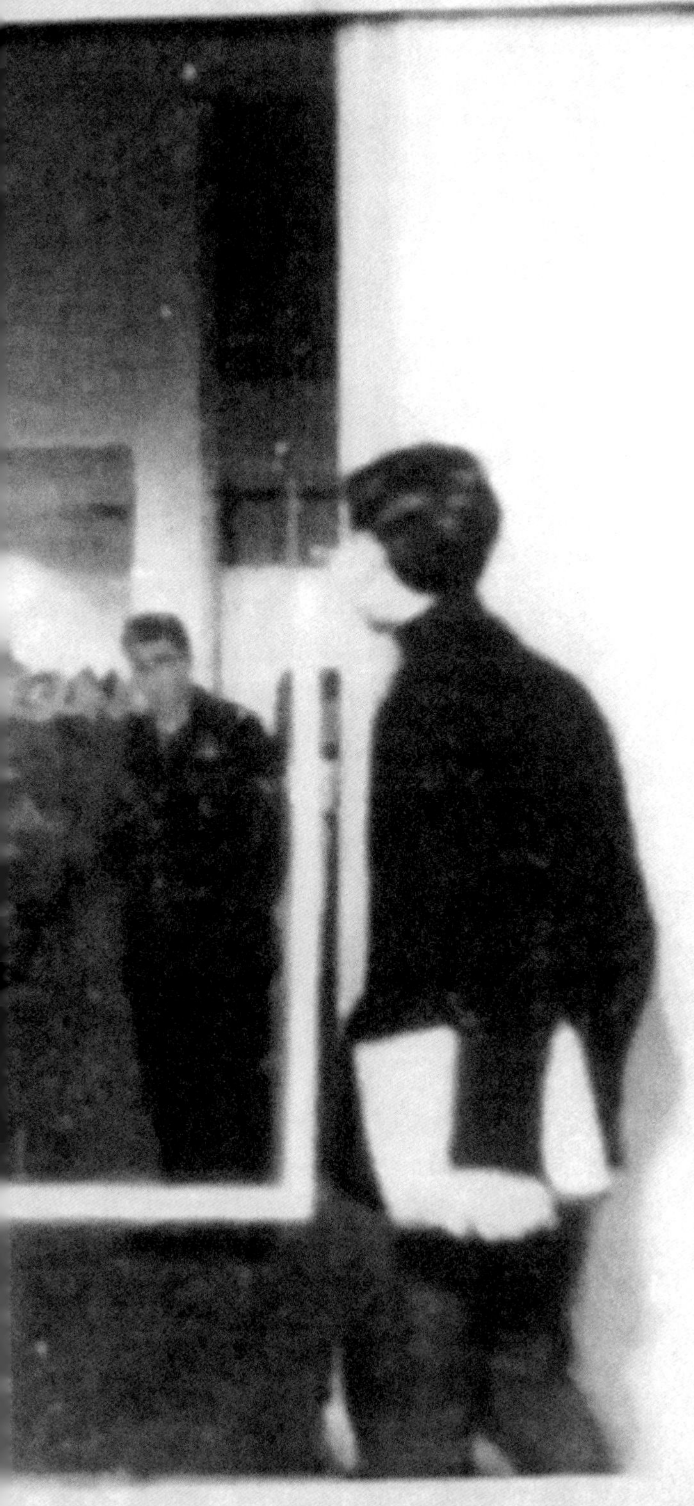
NCIA DE
O BREST

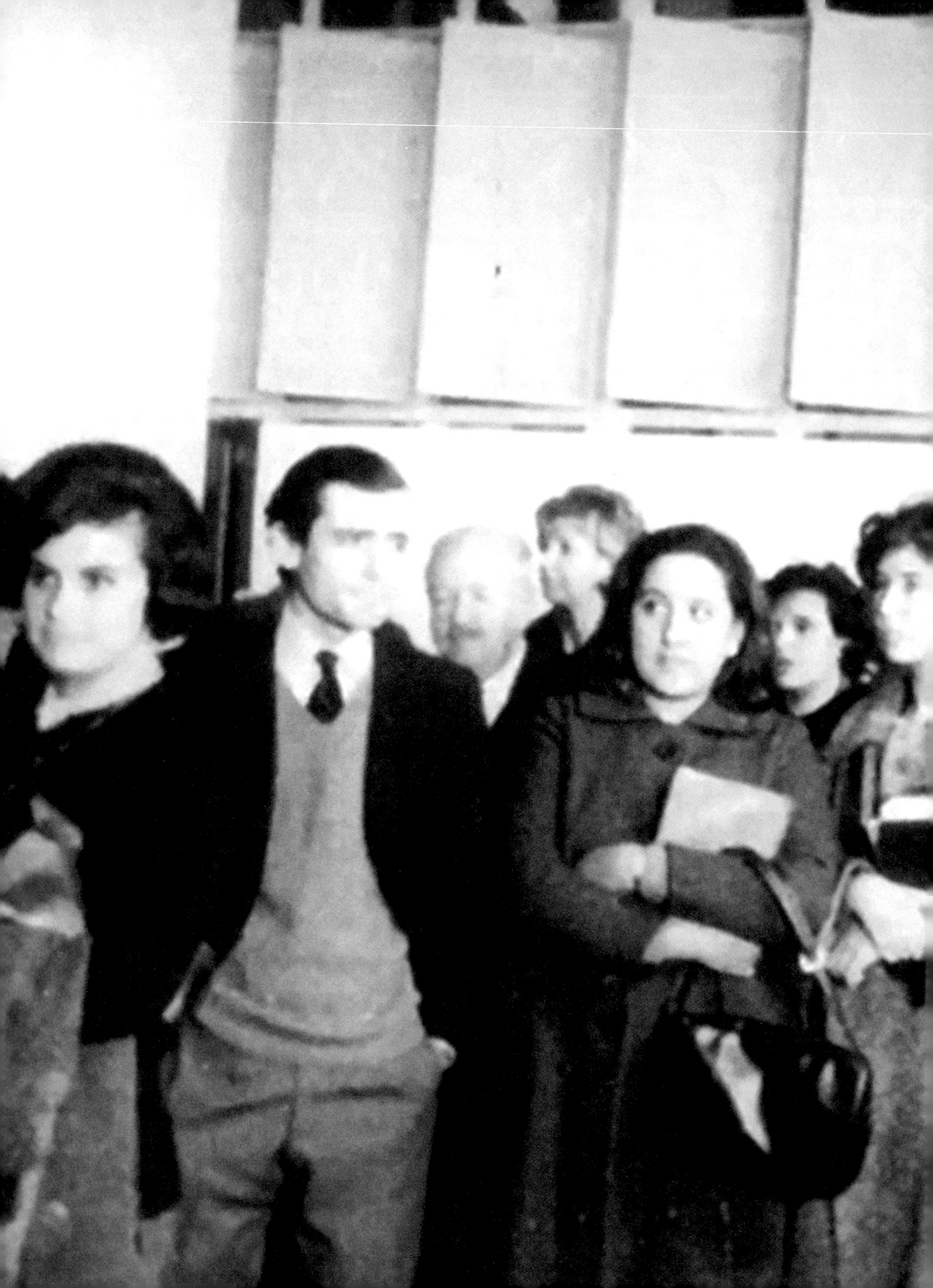

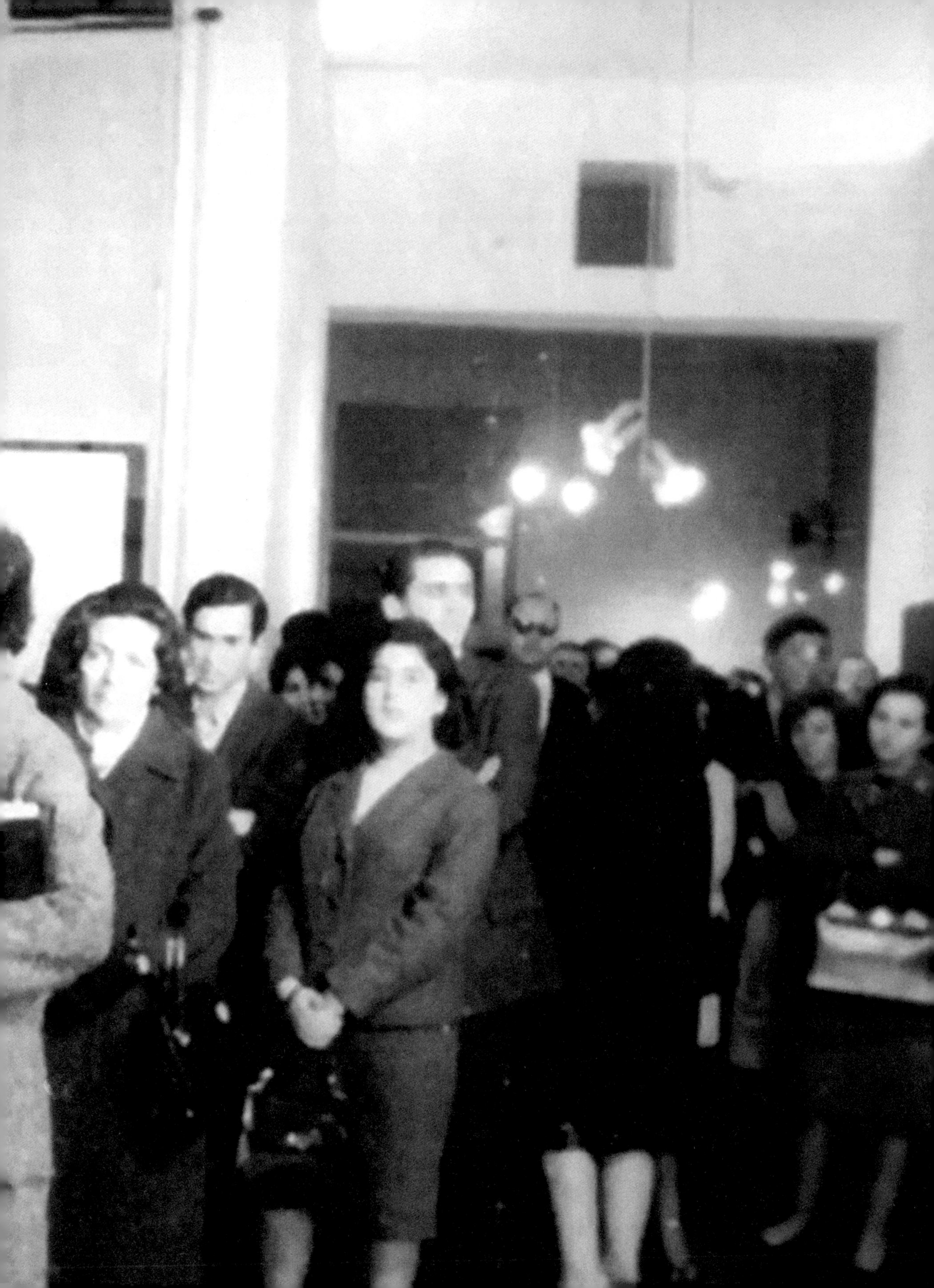

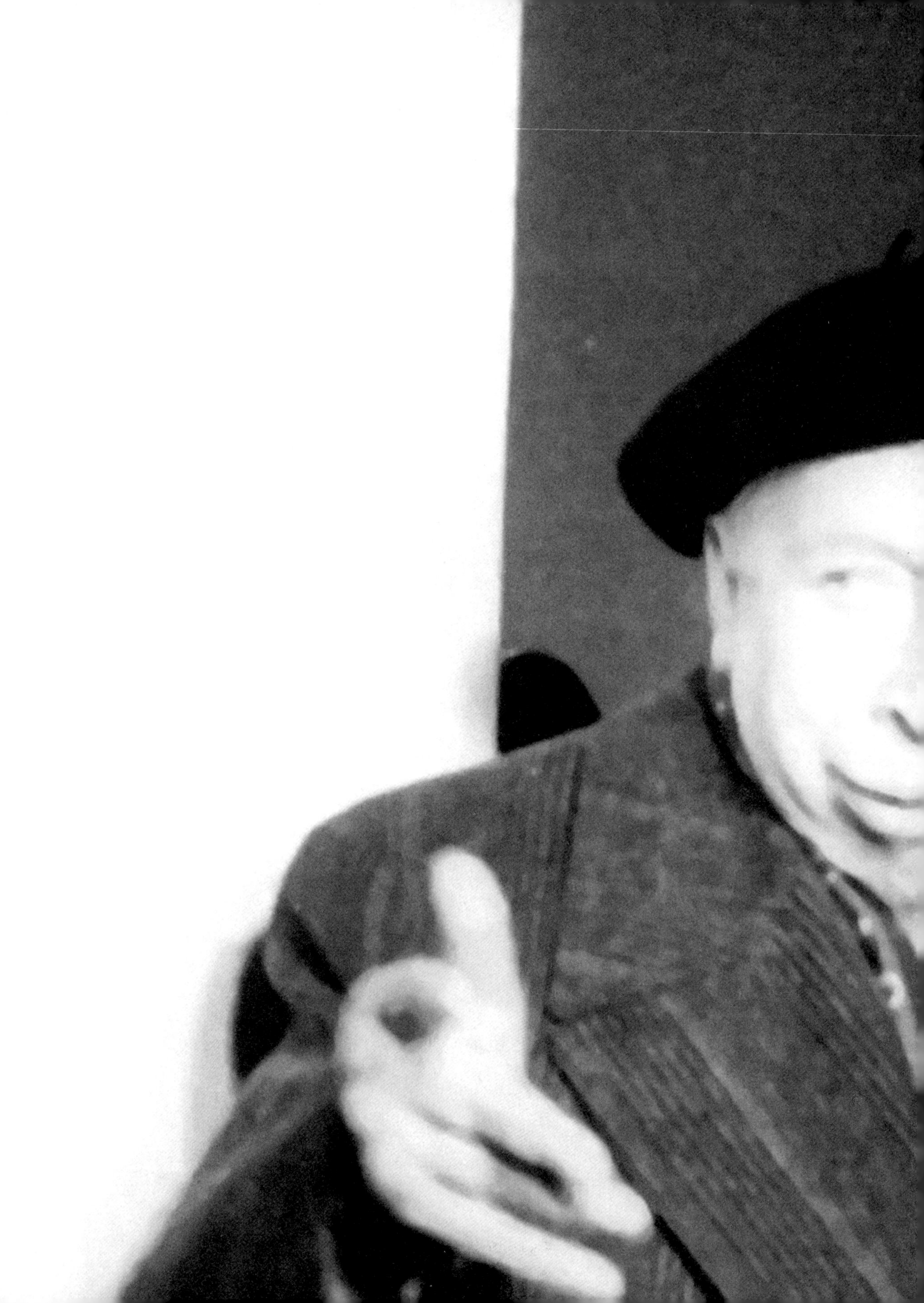

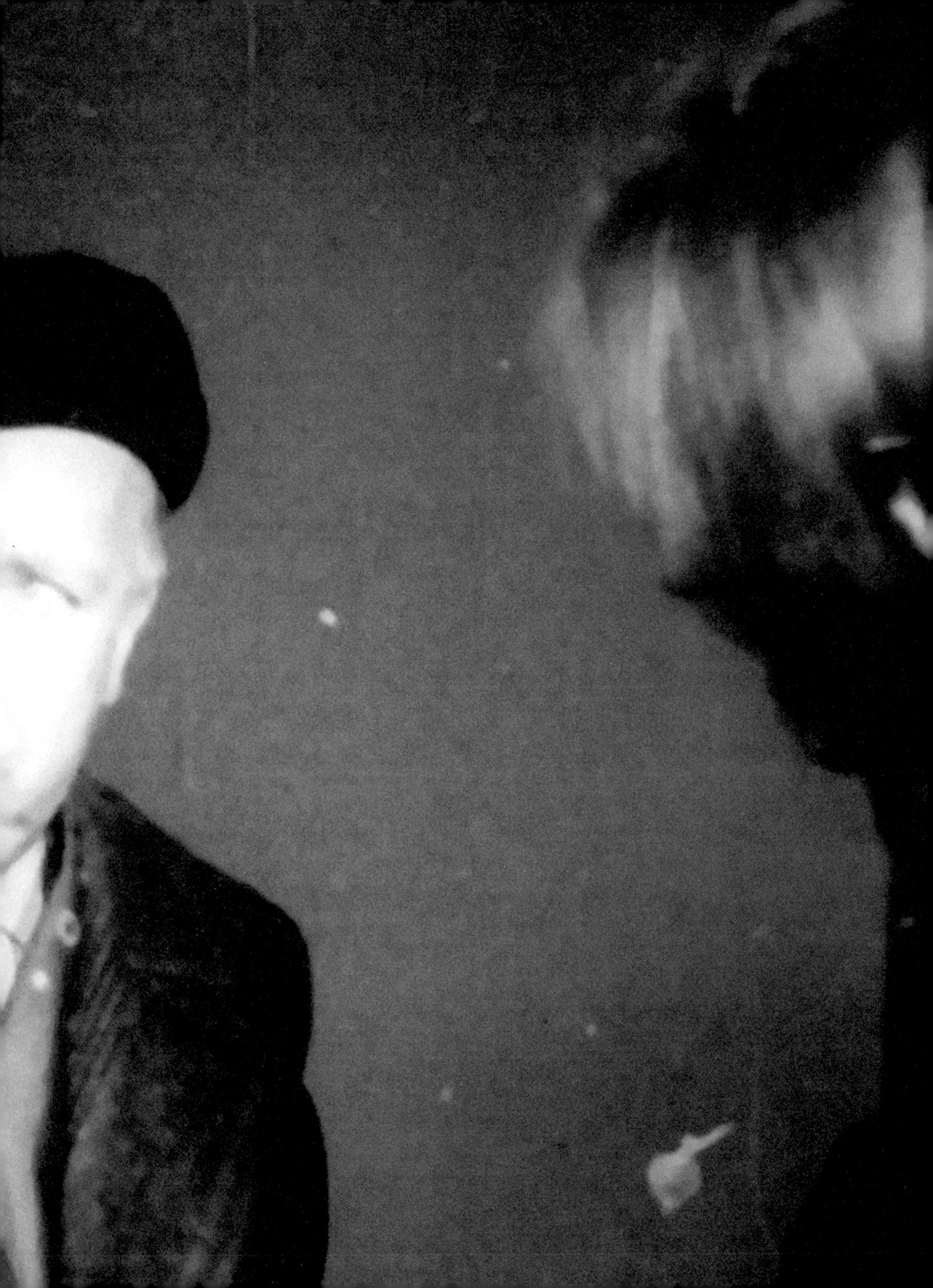

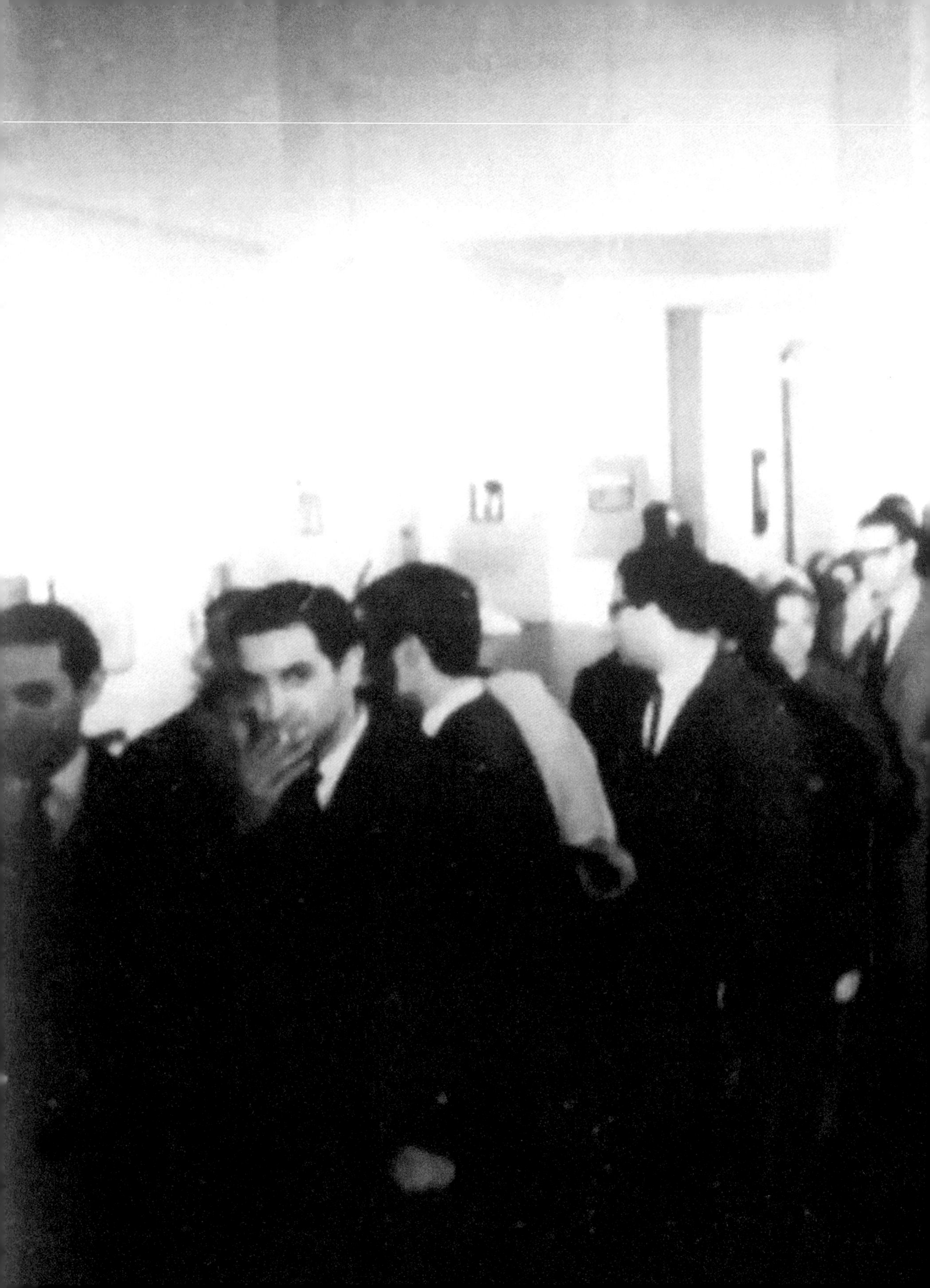

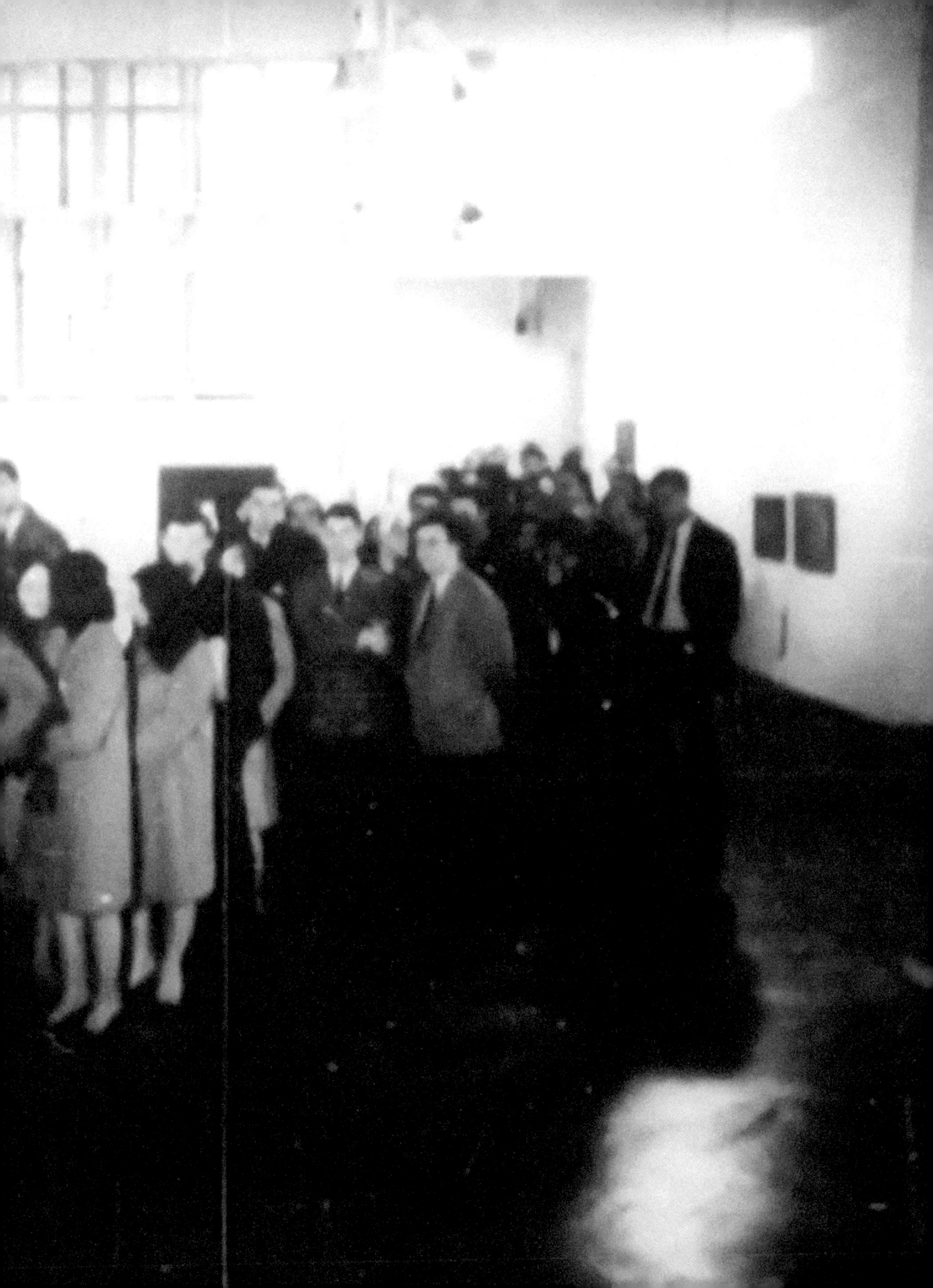

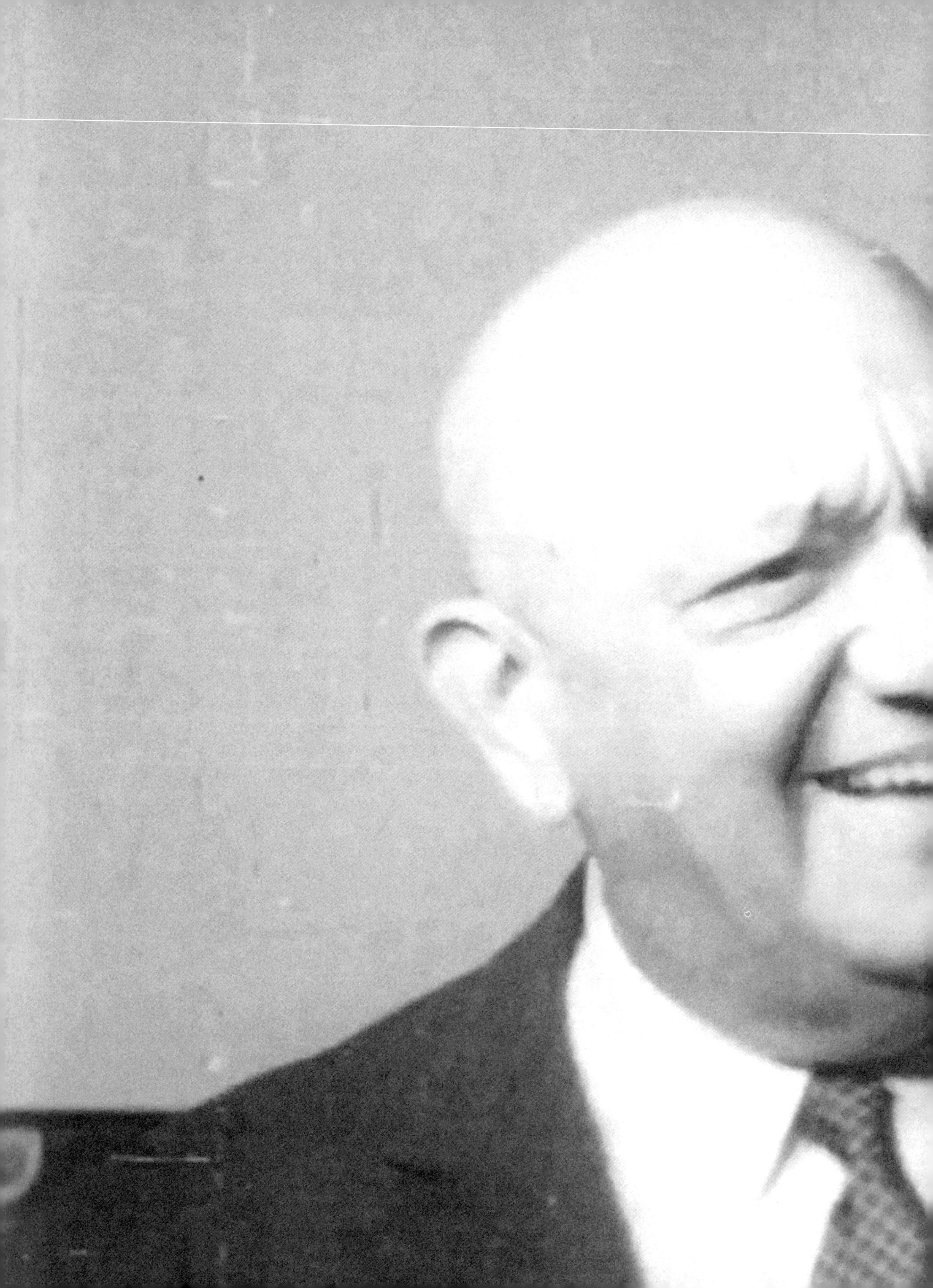

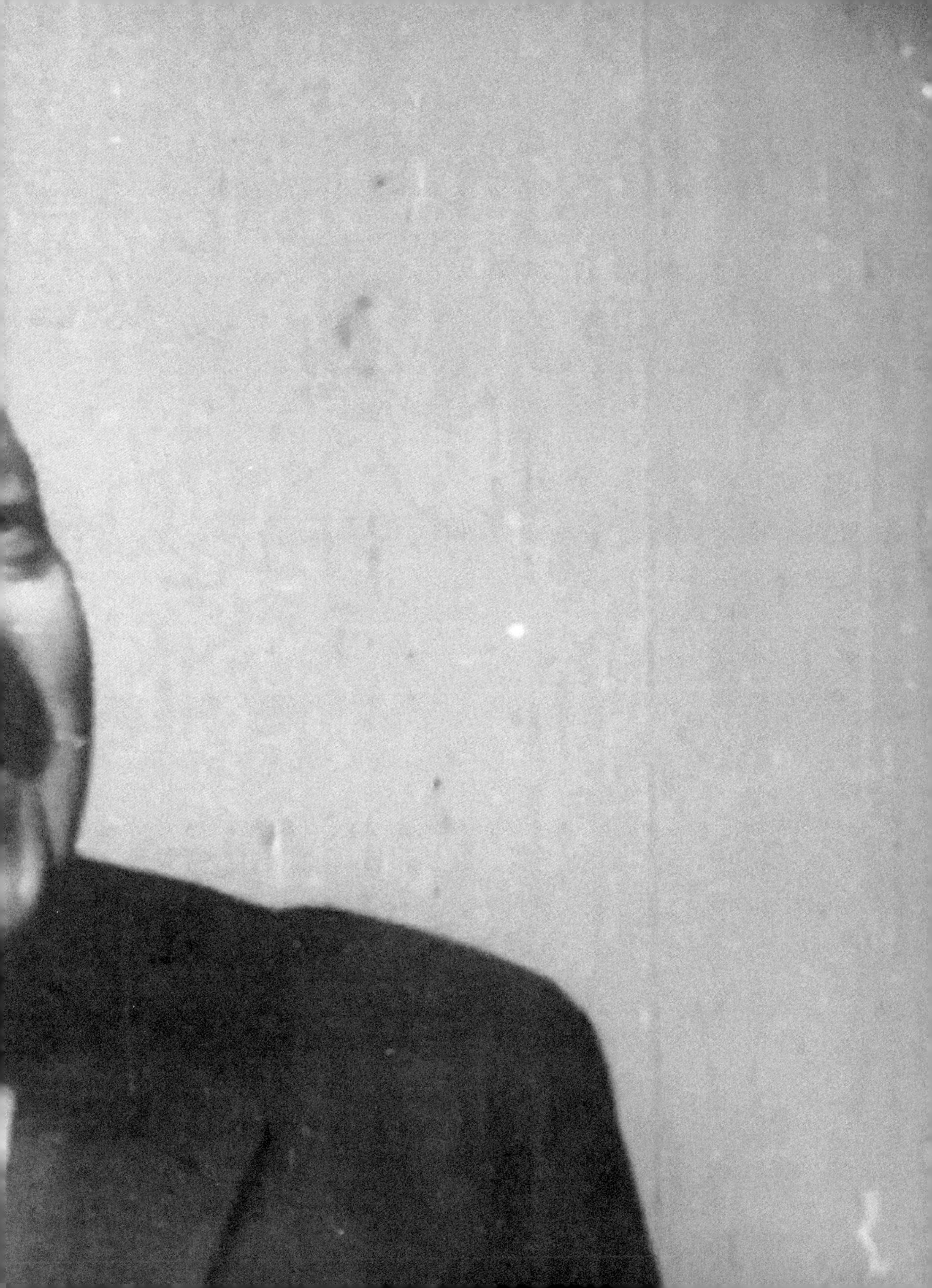

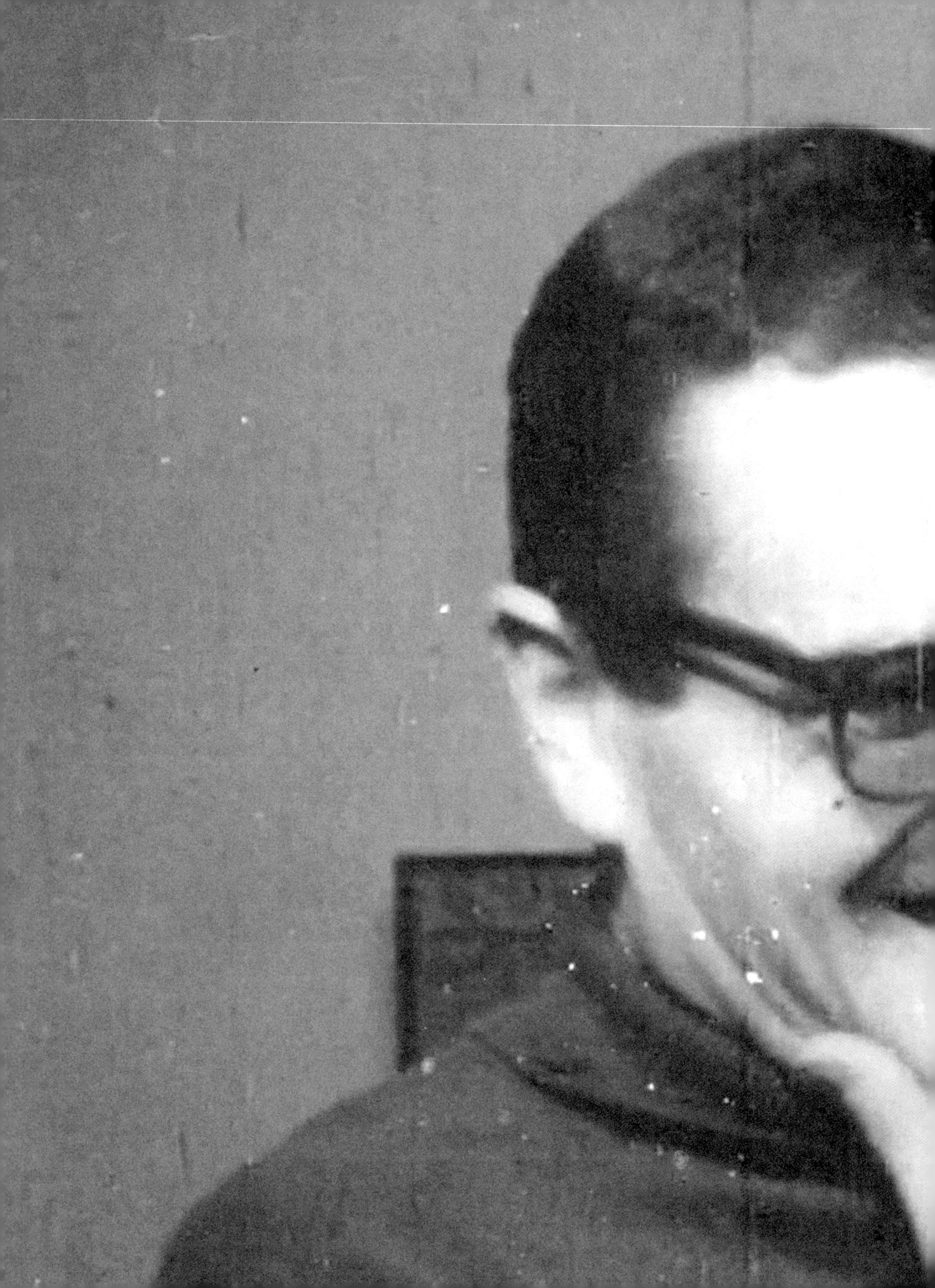

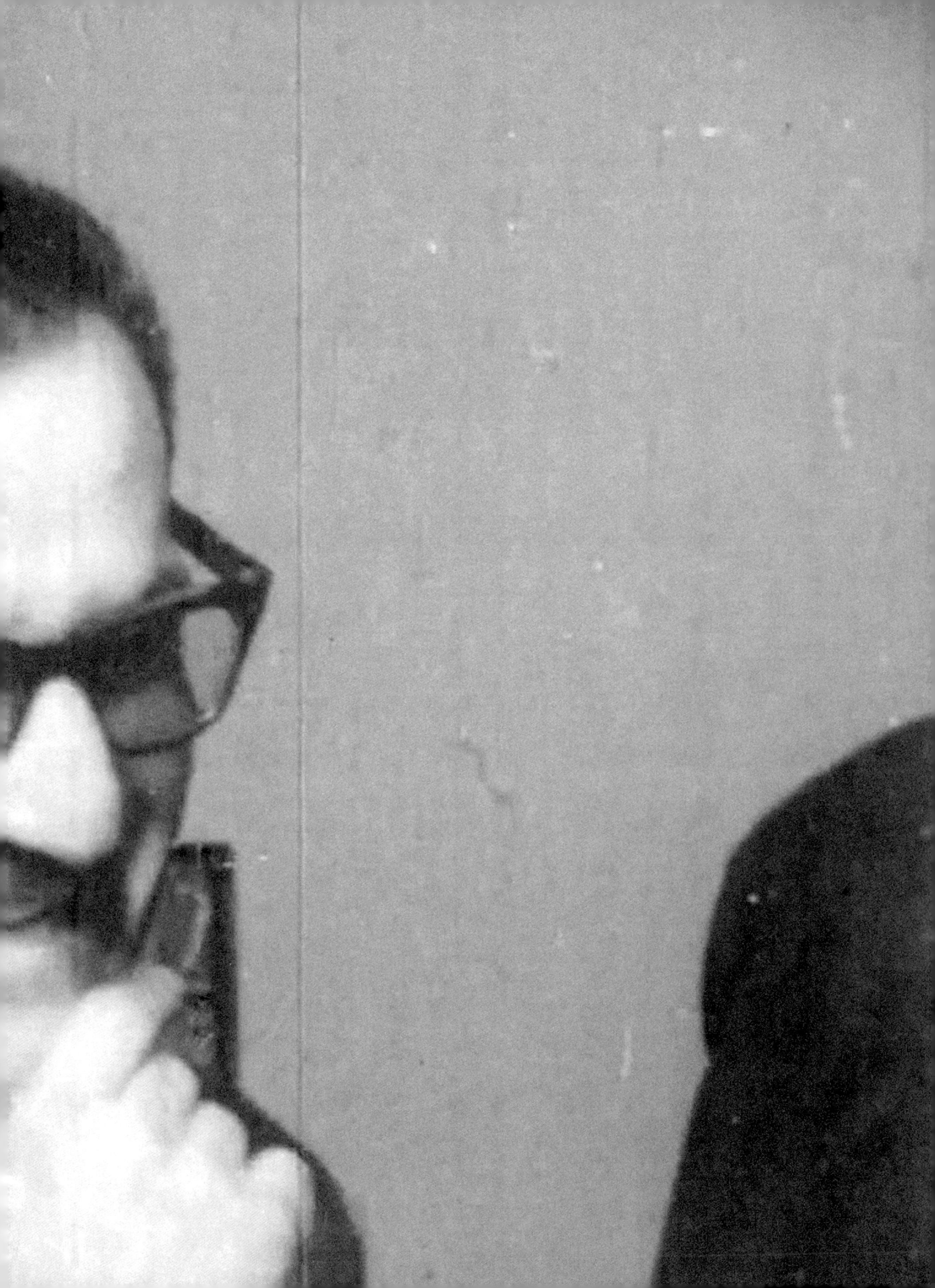

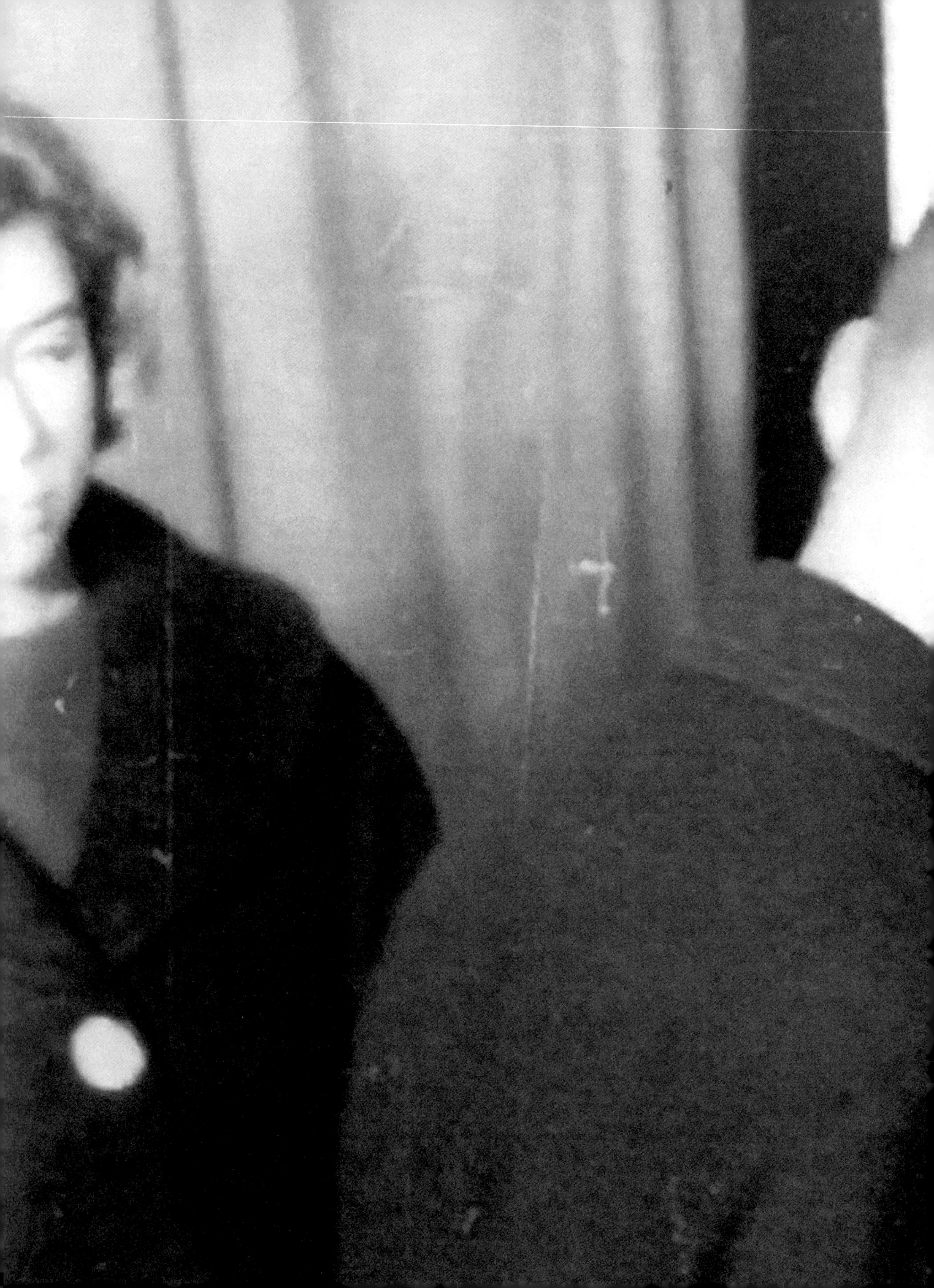

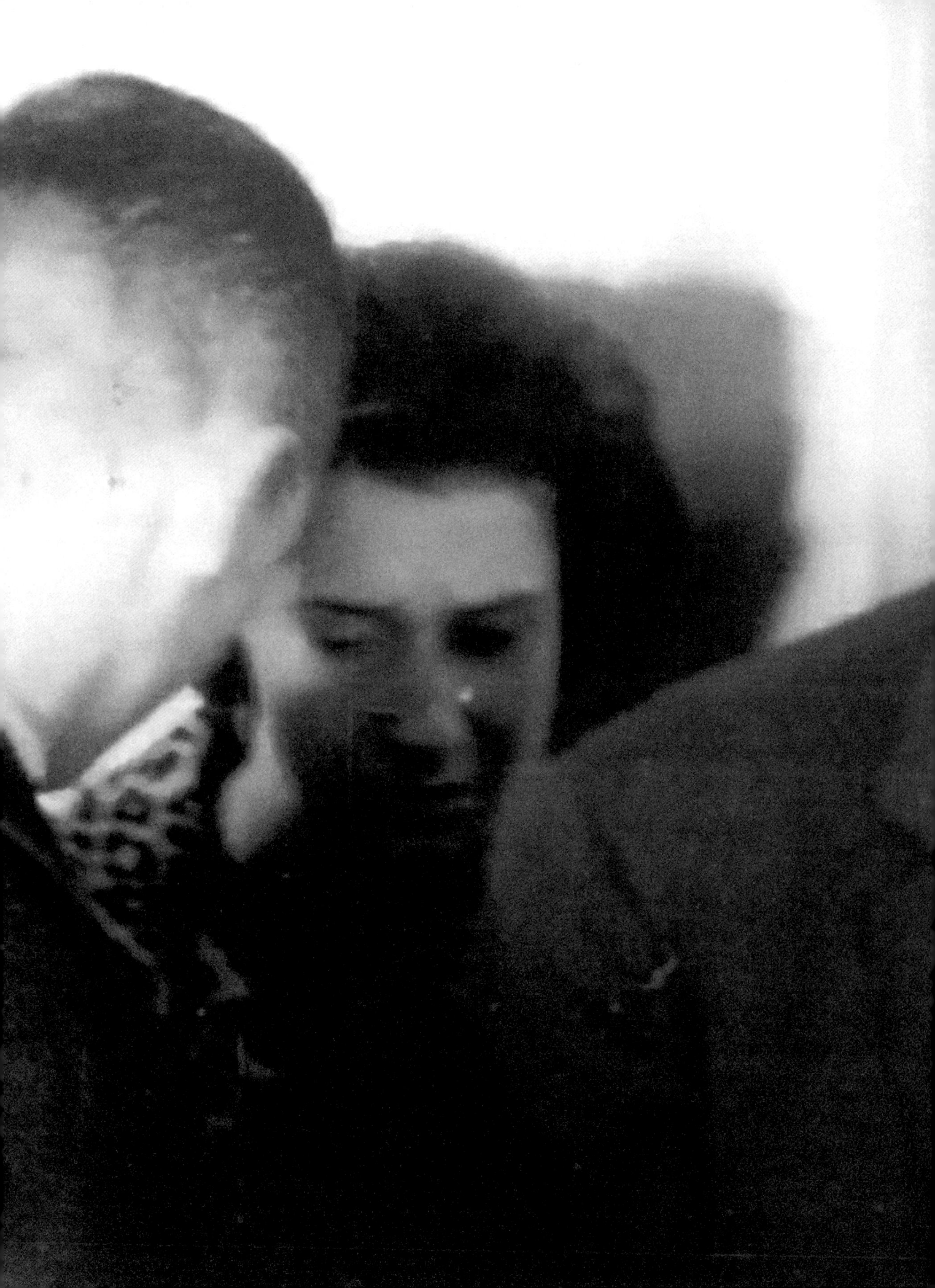

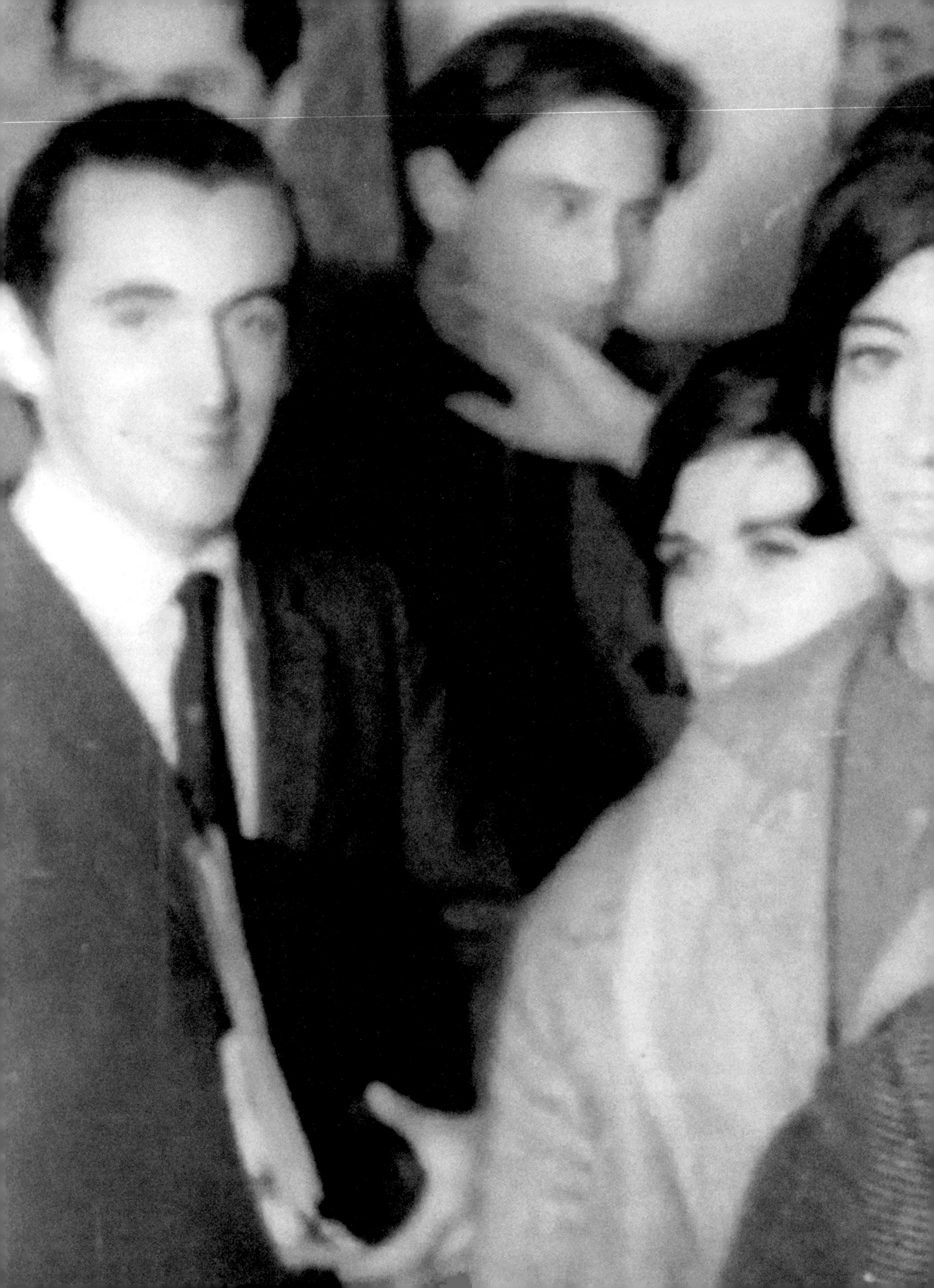

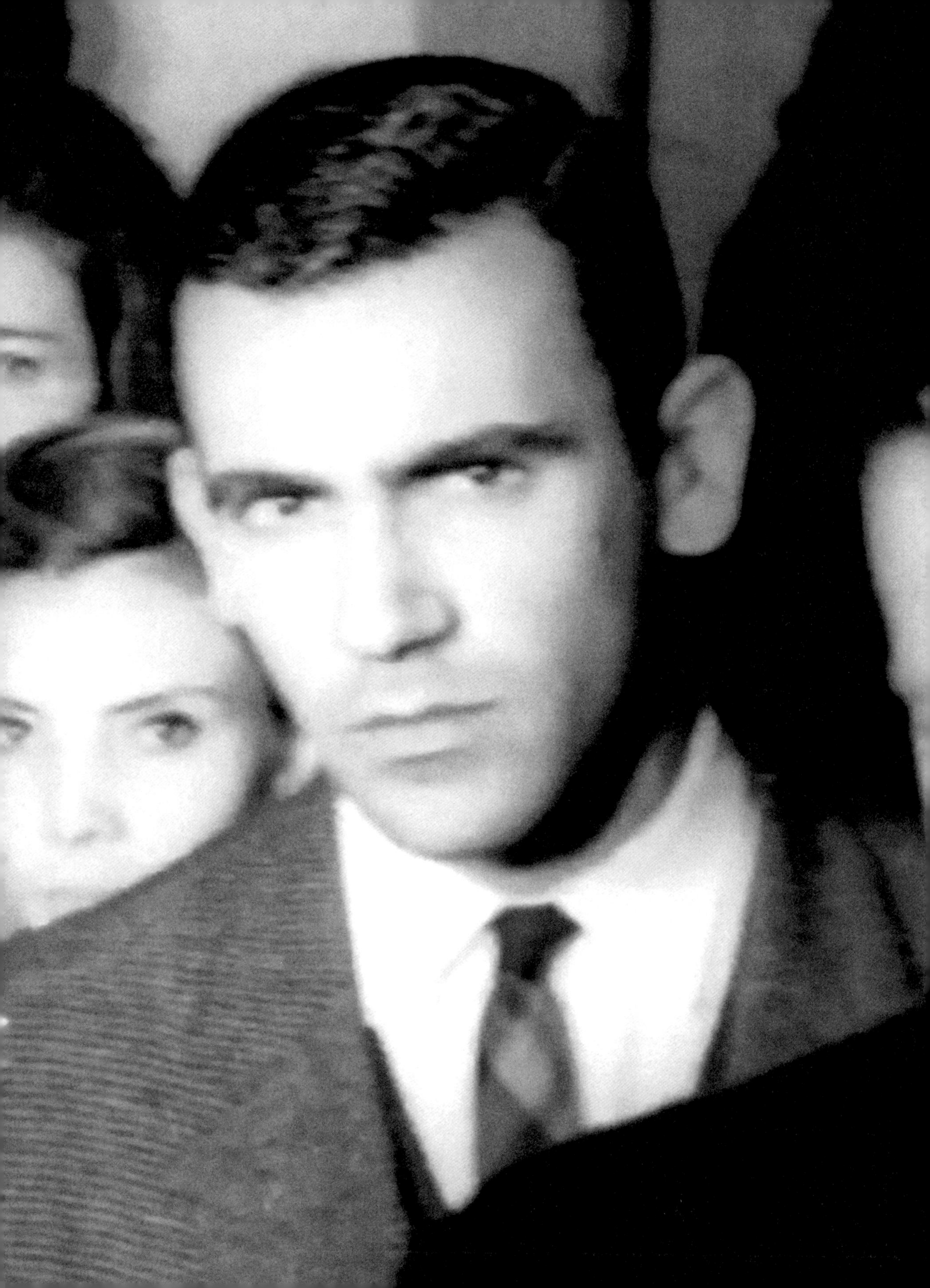

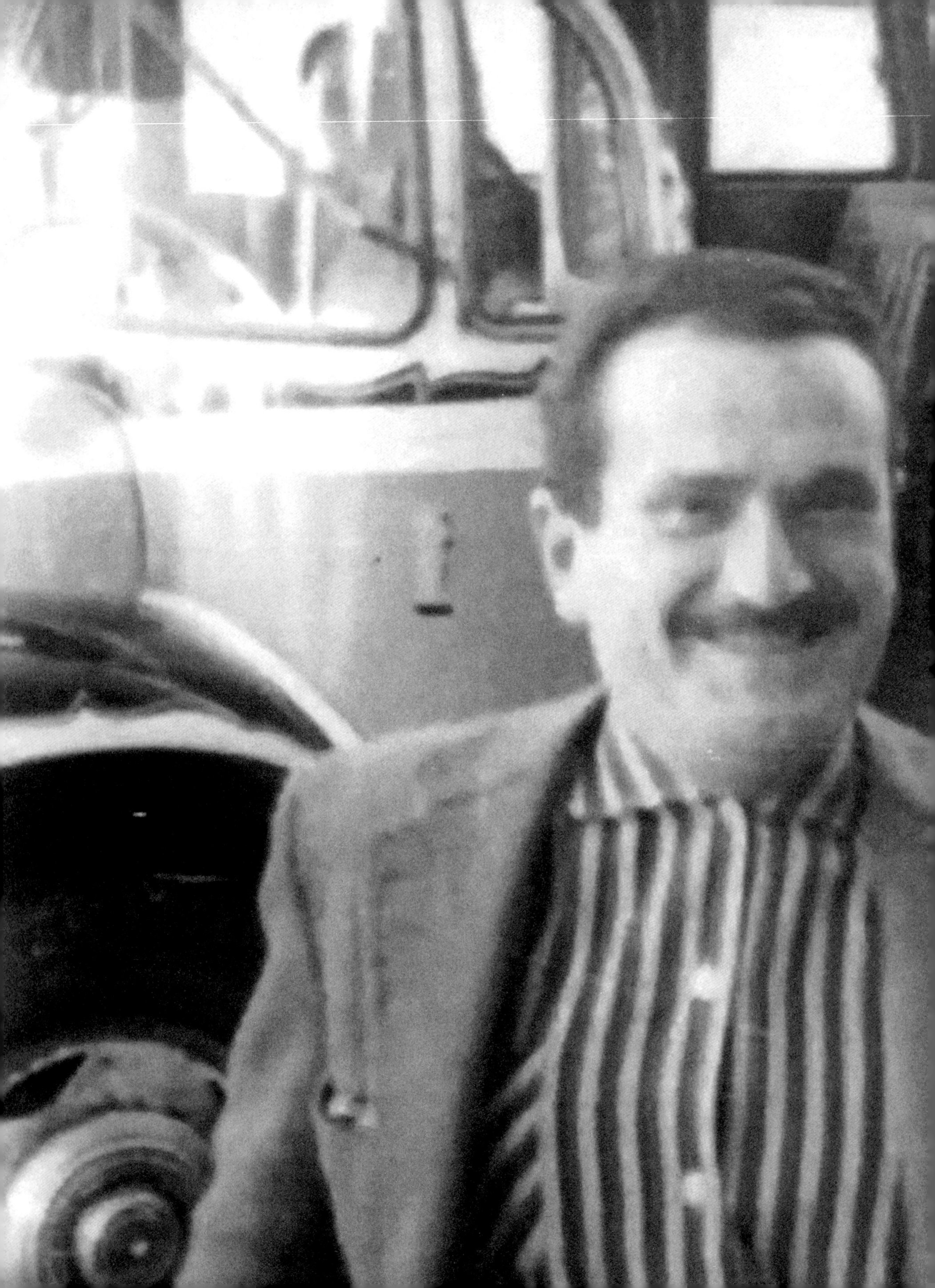

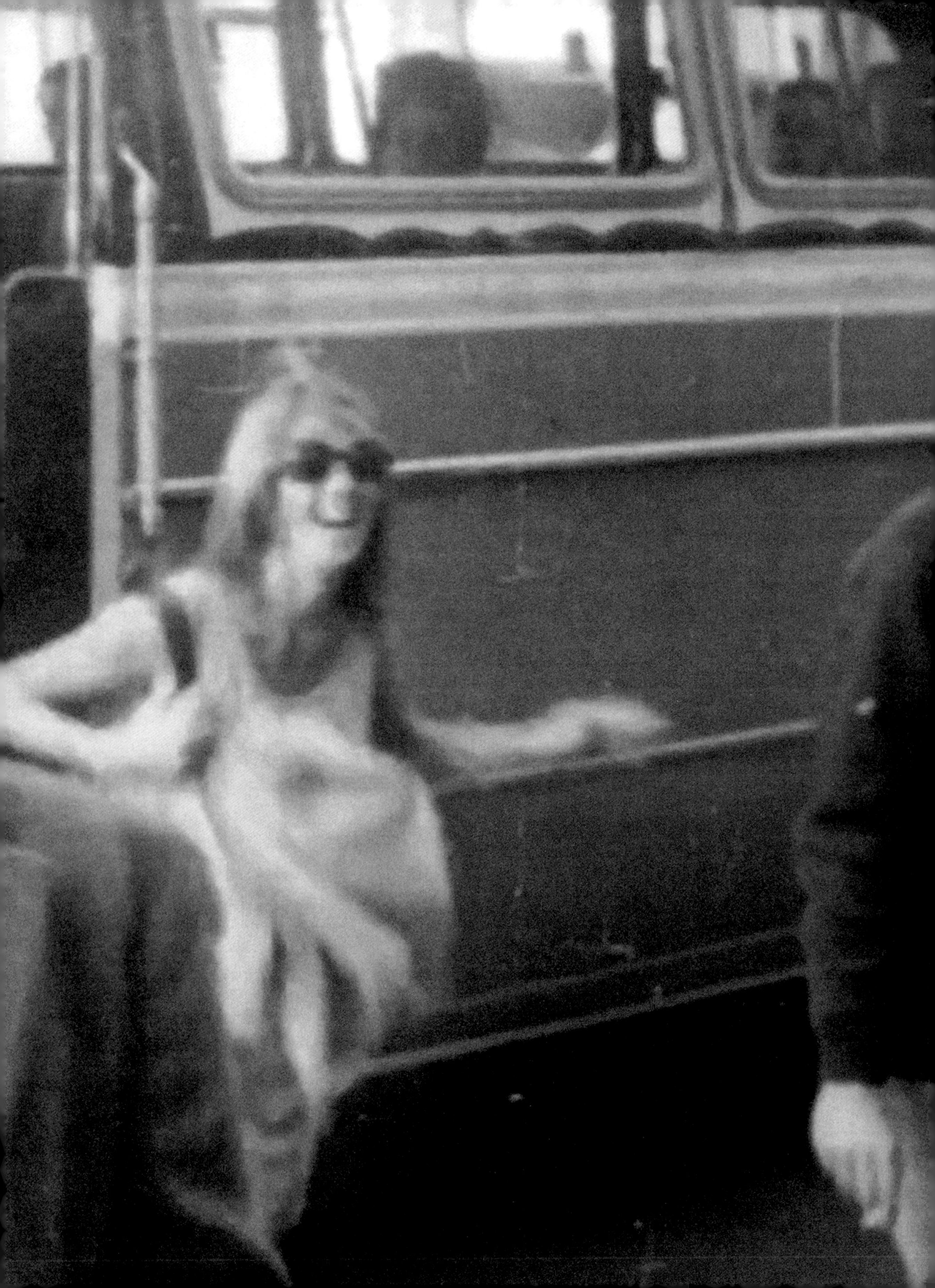

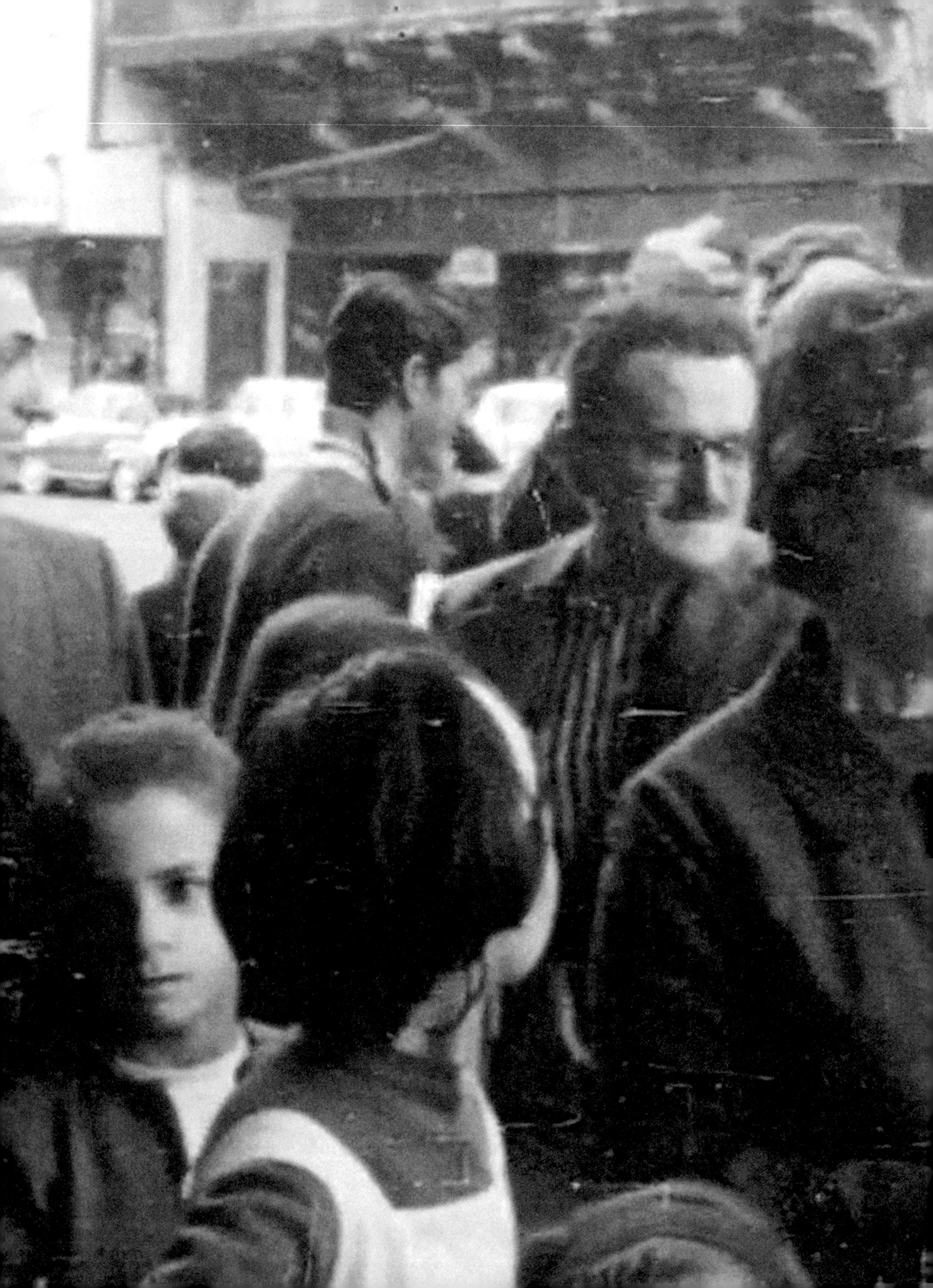

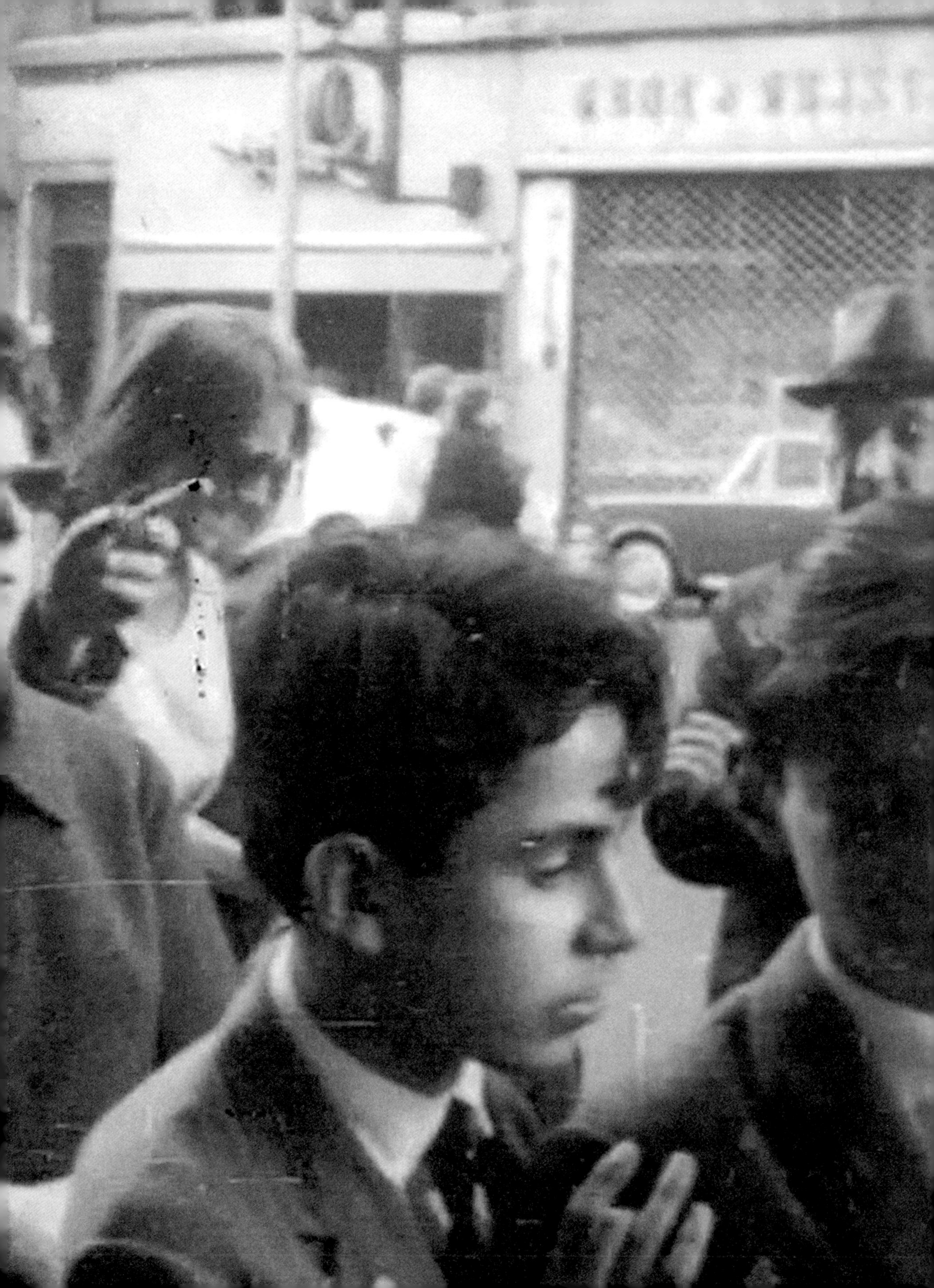

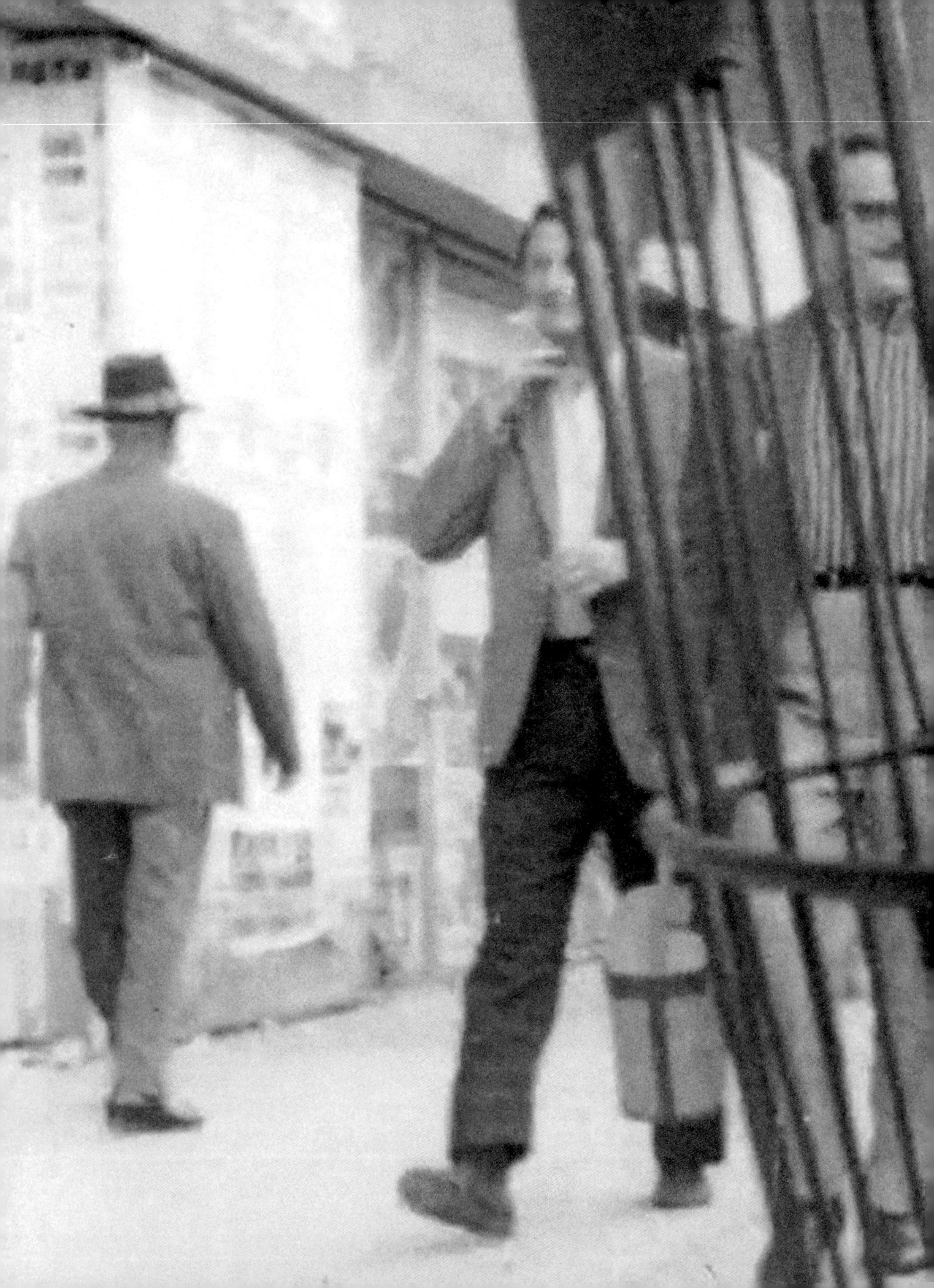

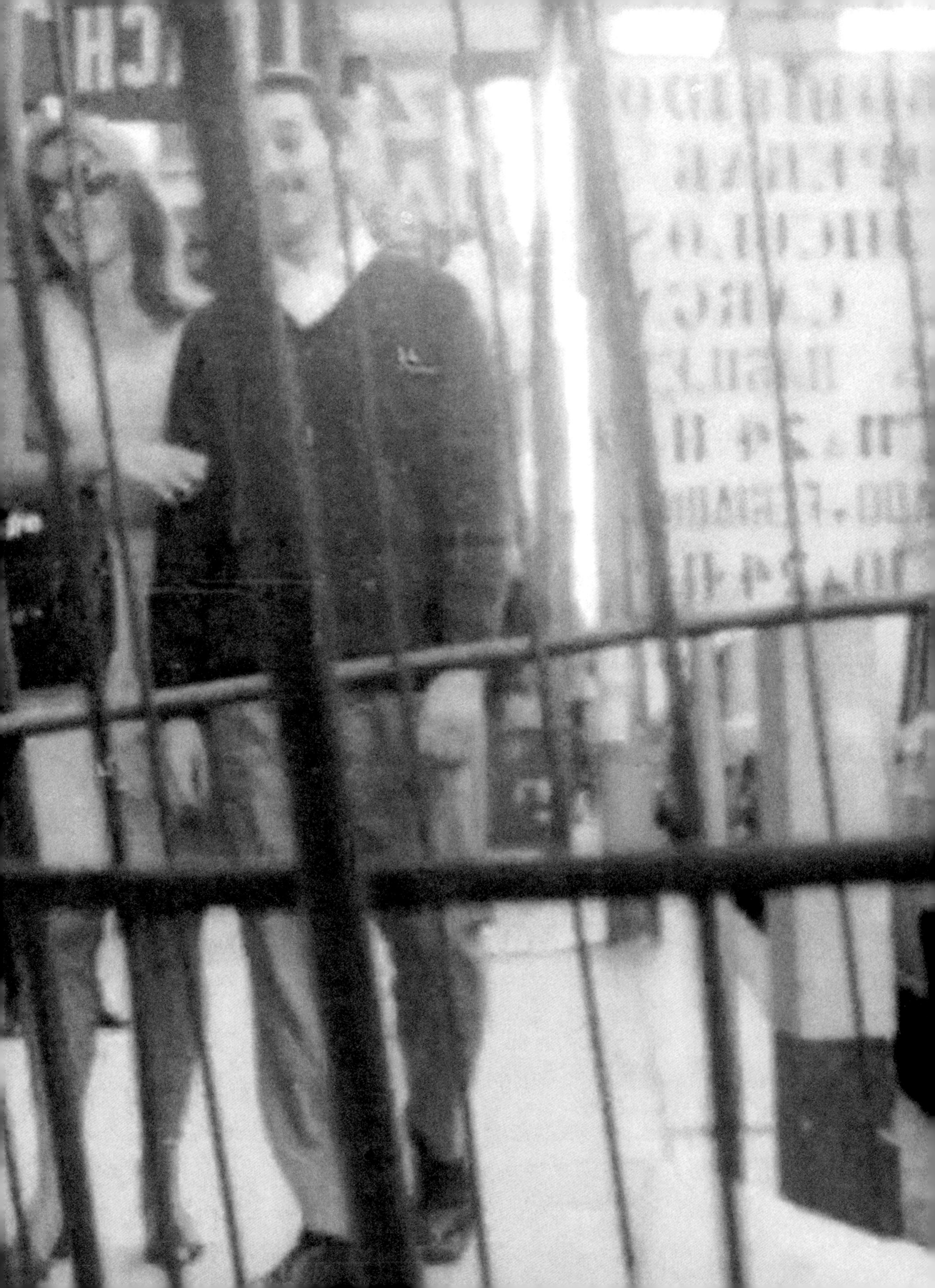

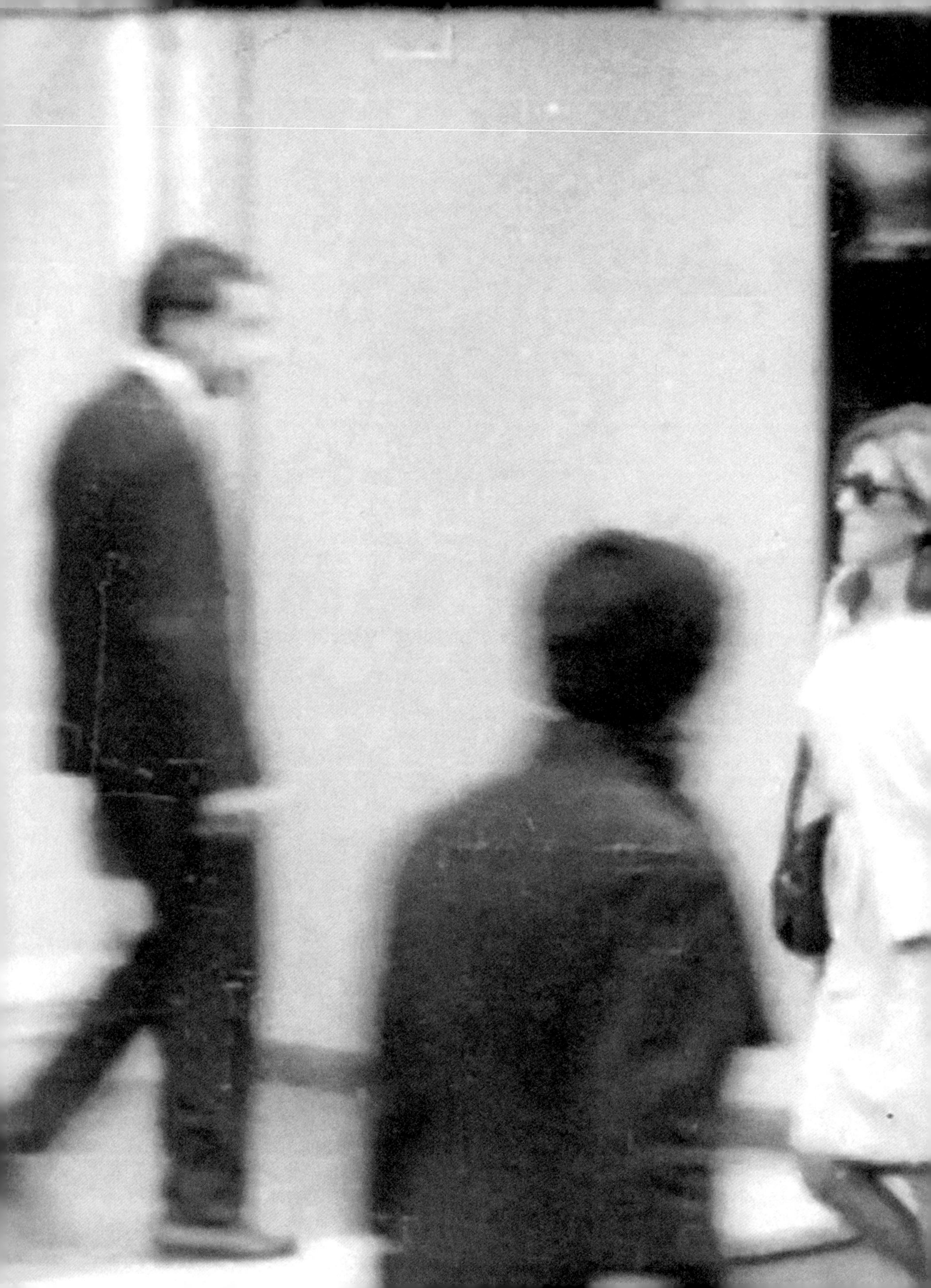

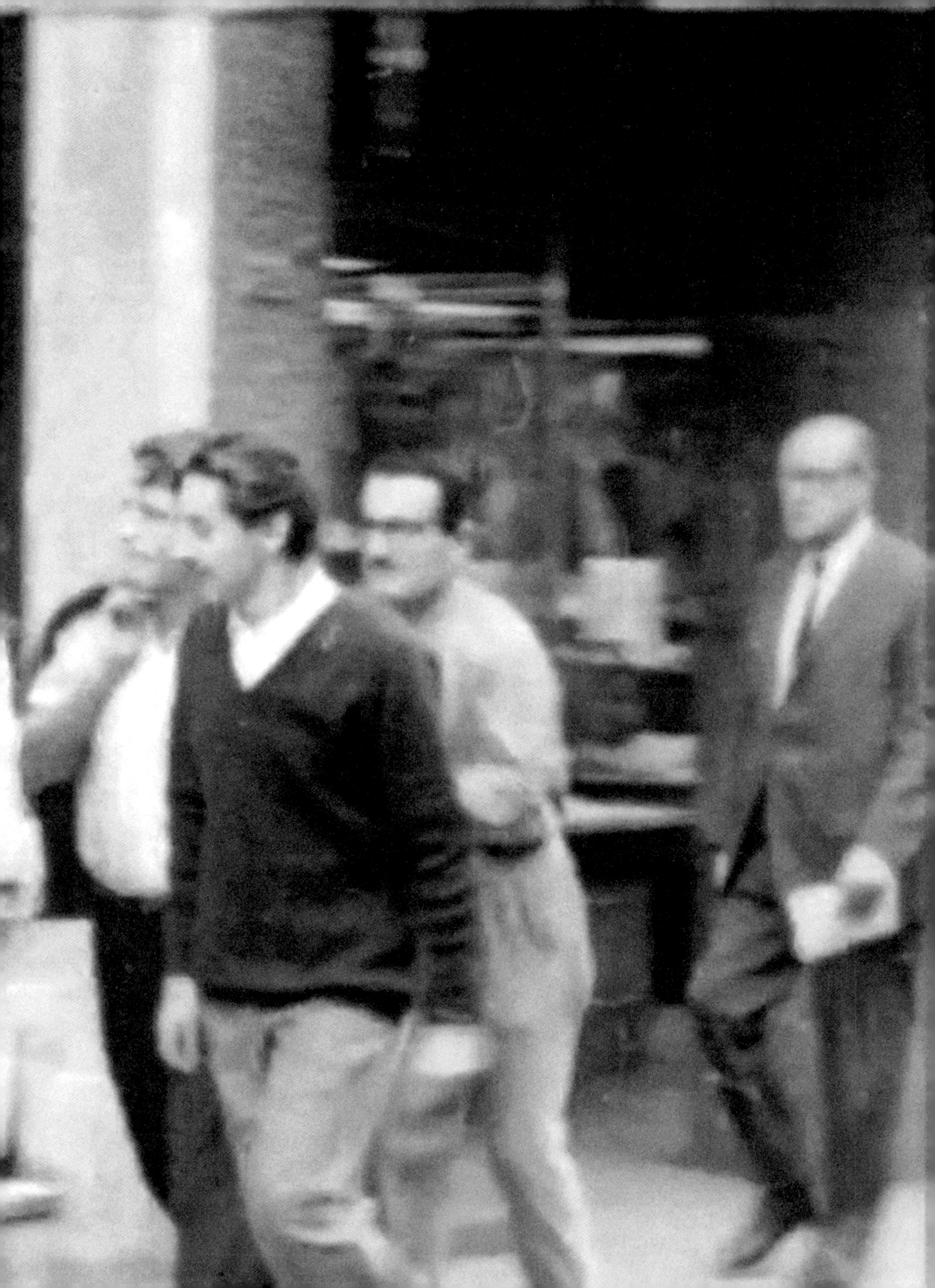

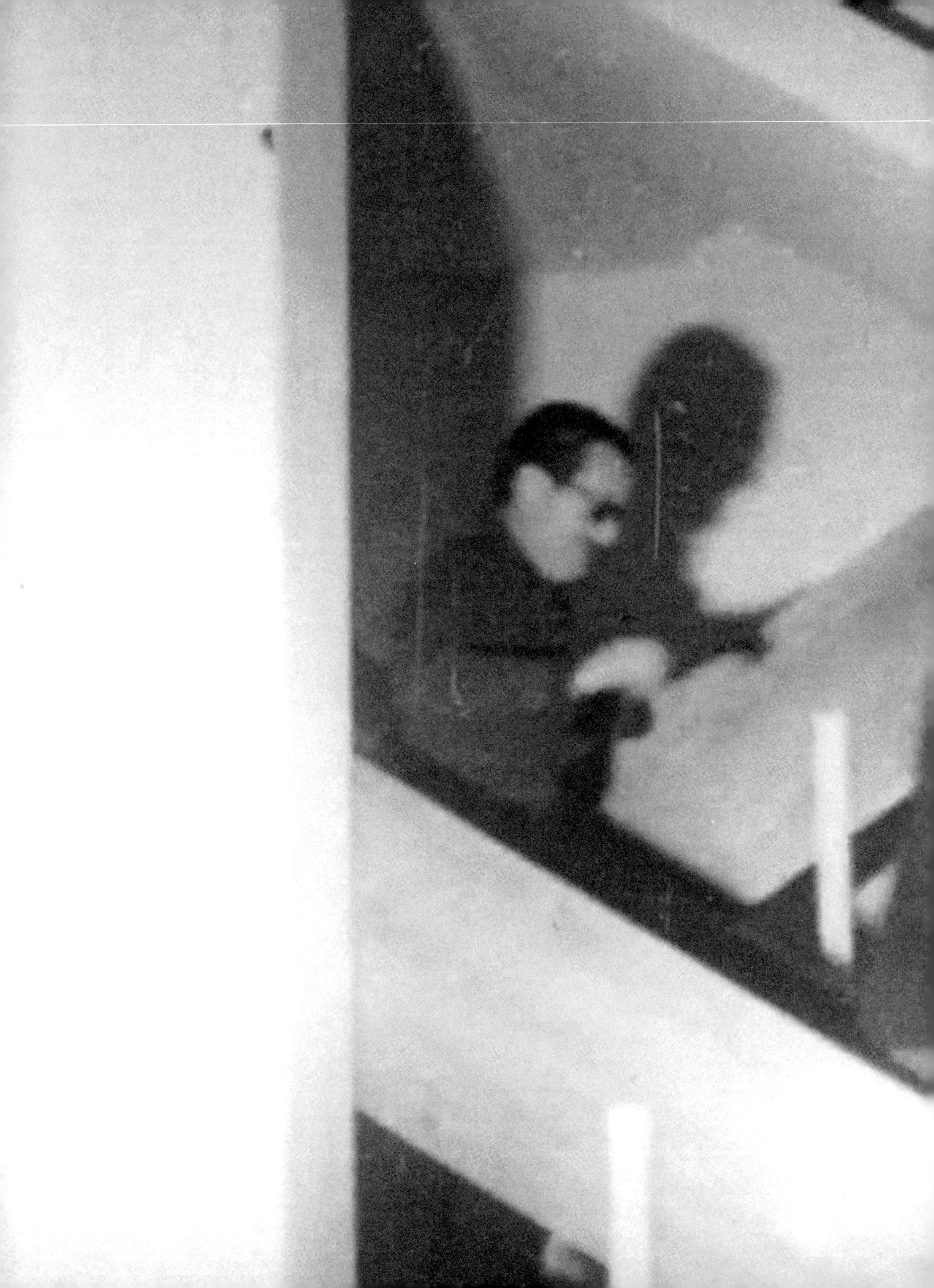

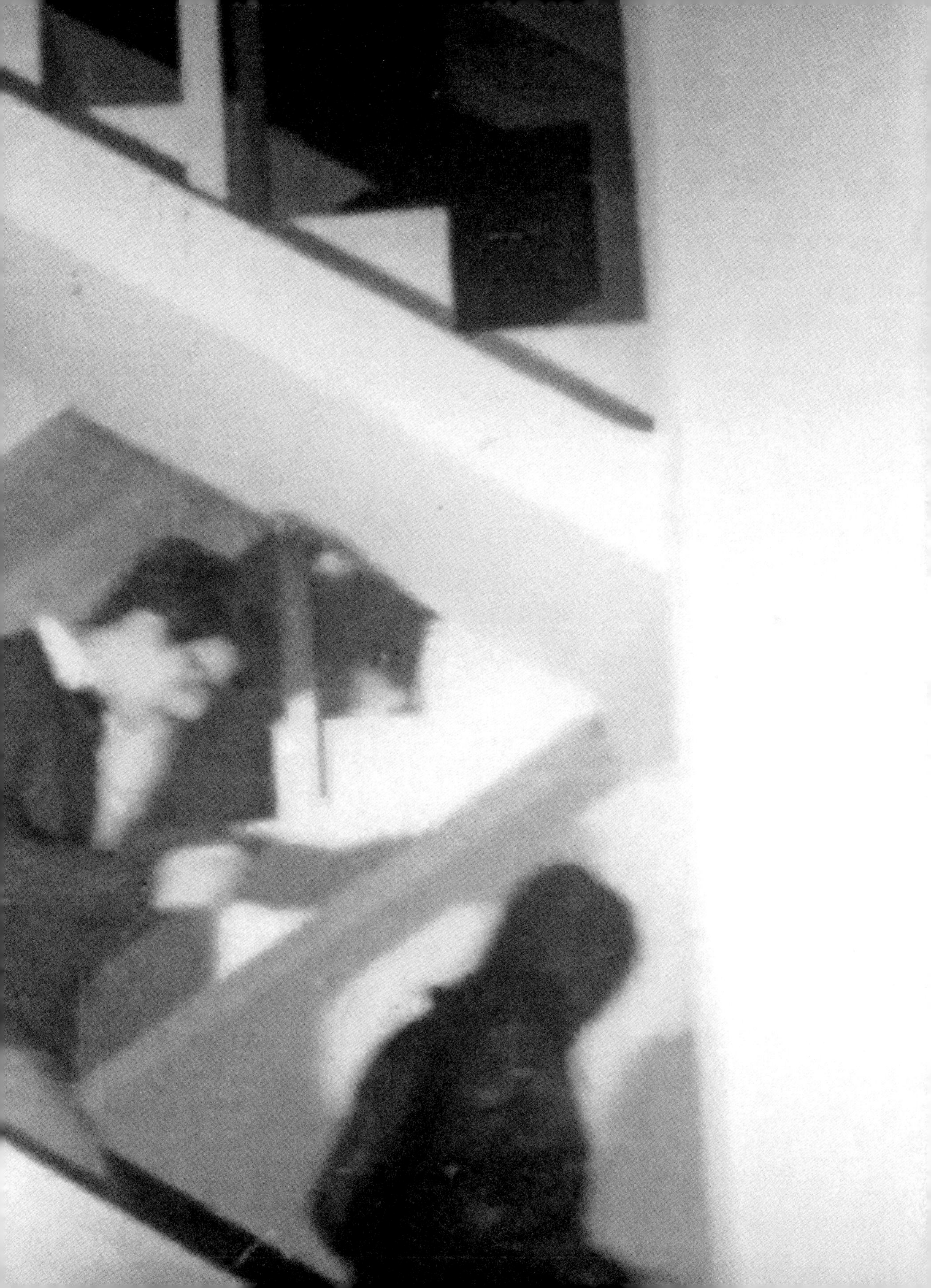

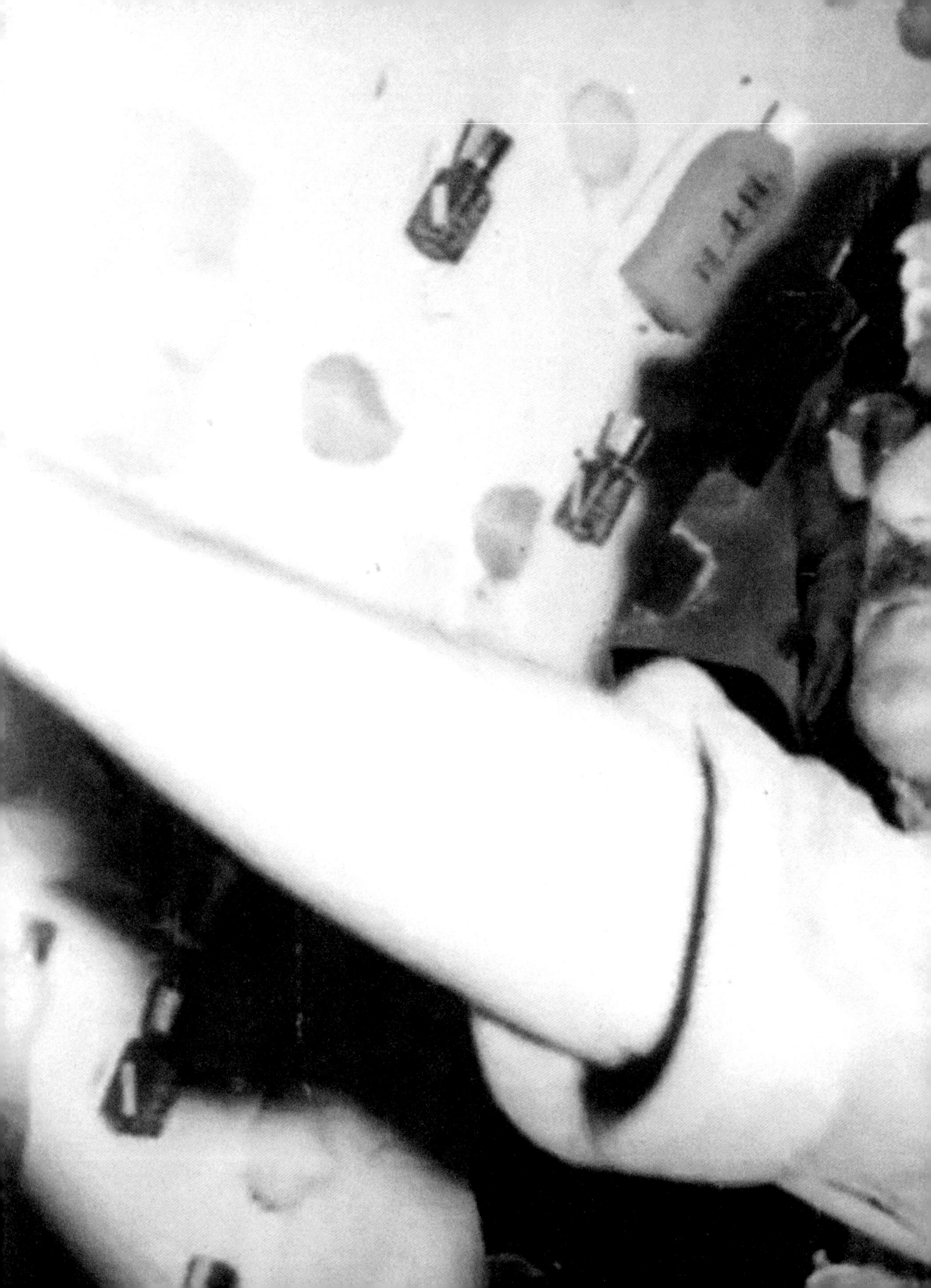

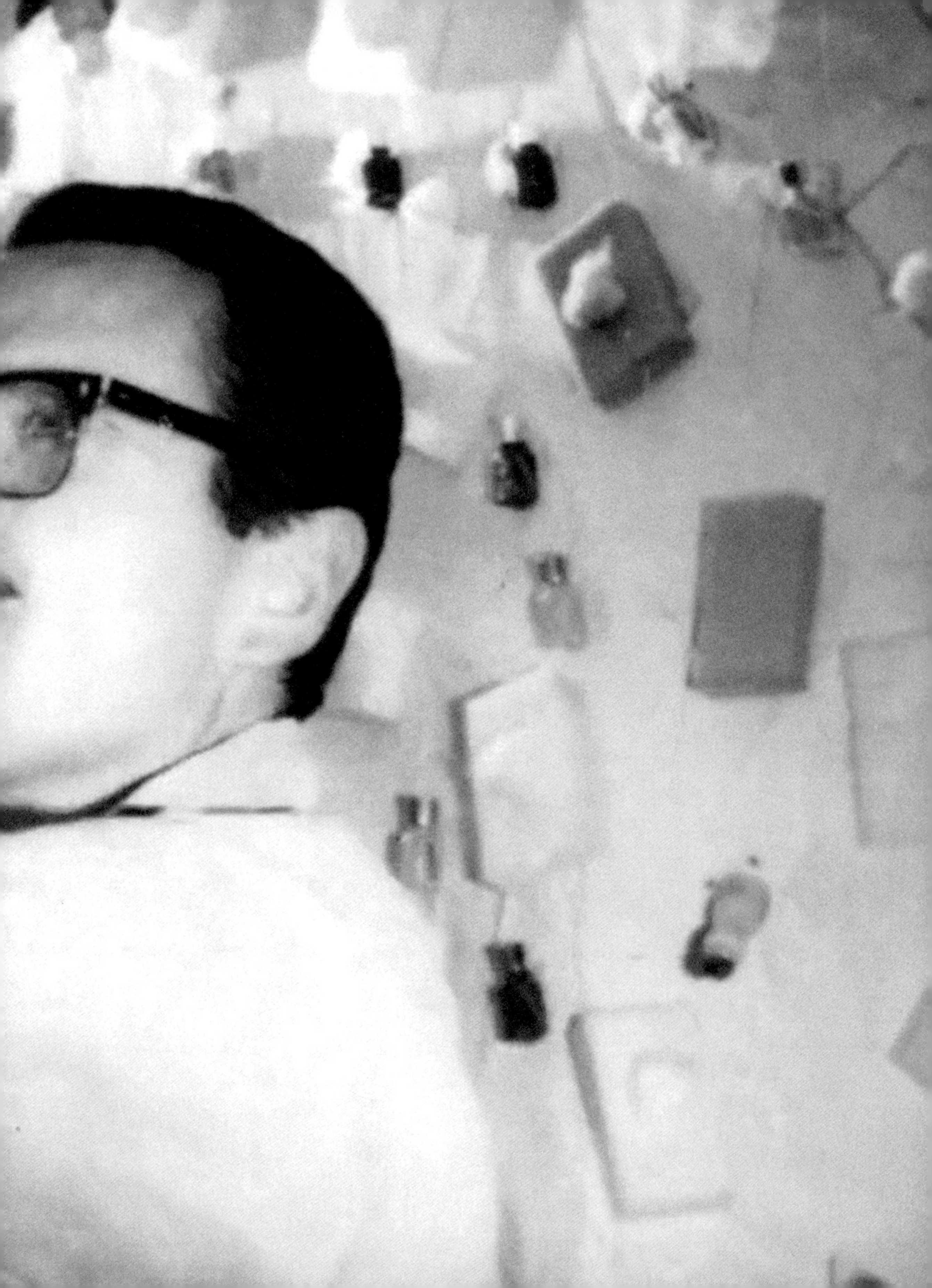

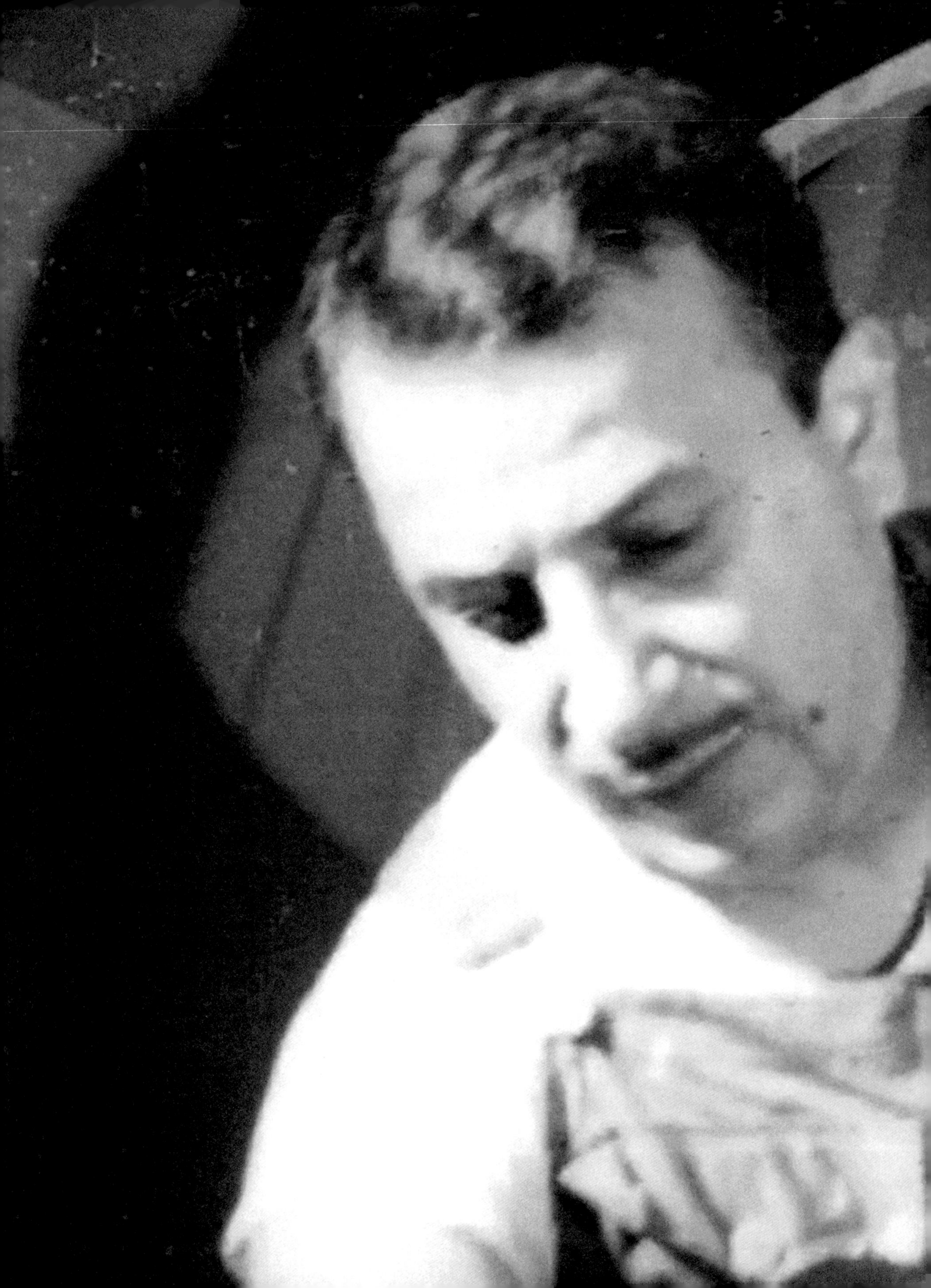

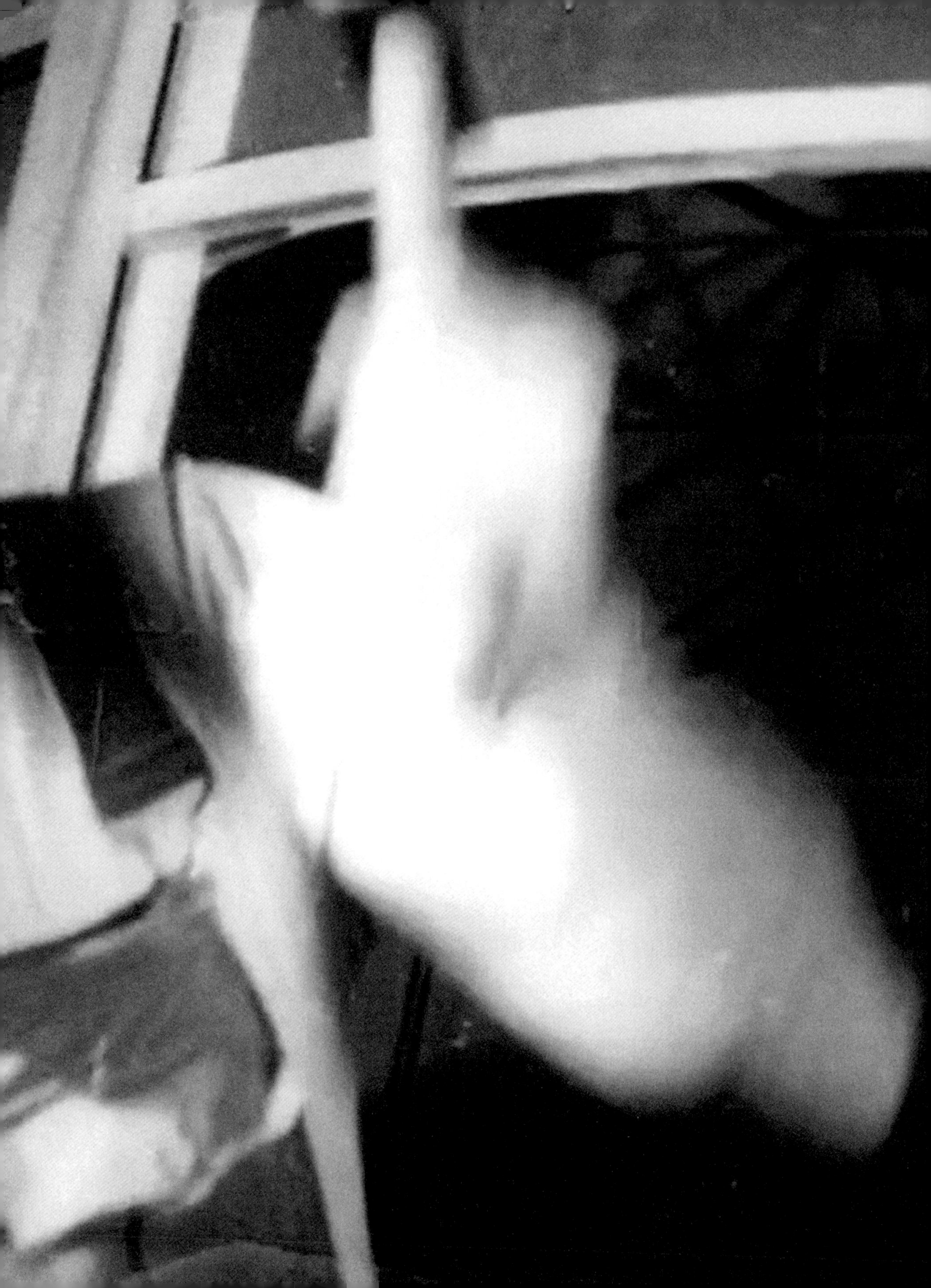

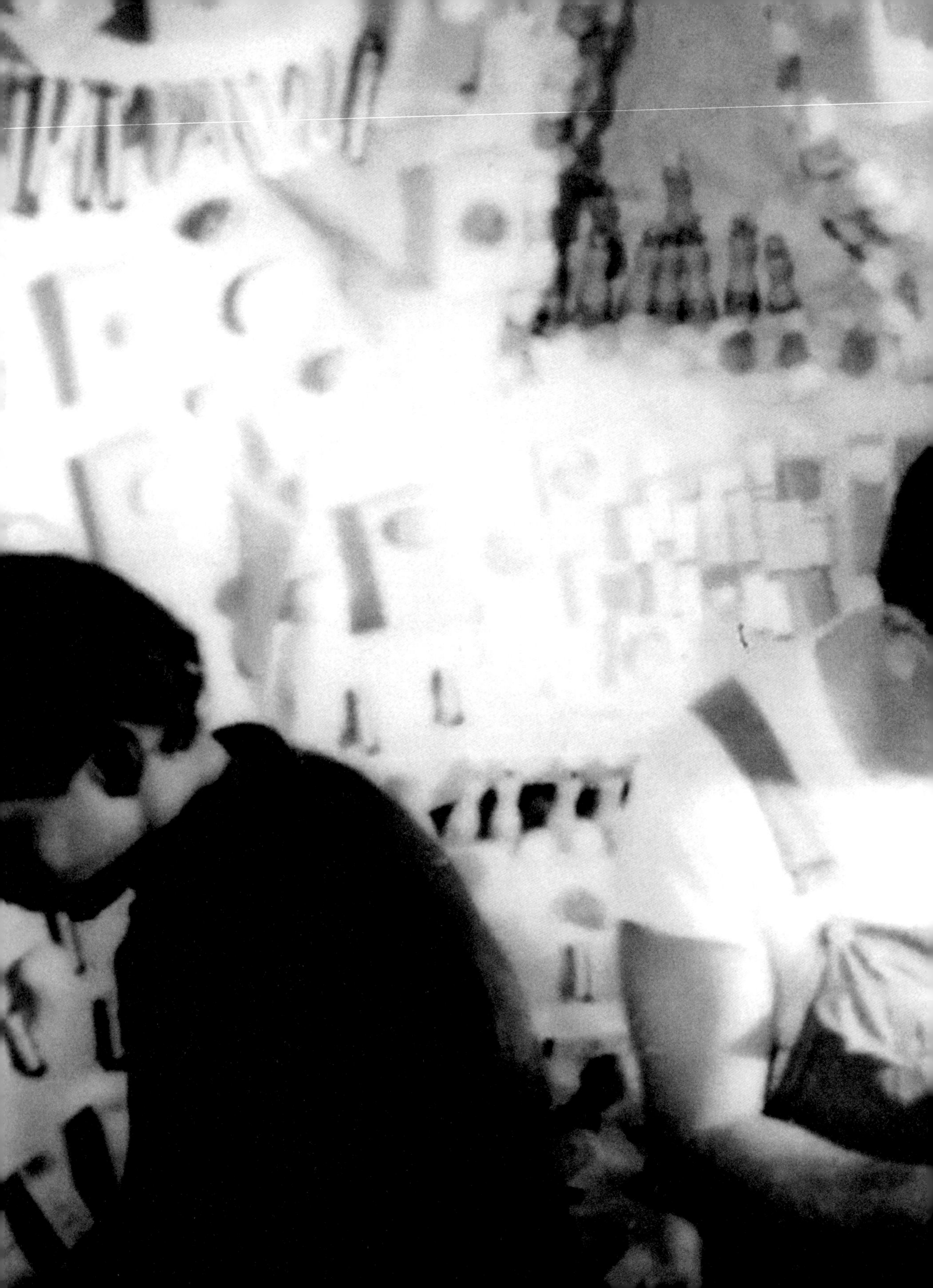

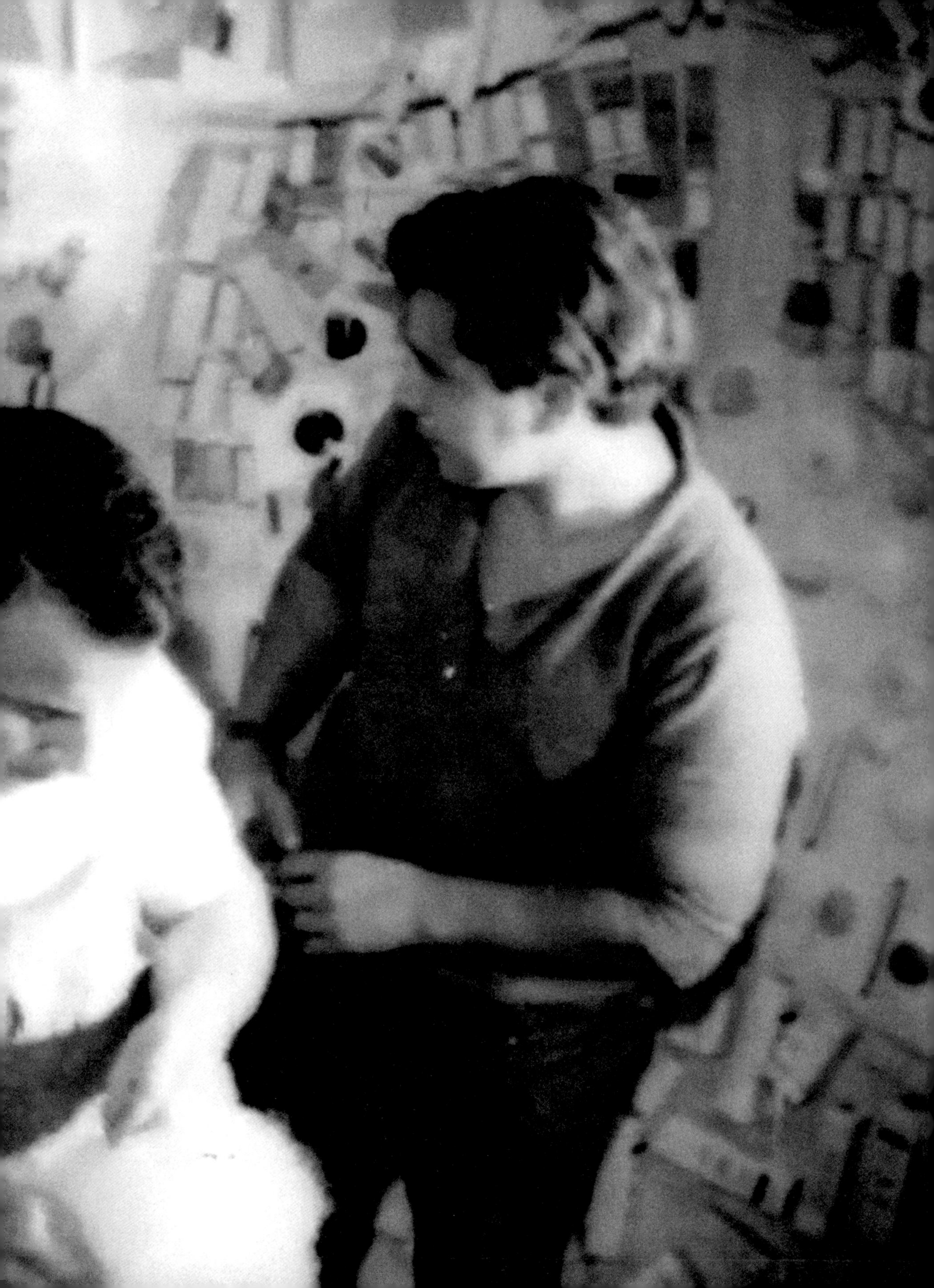

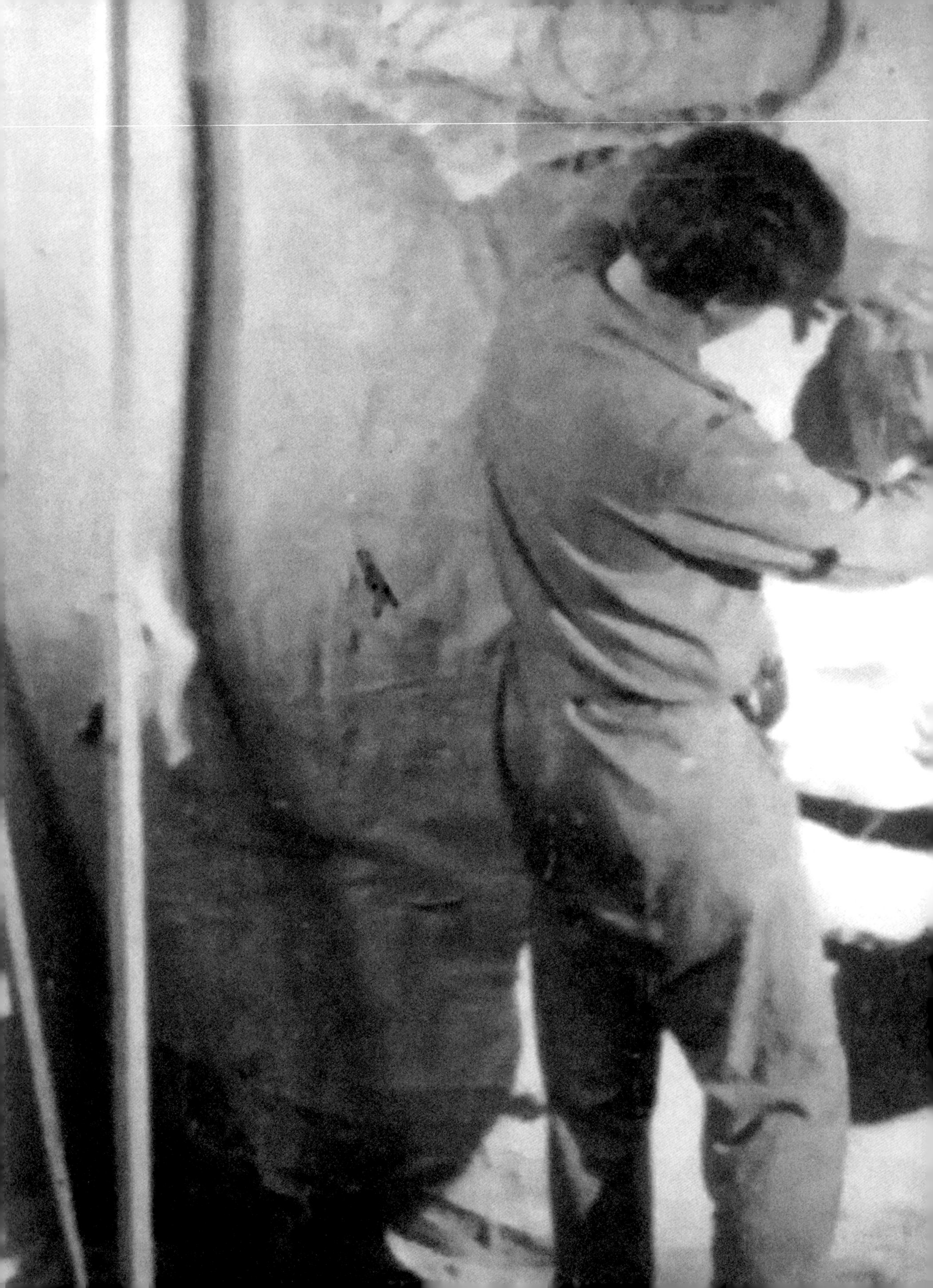

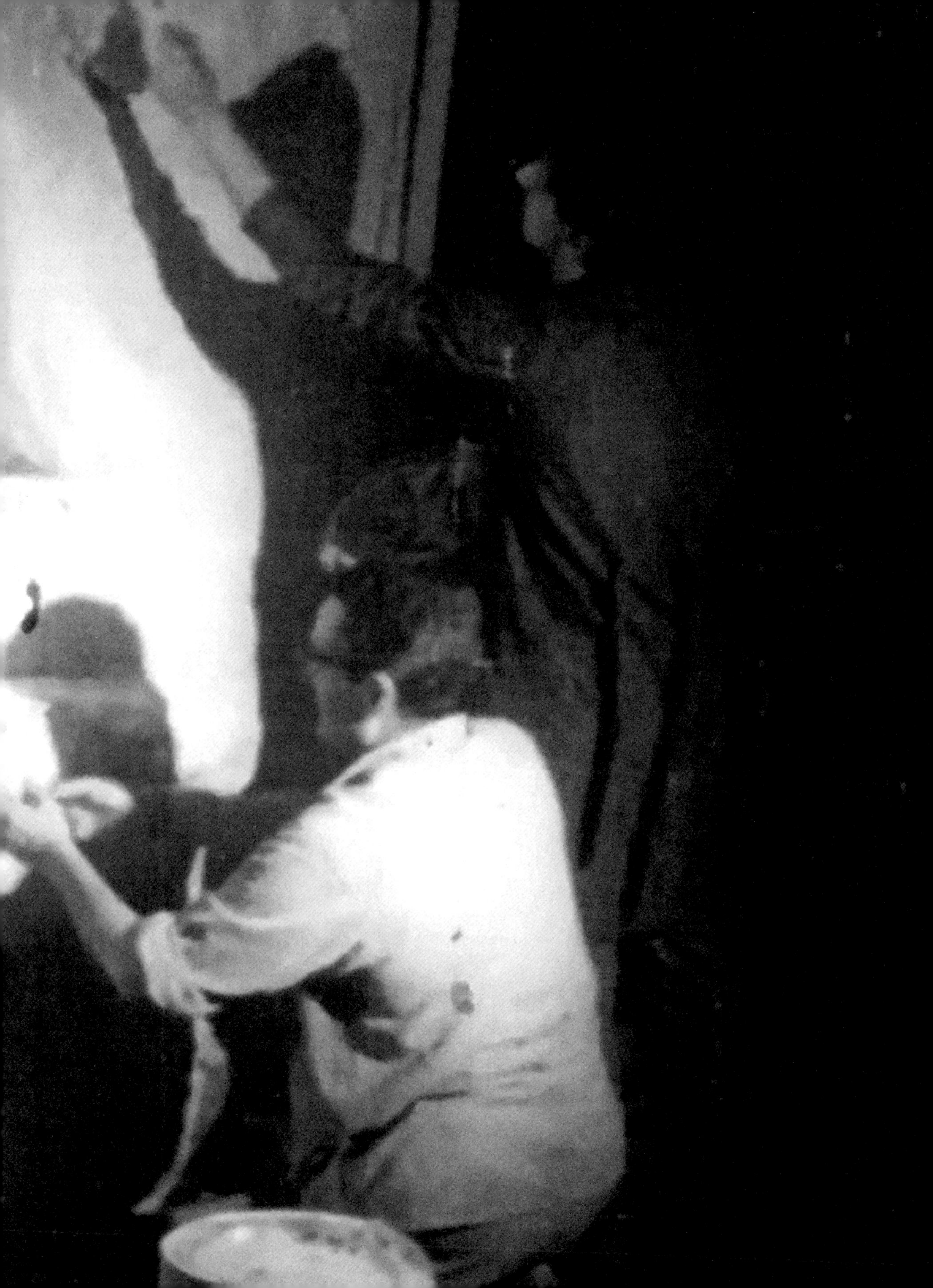

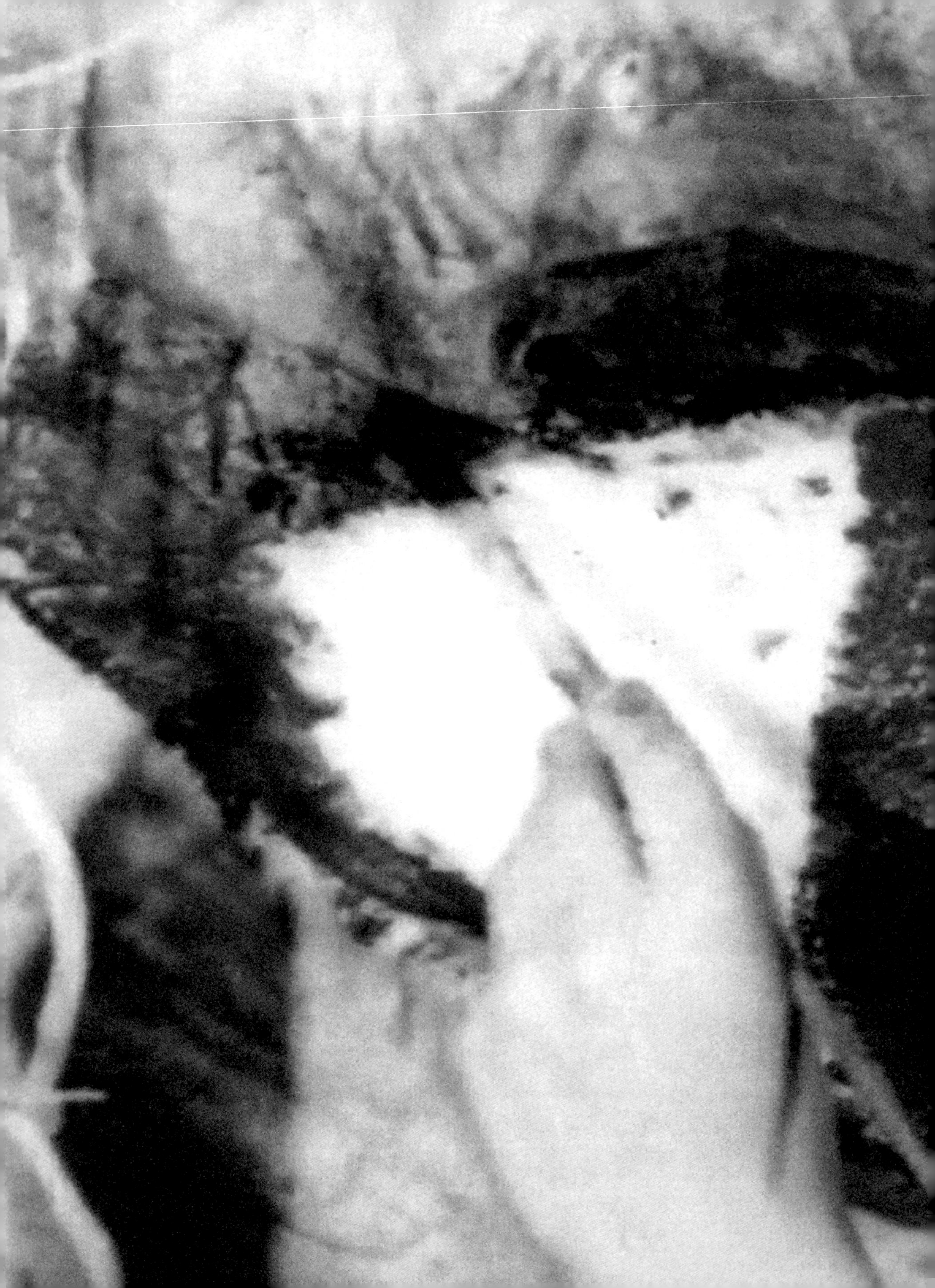

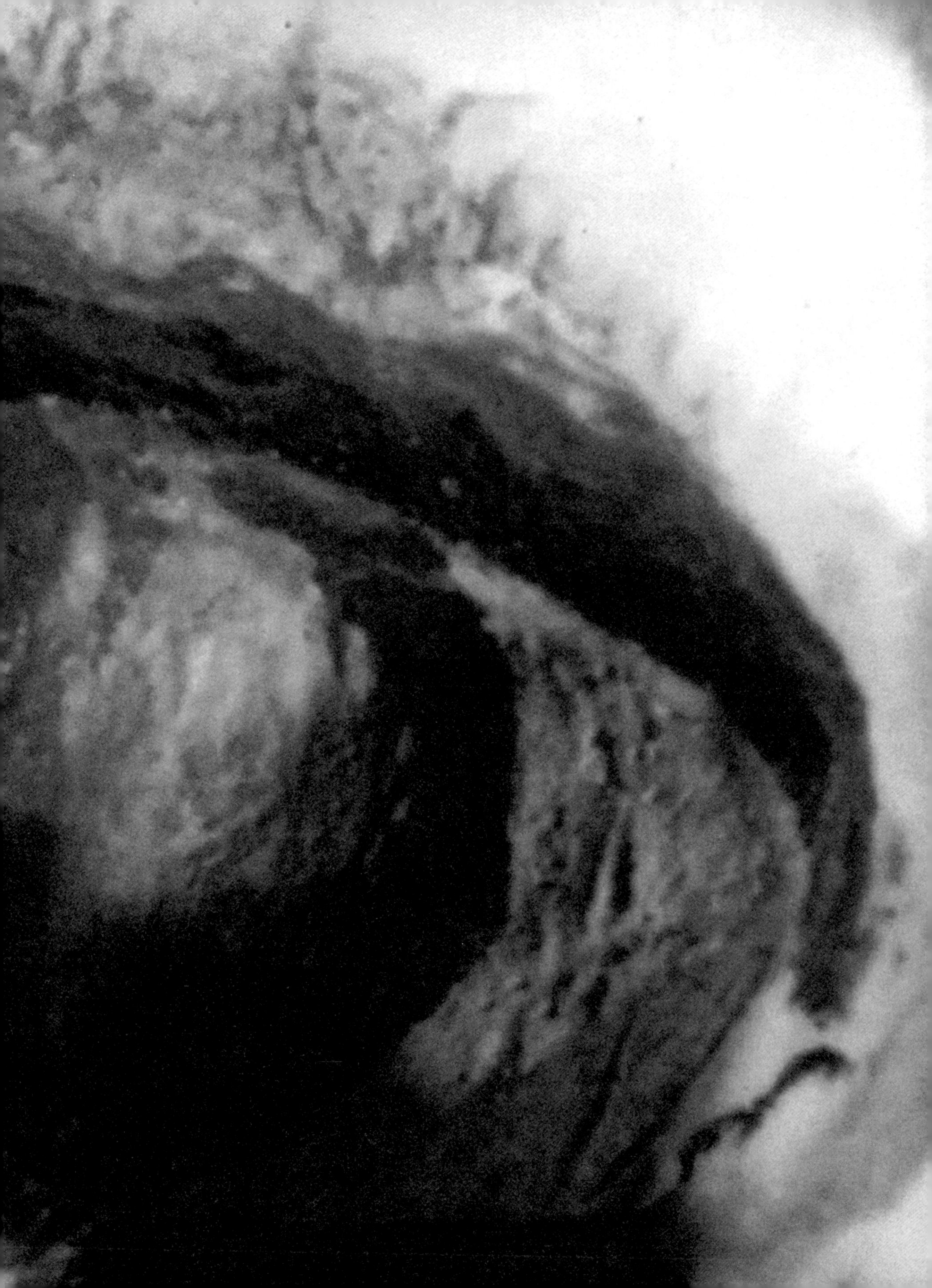

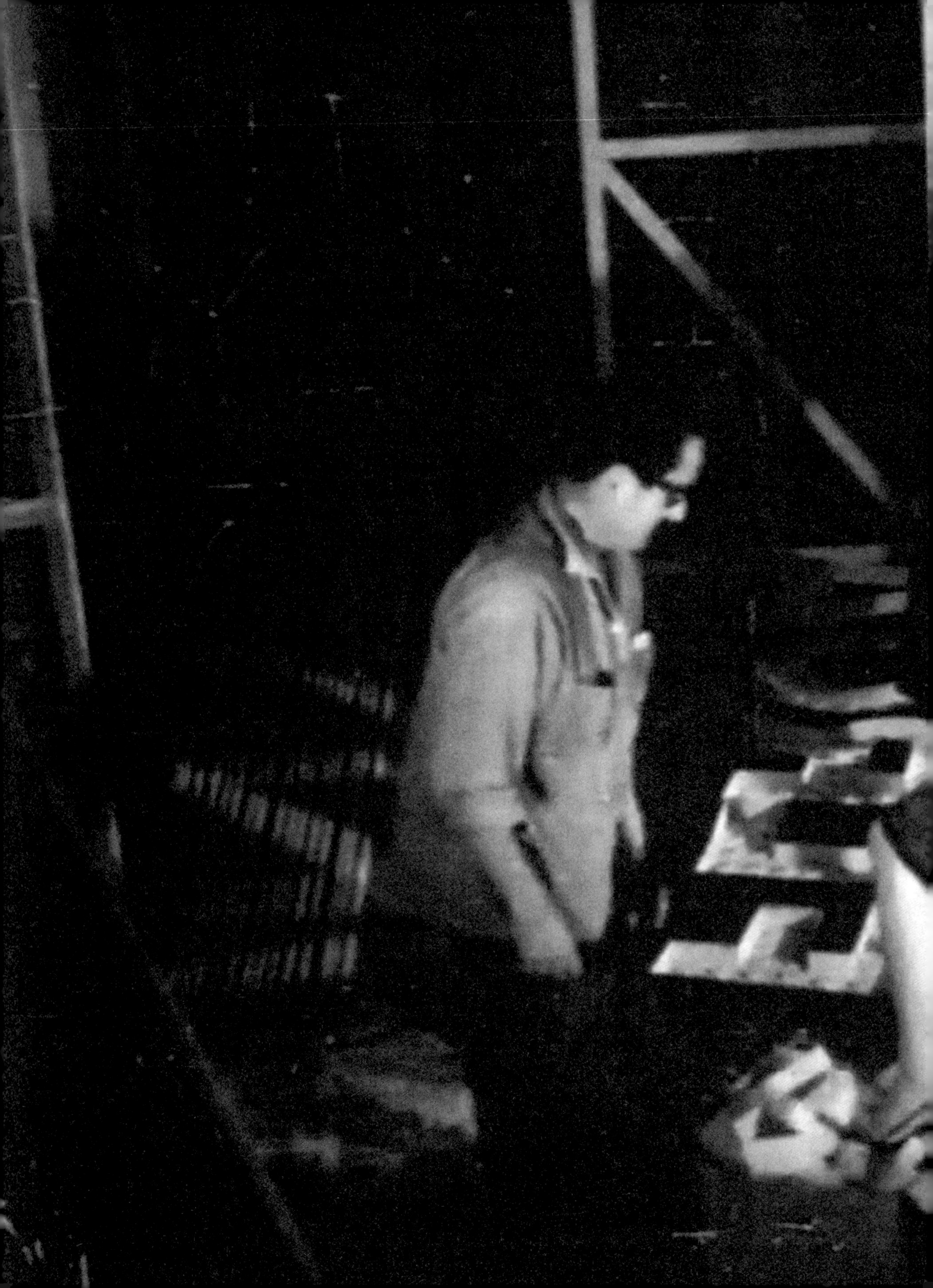

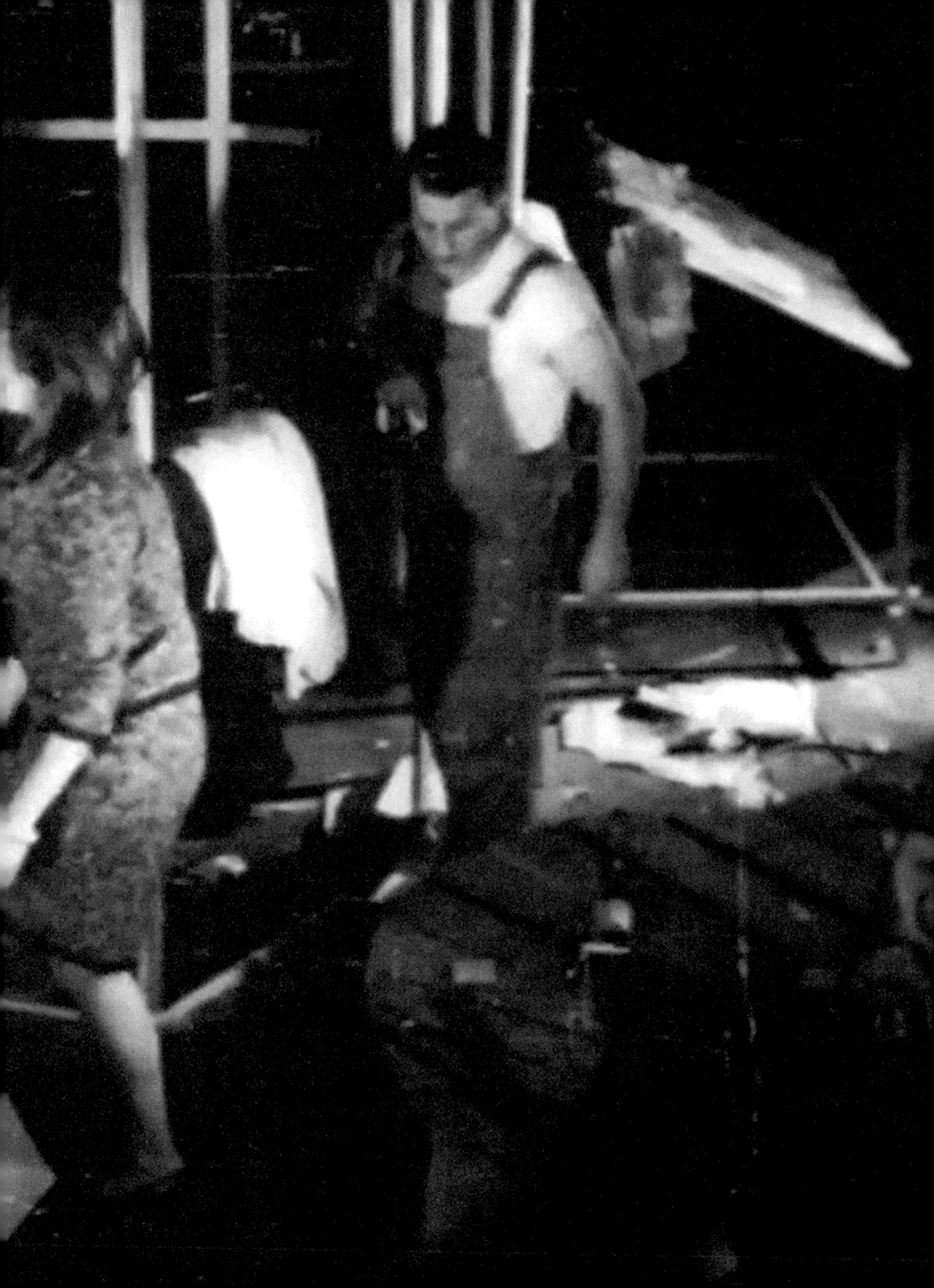

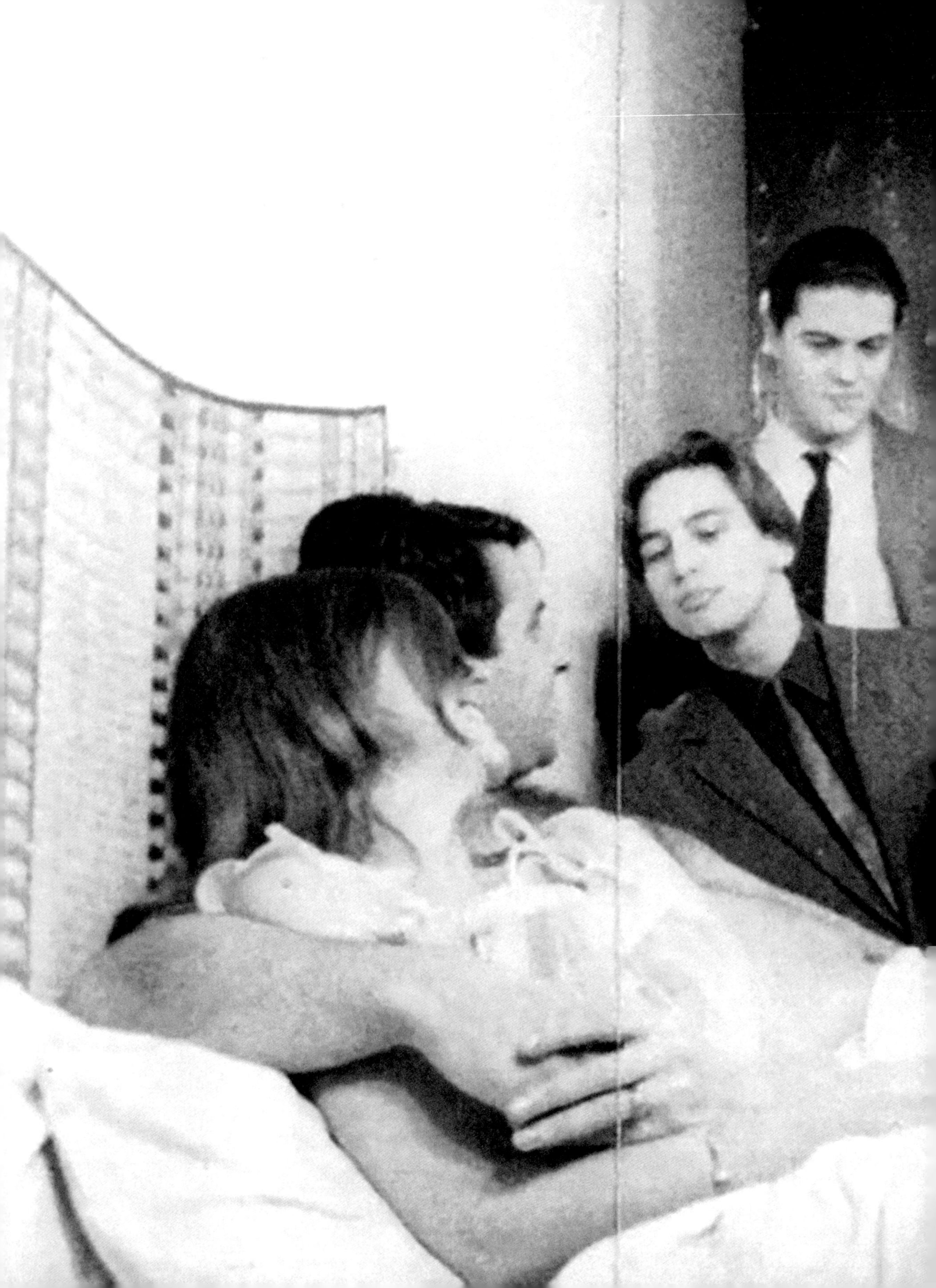

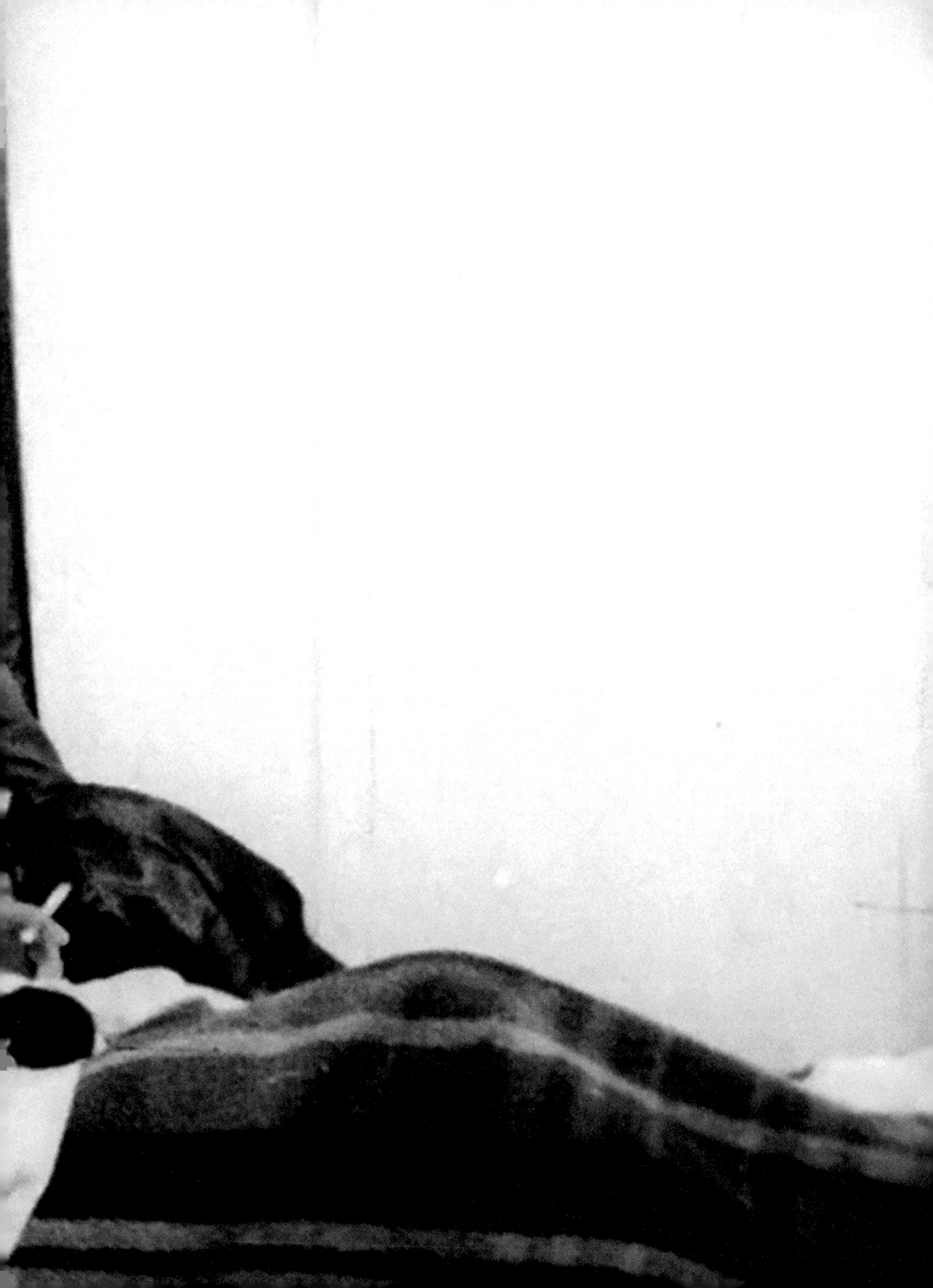

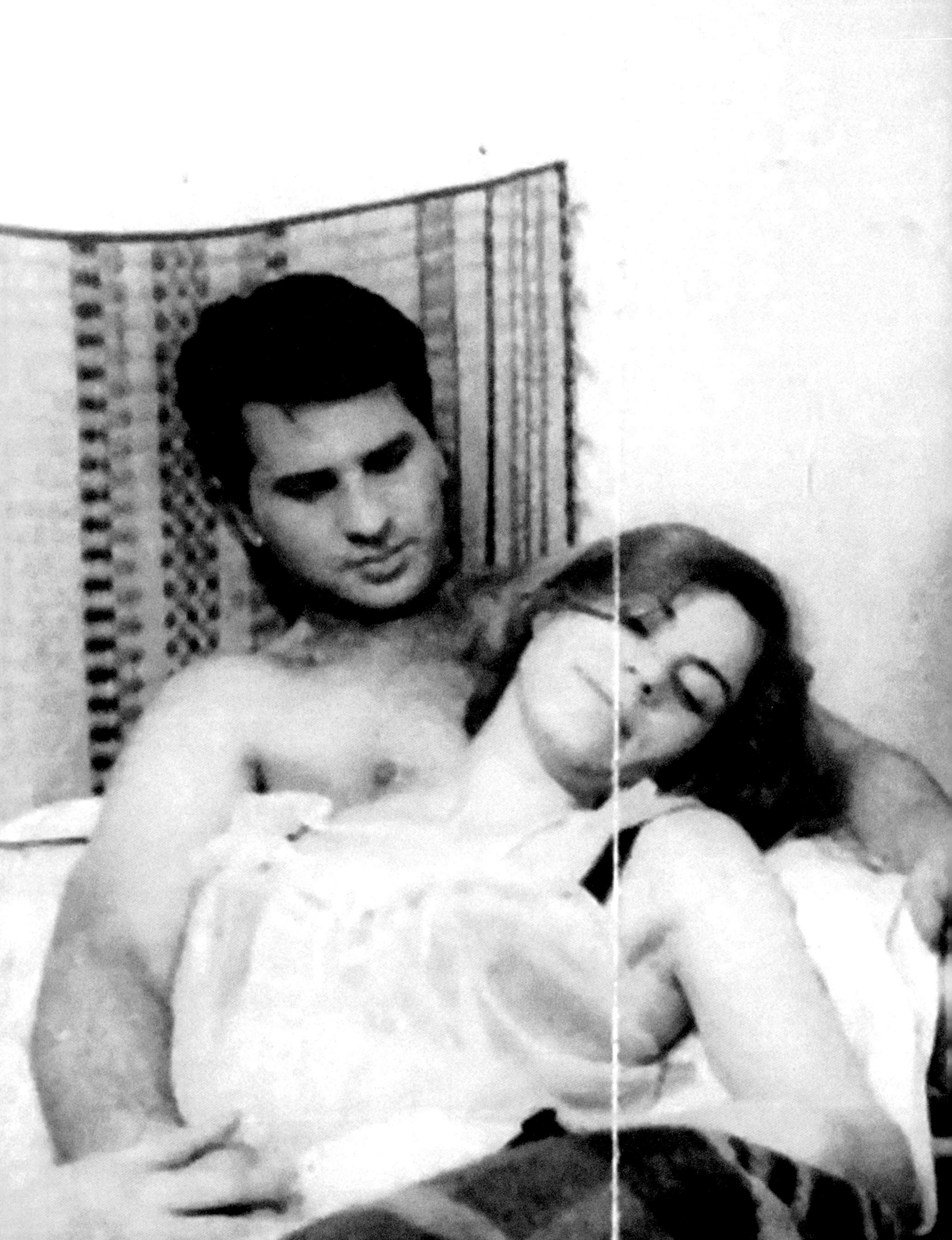

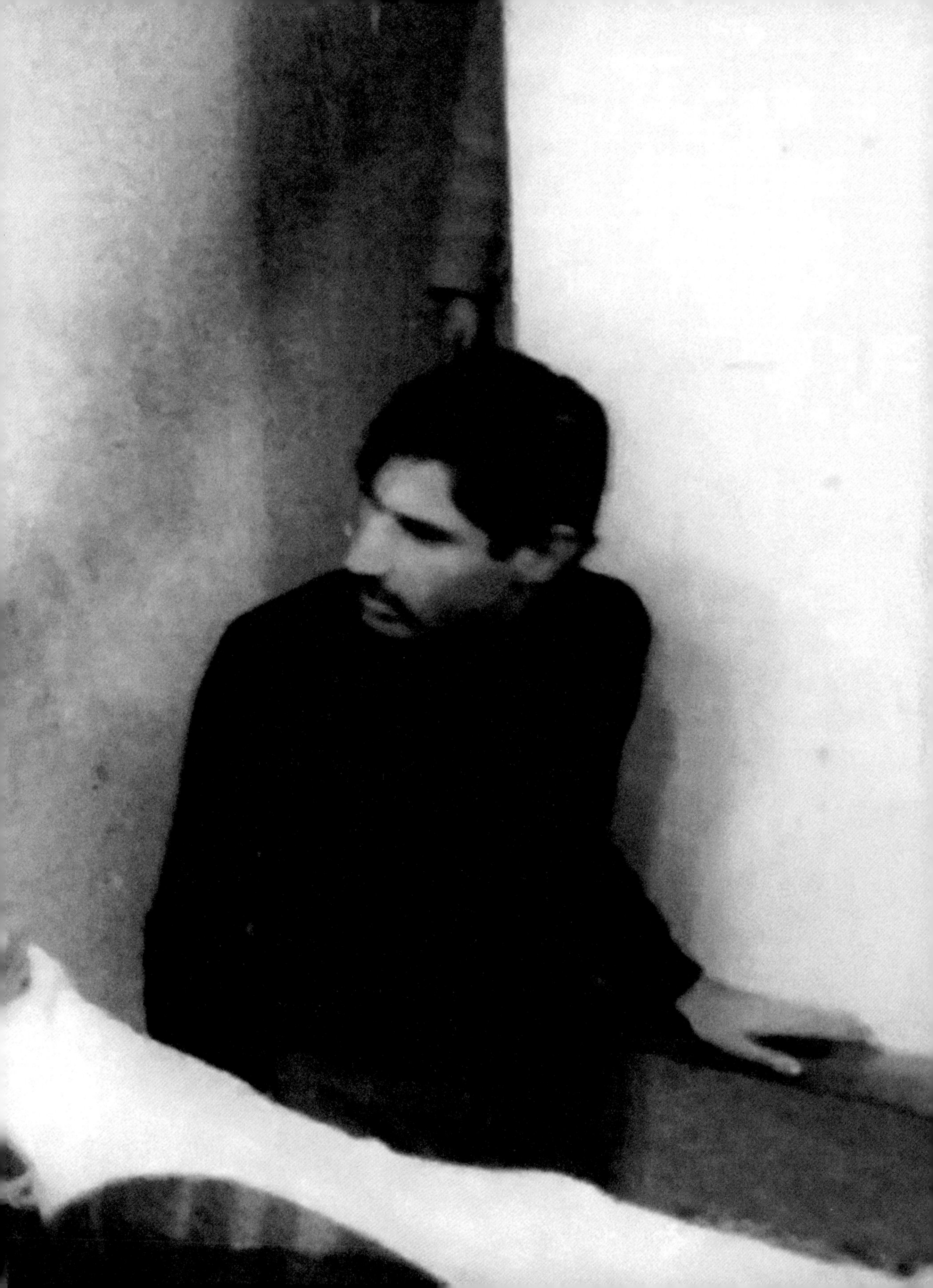

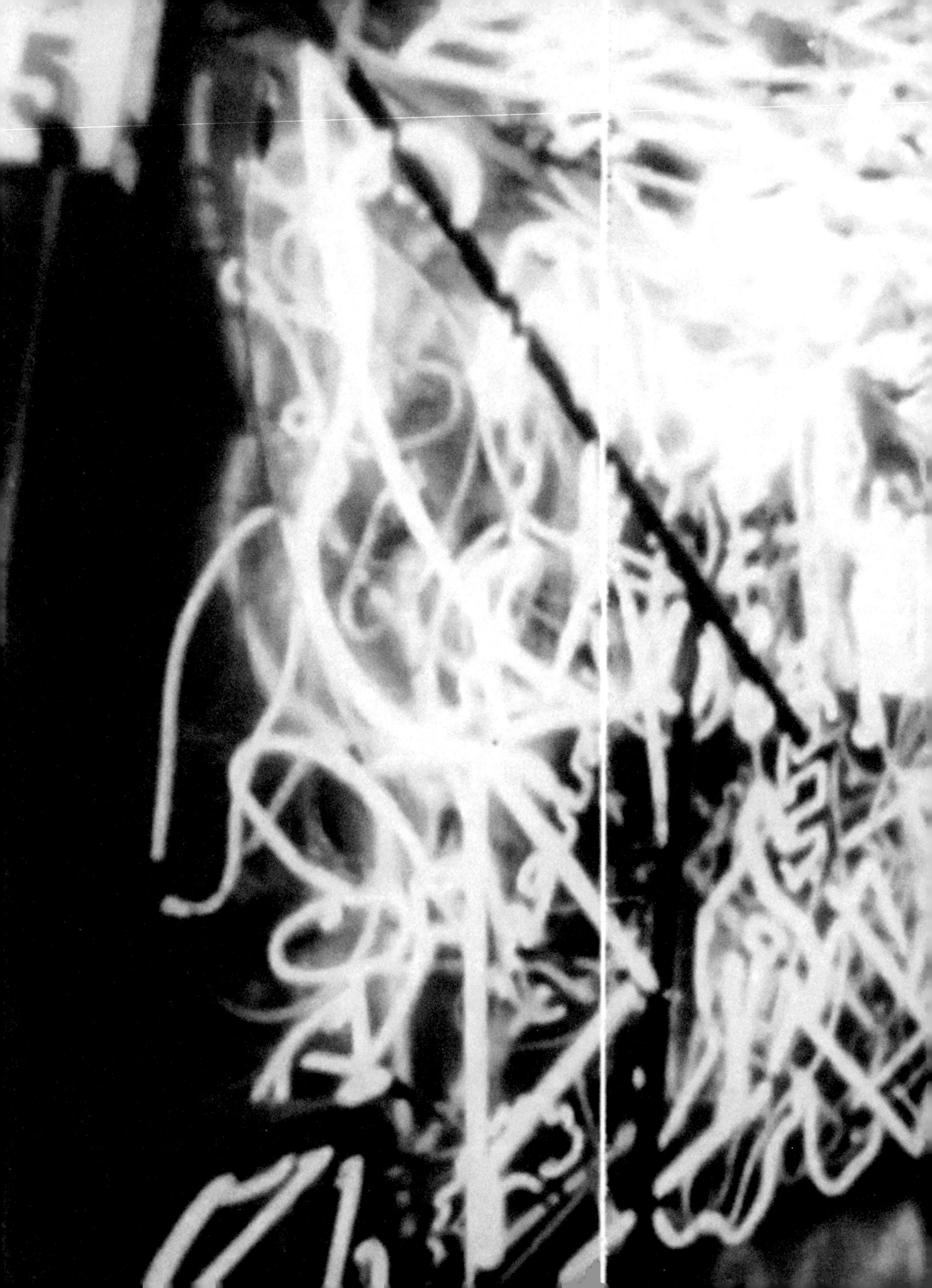

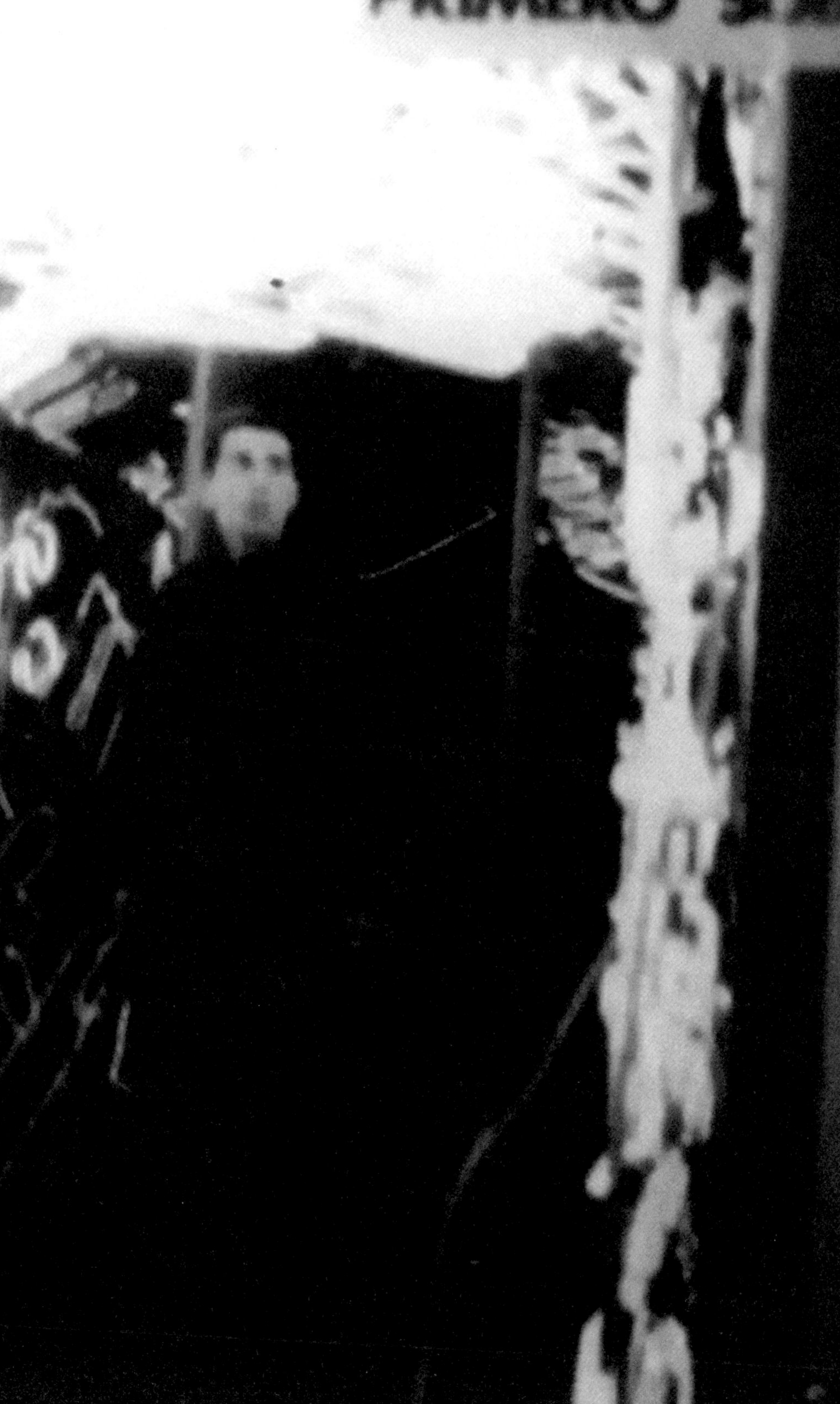
PRIMERO

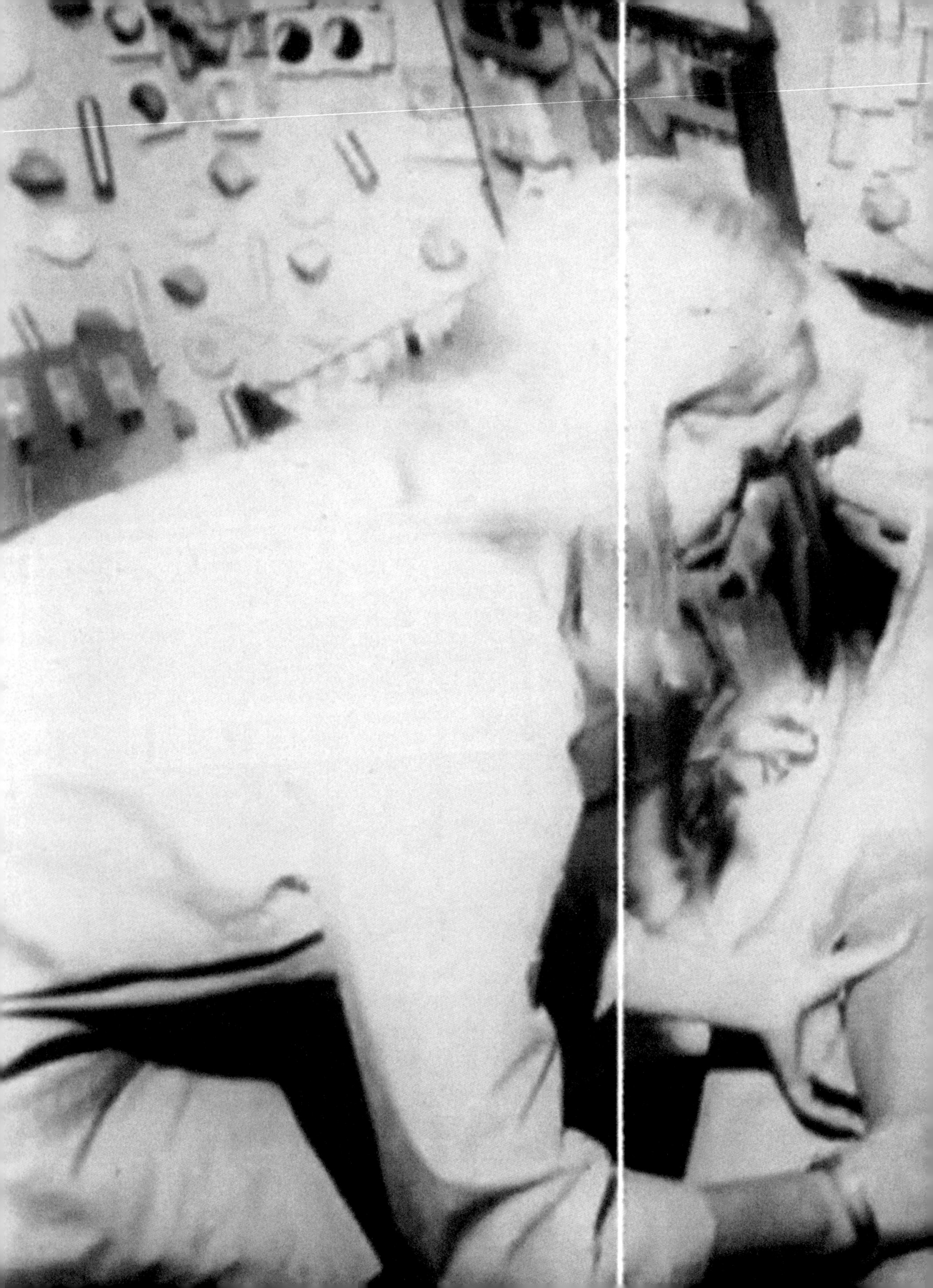

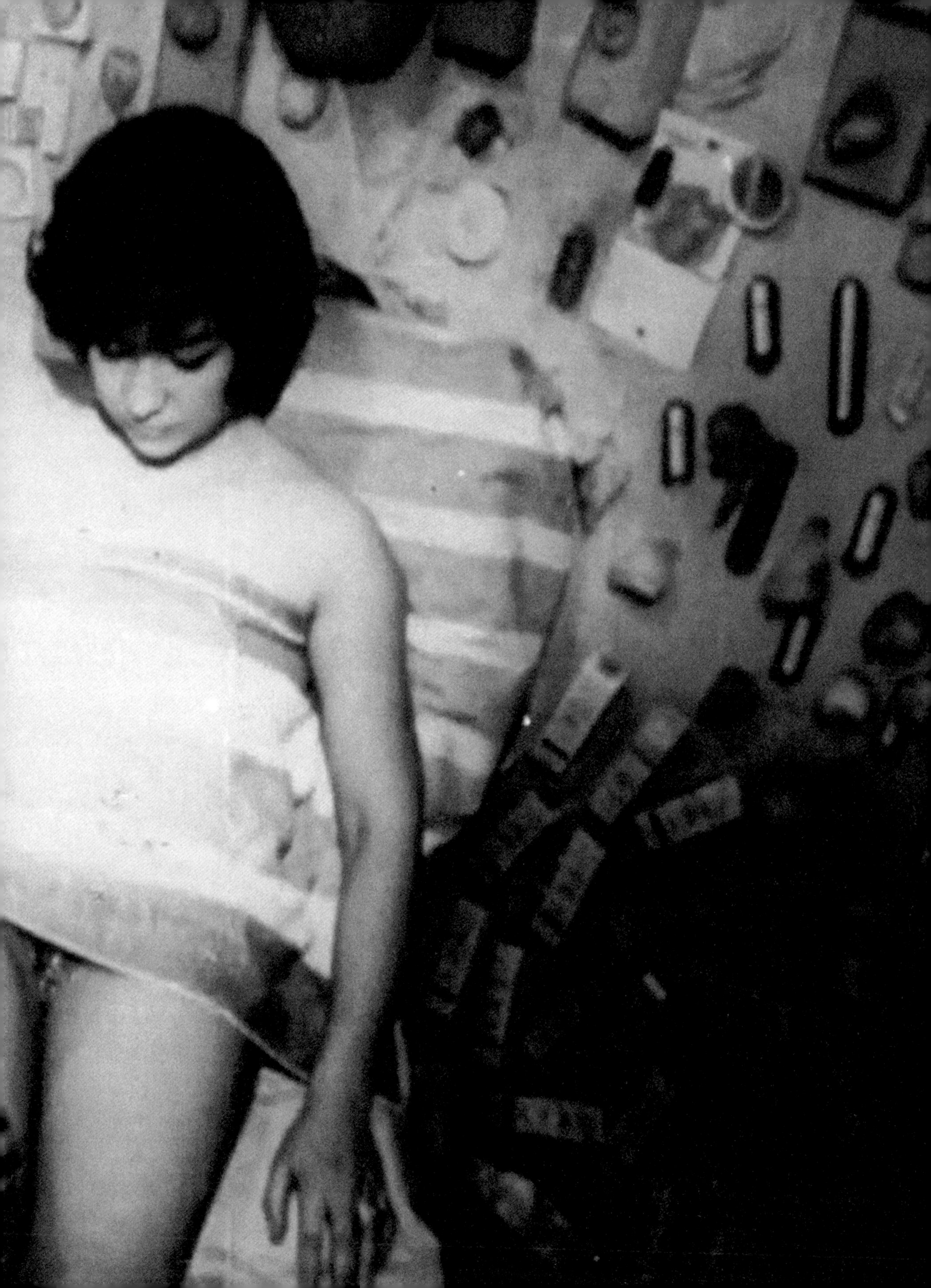

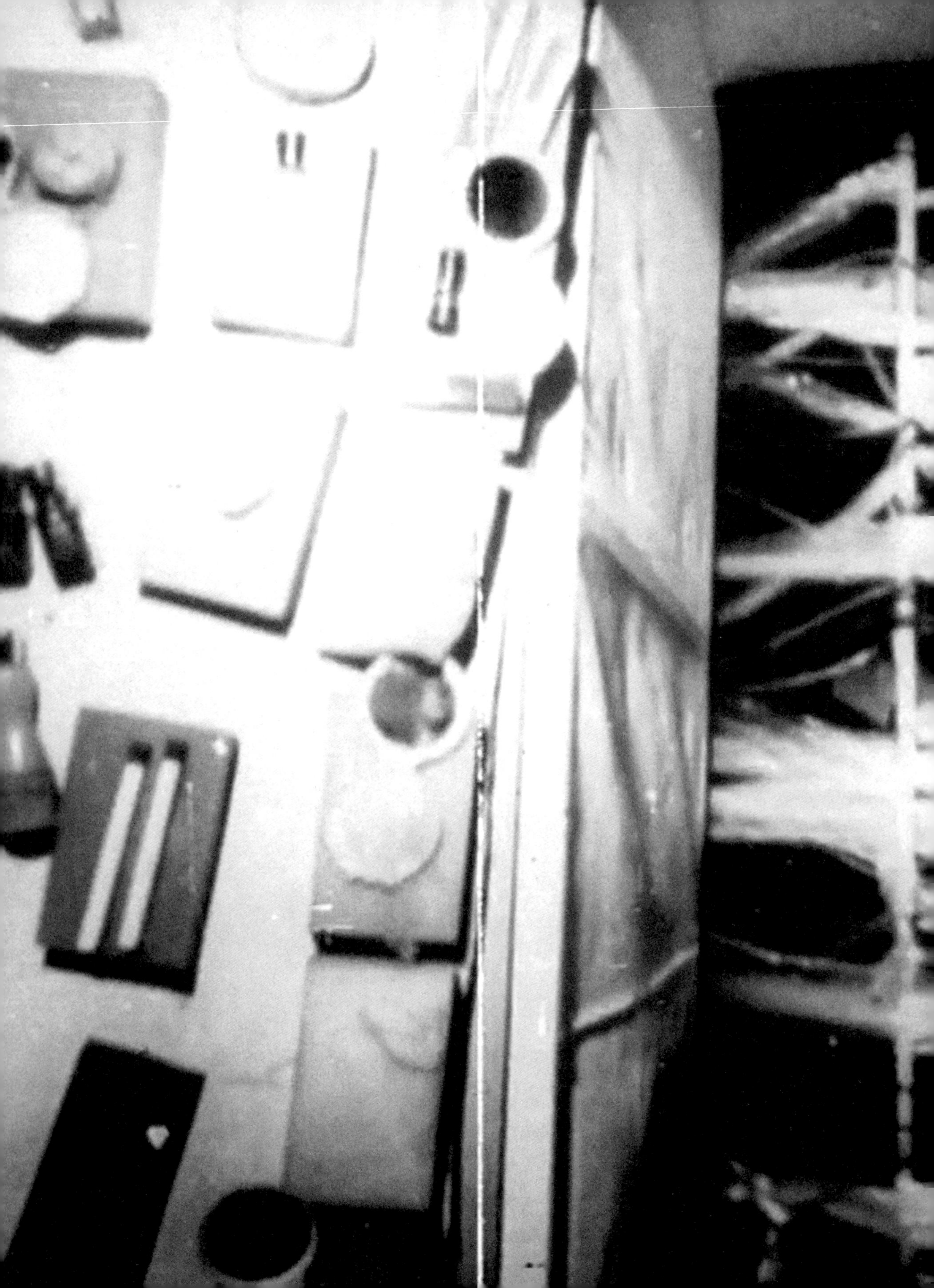

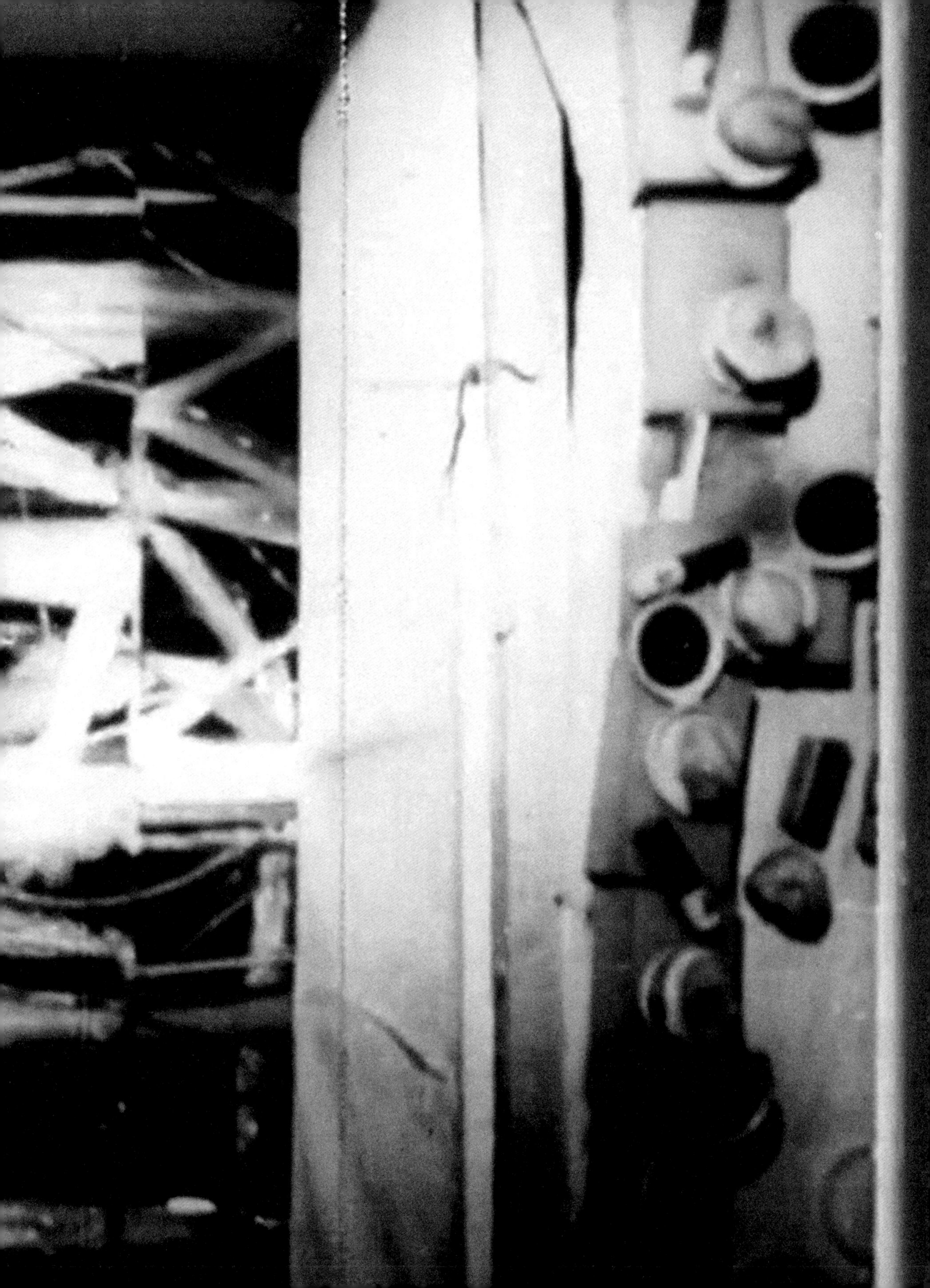

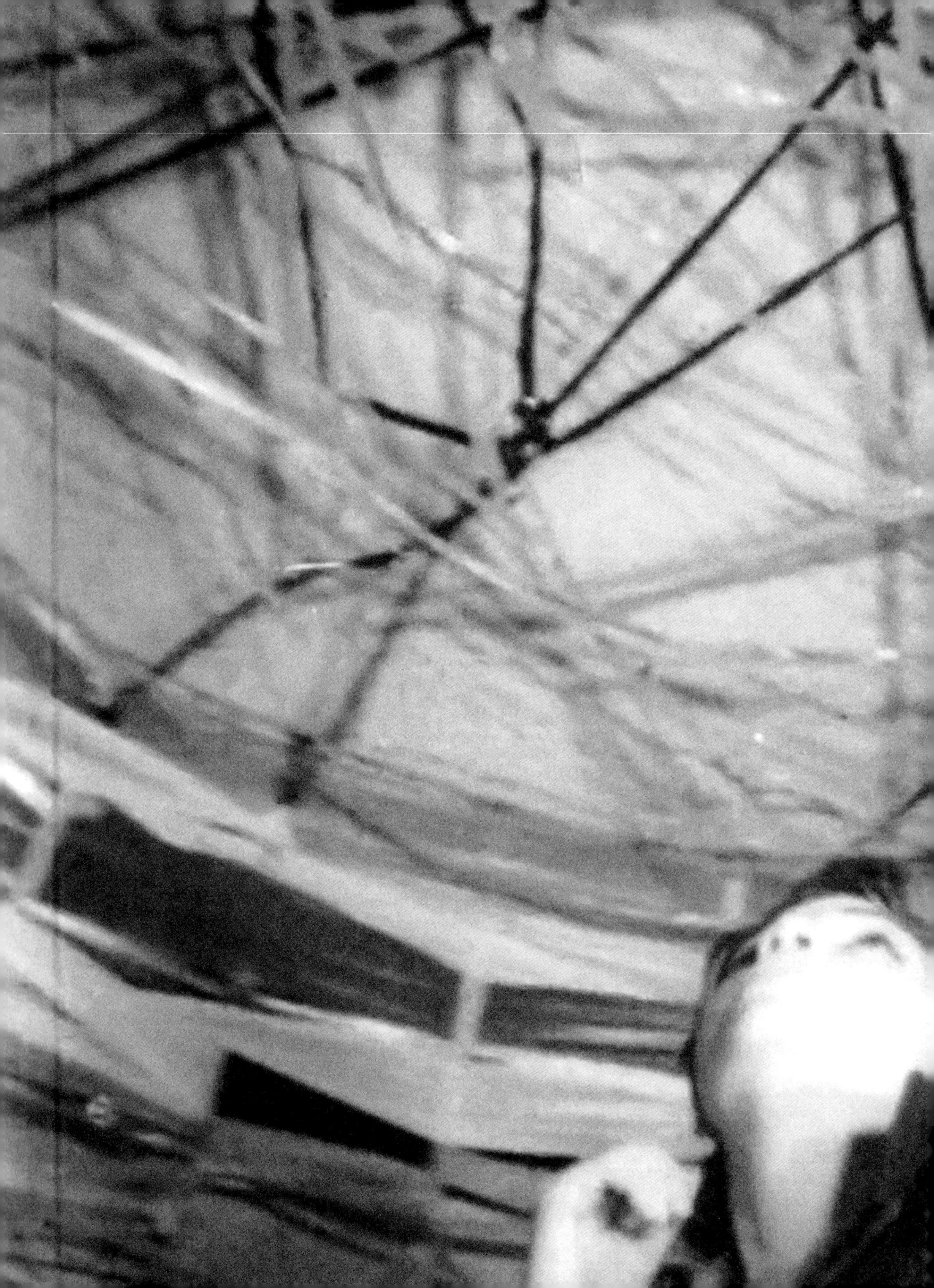

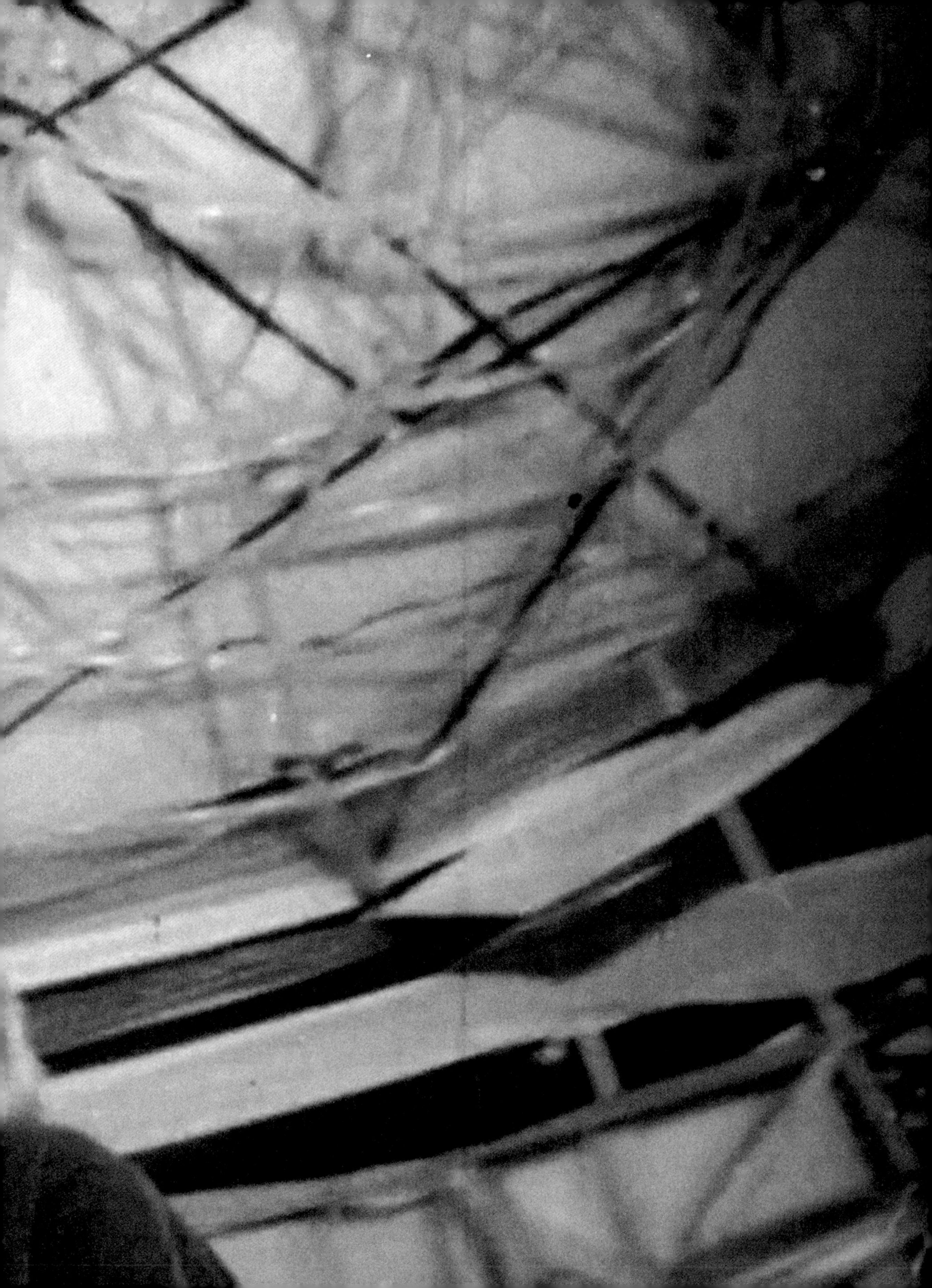

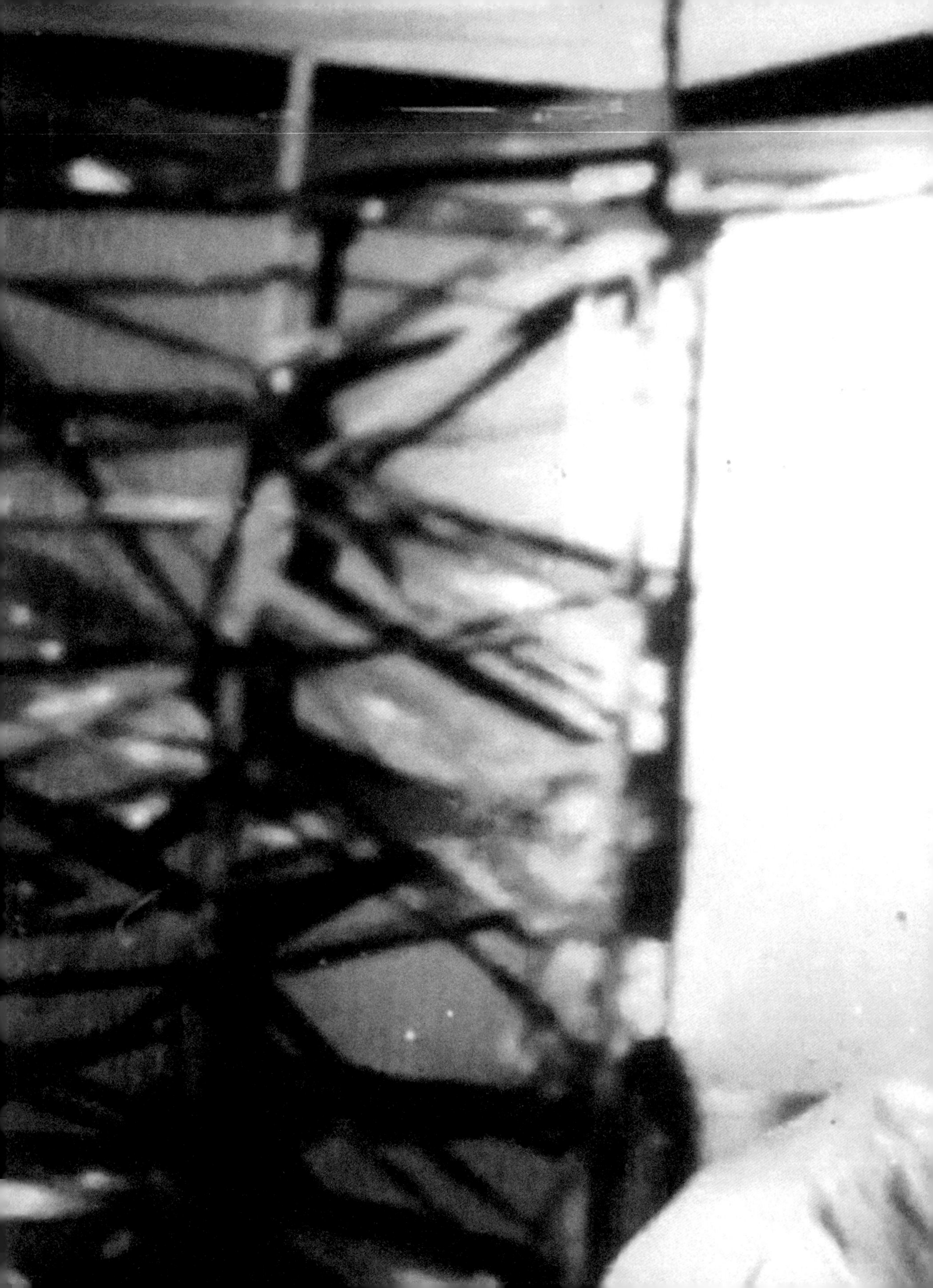

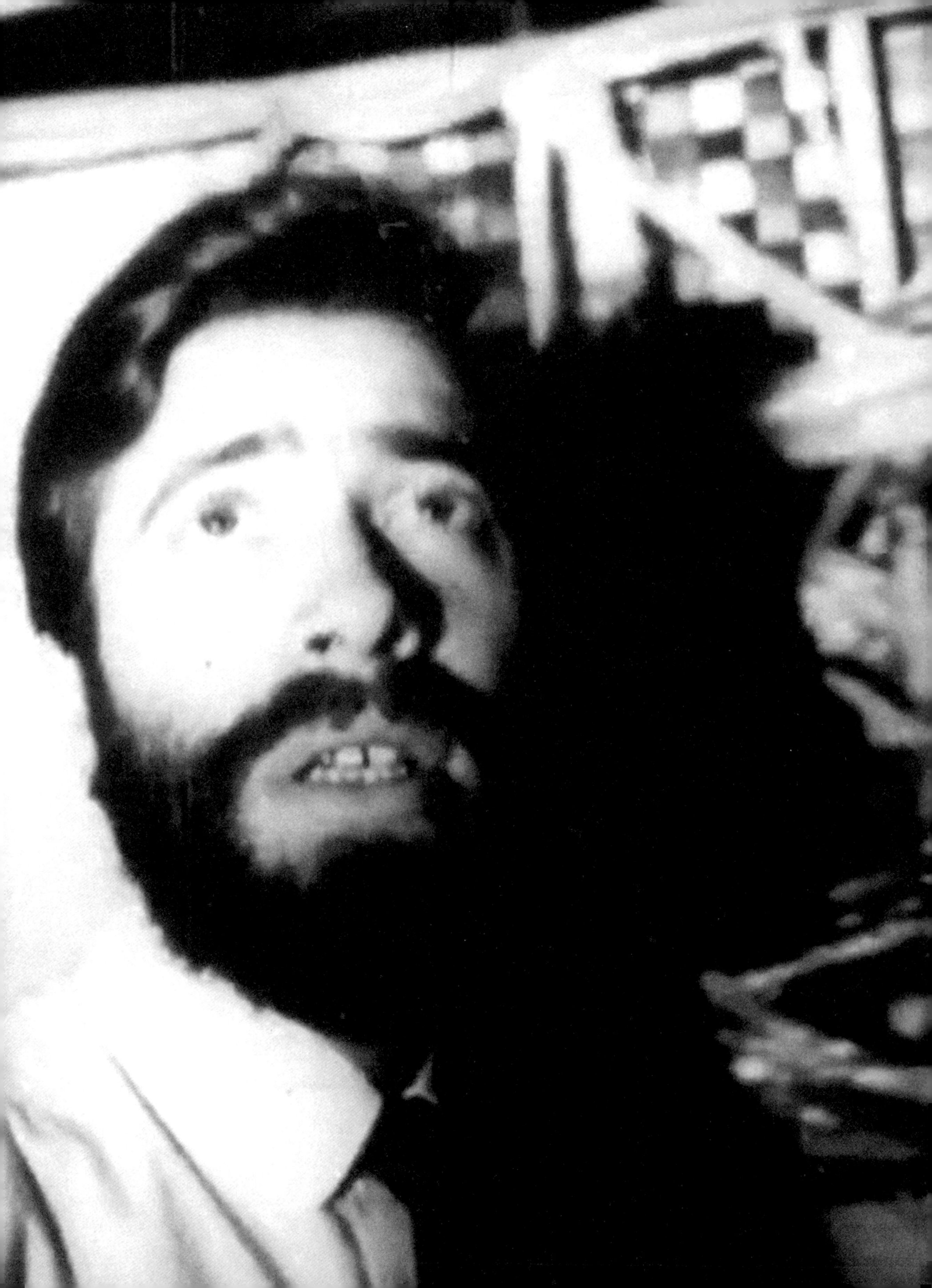

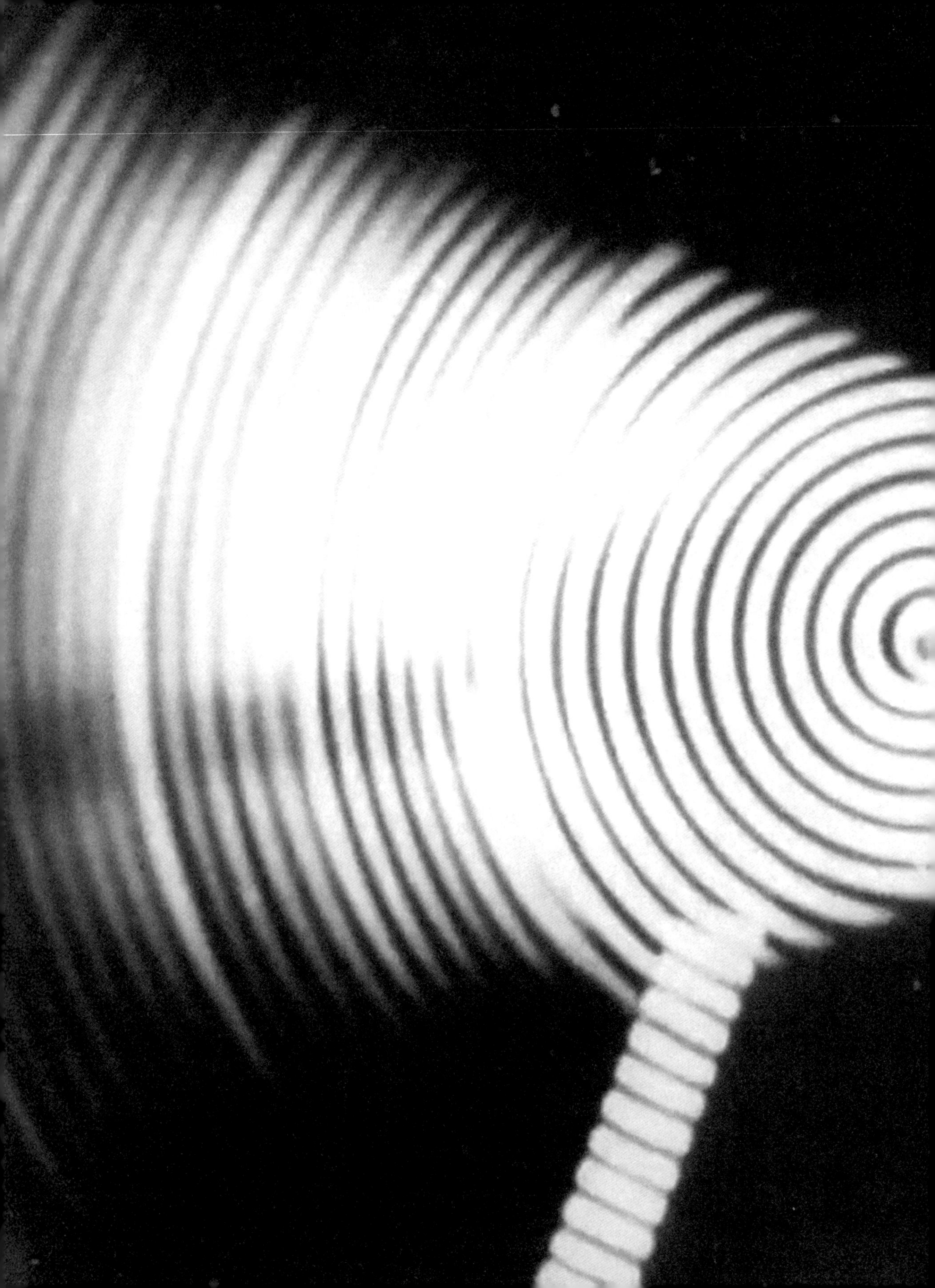

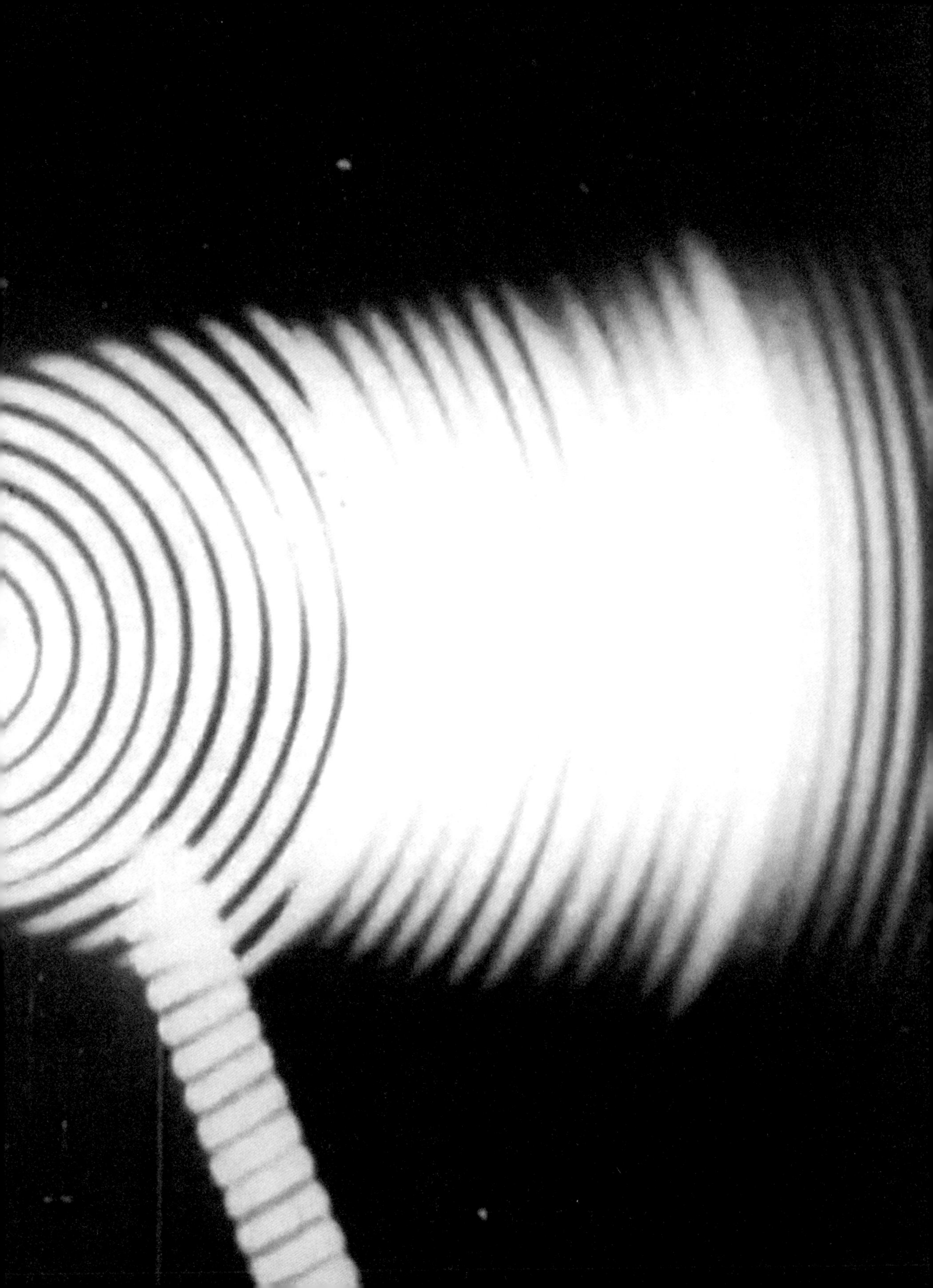

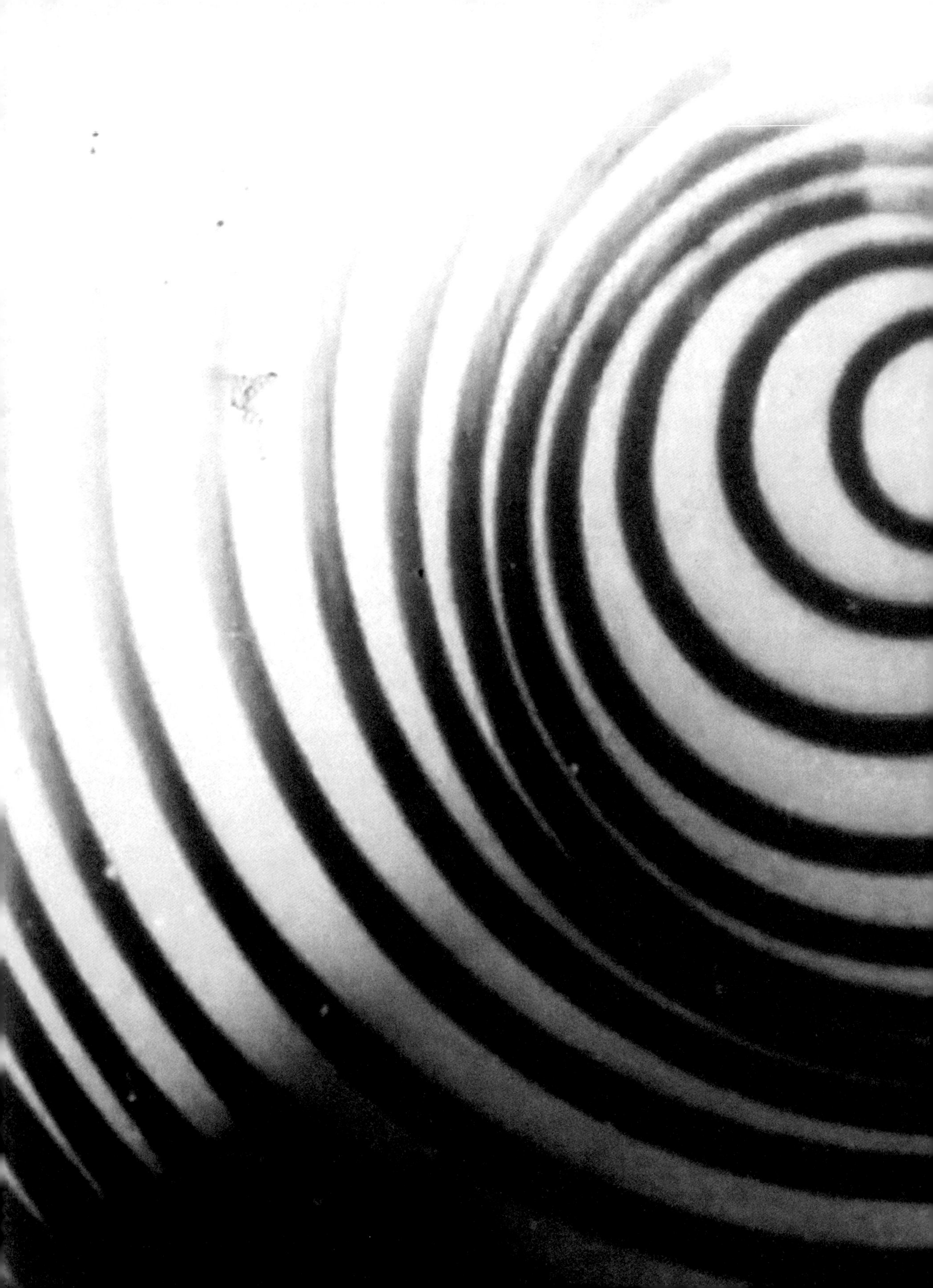

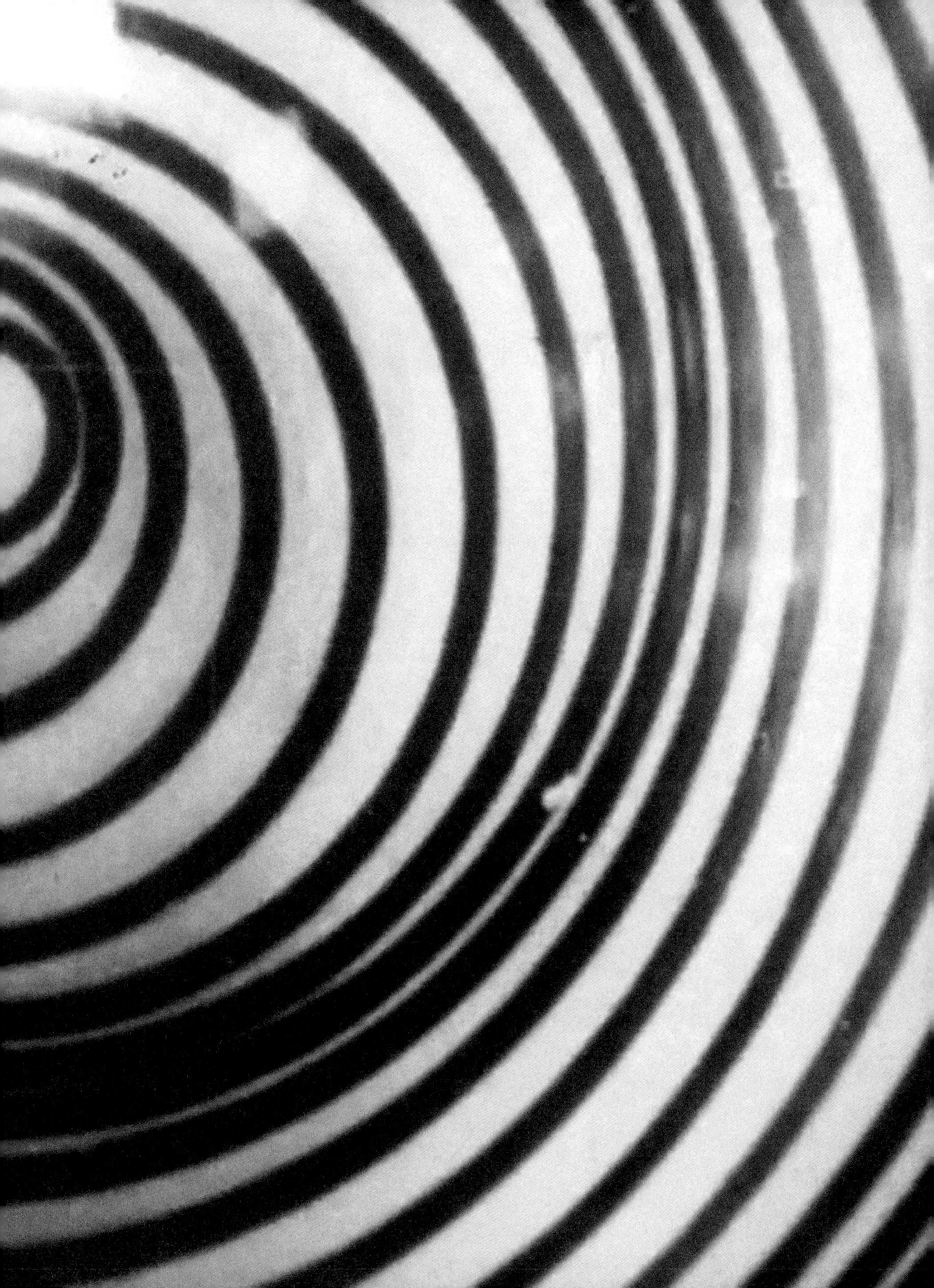

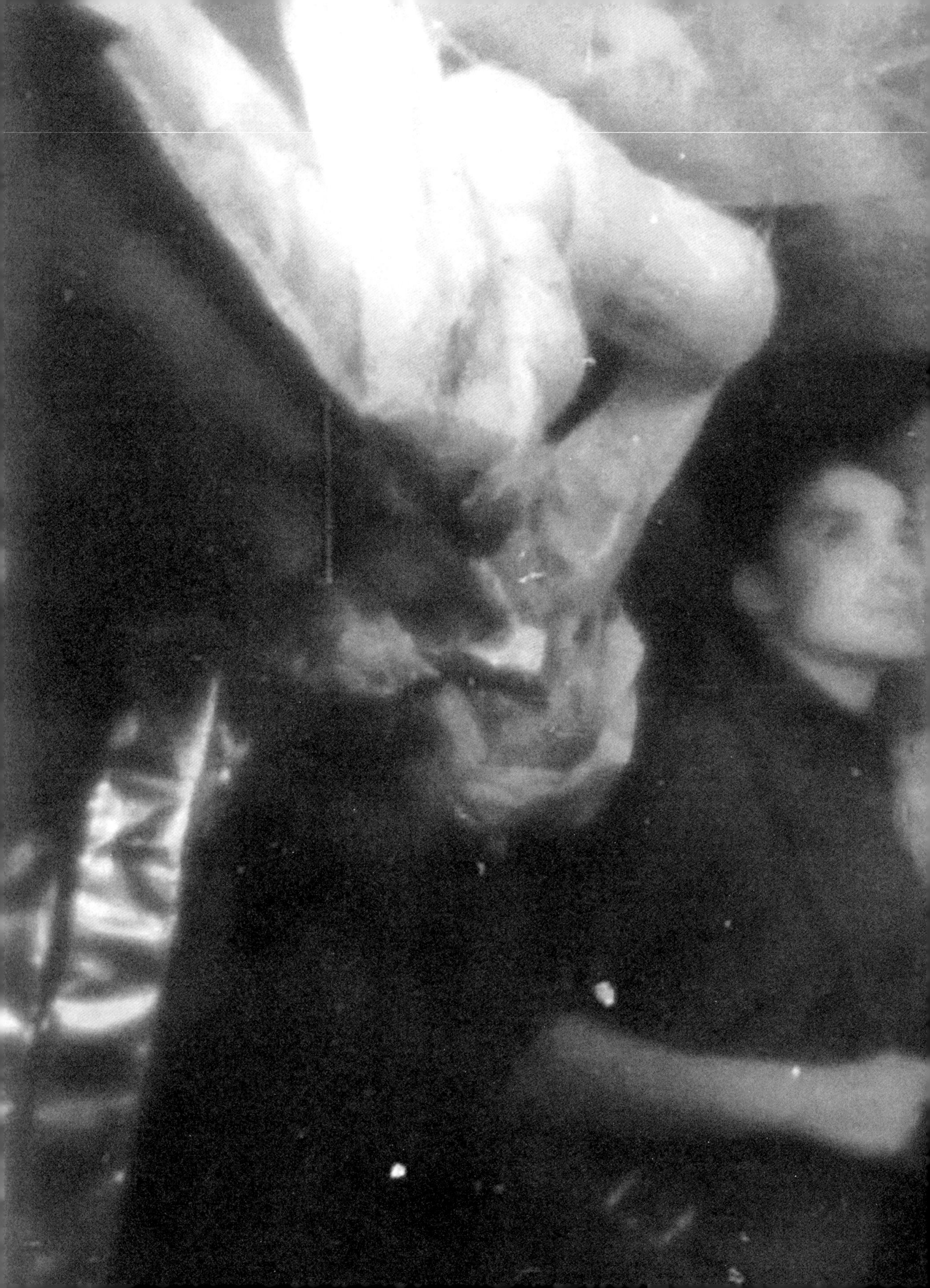

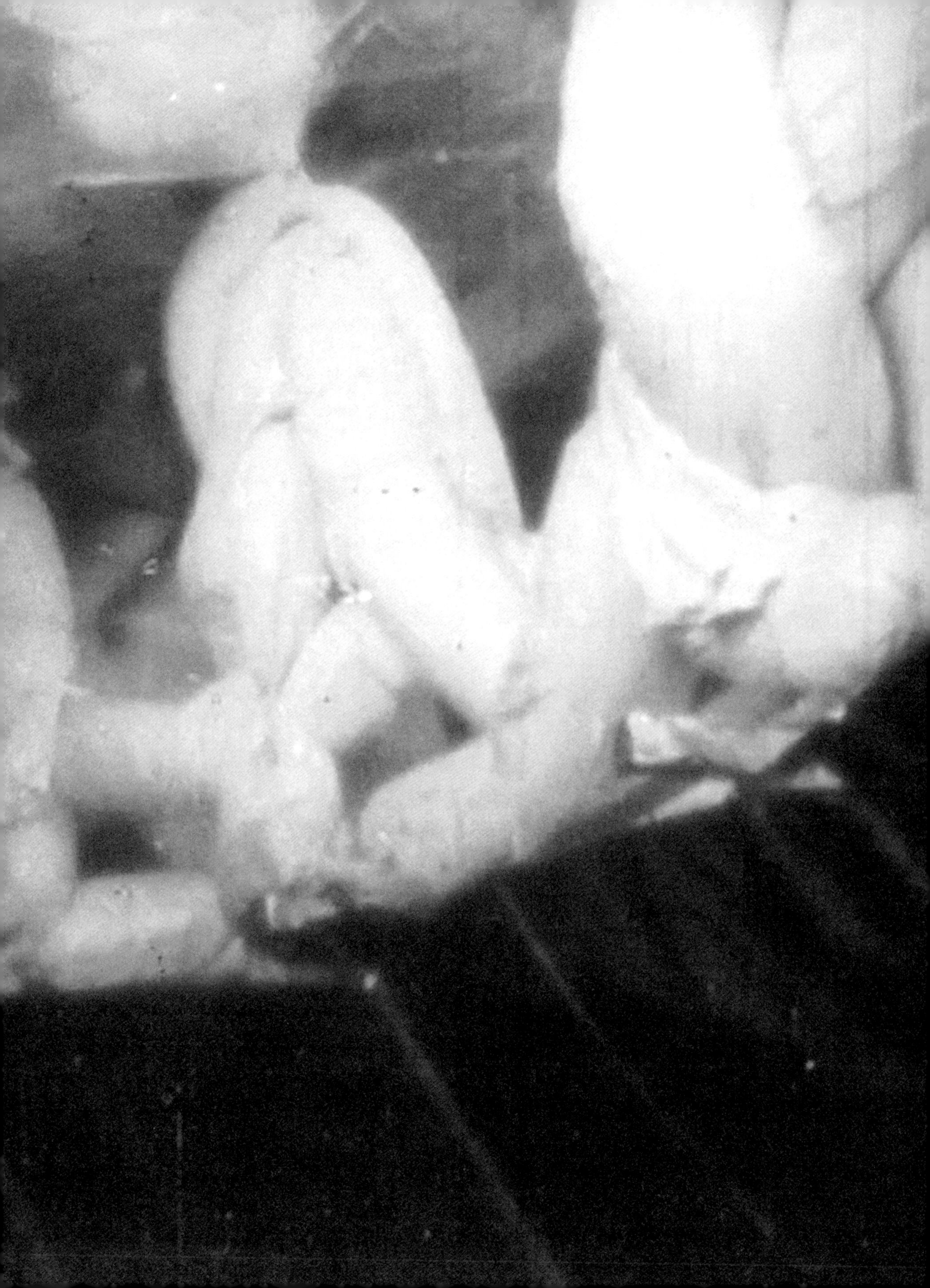

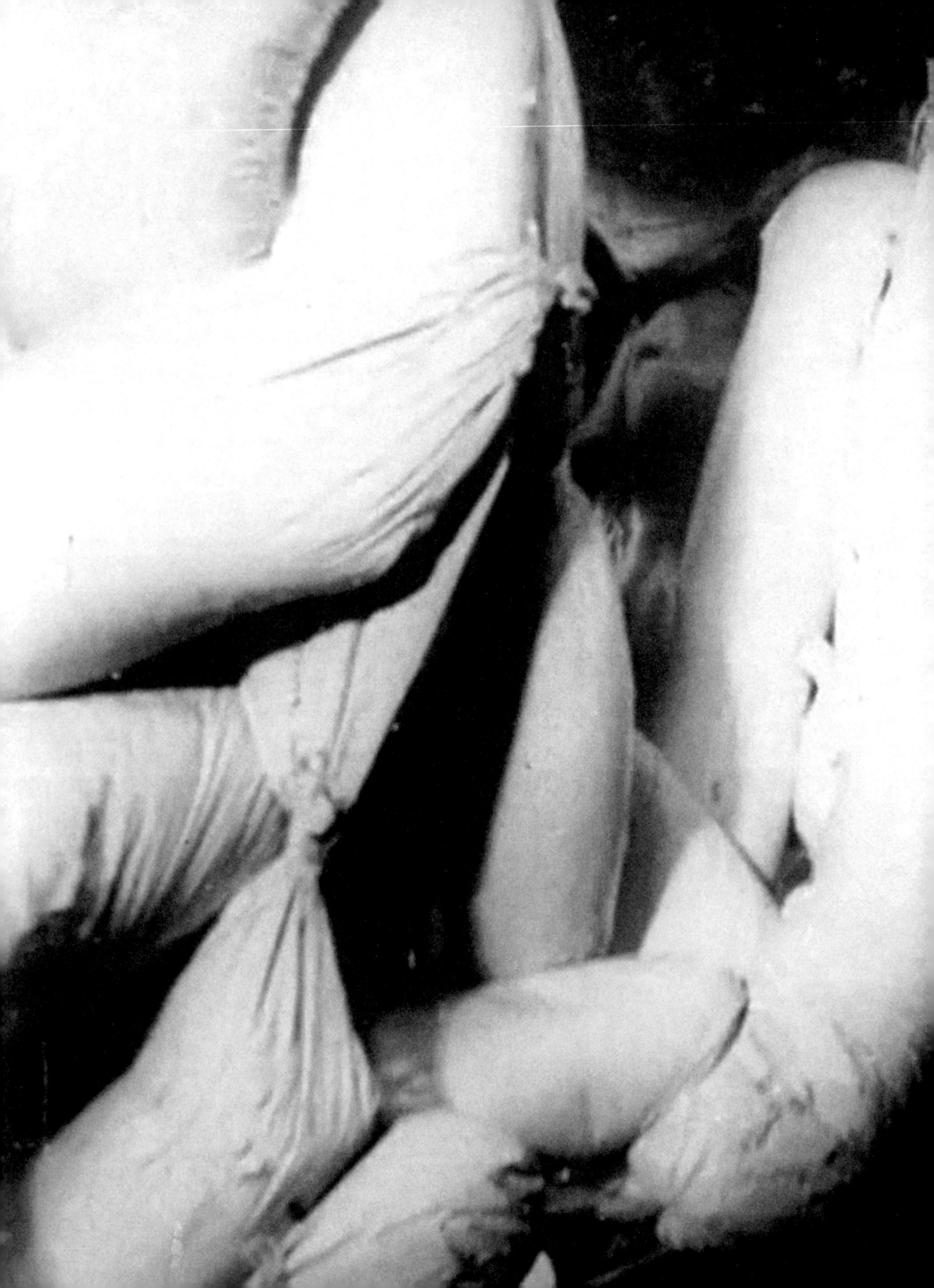

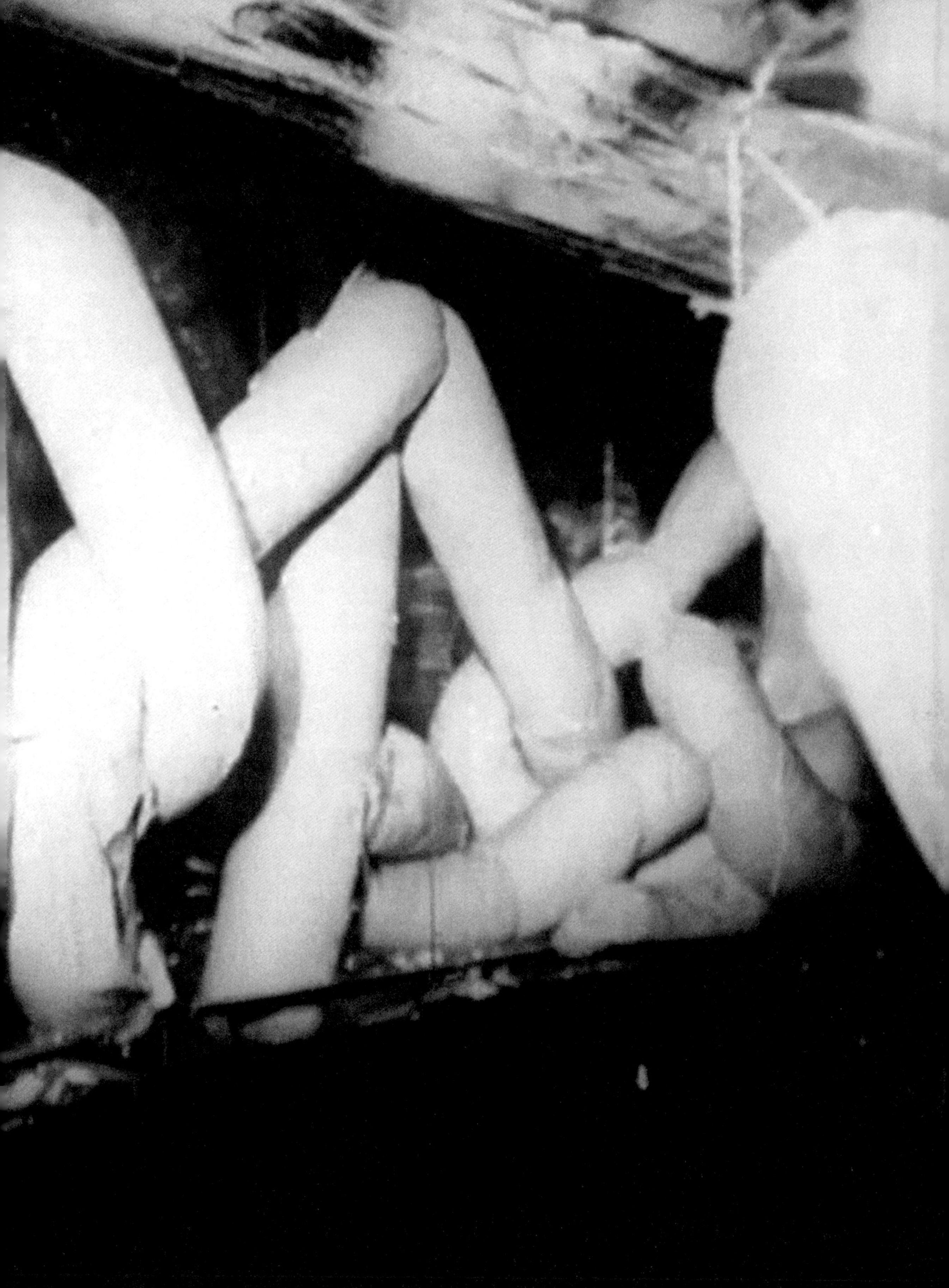

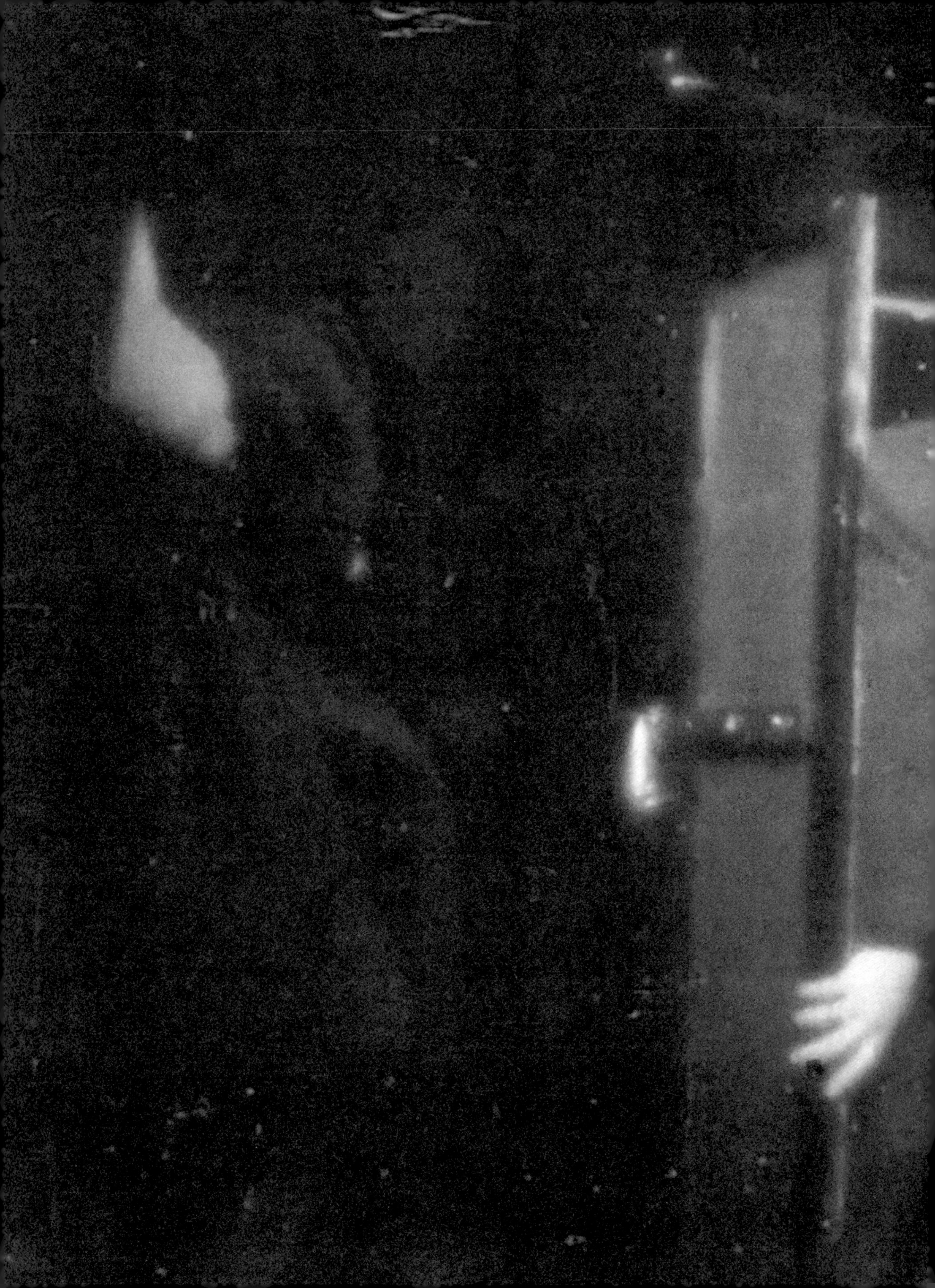

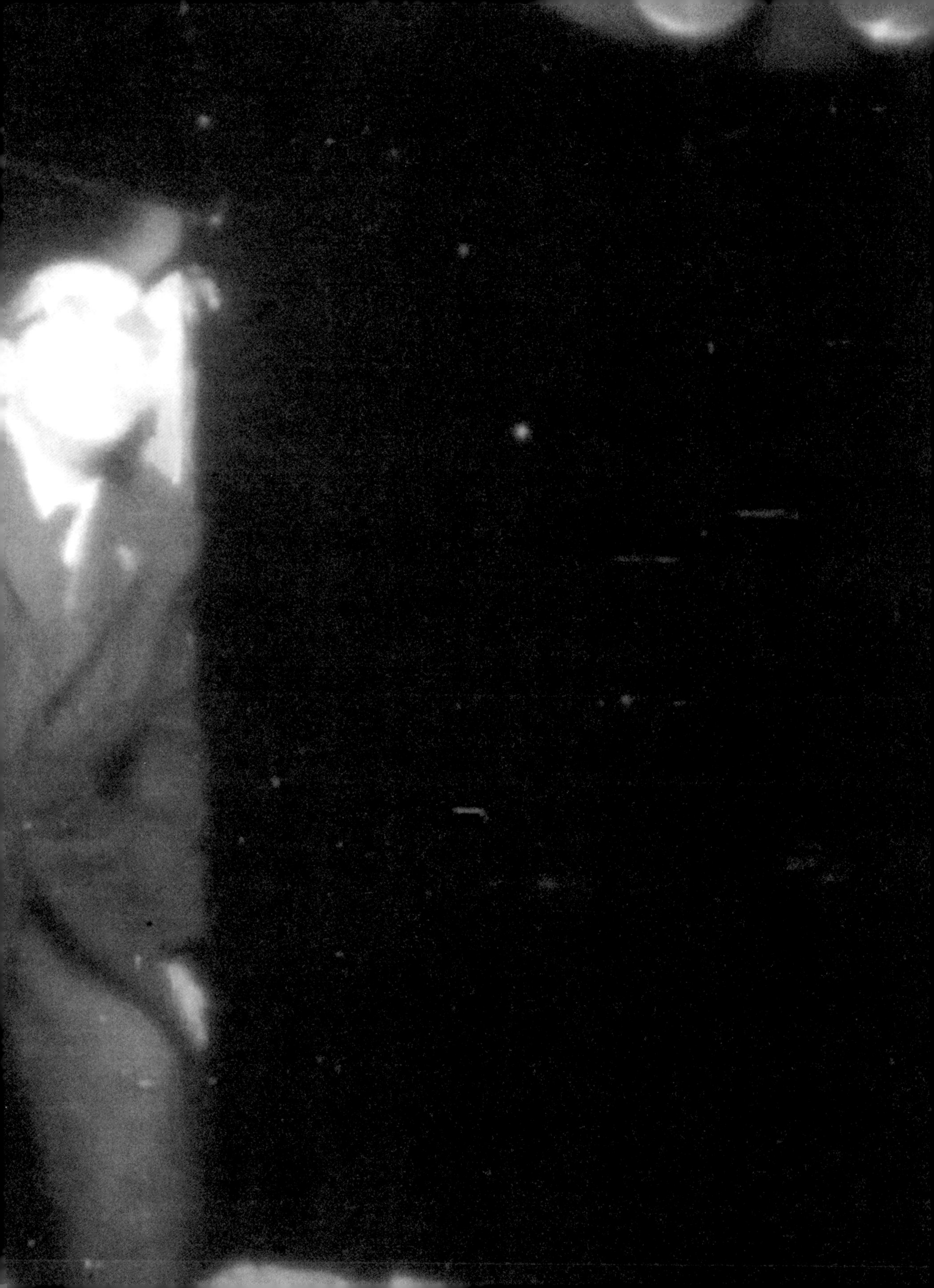

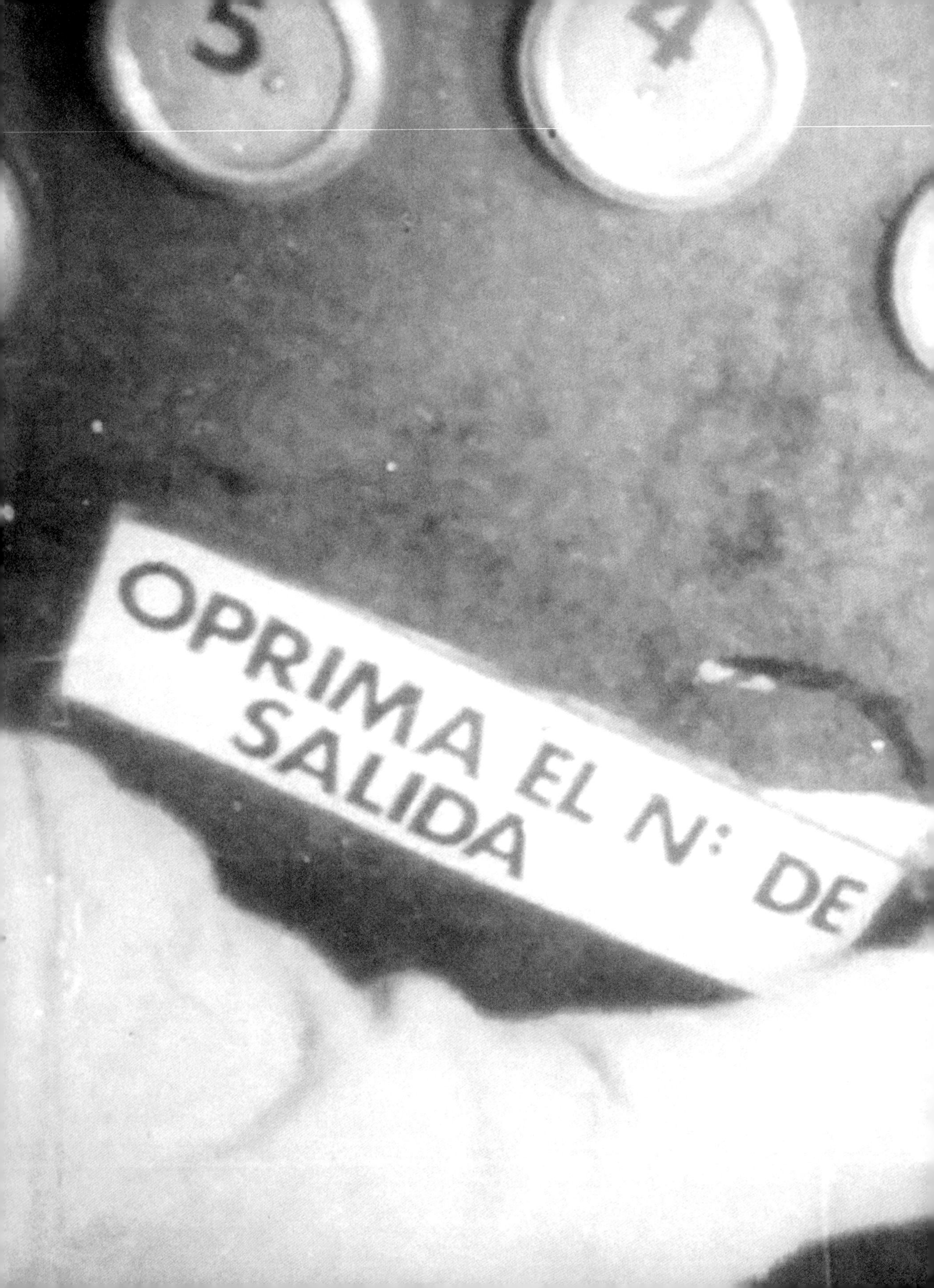
5
4
OPRIMA EL N: DE
SALIDA

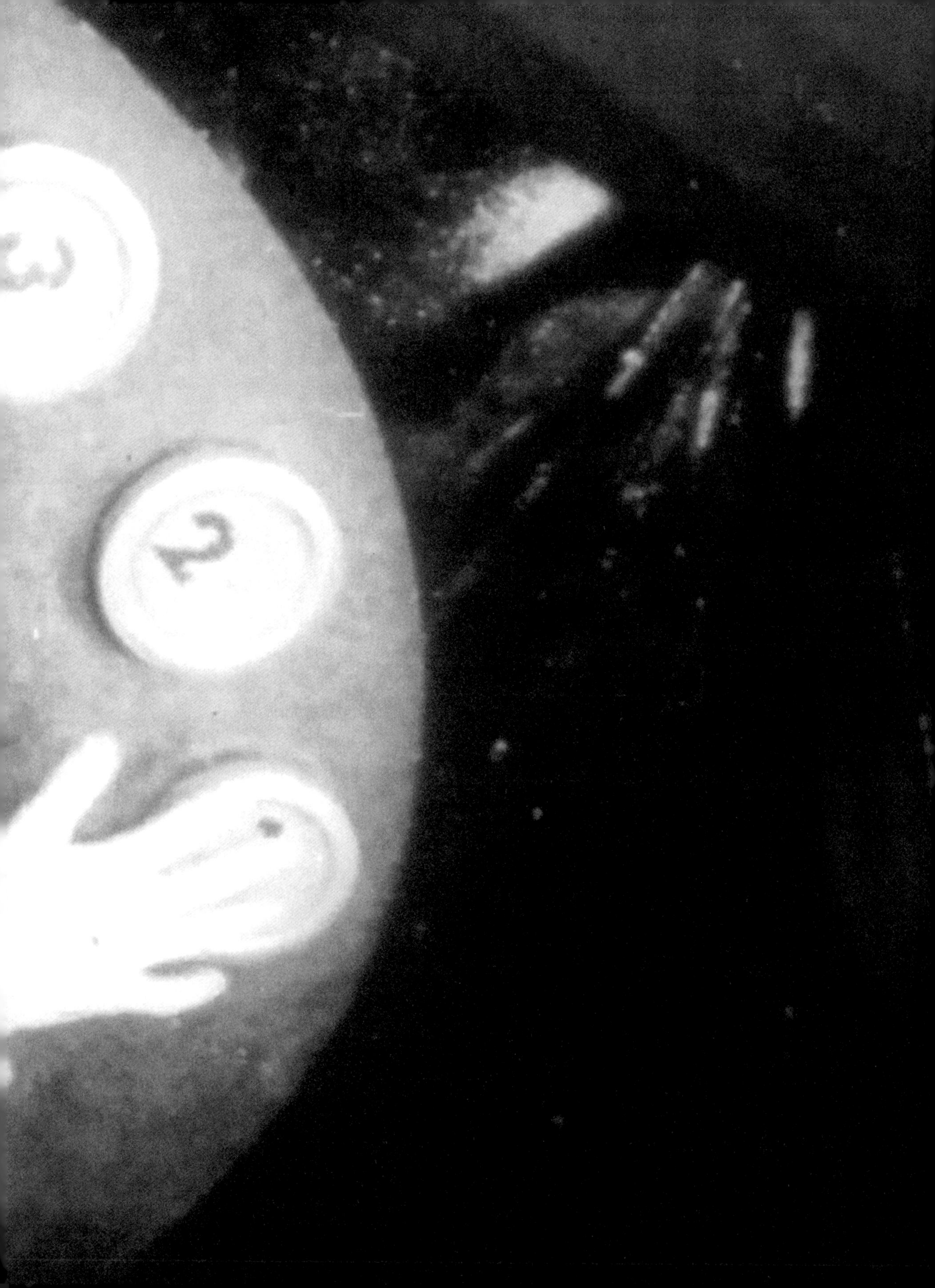

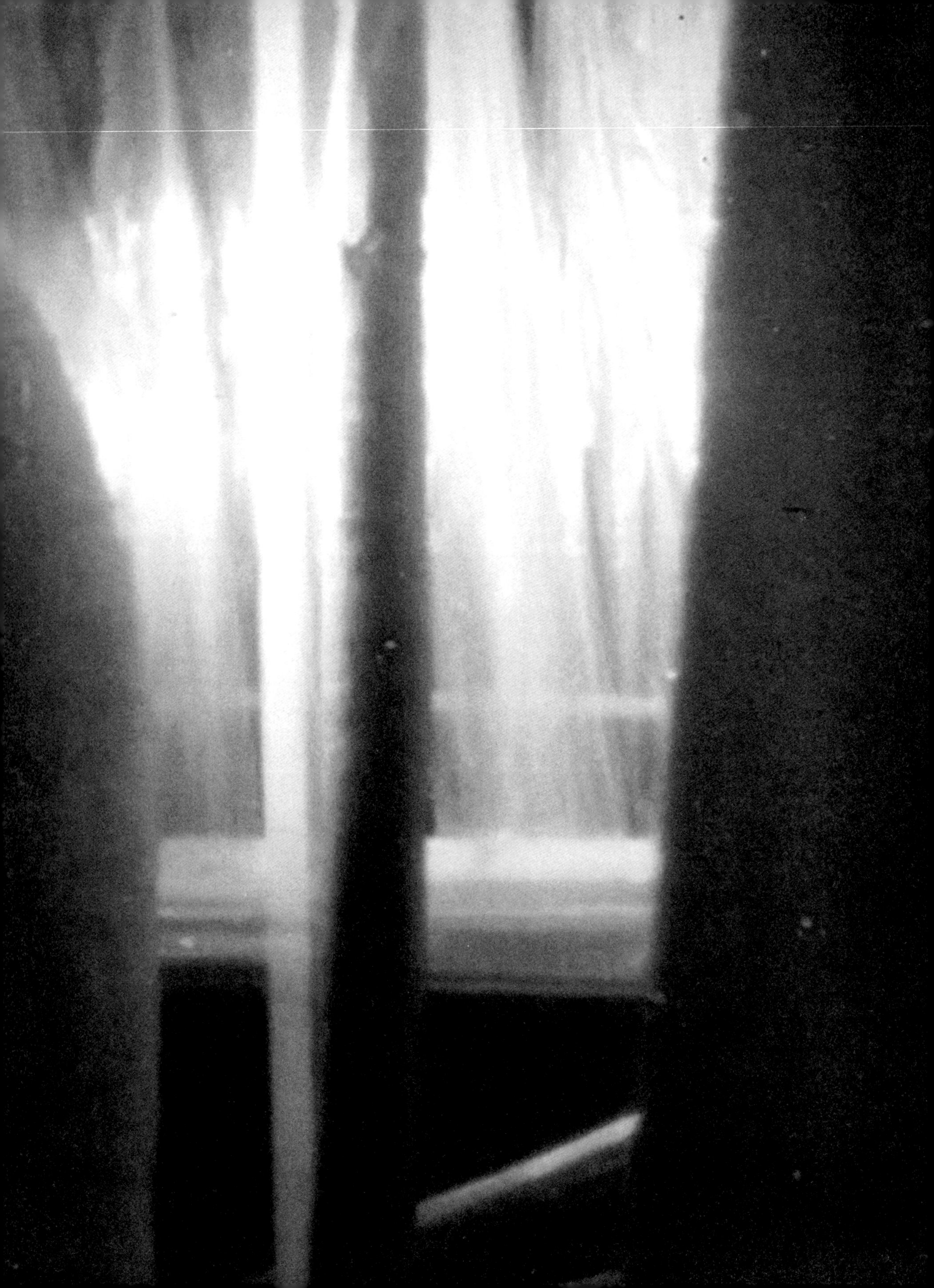

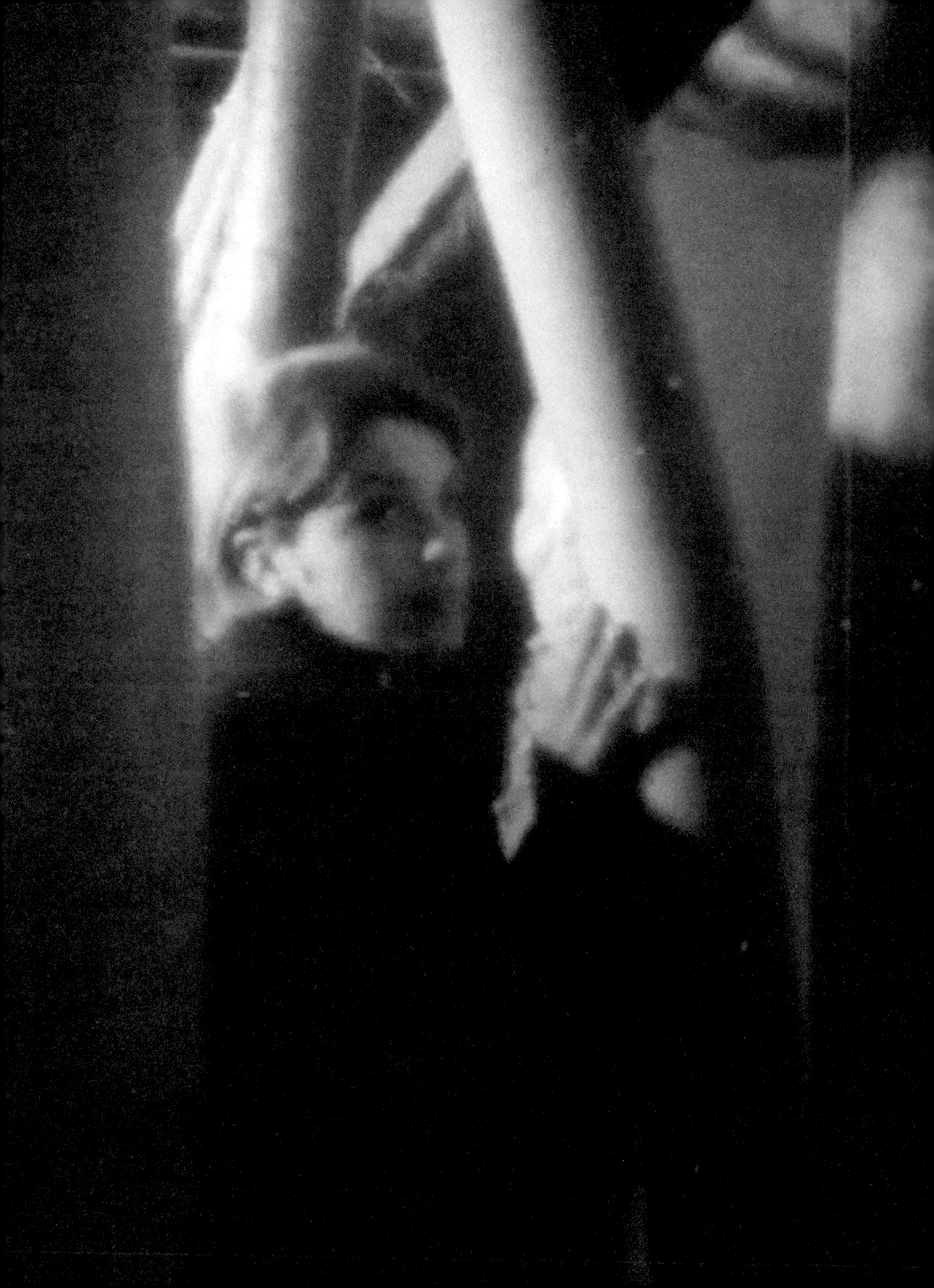

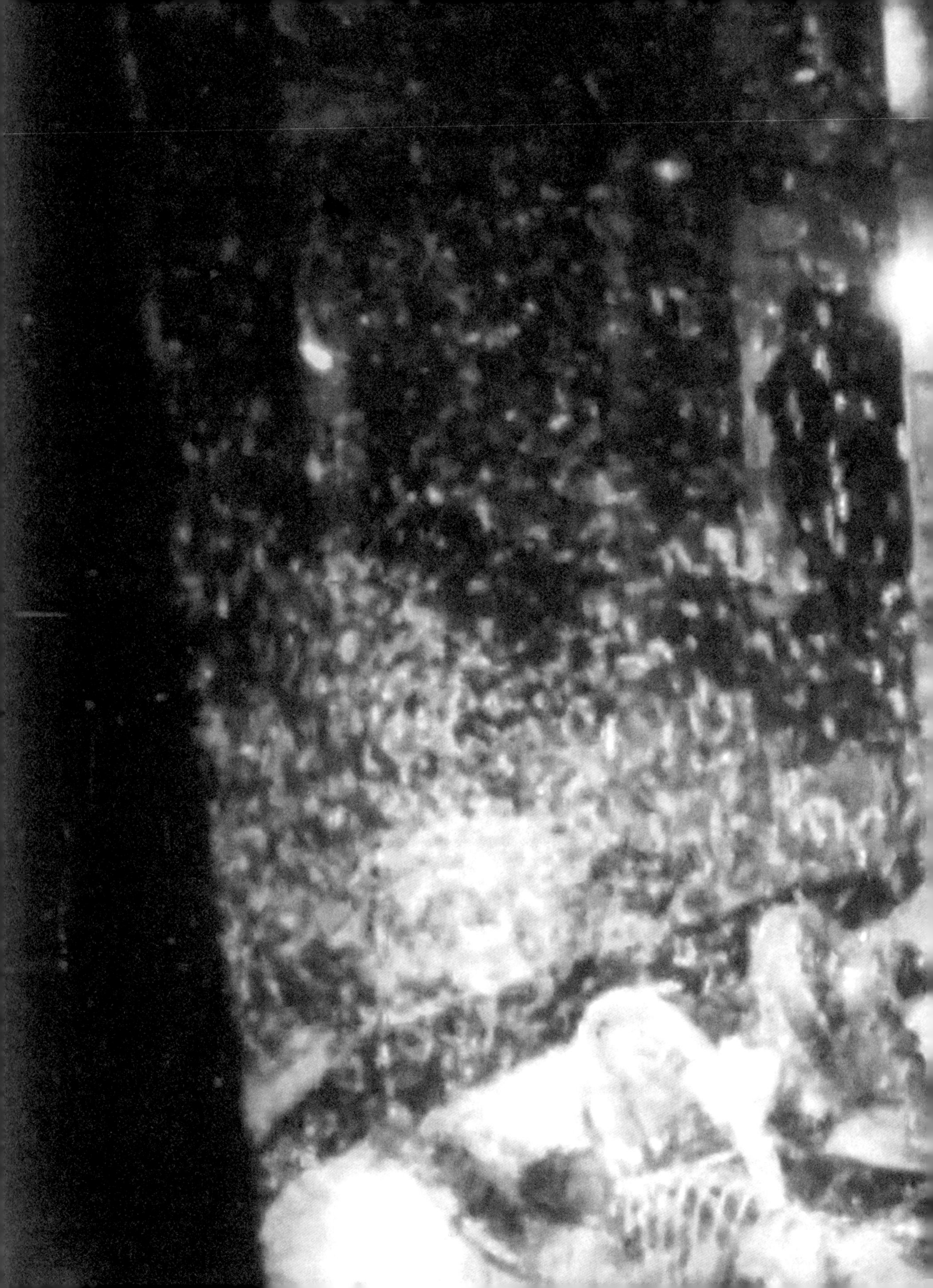

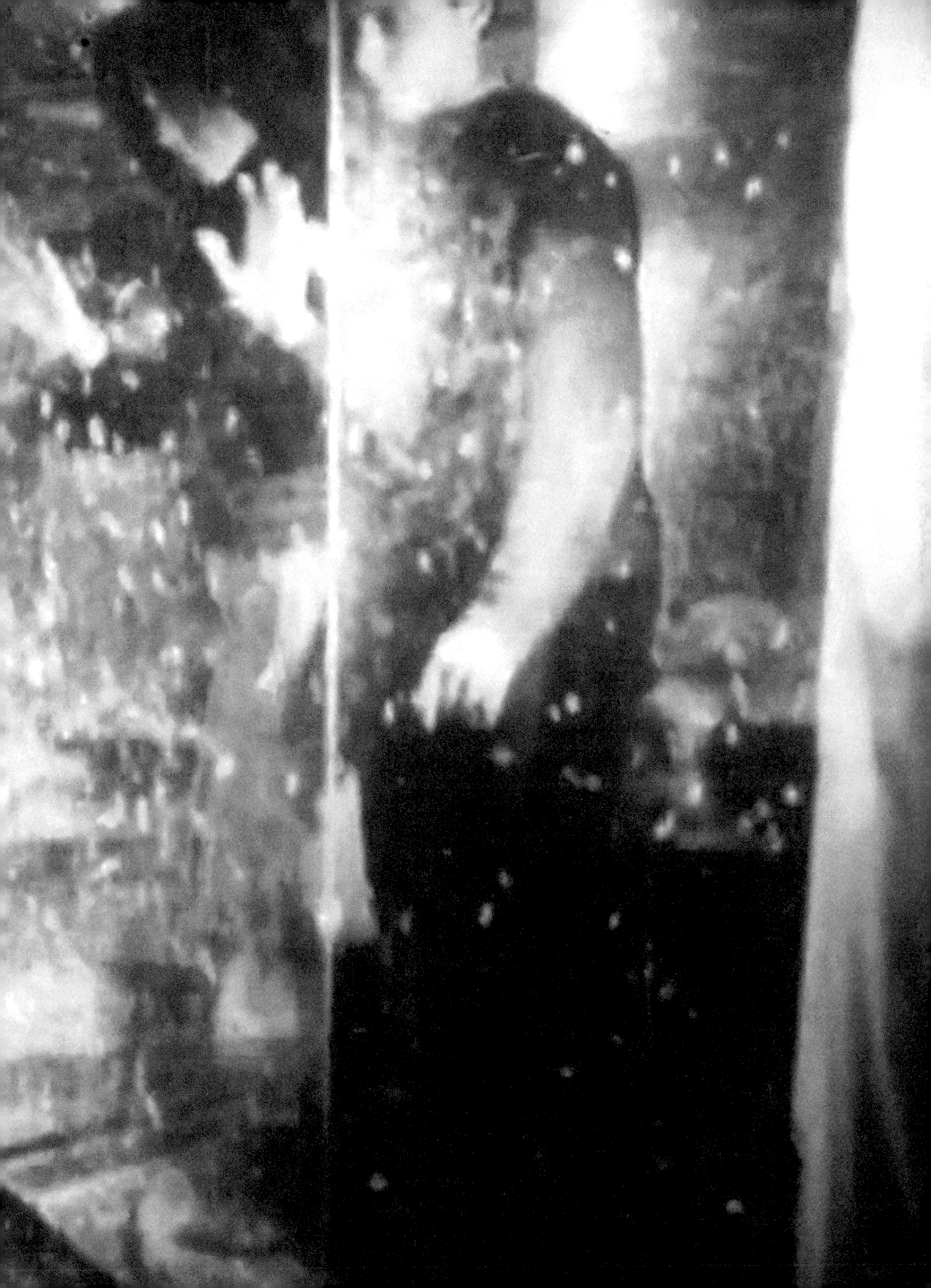

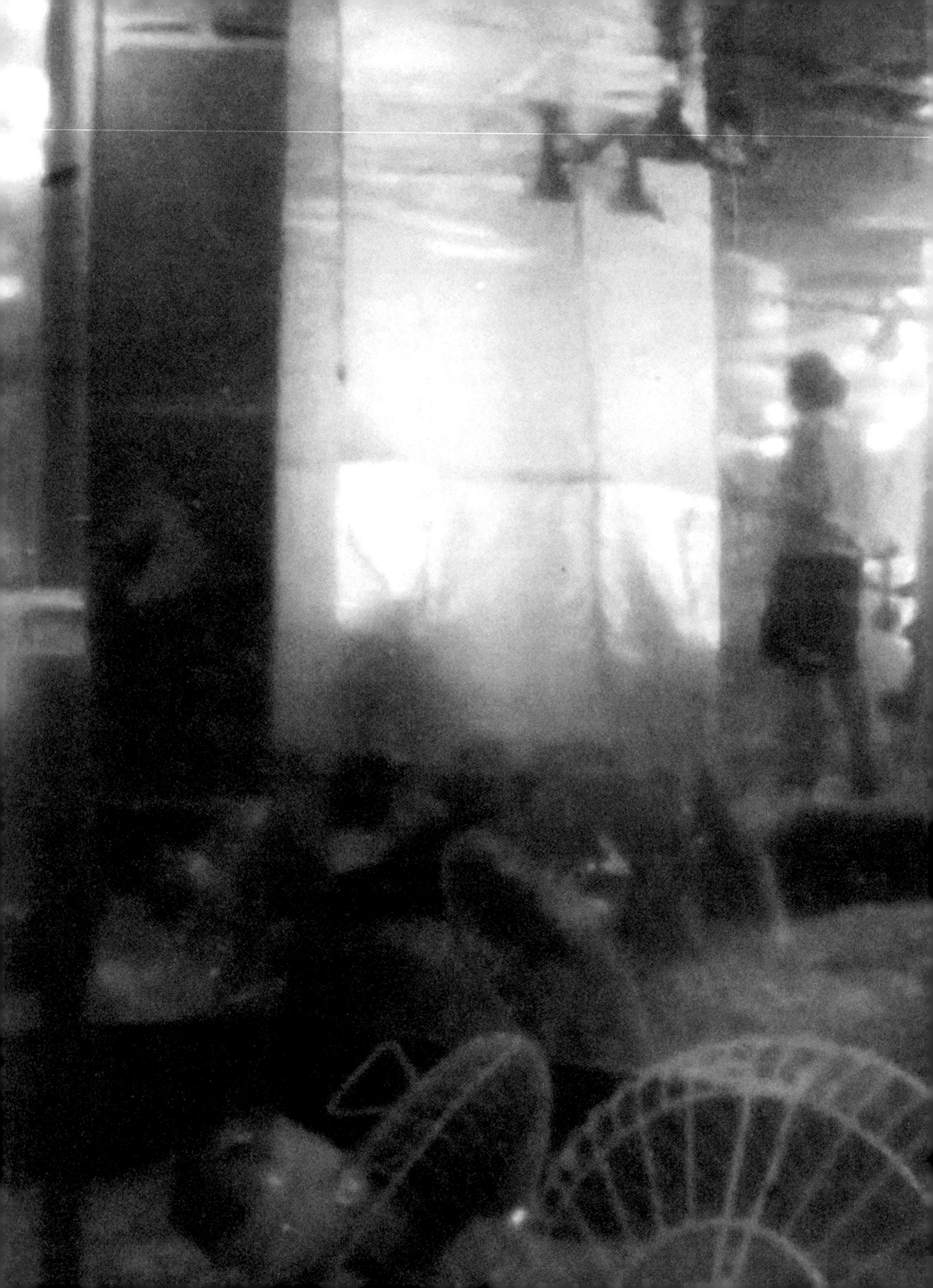

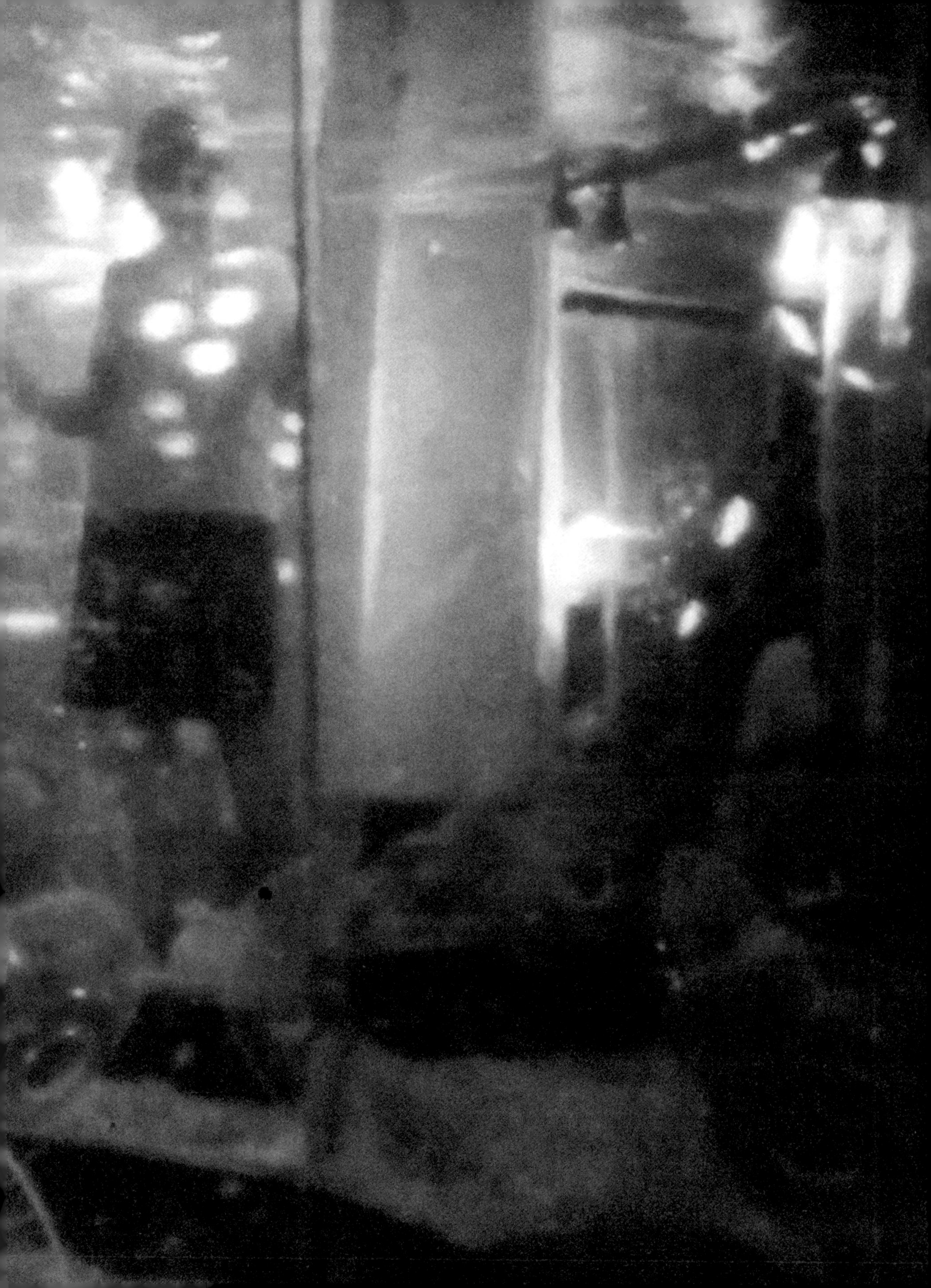

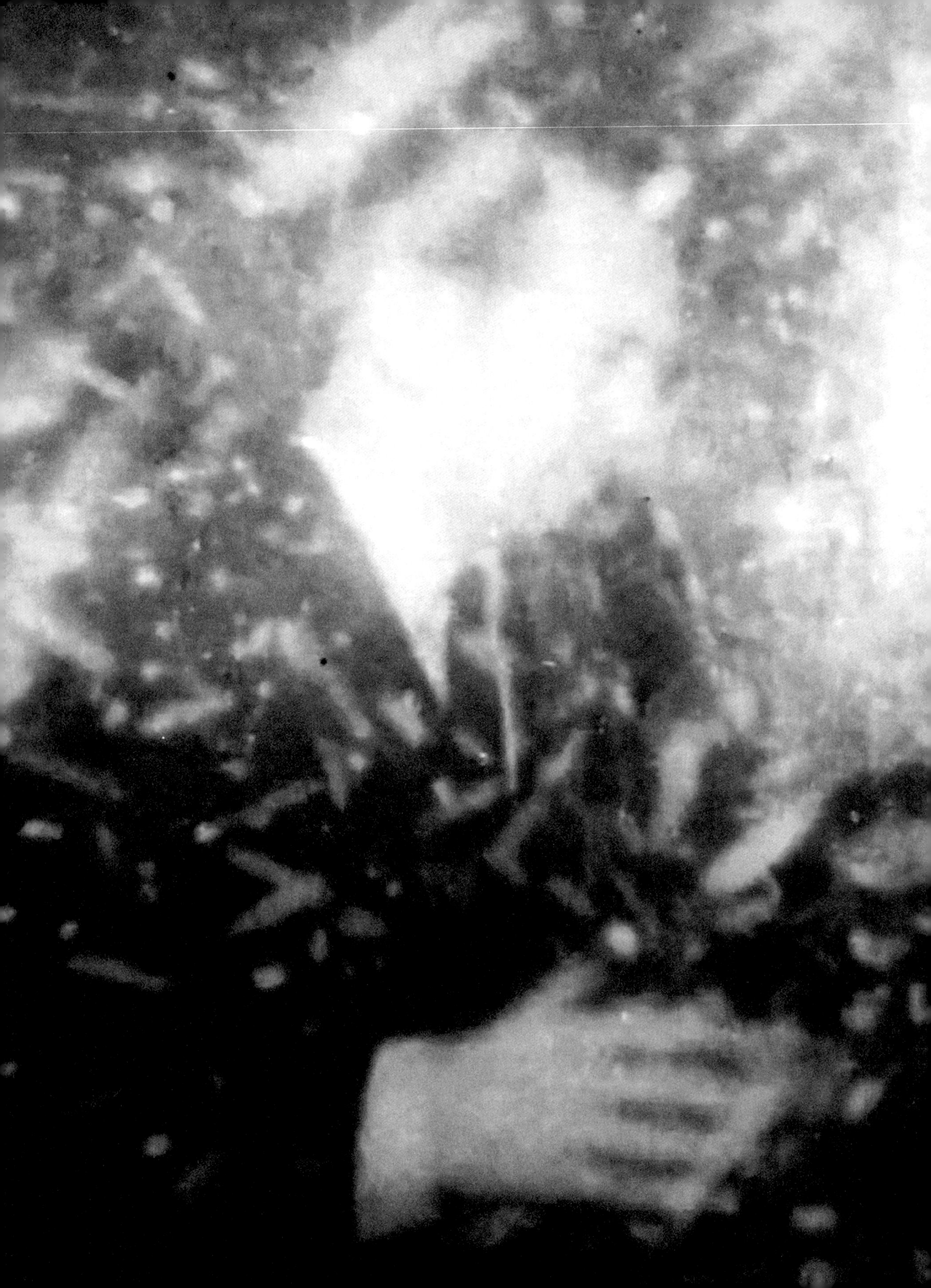

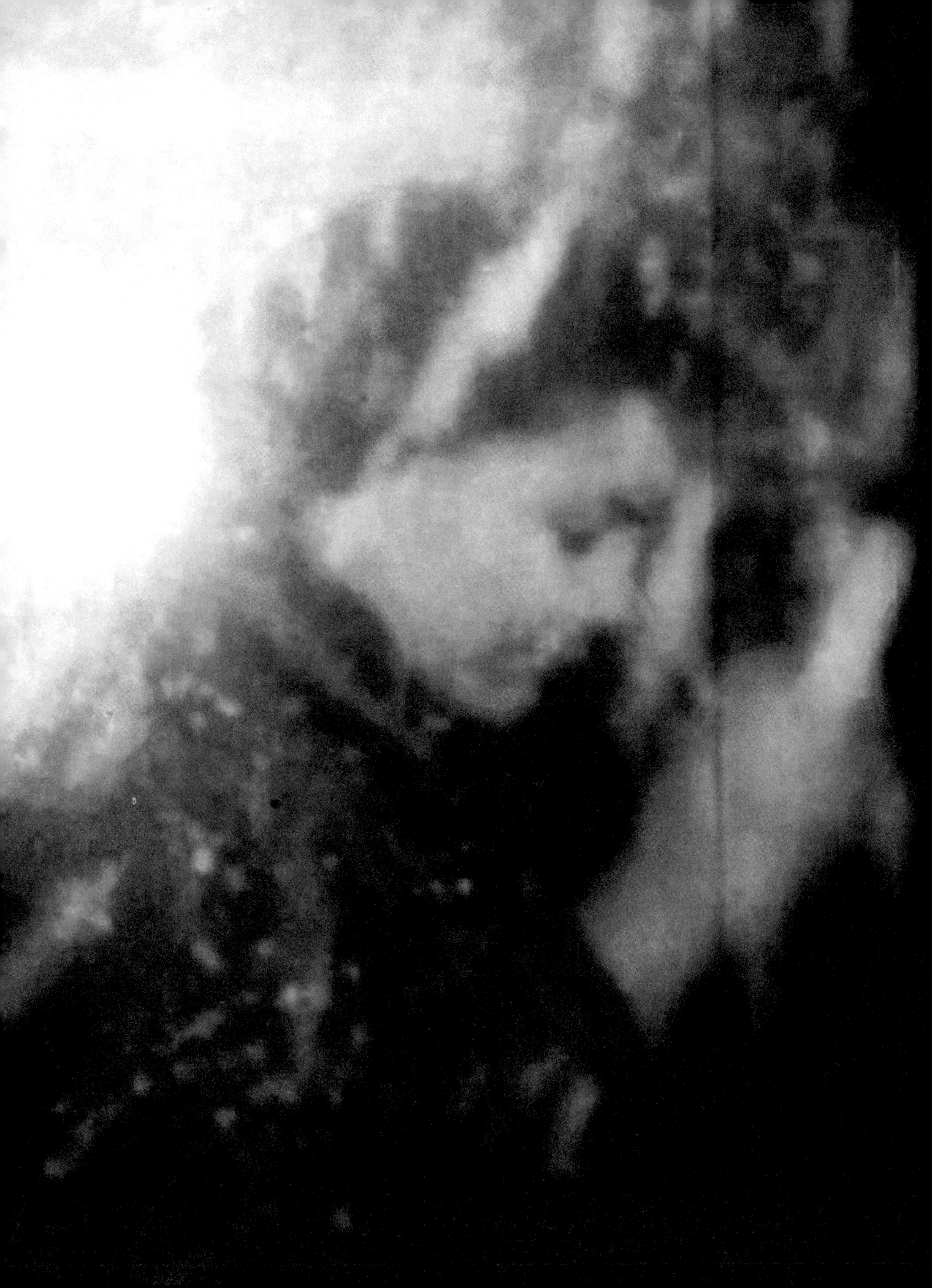

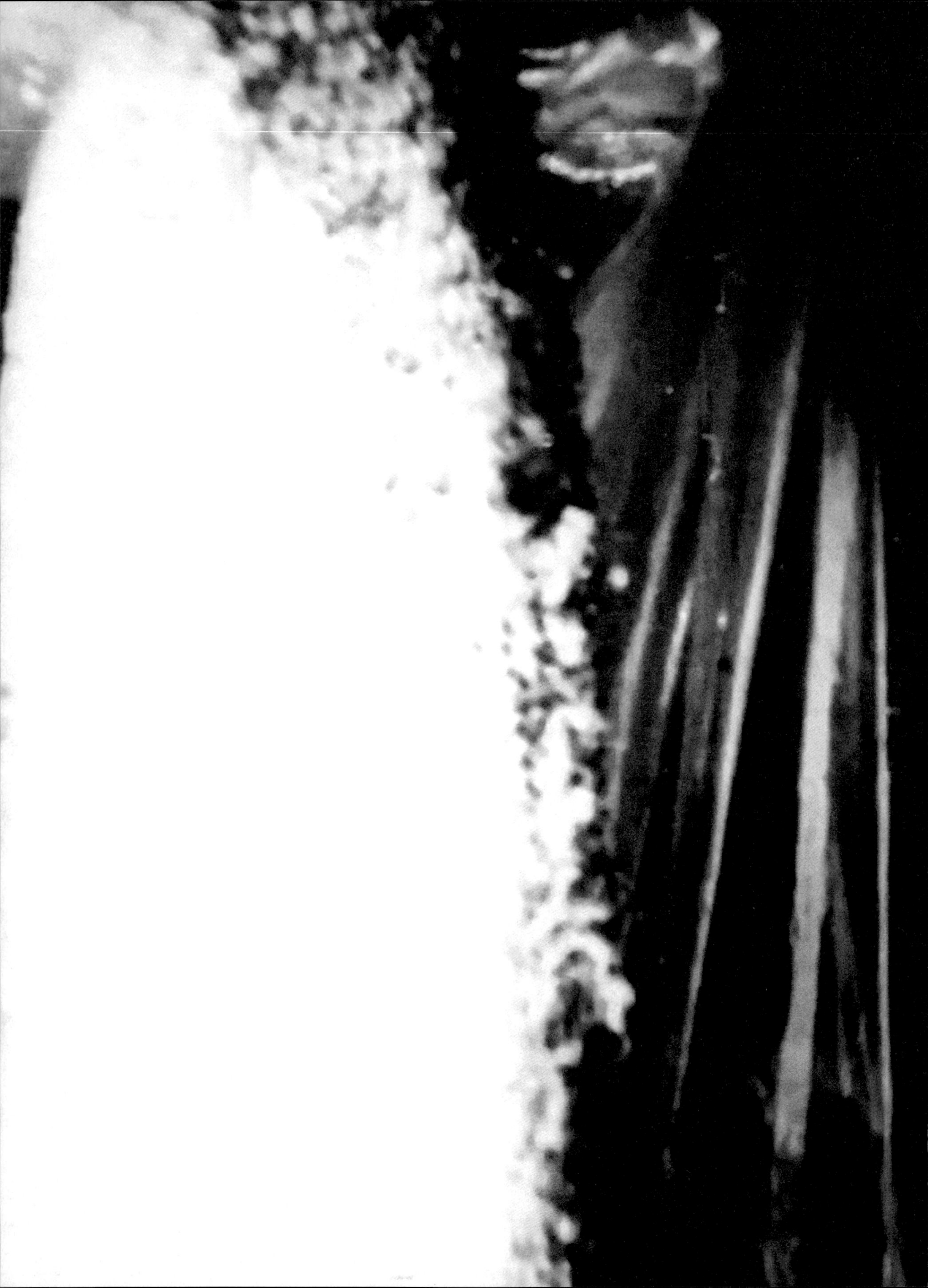

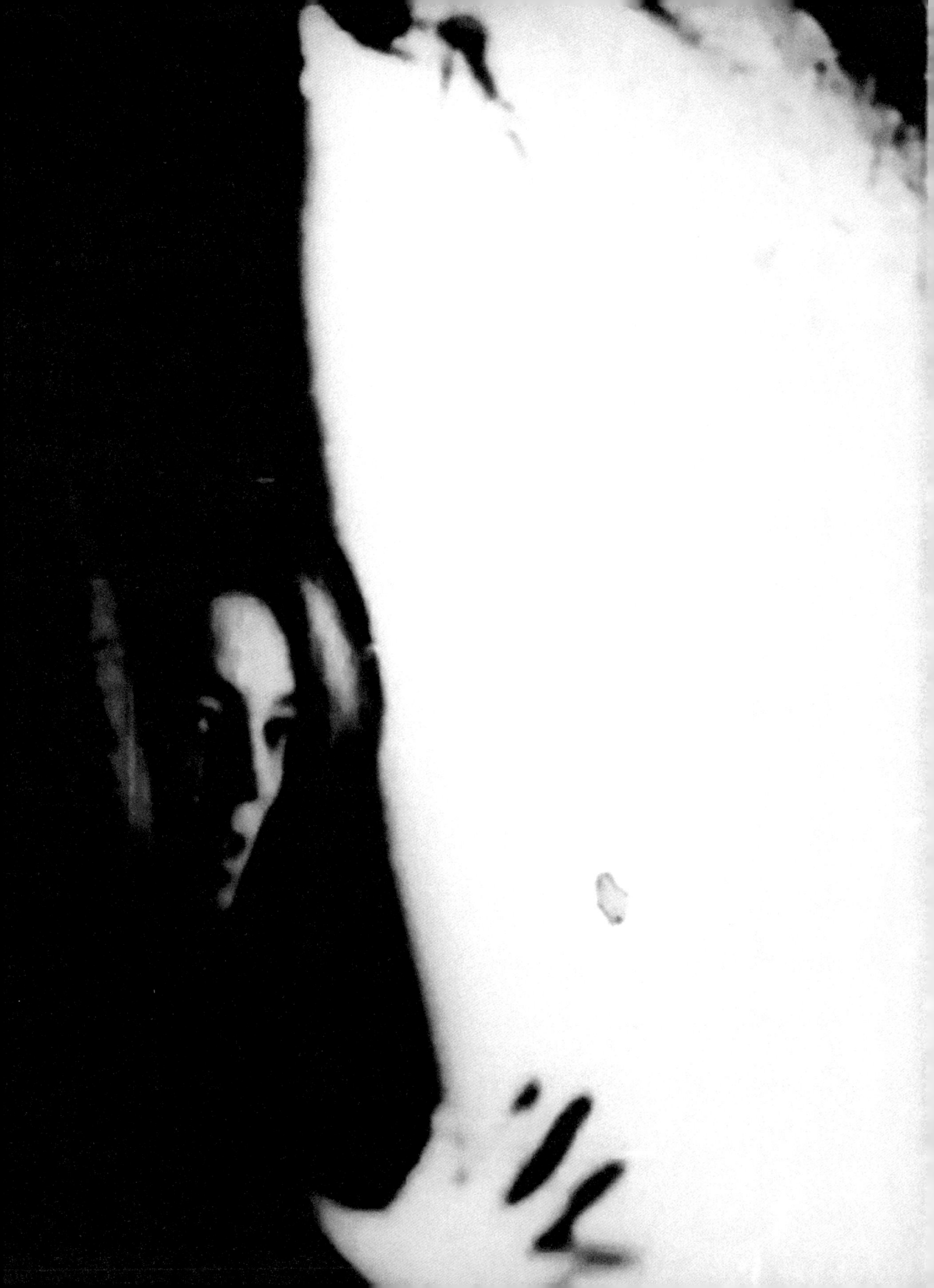

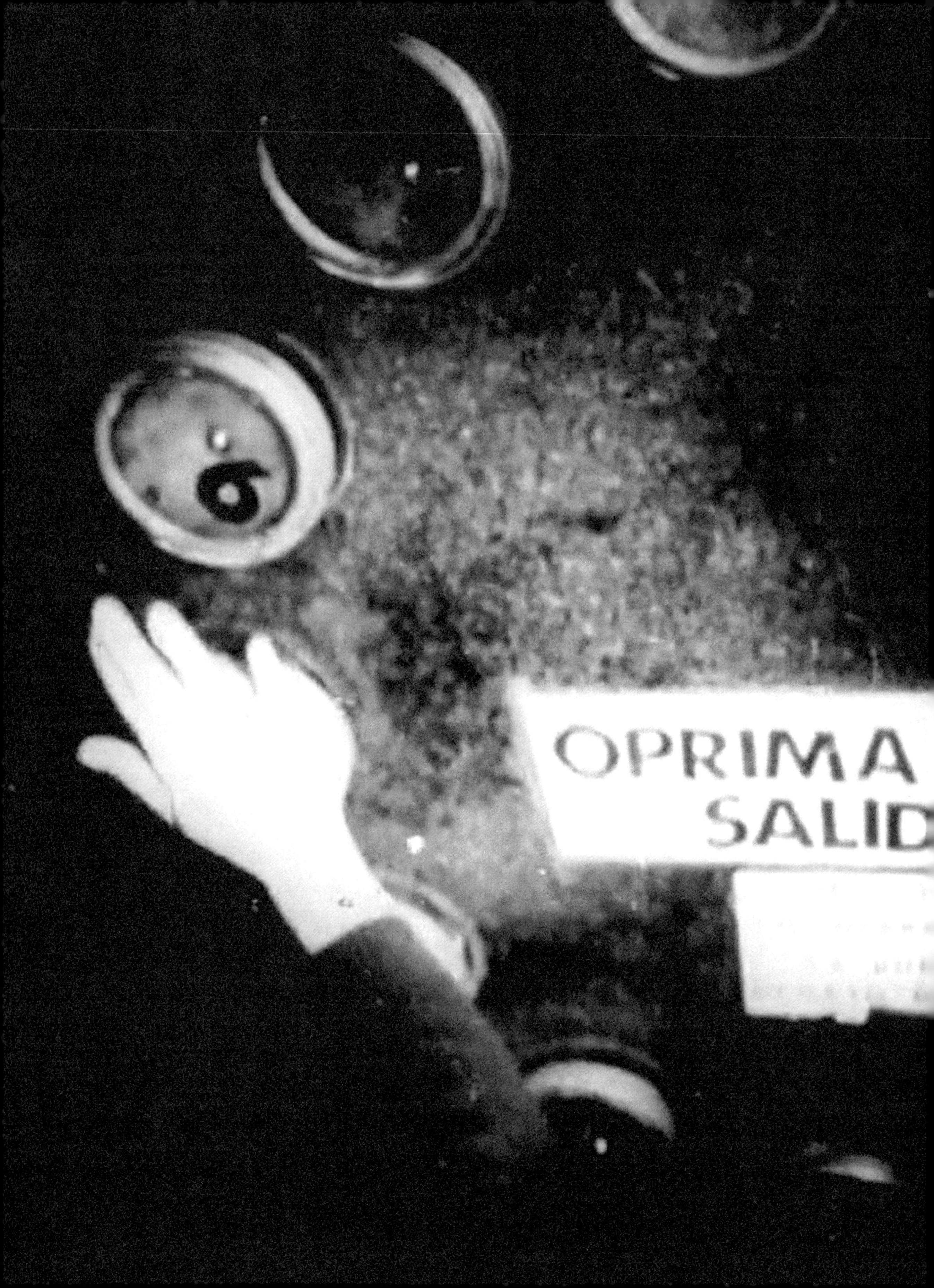

OPRIMA
SALID

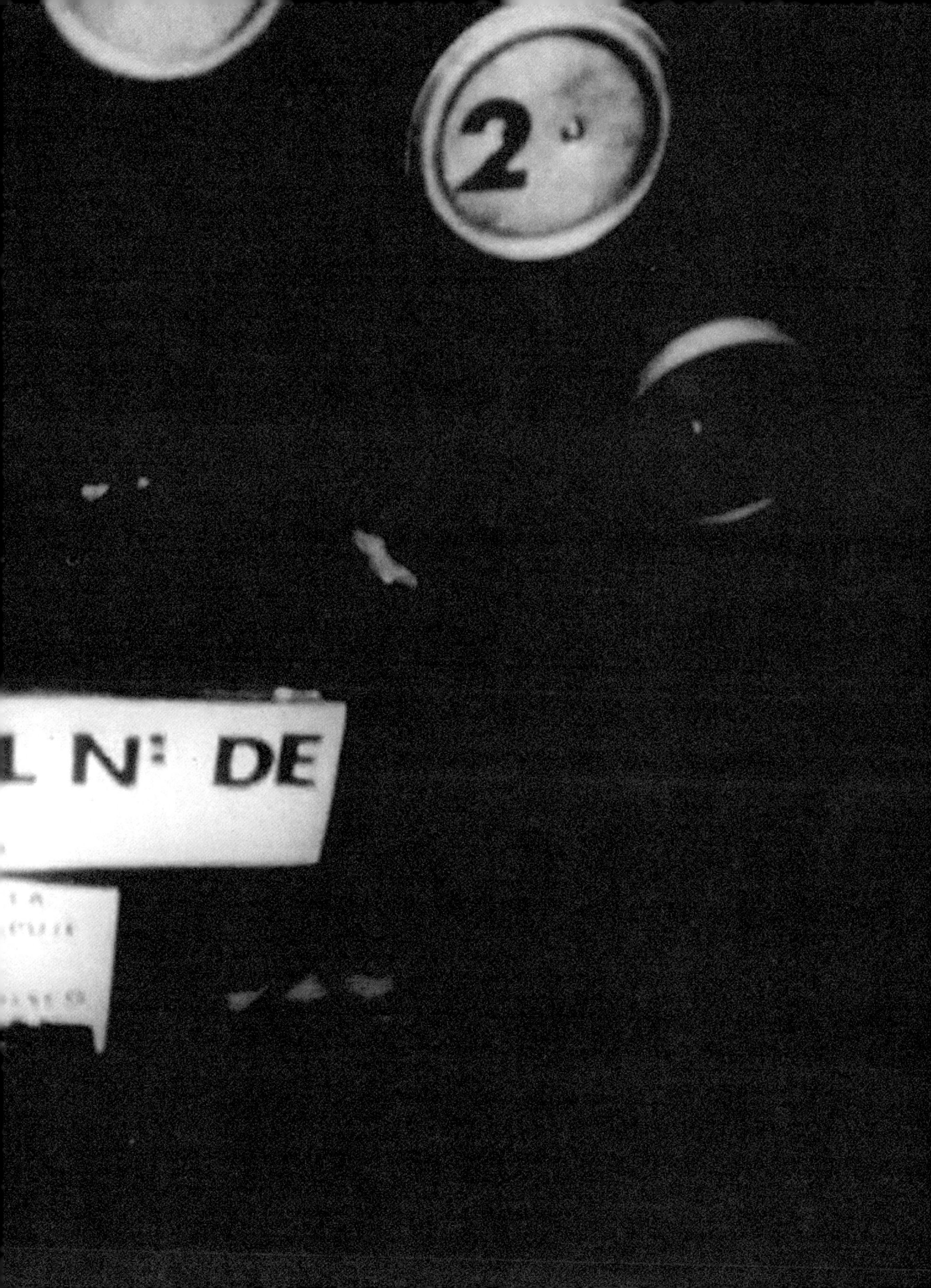
2
N: DE

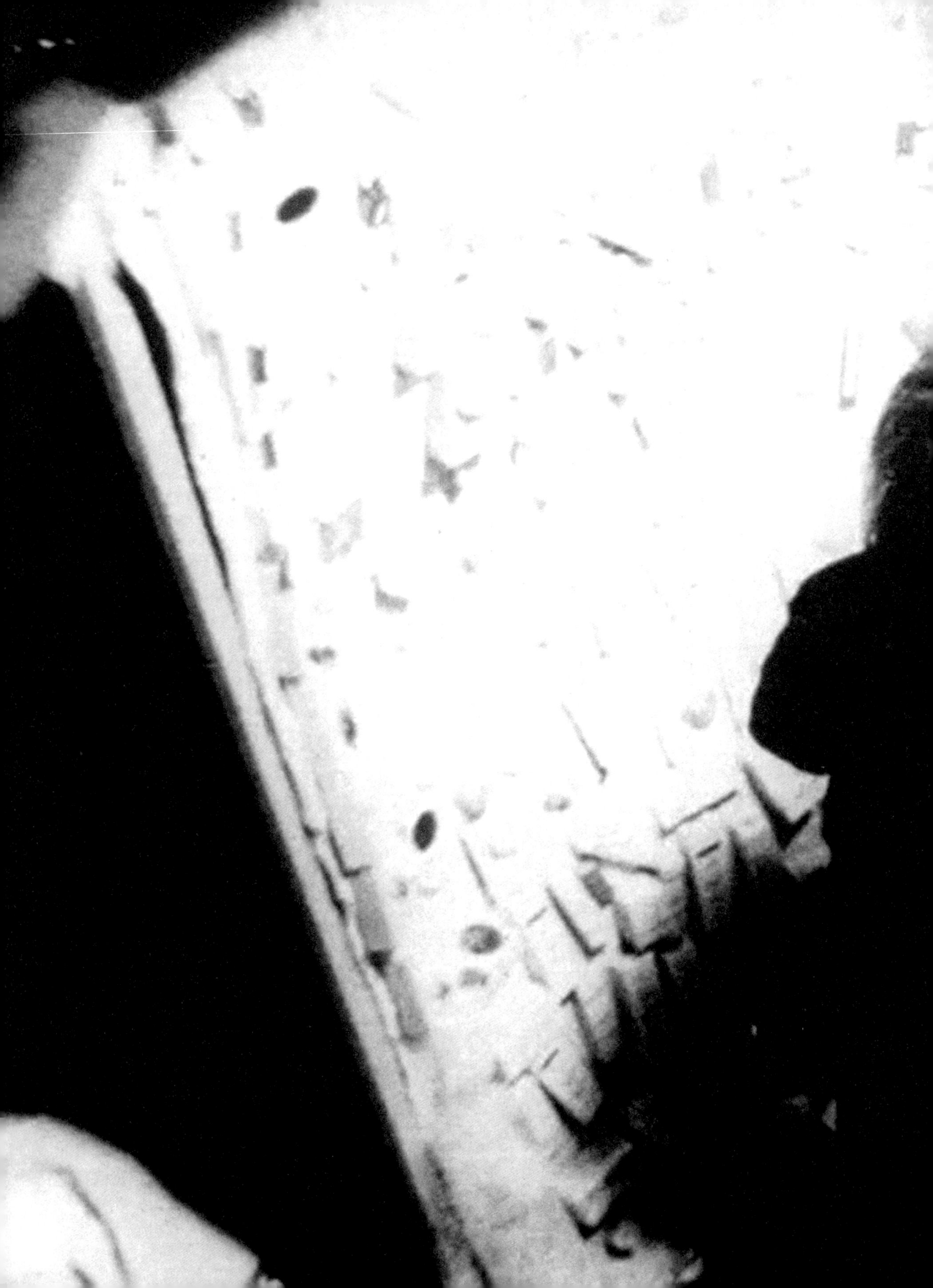

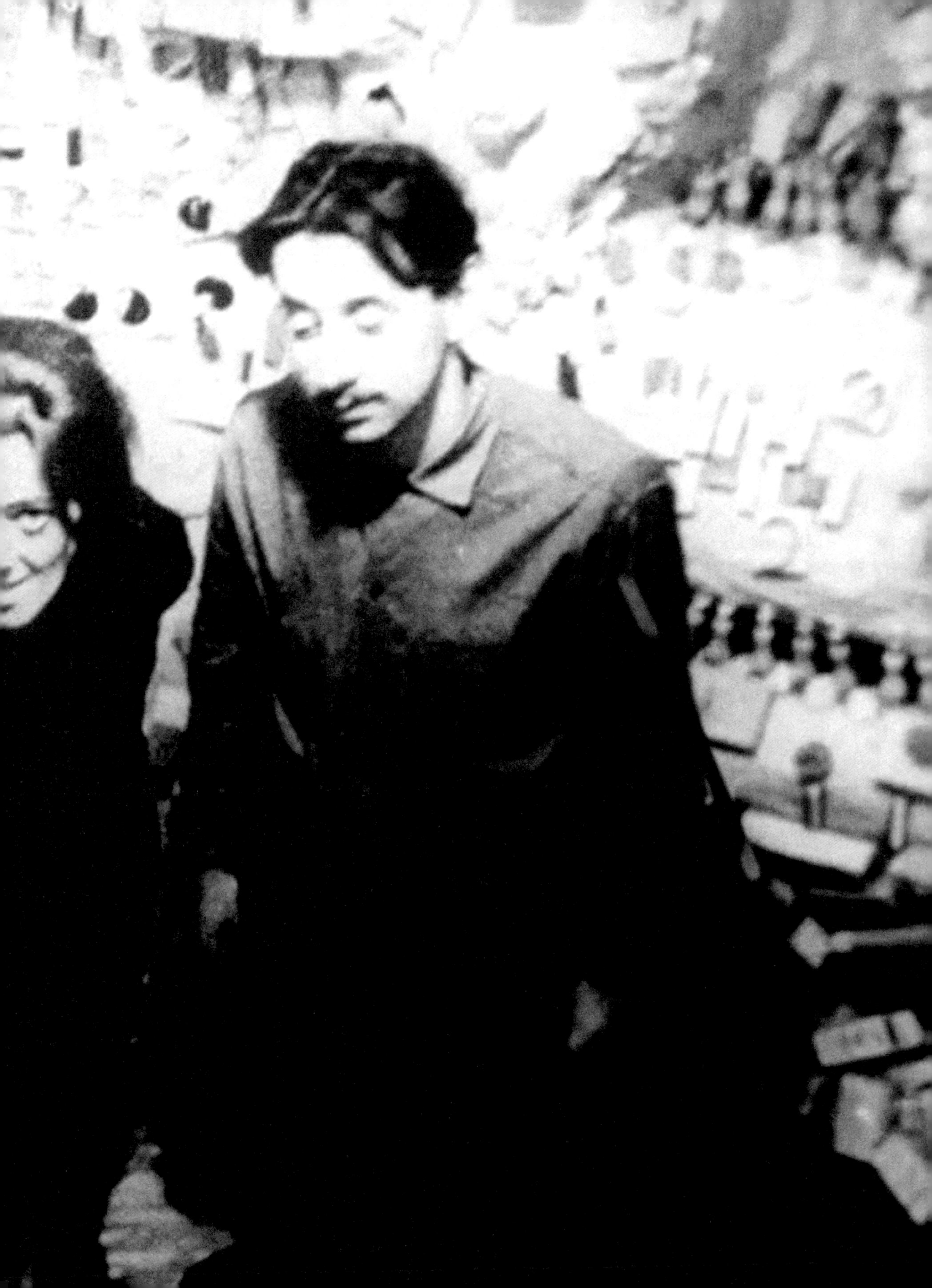

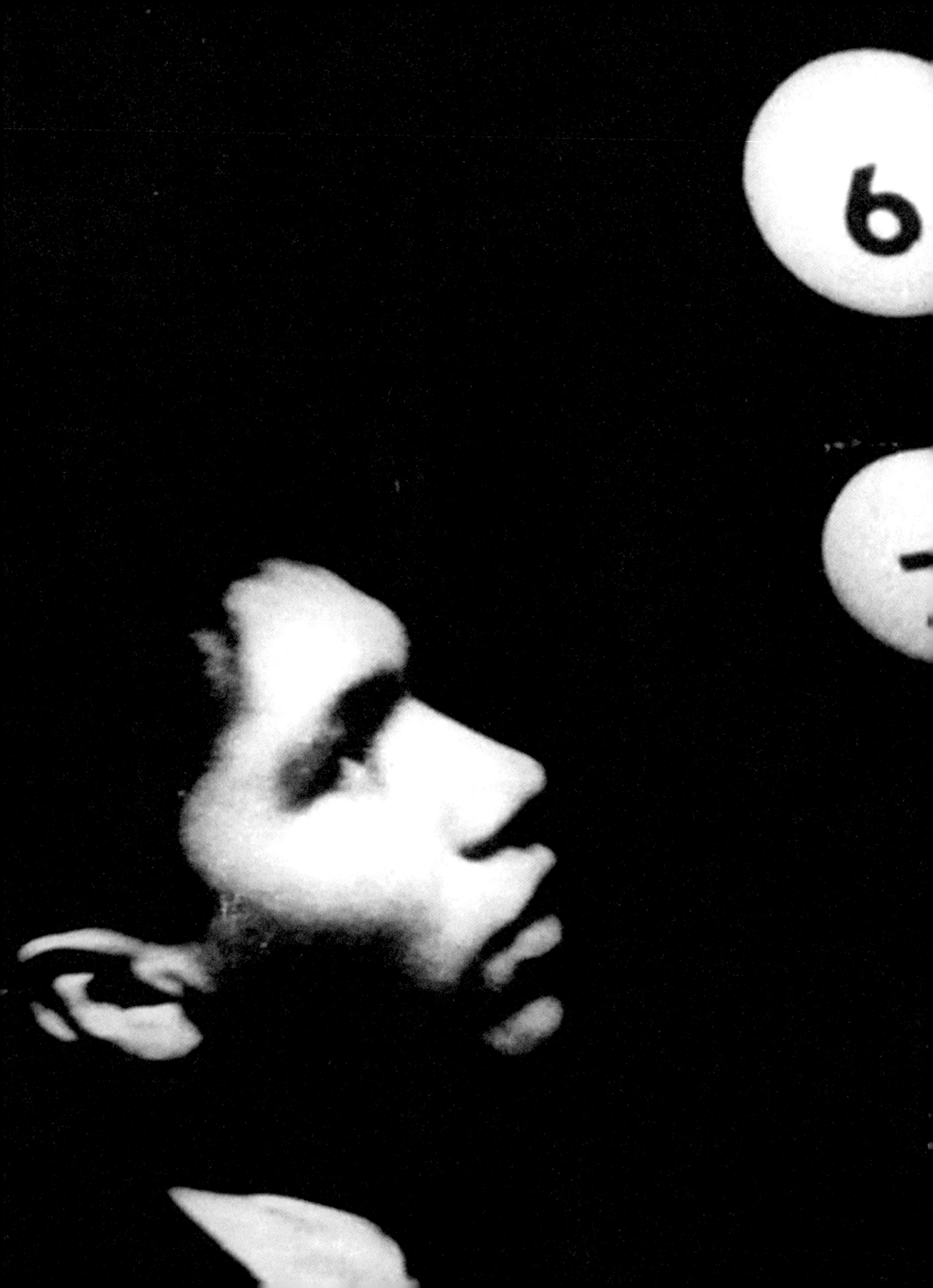
6

OPRIMA
SALID

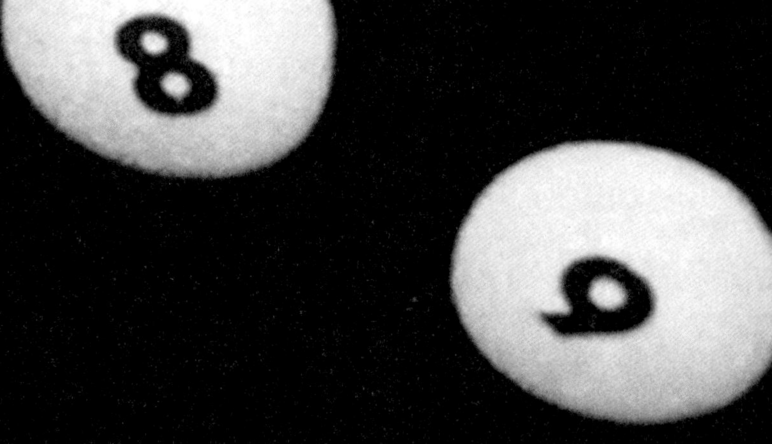
8
9

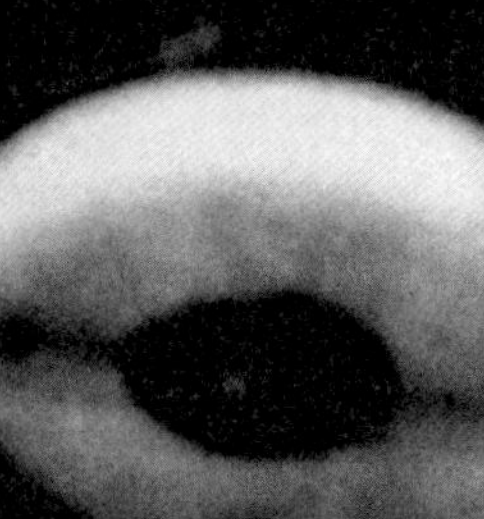

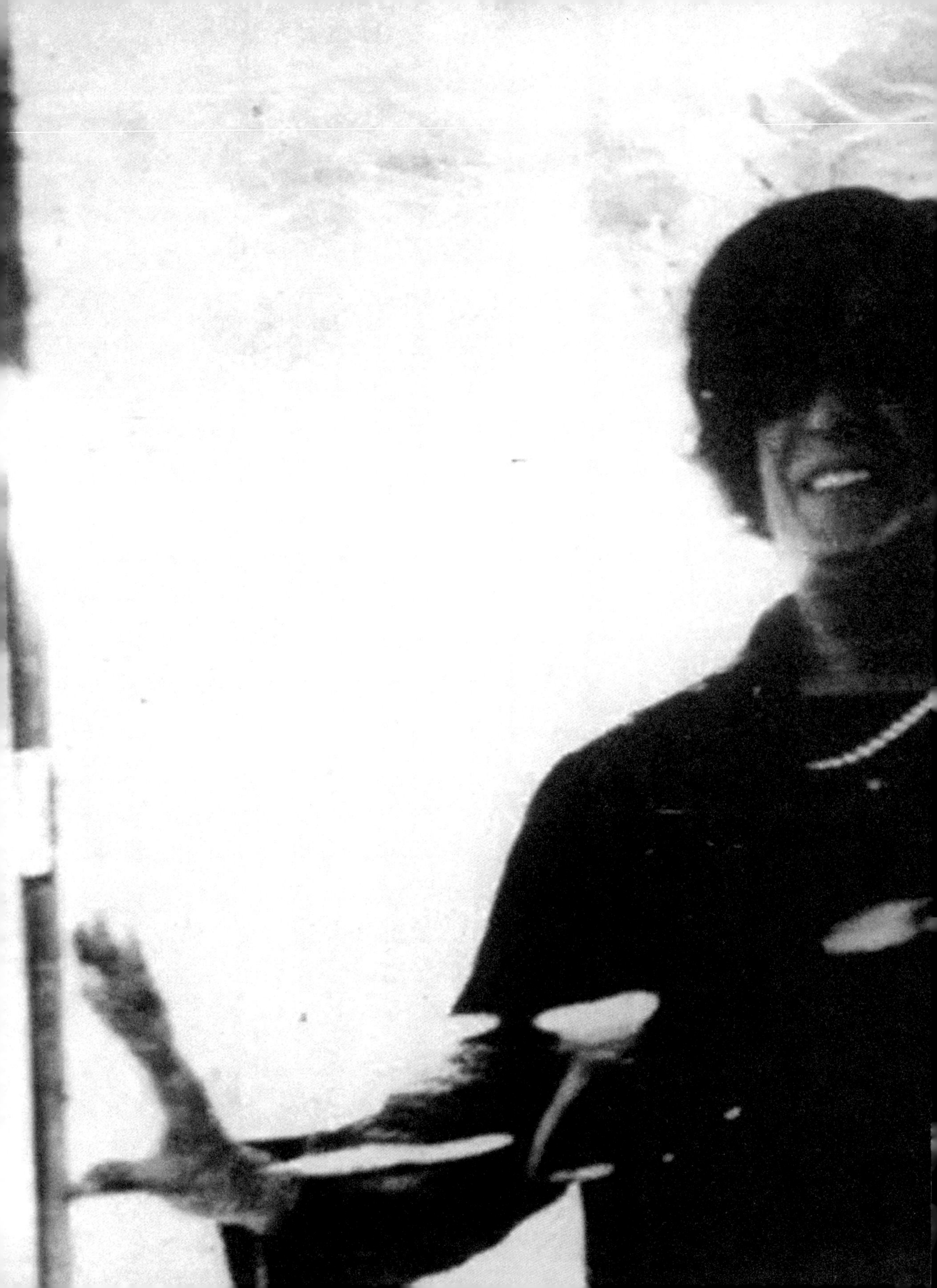

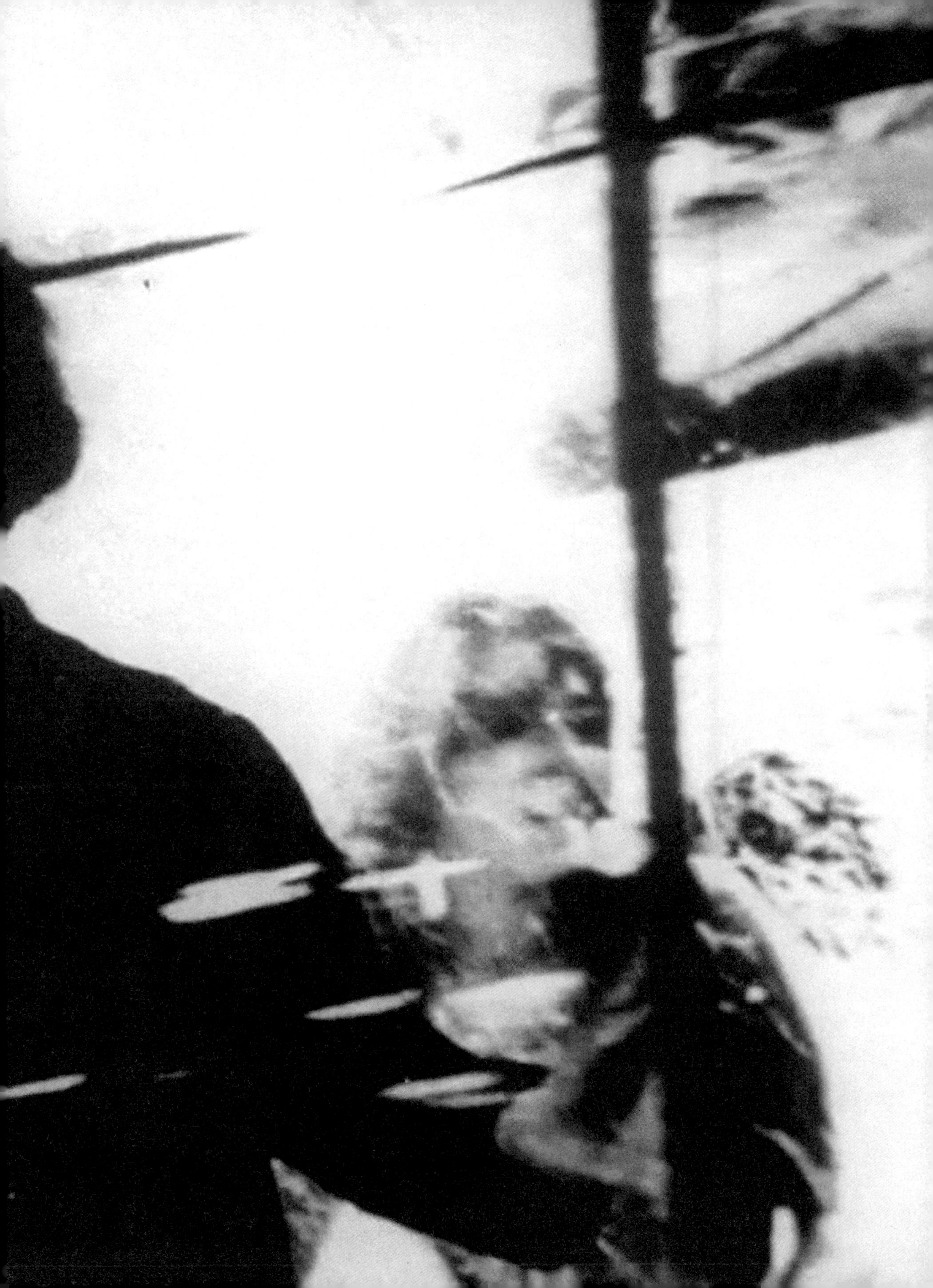

Buenos Aires
por un escá
que tiene ba
dosis de in
¿mito o

¿ART
O ARTE

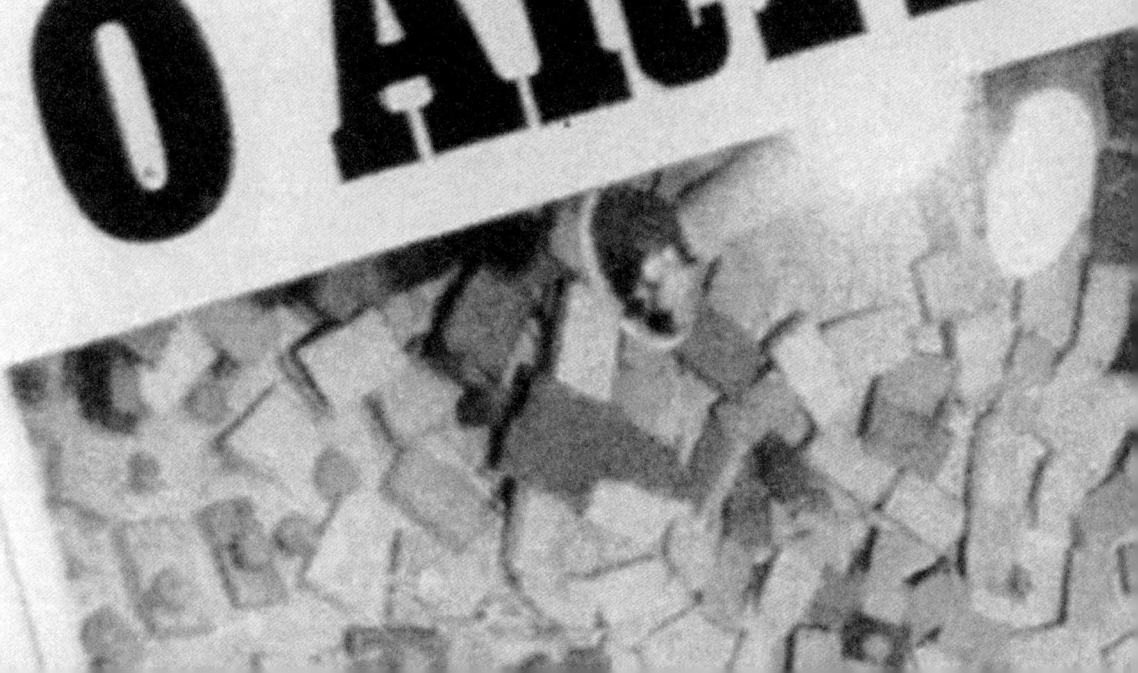

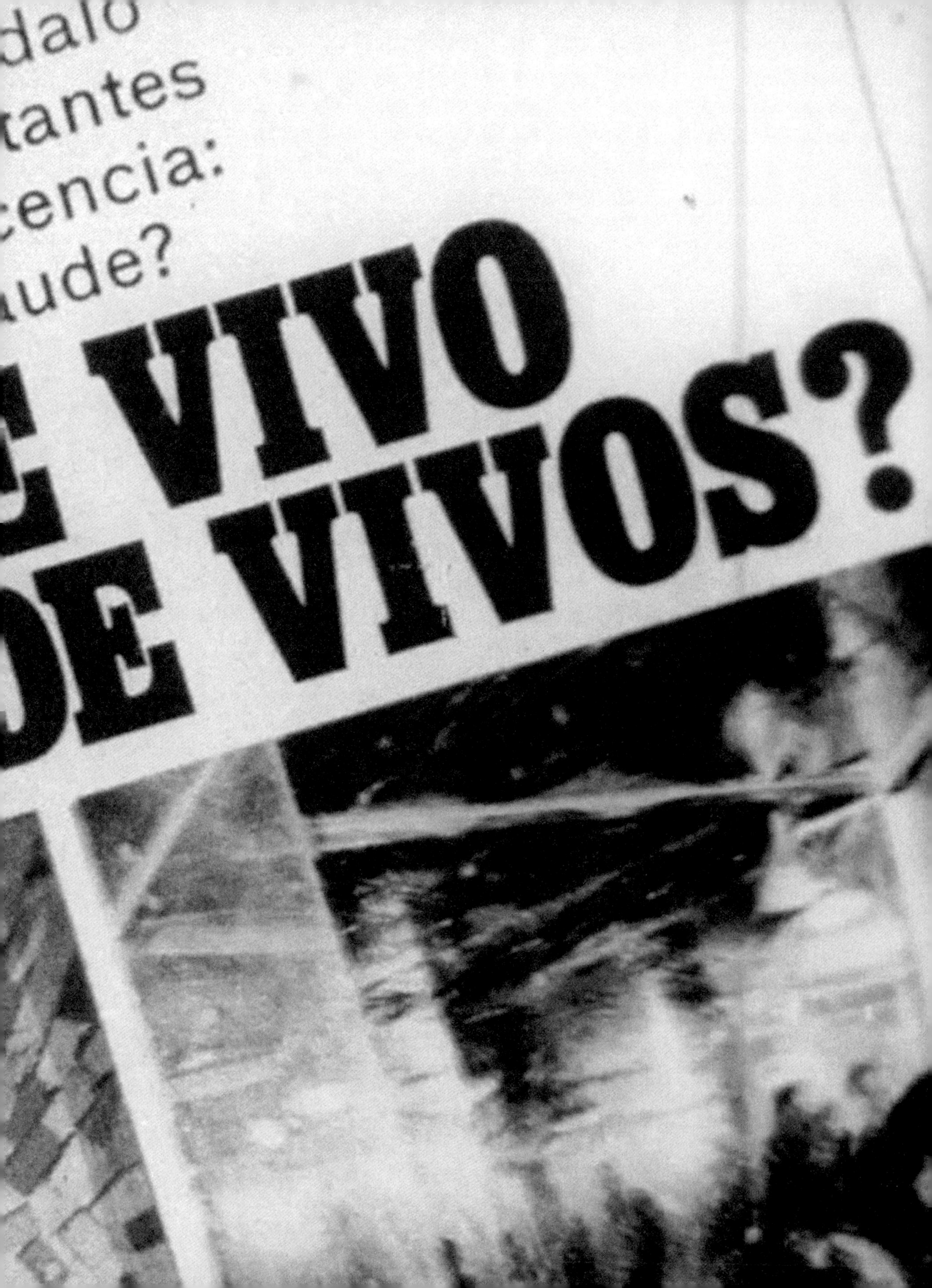

dalo
tantes
cencia:
ude?

VIVO
DE VIVOS?

¡Salud Fidias, Rafa

Arte
“Pal
Men

lada sobre la tela.

“MENESUNDA” (1) es u

“es”. Estuvo ayer en el Cen

Picasso!

Viejo

oma”,

esunda

alabra que no existe pero sin embargo
eraneando en pleno calendario invernal.

CUADROS C
MODELOS VI
EN FLORI

UNA BOMBA EN LAS ARTES PL
HA ESTALLADO EN PLENO CEI

ON
VOS
DA

TICAS
RO

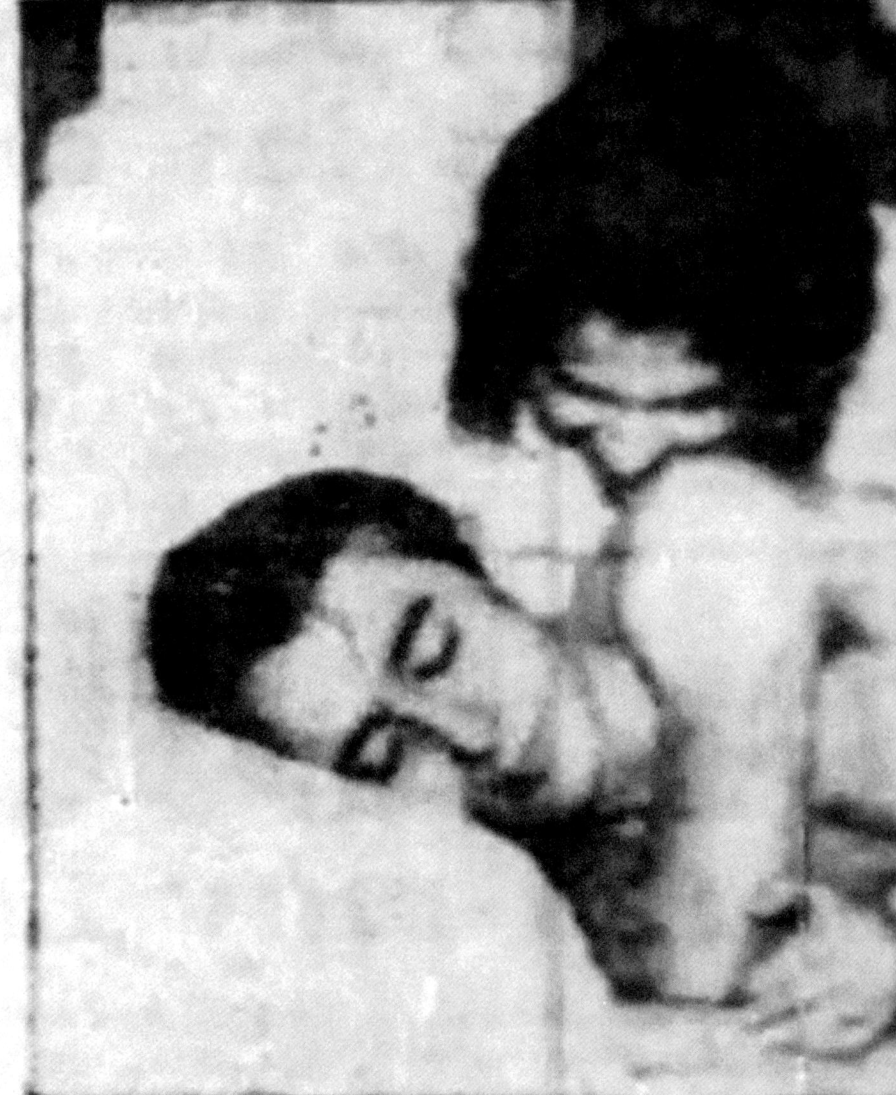

EN PLENA INTIMIDAD. Esta escen
a los espectadores de "La Mamers
introducir a quien la v

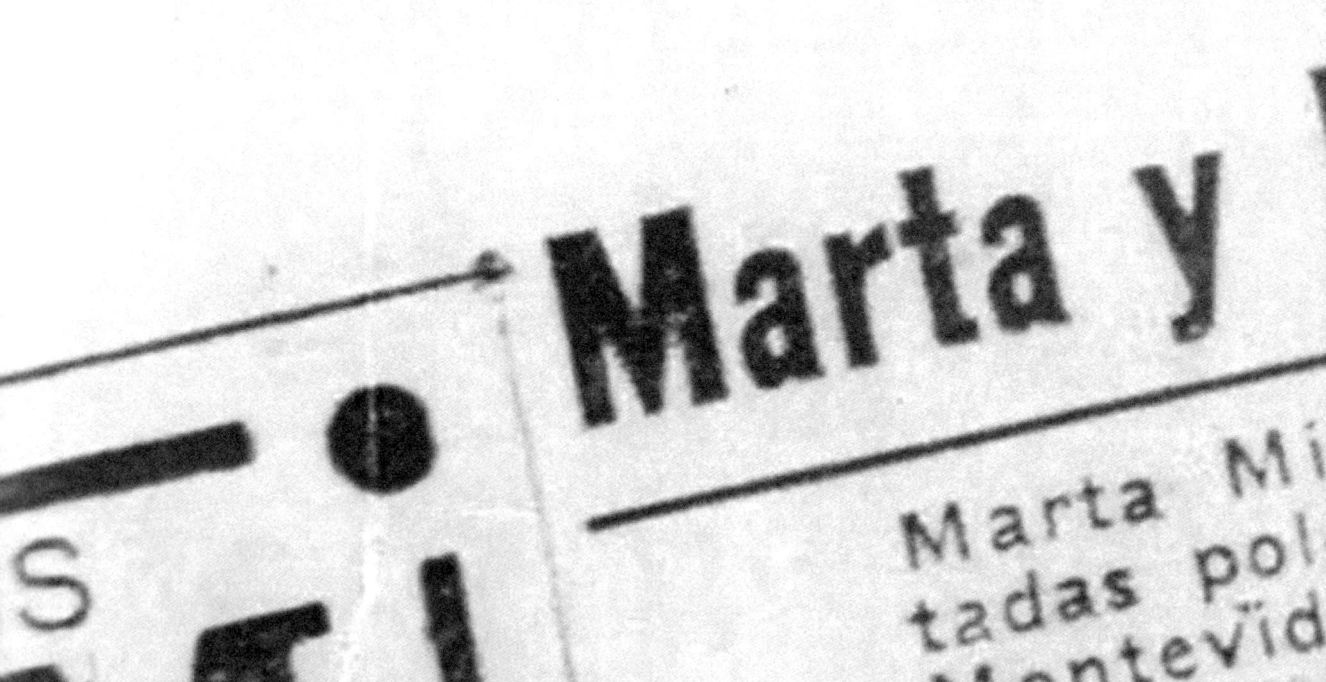

Mi

Marta y

Marta Mi
tadas pol
Montevid
sibles "s
El diario

a Menesunda

jin, la artista argentina que
nicas con su famosa "menesu
, donde llevará a cabo uno de
cesos plásticos" en una canc
"El País" publica una extens
y ésta, al ser interrogada ac
n "suceso plástico", dijo
través de situaci
porqu

"La Menesun
Plástico d

Una de las autores de la Menesunda Marta Minuj
cultura. Becada por el gobierno francés en 1962.
y 1962, en Galería Lirolay. Principales exposiciones
1960); Premio Ver y Estimar (1960); El hombre ante
Treinta argentinos en París (1962); Salón de relieve
ricanos en París (1963); Exposición y destrucción de
rededor del juguete; Salón de la joven pintura (1964
en una escultura expuesta en Galería Le Gendre, Co
puesta en la exposición "Del laberinto a la pieza de
oa Minneapolis, EE. UU. 1964); Exposición Pepsi Cola,
Suiza: en París y Minneapolis, EE. UU.

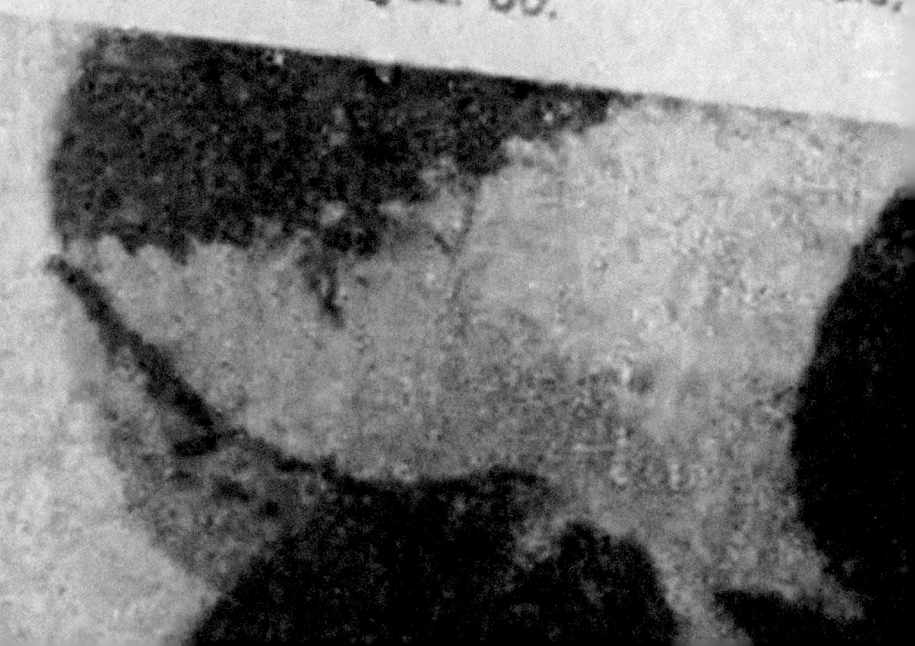

...da", Suceso ...e Buenos Aires

...nació en Buenos Aires en 1941. Estudia pintura y es-
...posiciones individuales a partir de 1957, 1959, 1960
...ectivas: Premio de Ridder (1959); Arte Nuevo (1959-
...el hombre (1962); Bienal de Jóvenes de París (1961);
...962); Salón de la joven escultura (1962); Latinoame-
...as en el impasse Ronsin; La caja y su contenido; Al-
...alón Comparación; Colaboración con Francois Arnal,
...oración con Marc Brusse en una escultura a ser ex-
...mor", en Tokio, Japón; Arte Nuevo de la Argenti-
...ueva York (1964). Sus obras se exponen en St. Galle,

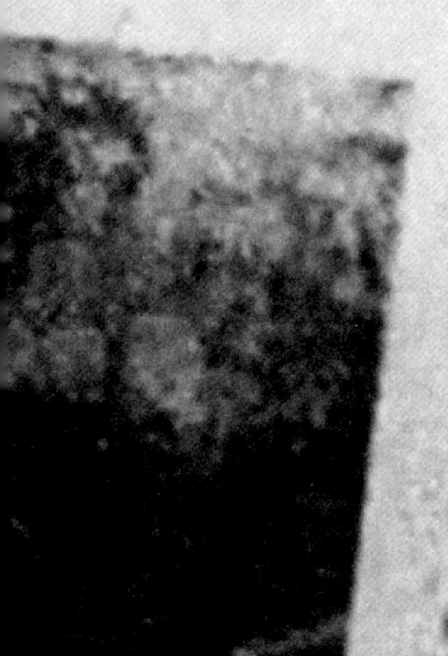

es siempre la misma para todos el número que se debe discar en el de-te, misterio que debe descubrir o la presión sobre el piso del prisma de cristal desencadena violentas ráfagas.

En parte se logran los fines de Minujín y Santantonín, particularmente el de "impulsar la imaginación".

Un hecho frecuente es que gran parte de los espectadores finalizan la experiencia concibiendo...

New Museum Third Floor

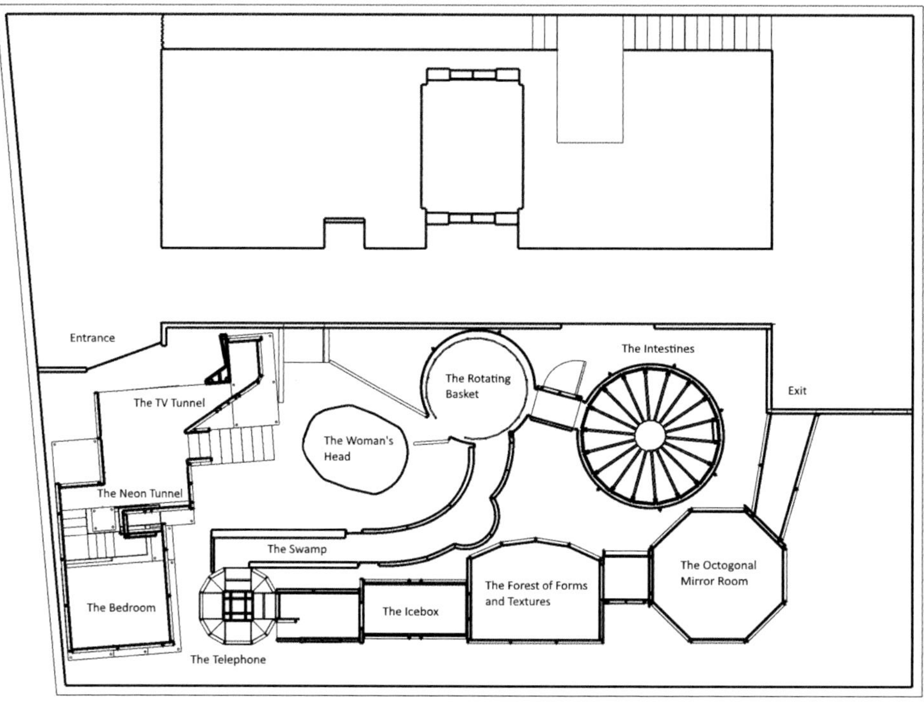

List of Works

Marta Minujín
Menesunda Reloaded, 2019
Total environment comprising eleven distinct rooms and situations: wood, mdf, metal, neon lights, textiles, foam, plastic, paper, hardboard, cardboard, mirror, acrylic, styrofoam, resin, straw, makeup, polyethylene crystal, TV monitors, air conditioning, digital projection, lights, sound, smells, and performers
Dimensions variable
Courtesy the artist

This reconstruction was coproduced by the New Museum and the Museo de Arte Moderno de Buenos Aires.

La Menesunda was originally created in 1965 by Marta Minujín and Rubén Santantonín at the Instituto Torcuato Di Tella in Buenos Aires.

About the Artist

Marta Minujín (b. 1943, Buenos Aires, Argentina) lives and works in Buenos Aires. She studied at the Escuela Superior de Bellas Artes Manuel Belgrano and the Escuela Nacional de Bellas Artes Prilidiano Pueyrredón Buenos Aires. In 1961, she received a scholarship to study in Paris, where she carried out her first performance, *La destrucción* [The Destruction] in 1963. Returning to Buenos Aires in 1964, she was awarded the Premio Nacional Instituto Torcuato Di Tella for the work *¡Revuélquese y viva!* [Wallow Around and Live!] (1964), her first interactive installation. Minujín received a Guggenheim Fellowship in 1966. During the 1970s, she lived between the United States and Argentina, exhibiting her work in major institutions such as the Museum of Modern Art, New York (1973), and Centro de Arte y Comunicación, Buenos Aires (1975, 1976). A retrospective of Minujín's work was presented at the Museo de Arte Latinoamericano de Buenos Aires in 2010, and her work has been included in documenta 14, Kassel (2017), and in exhibitions at Tate Modern, London (2015); Museum of Modern Art, New York (2015); Walker Art Center, Minneapolis (2015); Centre Pompidou, Paris (2001); and elsewhere.

Board of Trustees

Photography Credits

Pp. 12–13, 16, 17 (top), 66–67, 70–71, 74, 75 (bottom), 99, 100–101, 103–5, 108–13, 115, 117–21, 123–25, 127, 129, 132–35, 136, 144–47, 149–63, 166–67, 173, 179–87, 189, 190–290: Courtesy Marta Minujín Archive; pp. 106–7, 130–31, 137, 138–43, 164–65, 170–71: Courtesy Centro de Artes Visuales Archive, Universidad Torcuato Di Tella; p. 17 (bottom): Courtesy Robert Jacoby Archive; p. 75 (top): © Marta Minujín. Courtesy Marta Minujín and the Guggenheim Museum, New York; p. 169: Courtesy Museo de Arte Moderno de Buenos Aires. Photo: Josefina Tommasi; pp. 174–77: Courtesy Museo de Arte Moderno de Buenos Aires. Photo: Agustina Vizcarra

Published by
New Museum
235 Bowery
New York, NY 10002

On the occasion of the exhibition
"Marta Minujín: Menesunda Reloaded"

June 26–September 29, 2019

ISBN: 978-0-915557-22-6

Curators: Massimiliano Gioni, *Edlis Neeson Artistic Director*, and Helga Christoffersen, Associate Curator
Curatorial Assistant: Francesca Altamura
Editor: Lily Bartle, Editor, with Dana Kopel, Senior Editor and Publications Coordinator
Design: An Art Service

Contributors:
Christo
Helga Christoffersen
Zanna Gilbert
Massimiliano Gioni
Aimé Iglesias Lukin

Printed by Zakład Poligraficzny Moś & Łuczak in Poland

Front cover: Marta Minujín and Rubén Santantonín, *The Icebox*, from *La Menesunda*, 1965 (detail). Courtesy Marta Minujín Archive

Back cover: Marta Minujín and Rubén Santantonín, *The Telephone*, from *La Menesunda*, 1965 (detail). Courtesy Marta Minujín Archive

Lead support for this exhibition is provided by the Artemis Council of the New Museum.
Maria Baibakova, *Chair*; Dr. Shelley Fox Aarons; Stacey Bendet Eisner; Valerie Biberaj; Radhika Chanana and Amira Chanana; Robin Cofer-D'Alleva; Belma Gaudio; Stacey Goergen; Agnes Gund; Lynn Ingrassia; Shanyan Koder; Randi Charno Levine; Marley Blue Lewis; Margaret Munzer Loeb; Nazy Nazhand; Nicole Nunag; Bettina Prentice; Debbie Rechler; Nancy Rogers; Barrie Roman; Nicole Salmasi; Lisa Schiff; Jennifer Soros; Sara Story; Vicki Match Suna; Stacy Van Praagh; Olivia Walton; Madeline Weinrib; Tiffany Zabludowicz; Ruoqi Amy Zhou; Aimee Mullins, *Ambassador*; H.R.H. Princess Eugenie of York, *Ambassador*

Major support is provided by the Federal System of Public Media and Contents of Argentina through the Centro Cultural Kirchner.

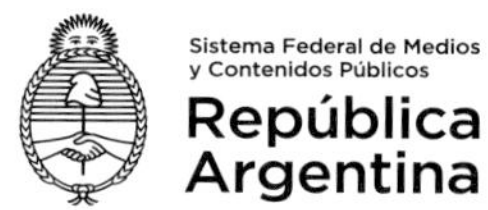

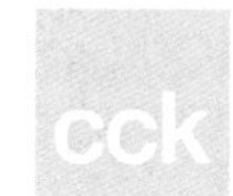

Generous support is provided by:
Fundación Proa
Maria Belen Avellaneda, Compass
Estrellita B. Brodsky
Kathleen O'Grady, The O'Grady Foundation

Additional support is provided by Amalia A. Amoedo.

Special thanks to Herlitzka + Faria, Buenos Aires, and Henrique Faria Fine Art, New York.

Thanks to the Bowery Hotel.

Support for this publication has been provided by the J. McSweeney and G. Mills Publications Fund at the New Museum.

La Menesunda is coproduced by the New Museum and the Museo de Arte Moderno de Buenos Aires.

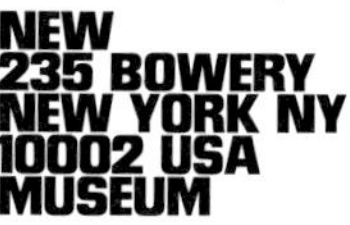